The
Challenge
of the
American
Presidency

Philip Abbott

Wayne State University

WAVELAND
PRESS, INC.
Prospect Heights, Illinois

For information about this book, contact:
Waveland Press, Inc.
P.O. Box 400
Prospect Heights, Illinois 60070
(847) 634-0081
info@waveland.com
www.waveland.com

To Patricia

Hail, wedded love.

—John Milton

CONTENTS

PREFACE

Niccolò Machiavelli wrote *The Prince* in 1513, shortly after he was released from prison and exiled by the Medici family. *The Prince* is filled with the bold exploits of political leaders, but late in the work Machiavelli reveals an uncharacteristic moment of resignation. "It is not unknown to me," he begins chapter 25, "that many have held and hold the opinion that worldly things are so governed by fortune and by God, that men cannot correct them . . . indeed they have no remedy at all." He continues, "When I have thought about this sometimes, I have in some part inclined to their opinion." Machiavelli soon concludes that fortune may be "the arbiter of half of our actions but she leaves the other half, or close to it, for us to govern." Nevertheless, leaders must always be prepared for change, even in violent and dramatic forms, in order to retain some control of their fate.

Many presidents have expressed the same views as Machiavelli's. In 1864, Abraham Lincoln defended his extraordinary Civil War measures to Albert G. Hodges, a newspaper editor, but closed by saying, "I claim not to have controlled events, but confess plainly that events have controlled me." One hundred years later, just after his landslide victory, Lyndon Johnson told Assistant Secretary of Health, Education and Welfare Wilbur Cohen:

> . . . every day while I'm in office, I'm going to lose votes. I'm going to alienate somebody. . . . So I want you guys . . . to get everything in my program passed as soon as possible, before the aura and the halo that surround me disappear. Don't waste a second. Get going *right* now. . . .

Sometimes presidents appear to be helpless figures, controlled by events. At other times they appear to be powerful figures (perhaps too much so) who change the course of history. This book argues that power and impotence are largely determined by how presidents respond to changes in the political system, including the presidency itself; changes in the economic system; and changes in the international system. With this basic framework, I examine each president's responses to these challenges. In this survey, individual presidencies are divided into six periods: the "founding presidency," from Washington to John Quincy Adams; the "partisan presidency," from Jackson to Lincoln; the "eclipsed presidency," from Johnson to Cleveland; the "modern presidency," from McKinley to FDR; the "Cold War presidency," from Truman to Bush; and the "postmodern presidency," from Clinton to the present. Each of these presidential periods embodies certain rules of behavior that shift and vary in the political system, the economy, and the international system. Presidents must learn how to adapt to these changes and/or alter them in order to excel, or even to survive, politically.

I am very grateful to Gayle Zawilla, who helped me formulate this project. She has truly been an ideal editor. I have benefited greatly from discussions of the presidency with Don Lutz, Cal Jillison, Charles Elder, Arthur M. Schlesinger, Jr., Fred Greenstein, Jeffrey Tulis, Betty Glad, Bruce Miroff, Christopher Duncan, George C. Edwards III, James Caesar, and Martin Medhurst. My wife Patricia happily took time away from her own writing to discuss and read the manuscript. Family members— Megan and Josh Abbott; Julie, Paul, Maryn, Karen, Chuck, and Susan Nichols; Jeff, Ruth, Stephen, Janet, and Ralph Nase; and Josh Gaylord— have been patient listeners as well as lively discussants in this effort. I offer a special note of thanks to my son, Josh, who spent endless hours with me at Detroit Tiger games, for engaging in another American pastime, "rate the presidents."

Philip Abbott

INTRODUCTION

Consider the following challenges that American presidents have faced and how they responded:

—When war broke out between England and France in 1793, George Washington was fearful that America would be drawn into the conflict. As he pondered what action to take, he considered the fact that domestic opinion was divided and that some, even in his administration, believed that the power to decide this kind of question rested in Congress and not in the presidency. Washington issued a "Proclamation of Neutrality" declaring that the United States would not support either nation, although the decision increased tension in his cabinet and his critics charged that he exceeded his constitutional authority.

—In 1806, Thomas Jefferson received an offer from Napoleon to buy the Louisiana Territory. Jefferson understood that Napoleon's offer was an unparalleled opportunity not only to protect America's western borders but also to provide an outlet for economic opportunity. On the other hand, he had a "gagging conviction" that such a purchase was unconstitutional. Jefferson actually drafted a constitutional amendment for the consideration of Congress, finally rejecting the plan since the international situation was so fluid. Instead he submitted a treaty to Congress. The act was the most popular measure of his administration.

—In 1832, Jackson's rival in the House of Representatives, Henry Clay, supported the passage of legislation rechartering the Bank of the United States four years before its commission was to expire. Because it was an election year, Clay believed Jackson would acquiesce to the legislation despite his opposition to the bank. Jackson knew that Madison and Monroe were opposed to the bank but had nevertheless accepted its recharter. He also knew that he could only effectively oppose the measure by invoking a little used presidential power, the veto. Jackson decided to veto the legislation, and Congress was unable to override the action despite claims that the president acted unconstitutionally. Jackson was subsequently reelected with 54 percent of the popular vote in a three-person race.

—John Tyler, the first vice president to assume the presidency, was a nominee of the Whig Party in 1840 despite his life-long affiliation with the Democrats. While Tyler left the Democratic Party in 1833, he still retained commitments to many of his old party's positions. Whigs in Congress insisted that Tyler was only an "acting president" with limited powers. Despite this opposition, Tyler negotiated a treaty to annex Texas that the Whig-controlled Senate refused to approve. Tyler was forced to reconsider his options. He decided to send a simple annexation bill to both Houses and requested a joint decision. The legislation was passed when Tyler agreed to a compromise measure that authorized the creation of as many as four states from the territory, although he was unable to secure nomination by either party for reelection.

—In 1861, the entire lower South had seceded from the Union. Lincoln's predecessor, James Buchanan, had declared that neither Congress nor the president could constitutionally prevent secession. One immediate particular question, however, involved the question of federal property in the South. Lincoln announced that he was prepared to give up Fort Sumter in South Carolina if Virginia gave assurance that it would remain in the Union. When Virginia did not act, Lincoln reconsidered his other options. He announced that he would send supplies to the fort. South Carolina responded by ordering artillery bombardment. Fort Sumter surrendered, but Lincoln could assert that the South had started the Civil War. The president is reported to have said, "The plan has succeeded. They attacked Sumter—it fell and thus, did more service than it otherwise could."

—Andrew Johnson, a Democratic vice president in Lincoln's wartime National Union Party, engaged in numerous acrimonious battles with Congress after he assumed the presidency after Lincoln's assassination. Extremely suspicious of the president's plans for the defeated South, Congress passed the Tenure of Office Act that required Senate approval before the president could remove any executive official. Johnson argued that the act was unconstitutional and considered what action to take. He fired his secretary of war, Edwin Stanton, but appointed the popular General Grant in his place. Johnson hoped this appointment would protect him from congressional action. Grant, however, withdrew from consideration, and impeachment proceedings began.

—After winning a very close election, James A. Garfield nominated a reformer for the head of the New York Port Authority, a major dispensary of patronage. Republican Party members in the Senate objected and offered him the option of approving all his appointments immediately—except this one. Garfield, though not known as a courageous politician, was concerned that the presidency was being treated as "the registering clerk of the Senate." He responded in protest by withdrawing *all* of his appointments. The public supported the president, and the majority leader, Roscoe Conkling, resigned.

—Theodore Roosevelt supported legislation to regulate railroads, an enthusiasm that the leaders of both the House and the Senate did not share. Roosevelt considered his options and formulated a plan. Although he was less committed to tariff reduction than to rail regulation, he threatened to send a tariff-reduction proposal to the House and then brokered a trade: abandonment of the tariff bill (which was unpopular with the House and Senate) for passage of the Hepburn Act. When the Senate delayed action, Roosevelt feigned defeat, announcing that he was taking a vacation. The trip actually was an excuse to deliver a series of rousing public speeches in support of rail regulation. The Senate responded to public opinion and passed the legislation.

—After returning from a triumphal public reception in Europe, Woodrow Wilson submitted the Versailles Treaty, which included a provision for a League of Nations, to the Senate. Now under Republican control, the Senate twice refused to approve the treaty. When advisors urged Wilson to accept some amendments in order to win over some of his opponents, he refused. Instead, he canceled all his engagements and went on an 8,000-mile speaking tour. While some evidence indicates that the president was influencing public opinion, he suffered a stroke in Colorado and was unable to continue his effort. Wilson had hoped he would be renominated by his party in 1920, or at least that the question of American participation in the League would be the central issue of the campaign. Neither scenario happened.

—Franklin Roosevelt was angry and concerned that the Supreme Court had declared important parts of his program of economic recovery unconstitutional. Rather than try to accommodate judicial objections or introduce the issue during the election campaign, FDR waited. After a record landslide victory, he sent legislation to Congress that required judges over the age of seventy to retire. Despite huge Democratic majorities in both Houses, Congress never passed his proposal—although subsequent judicial decisions favored the administration.

—During the Korean War, a strike broke out in the steel industry. Harry Truman could have invoked a provision of the Taft-Hartley Act that would send the workers back to the plants in 80 days. The president, however, was reluctant to use a measure he had publicly opposed as anti-labor legislation. Instead, Truman seized the steel mills on the grounds that as commander in chief he could take extraordinary actions in a national emergency. Two months later the Supreme Court declared Truman's action unconstitutional. Truman complained about the decision but nevertheless returned the steel mills to their owners. He then asked Congress to give him direct authority to re-seize them. Congress refused. Owners and labor reached a settlement six weeks later.

—At the end of his second term, Dwight D. Eisenhower hoped to make a major contribution to world peace. He proposed a new summit meeting in Paris and was also scheduled to visit the Soviet Union. Although flights by small U-2 airplanes over the Soviet Union were dangerous, intelligence officials urged the president to approve one more flight before the summit. Eisenhower agreed. The plane was shot down by the Soviets. Eisenhower, who believed the pilot had been killed, denied that the flight was a spy mission. Khrushchev immediately announced that the pilot was alive and under arrest. The summit was a failure, Eisenhower's visit to the U.S.S.R. was canceled, and the Cold War once again accelerated.

—In the fall of 1962, John F. Kennedy was presented with aerial evidence of Soviet missile installations in Cuba. Aside from the possible military significance, Kennedy felt he could not afford to acquiesce before upcoming elections, especially after the Bay of Pigs incident and Soviet construction of the Berlin Wall. The president set up a group of advisors that met in secret and presented him with options. Rather than send in ground troops and begin air raids, Kennedy initiated a blockade of the island and demanded removal of the missiles. After a complicated set of exchanges, Khrushchev agreed to Kennedy's demands.

—In 1996, the Republican-controlled Congress was about to present Bill Clinton with a welfare reform bill that eliminated federal Aid to Dependent Children (ADC) benefits (in place since 1935) as well as aid to legal immigrants. Several advisors in his administration as well as many congressional Democrats urged him to indicate that he would veto the legislation. His polling expert, Dick Morris, recommended that he sign the bill, since he had already vetoed two other versions and his acceptance would take the issue off the table for the upcoming reelection campaign. Clinton considered his options. He indicated that he would sign the Welfare Reform Act and began his reelection campaign with the theme of building a bridge to the future.

Some of these presidential decisions were very popular (Jefferson's decision to purchase the Louisiana Territory), and some were widely criticized (Andrew Johnson's decision to fire his secretary of war). Some were successful (Washington's effort to avoid war with England or

France, Theodore Roosevelt's effort to gain congressional passage of the Hepburn Act) and some were failures (Wilson's effort to gain Senate ratification of the Versailles Treaty, Roosevelt's effort to change the composition of the Supreme Court). Some were bold (Jackson's veto of legislation rechartering the Bank of the United States, Truman's seizure of the steel mills) and some indirect (Tyler's alternative to the Senate's refusal to annex Texas, Lincoln's response to Confederate occupation of Fort Sumter).

In all of these cases, the ways in which presidents responded to the challenges before them produced important, and often unanticipated, ramifications. Jefferson's decision to purchase the Louisiana Territory was cited by later presidents as a precedent for the expansive exercise of presidential power, despite the fact that Jefferson himself espoused a limited view of the office. Andrew Jackson's decision to veto the recharter of the Bank of the United States left his successors with the task of finding acceptable new ways to foster economic development. Andrew Johnson's actions and his subsequent impeachment were partially responsible for reducing the power of many future presidents. Theodore Roosevelt's speeches in support of the Hepburn Act led other presidents to rely more heavily on rhetorical resources of power. Wilson's refusal to negotiate a compromise with the Senate changed the future of Europe.

Although these presidents were certainly aware that their decisions were likely to have a far-ranging impact, each one felt that action was necessary. These and many other examples have always led to questions: How much power should presidents possess to make decisions? How wisely do presidents decide? Are there general standards for presidents to follow in making decisions?

MACHIAVELLI ON EXECUTIVE POWER

Niccolo Machiavelli, a sixteenth-century Italian writer and diplomat, would have appreciated these dilemmas. Perhaps no other person both celebrated and explored executive power more thoroughly. Machiavelli studied the nature of executive power in dictatorships in *The Prince*, and in republics in *The Discourses*. While he noted the important differences between the exercise of executive power in a dictatorship and in a republic, Machiavelli's analyses suggest that he believed there were some essential common features. In both *The Prince* and *Discourses*, he argued that leaders must mask their true intentions from the public, and even from their advisors, in order to be successful. In *The Prince*, Machiavelli said that "men in general judge more by their eyes than by their hands, because seeing is given to everyone, touching to few. Everyone sees how you appear, few touch what you are; and these few dare not oppose the opinion of the many, who have the majesty of the state to defend them. . . ." In

The Discourses, he noted how the founders of the Roman republic used religious myths to establish their authority.

Machiavelli offers several reasons why it is necessary for leaders to hide their true intentions. In *The Discourses*, he asserted that "human appetites are insatiable. It is in man's nature to be able to and want to desire all things; it is in the nature of circumstances that he can only realize a few of these desires. The result is that men are always finding themselves discontented. . . ." Leaders, therefore, must find ways to restrain and direct these desires. A truthful and open leader learns that he is unable to satisfy anyone. In *The Prince*, in particular, Machiavelli claims that adherence to moral qualities such as piety, mercy, and honesty will lead to a leader's ruin. Generosity, for example, will create public debt, the need for more taxes, and finally rebellion. Thus, a prince must appear to be good, "tak[ing] care that nothing escape his mouth that is not full" of moral virtues, while recognizing that "human conditions do not permit" their observance.

Machiavelli also discussed how both subjects (or citizens) and leaders are resistant to change. People are fearful that new circumstances will place them in a worse situation than the one in which they currently are, no matter how extreme their circumstances. For Machiavelli the inevitability of change, sometimes gradual but often dramatic like "violent rivers," is an enormous challenge to any leader. He conceptualized the problem as one of confronting "Fortuna" (the Roman goddess of Luck or Fate). One must anticipate that Fortuna will intervene, but one never knows exactly when and how. One way for an adept leader to deal with this problem is to study and imitate how other great leaders have dealt with crises. While Machiavelli acknowledges that one might never fully be able to attain greatness, he can act like the "prudent archer" who aims his bow high in order to hit a distant target.

In addition to learning from the actions of others, Machiavelli offered his famous dictum that a leader behave both like a "lion and a fox." Sometimes indirection and compromise are necessary in politics, and at other times the use of force is more appropriate. For Machiavelli, a virtuous leader knows when to bargain with and/or deceive his opponents and when to overwhelm them. Most political leaders are skilled at one tactic or the other, but Machiavelli notes that "the lion does not defend itself from snares and the fox does not defend itself from wolves." Great leaders thus act both as a lion and a fox and intuitively know when to select each strategy.

Machiavelli certainly valued the tactic of deception. (The very term "Machiavellian" now denotes cunning.) But Machiavelli recommended "impetuousness" and high risk-taking as the best strategy for confronting change. He was especially interested in the use of force, particularly when overwhelming and unanticipated, as an exercise of executive power. The Italian phrase *ad uno tratto* (with one swift stroke) is the basis for chilling examples in both *The Prince* and *The Discourses*. For example, when Caesare Borgia acquired the province of Romagna, he appointed Remiro de Orco, "a cruel and ready man," as administrator. Because Remiro brutally quelled lawlessness in the province, Borgia knew his minister was hated by the people. He ordered the assassination of Remiro and displayed his body "in two pieces with a piece of wood and a bloody knife beside him." According to Machiavelli, "the ferocity of this spectacle left the people at once satisfied and stupefied." In *The Discourses*, Machiavelli speaks approvingly of the decision to torture captured nobles who had attempted to take away the liberties of citizens of Corcyra and Brutus's decision to execute his own son for conspiring to restore the monarchy.

Whether a leader employed the tactics of the lion or the fox was for Machiavelli a question of circumstance. He was adamant, however, in both works that the justification for executive power lay in its capacity to undertake great projects. In *The Prince*, the goal is to free Italy from foreign occupation and in *The Discourses*, it is to restore and maintain liberty and a sense of the "common good." "When a citizen gains reputation and influence by serving the state well with his counsels and actions," he should be offered "suitable rewards . . . that will be satisfactory and honorable. . . ." Founders and restorers of republics are, according to Machiavelli, like great poets and religious figures who enjoy the acclaim of many generations.

THE INVENTION OF THE PRESIDENCY

Americans of the revolutionary generation were acutely aware of the observations Machiavelli made about executive power. They knew leaders masked their intentions, acted like both the lion and the fox, and imitated past leaders. They knew executive power could be used for vast political projects, some evil and some good. Unlike Machiavelli, however, these Americans were very suspicious of executive power. They had directly experienced the actions of monarchy and its colonial governors and administrators. To them, executive power was synonymous with arrogance, force, cooptation through fear and patronage, corruption, bribery, seizure of private property, and loss of basic liberties. Although Great Britain was certainly moving toward a constitutional form of government in the eighteenth century, Mercy Otis Warren, a revolutionary pamphleteer and historian, believed that the indifference to colonial petitions arose from the "general spirit of all monarchies to discountenance every effort of the people in favor of republicanism." How could one expect a fair hearing "where a monarch sits enthroned with all the powers of despotism in his hands, a parliament at command to enforce his mandates, and a people ready to relinquish their own will to the caprice of the pride of a sovereign"?

This suspicion of executive power permeated all of the first constitutions created by the American revolutionaries. The first national constitution (The Articles of Confederation) had no chief executive at all. The "president" was the presiding officer of Congress, elected by the members for an annual term. Executive departments were created in 1781. Their heads reported to Congress. Thus, under the Articles of Confederation there was an executive branch without an executive. Pennsylvania dispensed with the governor entirely, while other states kept the office but with very limited powers. The governor of Virginia was elected by the legislature annually, with a term limited to three years, and was advised by an eight-member council (also elected by the legislature). Even in New York where the governor was popularly elected and given veto over legislation, he shared power with a "council of revision" in which he was only one member.

Postrevolutionary economic and political problems forced Americans to reexamine their attitudes toward executive power. None of the founders (except perhaps Alexander Hamilton) developed an admiration of the executive comparable to Machiavelli's, but each accepted some portions of his views.

Many influential leaders, including Washington, Madison, Franklin, Hamilton, and John Adams, wondered whether the Articles of Confederation was an adequate national constitution. To James Madison, the confederacy was a concession to the need to resolve problems such as defense and cooperation that seemed to require larger political structures. The confederate model had never achieved these goals and, in fact, had contributed to the decline of individual republics in the past. Madison took extensive notes on the operation of past confederacies, ranging from comments on the ancient Greek Lycian Confederacy to the Belgic Confederacy established in 1679. The result of this effort was published in the spring of 1786 as "Of Ancient and Modern Confederacies." To Madison, the evils to which republics are prone are projected and magnified by confederate arrangements. States trespass upon the rights of one another. (For example, Maryland passed legislation giving tax breaks to ships owned by Maryland's residents.) States encroach on national authority. (For example, Georgia negotiated its own treaties with the Indians.) States act independently with regard to foreign powers. (For example, the Treaty of Utrecht was violated by several states.)

Critics also wondered whether the various state constitutions were capable of meeting important challenges. Washington wrote that "there are combustibles in every State which a spark might set fire to. . . . Good God! Who besides a Tory, could have foreseen, or a Briton predicted them?" Hamilton worried about the ultimate ability of America to function as a nation:

> There is something . . . diminutive and contemptible in the prospect of a number of petty States, with the appearance only of union, jar-

ring, jealous and perverse, without any determined direction, fluctu-
ating and unhappy at home, weak and insignificant by their
dissensions in the eyes of other nations.

Adams concluded that Americans, in their propensity for faction and
self-interest, "were like all other people, and shall do like other nations."
To him, state legislatures could not by themselves be trusted to act
according to the common good. Although Adams's disenchantment with
the optimism of the revolutionary generation was more pronounced than
others', his new views were similar to those of his cohorts. Most importantly, he began to advance an outlook that was like Machiavelli's. One
simply could not rely on people to act virtuously, especially in politics.
All human life is a struggle for power, wealth, and deference, Adams concluded. "We may call this desire of distinction childish and silly but we
cannot alter the nature of men." The desire for praise is so intense that
"every man is miserable every moment when he does not snuff the
incense." Ambition "takes the whole soul so absolutely, that a man sees
nothing in the world of importance to others, but in his object." People
are, for Adams, extremely unequal in their ability and talents even as they
pursue distinction. This inequality "no human behavior can eradicate,"
although Adams recognized that this inequality is rarely accepted by
other individuals who possess the same desires, even if they do not possess the same means to fulfill them. In a society without formal titles that
attempt to justify inequality, each person who sees his neighbor "whom
he holds his equal" with a new house or clothing "cannot bear it; he must
and will be upon a level with him."

Given these assumptions, how can republics possibly survive, especially when there are more opportunities for people to act upon their "constant desires" in these regimes? Adams believed that some institutional
structure was necessary in any society to mediate between the people as a
whole and those who have excelled through talent or the advantages of
birth. To Adams a bicameral legislature represented both wings of the
results of "constant desire." For those human beings who aspired to greatness, there would be the lower chamber of the legislature. The Senate
would be reserved for the already successful. The executive functioned as
the balancer, the third part of a trinity of stability whose function was to
balance the other two forces in society. For without an independent executive, the people would overcome the aristocracy of talent out of resentment. And without full representation the aristocracy would repress those
less successful in the race for power and distinction. Thus, Adams reintroduced executive authority to American political discourse. According to
him, states that in their foundings failed to respect this triumvirate solution to the problems of republics were courting disaster.

The crisis of confidence that emerged during the 1780s might have
dissipated or led to amendments to the Articles of Confederation, had not
a tax revolt in Massachusetts created the specter of armed insurrection in

1786. The newly created Massachusetts legislature, unlike those in other states, had adopted a strict pay-as-you-go budget policy after the revolution. This sense of fiscal responsibility was financed in large part by a regressive poll tax. Dislocations in agricultural markets as a result of the revolution left farmers without outlets for their produce. Mortgage foreclosures and imprisonment for debts were the result. The farmers themselves began to interpret these policies as a plot on the part of eastern merchants to buy up the land and make the free farmers peasants. Many of the tactics formerly employed by the revolutionaries against the British, such as committees of correspondence and the forcible prevention of court proceedings, were now being used by the farmers. Hoping for a more sympathetic legislature, the protesters insisted in the fall of 1786 that no courts should meet until after new elections, which were scheduled for the spring.

When the governor issued a proclamation forbidding unlawful assembly, Daniel Shay, a former captain in the revolutionary army, formed two or three thousand men into a militia. A volunteer force was collected which then routed Shay's contingent. The Massachusetts legislature treated the defeated insurgents leniently, pardoning or reducing sentences and permitting hard-pressed farmers to meet tax bills from unpaid soldiers' receipts. But Shay's Rebellion, as it became known, was regarded as proof of the doubts about the viability of the existing founding. Jefferson, who was in Paris at the time, attempted to allay these fears by contending that "a little rebellion now and then is a good thing." In late February of 1787, however, Congress authorized a meeting in Philadelphia to "render the federal constitution adequate to the exigencies of government, and the preservation of the Union."

When the fifty-five delegates met in May, they were disposed to consider the importance of executive power in a republic. Their faith in legislatures had been shaken; they believed that a stronger national government was necessary, presumably with some kind of an executive component. Moreover, many delegates were developing theories similar to Adams's that emphasized the prominence of self-interest and desire for distinction in human nature.

The delegates to the Constitutional Convention in Philadelphia immediately decided not to amend the Articles of Confederation but instead to write an entirely new document. Once they made that commitment, the delegates never considered continuing the "executive-less" arrangement in the Articles. They were, however, faced with addressing a series of momentous questions about the nature and form of executive power in the new constitution. Sometimes the delegates copied from state constitutions, sometimes they revised them, sometimes they borrowed from other political systems of the past, and sometimes they incorporated wholly new practices. Taken together, the office of president (not so named until late July) was formed from so many eclectic sources and combined in so versatile a fashion that one could say the founders "invented" the institution.

Both of the competing general proposals first considered by the convention, the Virginia Plan and the New Jersey Plan, included a chief executive, but neither provided many details. (Hamilton's plan provided for an executive with life tenure and an absolute veto. However, his proposal received no interest, and he left the convention and did not return until late in the session.) The first issue addressed by the delegates was the question of whether the executive component should be one person or several. James Wilson proposed that the executive be singular on June 4 on the grounds that "only a single magistrate" could provide "energy, dispatch and responsibility to the office." John Randolph strongly objected. Why, he asked, should the delegates introduce the "fetus of monarchy" to America just after a revolution? Why can't a plural executive be just as vigorous as a single one? Three days later, the convention voted (7 states to 3) to add the phrase "single person" to the blank space in the Virginia Plan.

The idea of a plural executive was still considered a reasonable alternative to a single one in 1787, even though all states except Pennsylvania had a governor. Many delegates noted that with three or more executives the problem of incapacitation from illness and succession were diminished, and many of the older delegates still held vivid images of the arbitrary powers of colonial governors. The tide, however, had already turned toward the single model, so the decision by the convention on this matter was not surprising.

Less easily resolved was the question of whether some of the executive's powers should be shared with an executive council. Most states had executive councils to advise the governor on questions of appointments and vetoes. Even the more nationalist Virginia Plan proposed a "Council of Revision" composed of the executive and an unspecified number of judges to be responsible for decisions about vetoes. Many delegates who voted for a single executive assumed that a council would be included in the new constitution. Yet, by mid-August, no decision had been made on this question, and several delegates demanded that the issue be addressed. A proposal for a "Council of State" was referred to a committee of detail. The suggested members were the chief justice of the Supreme Court and five department heads. While the proposal had significant support among convention delegates, it was not presented to the entire body for consideration. On September 7, George Mason complained about the omission and charged that the convention was about to undertake "an experiment on which the most despotic governments had never ventured"; and he moved consideration of a council composed of six members, two from each region of the country, elected by the "legislature or by the Senate." Franklin seconded the motion and Madison spoke in favor, but the proposal was defeated by an 8–3 margin. All that survived of the council was the sentence in the constitution that the president shall "call for the opinions of the Heads of Departments in writing."

Why did the idea of an executive council fail to be included in the constitution, especially since it was such a widely used practice in state governments and since Mason's proposal made it advisory only? Gouverneur Morris reported that members of the Committee on Postponed Matters felt the president might use the council to support "wrong measures"—that is, a council might add to executive power. This supposition was probably the reason Madison supported the motion. Other delegates expressed reservations about including a chief justice in any Council of State. It is possible that the council idea failed because no consensus emerged on who its members should be. It is also likely that by the end of the summer, the convention had already given the Senate many of the powers of an executive council. In any case, the founders in this instance did depart significantly from past practice.

The questions of the length of the executive's term of office and his eligibility for reelection were discussed in great detail at the convention. In the Virginia Plan, the length of service was left blank with no eligibility for reelection. The New Jersey Plan also provided for only a single term. Hamilton proposed a life tenure, and Charles Pinckney offered an annual term. The convention adopted a single seven-year term when it met as the committee of the whole in early June, but so many delegates later expressed reservations that the issue was readdressed. In September, the Committee on Postponed Matters recommended a four-year term with no reelection restriction. The convention finally settled on this proposal.

The question of term length was certainly an issue amenable to compromise, although most states had annual elections for governor and none permitted terms longer than three years. The seven-year term was clearly outlying in terms of precedent, and so, too, for that matter was a term of four years. It was, however, the issue of "rotation in office" that generated the most controversy. States had very rigorous restrictions on reelection. Many not only limited reelection to two or three terms but also made governors ineligible for reelection without waiting for several years after expiration of their term. In Virginia and Maryland, a governor could serve three one-year terms and then was eligible to serve again only after a four-year hiatus. In North Carolina, a governor could serve no more than three years in six. In those few states without restrictions, governors were reelected continually.

Many delegates thus concluded that without rotation in office, the presidency would quickly evolve into a lifetime position. Indeed, during the ratification debate some opponents to the new constitution predicted that the presidential election of 1788 would be the first—and the last. Other delegates, however, adopted the Machiavellian view that the executive is a source of great projects for the republic and ought not to be deprived of continued service. In his defense of the absence of reelection restrictions during the ratification debate in New York, for example, Hamilton spoke of the Constitution as acknowledging the desire for reward as one of the strongest incentives of human conduct. Presidents would not take up "arduous projects" if no opportunity existed to see them brought to fruition. Great men, declared ineligible for future service, would sullenly roam the republic like "ghosts" and constitute a threat to the republic. Some delegates were no doubt influenced by the knowledge that George Washington would be the first president. Their confidence in him assuaged their doubts. Once again, the founders departed from current practice.

The delegates debated the method of presidential selection at the same time they considered terms of service. Both the Virginia and New Jersey Plans provided for the election of a president by Congress. Despite this apparent consensus, the convention did not reach a final decision about presidential selection until September 6. Delegates expressed concern about the independence of a chief executive who owed his election to Congress. Also, there was always the issue of the impact of selection on state loyalties. Would presidents all come from large states that enjoyed heavier representation in the House? Direct election by the citizens raised the same problem, which one proposal attempted to solve by drawing lots and then having those state delegations choose the president. Another presented a plan to give the Senate a veto on the choice reached by the House. On July 19, a plan to select a president by state governors was also proposed. The delegates were clearly concerned that they had not reached agreement on such an important question by this late date.

Finally they focused on a proposal made on June 2 by James Wilson. The Committee on Postponed Matters included an "electoral college" along with other recommendations in its report to the convention. Electors, selected by the states, would choose a president. Each state would receive the number of electoral votes equal to their congressional representation. If no candidate received a majority (and the delegates assumed none normally would), the Senate would select a president from the top five vote-getters. Lest each state would select its own citizens, the recommendation required electors to vote for two candidates from different states. (The second in terms of votes would be the vice president.) When objections were raised to final selection in the Senate where each state had two votes, a compromise was reached by changing the responsibility for selection to the House, with each state receiving a single vote and the Senate selecting a vice president.

The method of selecting a president was approved hurriedly in the midst of several other recommendations by the committee, including a provision for a vice presidency and terms of service. Nonetheless, this solution to the selection problem received less criticism than other provisions for the chief executive. Ironically, complaints about the procedure came later as critics raised questions about both its compatibility with democratic principles and its complexity. Had the delegates followed their initial formulations, the election of the American chief executive would have closely approximated a parliamentary system. From the standpoint of the founders, however, the electoral college was yet another innovation that was perhaps more the result of pure finesse than of compromise over competing principles.

In the course of determining how the president was to be elected, the convention invented many other features of the office. A major critique of executive power during the revolution centered on the right of the Crown and the colonial governors to appoint judges and administrative officials. After the revolution, many states systematically removed this power from governors by appointment either by state legislature or, as in the case of New York, through executive councils. Even military personnel were chosen by legislatures. The new Massachusetts and New Hampshire constitutions, however, provided for executive appointments. To prevent executives from using the appointment power to bribe legislators, states forbade "plural office holding." The practice of barring administrative officials from also serving as legislators was widespread. In New Jersey, officeholders could not also serve in the assembly in order "to be preserved from all suspicion of corruption." The convention delegates were therefore acutely aware that the doctrine of legislative supremacy represented conventional wisdom in regard to appointments, but they had also become suspicious of the legislative power. Were not legislatures just as prone to use appointments to advance self-interests as executives? The delegates thus retained the principle of barring plural officeholding, now justified more in terms of the doctrine of separation of powers, but saw appointments as an executive power.

In June a motion was presented that would give the legislature the power of judicial appointments. Wilson complained, however, that "intrigue, partiality, and concealment" were likely consequences and that the appointment power should rest with "a single, responsible person." John Rutledge responded by arguing that so much power in the hands of a single person was too great and that "the people will think we are leaning too much towards Monarchy." Madison suggested reserving the appointment power to the Senate since it was a "less numerous and more select body" and would be "more competent judges." In September David Brearly offered a compromise: The president would nominate ambassadors, other public Ministers, judges of the Supreme Court, and "all other officers of the US" with the "advice and consent of the Senate." Although neither side seemed particularly enthusiastic, this combination of legislative-executive control over appointments was adopted.

The convention was quite innovative in addressing the question of the removal of a president. Although impeachment had deep roots in British constitutional history, it was reserved for judges and the king's ministers. By applying impeachment to the chief executive, the delegates broke new ground. They faced problems, however, in determining who should exercise this power. For example, if the Supreme Court would try presidential impeachment, who would try judges? Also, was it wise to give judges the power to impeach, since some were appointed by the president? If the legislature were given the authority, would the convention be authorizing the criminalization of political disputes? The delegates eventually settled upon the Senate as the place where impeachment convictions would be heard (after charges had been made in the House), but they also attempted to give the proceedings a judicial air by requiring an oath by senators, with the chief justice presiding. A high threshold for an impeachment conviction (two-thirds) was also approved to make the process difficult.

The convention devoted relatively little time to debate on many issues of later import. All the delegates accepted the proposition that the president should be given a veto power over legislation. Madison preferred that the power be exercised in the context of a special executive council. Hamilton's proposal for an absolute veto was decisively dismissed, but the threshold for a legislative override was set at two-thirds, raised to three-quarters, and then restored to two-thirds. On the question of what standard the president should use in exercising the power (an issue of much later debate) the convention was silent.

Similarly, the convention spent relatively little time on the president's powers in the area of national defense. Only one delegate supported giving the president the right to declare war. War-making power, nearly universally regarded as the essence of tyranny, was placed in the hands of the legislature, although the convention altered the language from "make war" to "declare war" in August. There was more discussion of where the power to make treaties ought to reside. Near the close of the convention, the delegates approved language that shared power between the president and the Senate. Surprisingly, the delegates granted the president an absolute power to pardon, the only such unqualified power attached to the office, with only brief debate. Critics of the Constitution were appalled by this grant of power, but Hamilton provided an interesting Machiavellian defense in *Federalist* #74, citing Shay's Rebellion as a justification. Sometimes a quick and unrestricted use of executive authority can stop a rebellion, he argued. Suppose a group of military officers were to engage in an insurrection but come to see that they were mistaken and that their leaders were "villainous"? A president, through the use of a pardon, could immediately defuse the threat.

Later presidents would use portions of the Constitution that had been casually included by the founders to justify their exercise of executive power. The "commander in chief" clause was regarded as a simple declaration of civilian control of the military, and the oath-of-office language that the president "preserve, protect and defend the Constitution of the United States" too was treated as a simple declaration of good conduct. The executive vesting clause ("The executive Power shall be vested in the President of the United States of America) differed slightly from the vesting section in Article I on Congress, which also included the words "herein granted." The language was offered in final form by the Committee on Style. Presidential historians have wondered whether Gouverneur Morris, a strong advocate of the presidency, purposely made these stylistic changes at the last minute of the convention.

It is interesting to consider how the presidency might have developed had the founders "invented" the presidency differently. For example, had the delegates approved the election by Congress, terms limits, a plural executive, shorter terms, an executive council, and/or legislative control of appointments, all of which were items on the agenda, the presidency would have been a much more limited institution. Perhaps America would have evolved into a parliamentary system, or perhaps there might have been further constitutional changes—perhaps even a new model of democratic governance would have developed. Similarly, had the convention moved in the direction of giving the president more power, such as an unqualified veto (or one requiring a three-quarter legislative override), complete power of appointment, or longer terms of office, the presidency would have been a much more powerful institution. Although the convention did neither, its surveyors tended to focus on one of these alternatives.

Everywhere they looked, the Anti-Federalists, opponents of the new Constitution, saw movement toward monarchy or dictatorship. Anti-Federalists took Machiavelli's advice very seriously, for what they saw in the office was an opportunity for the concentration of power. Patrick Henry, for example, said:

> Your president may easily become a king . . . if your American chief be a man of ambition and abilities, how easy is it for him to render himself absolute! The army is in his hands, and if he be a man of address, it will be attached to him, and it will be the subject of long meditation with him to seize the first auspicious moment to accomplish his design; and sir, will the American spirit solely relieve you when this happens?

Henry and others argued that a monarchy would be preferable to the presidency, since "we may prescribe the rules by which he shall rule his people." Many Anti-Federalists saw the president's role as commander in chief as the road to executive tyranny. Others thought the president would collude with the Senate.

Federalists dismissed these fears as irrational and hysterical. Alexander Hamilton's famous rebuttal in *Federalist* #69 compared the powers of the president to those of the English monarch and the governor of New York. A president had far less power than the king: he was elected; he could be impeached; although commander in chief, he could not declare war or raise armies; he shared appointment- and treaty-making power with the Senate; and his power to receive ambassadors was more a matter of "dignity than of authority." The president's powers were more comparable to those of the governor of New York and, in some cases, such as the power of dissolving the legislature, considerably less restricted than those of the governor. On the other hand, Hamilton did accept another aspect of Machiavelli's advice. The Constitution provided the president with the capacity to bring "energy" to government. The president could act swiftly and decisively for the common good when the need arose. He could protect "the community against foreign attacks" and protect "property against those irregular and high-handed combinations which sometimes interrupt the ordinary course of justice." He could provide "security of liberty against the enterprises and assaults of ambition, of faction, and of anarchy."

In one sense, both critics and defenders were correct. The Constitution as written and ratified was elegantly poised between a restricted presidency and one which was open to significant expansion. Contemporary scholars continue to consider the question of whether the American presidency has a tendency to settle into a "clerkship" or to gravitate to the dominating center of the American political system. For example, Richard Neustadt, in his classic work *Presidential Power*, argued that in terms of formal powers the presidency is at best an "invaluable clerkship," since there are few opportunities for presidents to effectively issue commands. A president's power is fundamentally a "power to persuade." The exercise of this persuasive power is subtle and complex, and it is certainly "no place for amateurs." While Neustadt emphasizes the need for a president to act like a fox in order to avoid performing only as a clerk, Richard Pious (*The American Presidency*) emphasizes his constitutional authority as a source of political power. Presidents are engaged in a continual process of constitutional interpretation, claiming authority both when the constitution speaks and when it is silent. Successful presidents seize upon constitutional ambiguities like lions. Often, Pious argues, they are unsuccessful, as when Truman attempted to justify the seizure of steel mills during the Korean War on the basis of presidential "war powers." Sometimes, however, they succeed, as Lincoln did when he justified unilateral actions at the onset of the Civil War on the basis of his constitutional oath.

The questions that presidents face are the same as Machiavelli posed: When should one act like a fox, and when should one act like a lion? The founders attempted to give the president opportunities to do both within constitutional boundaries. However, as Machiavelli discussed, how does one know how to act when the world is constantly changing, particularly in moments when Fortuna strikes with great force and dramatic transformations occur?

THE SIX PRESIDENTIAL PERIODS

Presidents do, of course, confront the problems of governance in the context of certain basic parameters. The Constitution provides for their method of selection and removal as well as certain fundamental authorizations of power and restrictions. Every president knows that he is commander in chief, that he will provide Congress with an annual State of the Union address, that he must seek the advice and consent of the Senate on appointments and treaties, and that he will sign or veto legislation. He knows that he must retain some measure of support if he wishes to seek reelection and that he has supporters as well as critics. Presumably he knows what he hopes to achieve in office as well. What he does not know, however, is how the economic system will change, what situations will develop in other governments and in the international system in general, or even how the American political system itself will adjust to these and other alterations.

If one surveys individual presidencies, it is possible to classify them into identifiable periods that are outlined in Figure 1. Each of these presidential periods embodies certain rules of behavior in the political system, the economy, and the international system that shift and vary. Presidents must learn how to adapt to these changes and/or alter them in order to excel or even survive politically. They must outwardly conform to the standards set in each period, even while they may be engaged in subverting them. Also, it is not always clear that individual presidents accurately gauge these changes and, if they do, whether they respond effectively. Thus, we shall approach each administration with two questions inspired by Machiavelli's advice: "What did the president want?" and "How did he get it (or fail to get it)?"

The *founding presidency*, the first presidential period, includes six presidents who governed on a model that was considered the only acceptable one in a republic. Executives stood above factions and governed impartially in the public interest. Much of their authority depended on their ability to project, both to Congress and to the public, a persona of patriotic service that exhibited a genuine disinterestedness toward claims from particular regions or groups. George Washington was, of course, the master of this mode of governance. He always accepted power reluctantly and always framed his decisions in terms of civic duty. Even as Thomas Jefferson was organizing a political party whose objective was to significantly change the policies of the first two presidents, he did so on the grounds that his departure from the rules of republican leadership was only temporary. As president, he carefully avoided partisan speech, which was carried out in party newspapers at his direction; and he avoided open expressions of political recommendations, which were presented by his allies in Congress. Nevertheless, both Washington and Jefferson, as well as all the founding presidents, were challenged by critics who argued that a comprehensive political agenda was being promoted behind the façade of republican leadership. Washington was charged with attempting to facilitate a gradual movement toward the British monarchy (by none other than Jefferson himself), and Jefferson was charged with attempting to extend the French Revolution to America.

Figure 1 Presidential Periods

	Selection	Mode of Governance	Institutional Constraints	Economy	International System
Founding Presidency (1789–1829)	Congressional caucus	Nonpartisan; exemplar of republicanism	High	Rural with slave labor	Weak actor in unstable balance-of-power system
Partisan Presidency (1829–1865)	Party convention	Partisan	High to variable	Rural with slave labor	Weak actor in concert system
Eclipsed Presidency (1865–1897)	Party convention	Partisan	Very high	Industrializing	Weak actor in disintegrating concert system
Modern Presidency (1897–1945)	Party convention; limited primaries	Partisan; economic manager; diplomat and commander in chief (variable)	Variable to low	Industrial	Ascending to major actor in unstable balance-of-power system
Cold War Presidency (1945–1993)	Party convention and limited primaries to primaries	Partisan; economic manager; commander in chief; civil rights advocate/adjudicator	Low to variable	Industrial-Postindustrial	Major actor in a bipolar system
Postmodern Presidency (1993–)	Primaries	Partisan; economic manager; diplomat; commander in chief; media director	High to variable	Postindustrial	Hegemony to major actor in balance-of-power system

This mode of governance placed significant constraints on the exercise of executive power, which presidents sought to circumvent with varying degrees of success. John Adams, for example, attempted to govern as a "prudent archer," as Machiavelli advised; but in imitating Washington he found he faced new problems that his predecessor had not, including the rise of new and hostile factions within his own party. In addition to this constraint, the founding presidents were faced with major domestic problems, including the questions of whether it was proper for the federal government to engage in "internal improvements" for the economic benefit of citizens, of how to respond to the Native American population and, late in this period, the issue of slavery. Internationally the United States was in a precarious political situation, since the new nation faced stronger, more established powers who constantly challenged its very boundaries.

The *partisan presidency* lasted 36 years and included ten presidents. While there were, of course, political parties in the first period, presidents carefully avoided open association with partisan activity. Beginning with Jackson, who initiated the new system of partisan governance, and ending with Lincoln, who transformed it, this period freed presidents from governing through the republican model. However, it also tied them to party organizations and goals, making them directly vulnerable to organized partisan attacks. In the founding period, presidents sought to find ways to promote their partisan agendas without challenging their republican personas; in the partisan period they sought to find ways to promote the public interest while governing as party leaders. Jackson invented the concept of the president-as-tribune who sought to govern for all of the people, not just the rich and powerful. Lincoln, too, found a way to challenge the partisan mode of governance by focusing on slavery and secession as issues on which all Americans should take a stand. Both Jackson and Lincoln built party machines that rewarded friends and punished opponents.

Between the towering figures of Jackson and Lincoln, however, stood presidents who were less successful at finding ways to govern in this intense partisan environment. Many Democrats sought to imitate Jackson's success. Polk portrayed himself as the "Young Hickory" and Pierce the "Young Hickory of Granite Hill," both representing efforts to revitalize the Jackson coalition. The Whigs openly abandoned their image as the party of the rich and well-born in 1840 by depicting William Henry Harrison as the "log cabin" candidate. While international questions faded in salience, as America was able to avoid interacting with the concert system created by the dominant European powers, the issue of slavery challenged every president in this period. Each president struggled to remove the issue from the national political agenda. Pierce, for example, declared the question permanently "at rest" after the 1850 compromise, only to be confronted with the Kansas-Nebraska Act months later.

While the slavery issue was resolved by the Civil War, the new configuration of party competition helped produce a new presidential period. The *eclipsed presidency* still featured strong partisan behavior, but now the presidency was an office greatly reduced in power. Eclipsed presidents were constrained by their own parties, which were driven by the need to sustain their organizations through patronage and also were prone to factional splits. As presidents struggled to assert their authority, they confronted a powerful Senate that attempted to "shrink" presidential powers even further by claiming the right to approve cabinet changes and presidential appointments. Johnson was impeached (at least ostensibly) over his refusal to observe the Tenure of Office Act. Garfield and Arthur fought protracted battles with the Senate over appointments. In this environment, presidents were largely helpless in or indifferent to protecting the civil rights of African Americans in the South. The last president even to attempt to undertake this effort was Grant. Eclipsed presidents were also bystanders as momentous economic developments changed the face of America. Financial scandals and labor disputes plagued nearly every president in this period.

Despite diminished presidential powers during the period of the eclipsed presidency, the political system as a whole nevertheless met basic challenges. Southern nationalism was contained, and Westward expansion and economic development proceeded rapidly. The office of president, which had been eclipsed by other public and private institutions for thirty years, quickly recovered. Two factors influenced the transition into a new *modern presidency*. First, rapid industrial growth transformed America into a global economic power; and second, the instability of the world's new balance of power propelled the United States for the first time into roles as a major international actor. In both cases, Americans acknowledged these changes reluctantly.

William McKinley was the first president to present these new developments in positive terms. He argued that a nation with global economic and political interests need not be concerned that "our institutions" will "deteriorate by extension," and he reconfigured the presidency as both the agency for economic development and the locus for determining international political commitments. Subsequent occupants assumed these new presidential roles of national economic manager and international crisis manager, although, of course, in different ways. McKinley and other "New Era" presidents offered plans to supervise the economy by fostering corporate leadership, while Theodore Roosevelt, Woodrow Wilson, and Franklin Roosevelt sought more direct government involvement. In terms of international affairs, modern presidents differed in their approaches as well.

The new roles of economic manager and international crisis manager placed the president at the center of the American political system, not only because both required initiative and dispatch but also because both entailed a recognition of central aspects of modern life. Presidents were planners, innovators, and managers. Of course, while these new roles provided new opportunities for presidents, they also increased their liabilities as leaders. If the economy faltered or international crises occurred, the president's voice was the first heard but also the first to be challenged. Both Wilson and Hoover suffered from the consequences of this new political environment in dramatic ways, and later presidents have been quite aware of their alleged failures. Hoover systematically studied Wilson's decisions. FDR often focused on the impact of Wilson's inability to convince the Senate to join the League of Nations when he devised both his pre-war and post-war policies. Later, Richard Nixon ruminated on Wilson's "mistakes." No subsequent president could afford to ignore Hoover's image as failed economic manager. In 1980 both Jimmy Carter and Ronald Reagan claimed that their opponent acted like Herbert Hoover.

As was the case with the partisan presidency, more aspects of the presidency as we now know it were added in the next period. To date, the *Cold War presidency* in some ways represents the apogee of executive power. With the relative decline of great colonial powers such as Great Britain and France and the defeat of Germany and Japan, the United States and the Soviet Union stood alone as the two remaining dominant powers in a new international system. The framework of this bipolar configuration immediately became apparent as early as 1945, and its basic features changed little for the next 44 years. The United States and the Soviet Union engaged in direct and indirect economic and political competition with one another in a state of "cold war." At some points (in the late 1940s and in 1963) actual war between these "superpowers" seemed imminent, but for the most part military conflict occurred between surrogate states (such as North and South Korea and North and South Vietnam). Both powers engaged in a costly and dangerous arms race and in struggles to extend their own political and economic influence. Since the United States was engaged in a permanent war for over four decades, the power of the president expanded even beyond the new boundaries set by the modern presidents. The executive branch itself was bureaucratically enlarged, and presidents increasingly assumed the role of international crisis manager.

In some ways, however, the power of Cold War presidents was constrained. Not only did they realize that there would be no dramatic victory such as in World War II, but they also faced spirited partisan opposition to their domestic programs. Only once did a Cold War president enjoy the opportunity levels for domestic initiatives that FDR did in 1933 and 1937. Lyndon Johnson's case was unique. Significant but lesser opportunities in this period were relatively rare and limited to Eisenhower's and Reagan's first two years in office. Moreover, Cold War presidents faced nine periods of economic recession, and they also struggled to respond in an effective and politically successful manner to the civil rights movement that challenged racial inequality in the South and other regions of the nation.

When the Cold War ended abruptly and unexpectedly in 1989, a new presidential period seems to have emerged. In the *postmodern presidency*, occupants can no longer rely on the Cold War consensus to formulate support for international commitments. In an era in which all nation-states are porous, presidents may find it difficult to offer consistent policies on questions such as the spread of AIDS, economic integration, "hollowed out" states with little control of their territory, secession movements, nuclear proliferation, and terrorist threats. In addition, the postmodern president must govern in a context of extraordinary media coverage. Whether presidents will learn to manage media spectacles and deal with these new threats—and if so, on what terms in relation to democratic governance—remains to be seen.

Taken together, these six presidential periods illustrate certain basic features of American political development in general and of the presidency in particular. First, some aspects of change are *cyclical*. Historically, executive power seems to rise in some periods and decline in others. Lincoln's expansion of presidential authority collapsed immediately after his death and the end of the Civil War. Similarly, the enlargement of executive power under Wilson dramatically shrank. Although the young Woodrow Wilson reportedly concluded that he was convinced that "congressional government" would be a permanent feature of American politics, he began to revise his assessment after observing the actions of Grover Cleveland. Sometimes the resurgence of executive power is the result of war and economic distress, but at other times it results from the imaginative efforts of presidents themselves, as was the case with William McKinley.

Second, many changes are *layered*. Since Jackson initiated the partisan presidency in 1828, party systems, nominations, rules, and party realignments have certainly changed, but every subsequent president has been selected and has governed in large part as a leader of his party. Similarly, when McKinley added the role of chief economic manager to the presidency in 1896, all later presidencies have assumed major responsibility for the economy (although in different ways).

Third, changes in the presidency in relation to other American institutions are *uneven*. Presidents exercised only general control of departmental budgets until James Polk attempted to regularize estimates, and it was not until 1921 that the presidency received authorization from Congress for a Bureau of the Budget to assist him. Meanwhile, Congress developed effective management of its committee structure under Henry Clay's direction in 1811, and the Senate developed an intricate system of patronage under the leadership of Roscoe Conkling in Grant's administration. New cabinet posts and agencies are frequently created only after major changes occur in society (a recent example being the Office of

Homeland Security in the wake of the 9/11 terrorist attacks). Commerce and Labor were formed as separate departments in acknowledgement of problems in the new industrial economy. Most of the agencies dealing with defense in the executive office were created during the Cold War. Moreover, sometimes the president and Congress engage in balance-of-power strategies to recreate even playing fields. Congress, for example, created the Congressional Budget Office in 1974 in response to the president's apparent advantage in formulating the budget.

Fourth, some changes are *episodic*. Frequently, alterations in the office are made as a result of the individual inclinations of particular presidents. Thomas Jefferson abandoned the practice of delivering the State of the Union address in public, in part because it reminded him of monarchical practices and in part because he disliked public address as a form of communication. Some presidents like press conferences, and others attempt to avoid them as much as possible. Warren Harding, as a newspaper person and gregarious individual, was very adept at press conferences. Some presidents, such as FDR and Richard Nixon, were quite secretive; others were more outgoing in their expression of opinions. James David Barber, in fact, has attempted to categorize presidential personalities in terms of their personal attitudes toward the office and toward political life in general in order to predict their performance.

Confronted with these presidential periods and various patterns of development, presidents perform as both challenged and challenging individuals. Presidents in each period must be intimately acquainted with the rules specified for them. Each president is subject to the manner of presidential selection, the mode of governance, institutional constraints, and the state of the economy and the world in his own time. On the other hand, in order to respond effectively each president must also be alert to find ways to challenge the existing rules. Often presidents can govern quite well under the rules prescribed in their particular period, but at other moments presidents find, much as Machiavelli noted, that Fortuna requires a challenge to these rules.

Bibliographic Essay

There are many editions of Machiavelli's writings. Harvey Mansfield, ed., *The Prince*, (University of Chicago Press, 1998) and Harvey Mansfield and Nathan Tarcov, eds., *Discourses on Livy* (University of Chicago Press, 1996) contain helpful introductions. Mansfield examines the relationship between Machiavelli's views on executive power and those of the founders in *Taming the Prince* (New York: Fee Press, 1989). Sebastian de Grazia's biography, *Machiavelli in Hell* (Princeton: Princeton University Press, 1989), explores the relationship between the political life during Machiavelli's childhood and his writings, and Hannah Pitkin traces Machiavelli's outlook to the masculine sense of political impotence in sixteenth-century Florence in *Fortune is a Woman* (Berkeley: University of California Press, 1984).

One widely available edition of the Federalist Papers is Clinton Rossitor, ed., *The Federalist Papers* (New York: New American Library, 1961). Collen A. Sheldon and Gary L. McDowell have collected other defenses of the Constitution during the ratification period: *Friends of the Constitution* (Indianapolis: Liberty Fund, 1998). A useful one-volume edition of anti-federalist writings is Herbert J. Storing, ed., *The Anti-Federalist* (Chicago: University of Chicago Press, 1983). The debates at the Constitutional Convention are available in a collection edited by Max Farrand, *The Records of the Constitutional Convention 1787*, 3 vols. (New Haven, CT: Yale University Press, 1911). Richard Ellis has assembled those discussions at the convention dealing with the presidency with useful commentaries in *Founding the American Presidency* (New York: Roman Littlefield, 1999). Also see Forrest Mac-Donald's account in *The American Presidency: An Intellectual History* (Lawrence: University Press of Kansas, 1994), ch. 1–8.

Stephen Skowronek presents a classification of presidential periods in *The Politics Presidents Make* (Cambridge: Harvard University Press, 1993) that contains an influential model of presidential decision making in the context of "political time." Also see Michael P. Riccard's history, *The Ferocious Engine of Democracy*, two vols. (New York: Madison Books, 1995), which focuses on the relationship between presidential development and nation and empire building. Sidney Milkis and Michael Nelson examine presidential history in terms of institutional development in *The American Presidency: Origins and Development, 1778–1998* (Washington, DC: Congressional Quarterly Press, 1999).

For two different emphases on presidential power, see Richard Neustadt, *Presidential Power* (New York: Free Press, 1999) and Richard Pious, *The American Presidency* (New York: Basic Books, 1979).

CHAPTER 2

THE FOUNDING PRESIDENCY

Founding Presidents

President/ Political Party	Term of Office	Vice President	Percent Electoral Vote	Percent Popular Vote
George Washington (F)	1789–1793	John Adams	100	—
George Washington (F)	1793–1797	John Adams	98	—
John Adams (F)	1797–1801	Thomas Jefferson	51	—
Thomas Jefferson (D-R)	1801–1805	Aaron Burr	53	—
Thomas Jefferson (D-R)	1805–1809	George Clinton	92	—
James Madison (D-R)	1809–1813	George Clinton	69	—
James Madison (D-R)	1813–1817	Eldridge Gerry	59	—
James Monroe (D-R)	1817–1821	Daniel D. Tompkins	82	—
James Monroe (D-R)	1821–1825	Daniel D. Tompkins	98	—
John Q. Adams (D-R)	1825–1829	John C. Calhoun	32	31

The founding presidency lasted 40 years and included six presidents. Although Jefferson instituted important changes that he later called the "revolution of 1800," there is a remarkable similarity among the first of the founding presidents, George Washington, and the last, John Quincy Adams. Washington represented the American version of the quintessential republican hero. He was devoted exclusively to the public good and unwaveringly undertook his responsibility to maintain public virtue in the face of party factions and ambitious politicians, as did each of his successors. Even Jefferson only reluctantly broke the republican rule against encouraging party organization, with the goal of reversing the "commercialization of values" that he saw as characterizing the first two administrations. Once "pure republicanism" was returned, he believed that "political feuding would disappear." James Monroe attempted to reinstitute republican symbolism in his dress. His ceremonial clothing—blue coat with black breeches and hose—was meant to recall the uniform of revolutionary soldiers. John Quincy Adams, the last of the founding presidents, was horrified and furious that, after a lifetime of devotion to public service, he should be accused of political intrigue in the disputed election of 1824.

Each president experienced the difficulties of governing in the context of the model of the presidency as an institution that stood above factions and as an office occupied by a person who epitomized the highest commitment to national service. Factions within each administration, party conflict between Democratic-Republicans and Federalists, and (later) factions within parties were a fact of political life. For a president to ignore them was to risk political irrelevance, but for a president to openly acknowledge his political aims was to risk his legitimacy. Jefferson expressed the dilemma very clearly in a reply to a troubled supporter in 1806: "If we recommend measures in a public message, it may be said that members [of Congress] are not sent here . . . to register the edicts of a sovereign." If we say nothing, he continued, we are accused of having "no opinions, no plans, no cabinet." When James Monroe offered his views on pending congressional action, Henry Clay reminded him that it was the job of the president to react only to legislation "in the most matured form which Congress can give to it." Otherwise, so argued Clay (admittedly self-servingly), Congress would not benefit from the president's independent judgment.

The appearance of nonpartisanship extended to the electoral process as well. Before the passage of the Twelfth Amendment in 1804, presidential candidates were not identified as president and vice president. The second-place candidate simply became vice president, regardless of any party affiliation. Candidates were nominated by party caucuses in Congress. However, when the results were published, the fiction of nonpartisanship was upheld. Members involved told the public that they acted "only in their individual characters as citizens."

As we shall see, presidents employed different strategies to deal with this problem. Washington, for example, permitted his secretary of treasury, Alexander Hamilton, to be his political point man (his "aegis," as he called him). Jefferson promised a return to republican principles of governance once the real cause of faction ("monocrats," according to him) was exposed. He carefully worked with congressional majorities but avoided public appearances as a partisan leader. Other presidents were less successful. John Adams retained Washington's cabinet in part on the grounds that continuity of service was more important than factional loyalty and soon found that its members owed more loyalty to Hamilton than to him.

If the founding presidency defined the way presidential power could be exercised, there was nevertheless an element of novelty in the model. Because the institution was a new one, the founders had left numerous aspects of the office unspecified—to be shaped, as John Emmet Hughes has said, "by the live touch of history." Naturally, the newness of the presidency was most acutely felt by Washington, who announced upon assuming office that he walked on "untrodden ground." However, every other founding president faced novel circumstances as well. There were two disputed elections in this period. Jefferson was challenged by the opportunities (and burdens) of purchasing the Louisiana Territory and seriously questioned whether a constitutional amendment was required. Madison was the first president to face the question of how to be a leader in war. Monroe was the first to confront a serious economic crisis.

The founding presidency began and ended with America as a rural republic. (About 85% of the population was employed in agriculture in 1800, and about 75% 25 years later.) Nevertheless, each president during this period confronted difficult domestic problems. Washington's aegis, Hamilton, raised the question of whether the nation should prepare to be a commercial republic. Even if, as Jefferson argued, the maintenance of an agricultural nation was essential to the maintenance of republicanism, should the federal government assume a role in economic development? The "internal improvement" question (federal support for highways, canals, and bridges) bedeviled every single president. In general, Democratic-Republicans were opposed to federal support and Federalists were in favor, but Jefferson seemed to change his mind late in his second term. Madison and Monroe equivocated as a "nationalist" faction emerged in their administrations. Equally difficult was the Indian question. Washington asserted a primary presidential responsibility for Indian policy, and every subsequent president was faced with addressing new challenges. Madison was confronted with a resistance movement on the part of the Shawnee led by Tecumseh and his brother in the Northwest as he was dealing with war with Great Britain, and Monroe faced the difficult problem of Spanish support for the Seminoles in Florida.

Although the period is not usually characterized in these terms, perhaps the most central issue facing the founding presidents was war and the threat of war. Every president except John Quincy Adams was confronted with the possibility (and often, the likelihood) of war with a major European power. Washington was forced to issue a neutrality proclamation in an effort to avoid support for the French, which might lead to war. John Adams narrowly avoided war with France through last-minute negotiations. Jefferson issued an embargo against all shipping with France and Britain over the objections of many of his cabinet members and the Federalists. Madison asked for and received a declaration of war against Great Britain in 1812. Monroe avoided open hostilities with Spain despite the controversial military actions of General Jackson in Florida.

These encounters with European powers were in part the result of an extremely unstable international system in Europe during the period of founding presidency. First, the French Revolution and then the Napoleonic Wars (1800–1815), as well as the rapid decline in Spanish power, upset traditional security arrangements in Europe. America frequently became a battleground in this vortex. Also, the United States, though now an independent power, experienced all the political problems new nations confront. Although it had two oceans as protection, the United States was weak militarily and economically dependent on Great Britain. Its borders were not secure. Spain, France, and Great Britain controlled territory in the West, South, and North and were not adverse to allying with Indian tribes to promote their interests. Moreover, while the United States was not a rogue nation in the international system, its republican form of government was a novel one and treated with some suspicion among European monarchies.

The founding presidents enjoyed clear advantages as each took office. The revolution provided a source of political cohesion. The Constitution was popular. The nation was relatively homogeneous and prosperous. Yet, the newness of the presidency (and especially its configuration in republican terms), domestic disagreements, and a volatile international system provided significant challenges to effective governance. How did the founding presidents respond?

GEORGE WASHINGTON (1789–1797)

When George Washington died in 1799, eulogists compared him to nearly every great leader of the past: Moses, Joshua, David, Elijah, Noah, Josiah, Ezekiel, Hezekiah, Samuel, Solon, Cato, Cincinnatus, Fabius, Cicero, Cyrus, Darius, Mohamet, Alexander, Charlemagne, and Henry IV. Patrick Henry Lee captured the feelings of veneration and gratitude when he spoke of Washington as "first in war, first in peace, and first in the hearts of his countrymen," for this summary acknowledged his multiple leadership roles. Washington was the revolutionary commander in chief; he was the chair of the constitutional convention; he was the first president of the republic. What so awed Washington's generation, as well as later ones, was the manner in which the first president performed these tasks. A speaker from New England, Ebennezzer Marsh, compared Washington to Caesar and noted that the former's "great talents would have made him the first citizen of Rome; but he disdained the condition of subject." For Marsh, Washington was "superior to ancient and modern examples" of great leaders. While others may have rejected opportunities "to abdicate power, which they found inadequate to their ambition," Washington voluntarily stepped down from powerful positions. This reticence to assume and exercise power especially charmed his generation. In his recent study of Washington (*Cincinnatus: George Washington and the Enlightenment*), Garry Wills describes Washington as "a virtuoso of resignations. He perfected the art of getting power by giving it away."

This reputation for calm deliberation and commitment to public service as the sole motivation for the exercise of power did not come easily to Washington. As a young man he was an ambitious figure who resented the obedience to political and military superiors expected of young men in colonial America. Marcus Cunliffe writes, "there is something unlikable" about the George Washington of 1753–1758 since he is "raw and strident, too much on his dignity, too ready to complain, too nakedly concerned with promotion." He finds in the 1772 Peale portrait a man grown in "moral stature," a man "poised, almost benign—the master of himself and his surroundings." The military historian Donald Higgenbotham supports this assessment: "Thank goodness Washington in 1775 was forty-three rather than twenty-six. Everything we know about him indicates that during those intervening seventeen years he became a more sober and judicious person."

No biographer can identify the source of Washington's transformation. Cunliffe concludes, "The most we can say (and it is a good deal) is that, like Loyola or Saint Francis, he showed a capacity for growth; his character improved, if not to the point of sanctity." In the first of Washington's great leadership roles, commander in chief of the revolutionary army, he established the tactics he would use throughout his career. Washington alone attended meetings of the Continental Congresses in uniform (one which he designed) and impressed a delegate with his "easy, soldier like air and gesture." At the first Congress, Washington is reported to have offered to raise and financially support a regiment from Virginia. The gesture overwhelmed the delegate, who noted breathlessly that "his fortune is said to be equal to his undertaking." At the second Congress, Washington made no such offer (although he spent his time when the Congress was in adjournment training a militia with his own funds) but chaired two committees dealing with military questions in 1775. Washington thus advertised his availability and suitability in a variety of ways: He visibly promoted his persona as soldier in both appearance and behavior; he illustrated grandly his economic status by lending his fortune to the cause; and he demonstrated his competence in military issues in congressional committee. The appointment still required more than a little bit of luck. Fate required a commander from the South to solidify national resistance.

Washington's statement accepting the command was very brief (just three paragraphs). He noted that the "extensive and important Trust" was evidence of congressional recognition of his talents for which he gave "cordial thanks." However, he cautioned his audience that he "may not be equal" to the task: "But lest some unlucky event should happen unfavourable to my reputation, I beg it may be remembered by every Gentn. in the room, that I this day declare with utmost sincerity, I do not think my self equal to the Command I am honored with." The address concluded with a gesture: Washington refused to accept any pay for the command.

As commander in chief, Washington carefully built a modern army with a class of professional officers, which were essential to any army. "An Army formed of good Officers moves like Clock-work," Washington informed Congress, and good officers were "Gentlemen" and "Men of Character" who were "actuated by Principles of honour, and a spirit of enterprize."

All the more remarkable in terms of Washington's achievement is the fact that colonial Americans were extremely suspicious of professional military structures. A standing army was an "armed monster," an "infernal engine" from the "powers of hell" that stripped a free people of their freedom and bent government to its own will. Americans much preferred citizen militias. In fact, American pride in its militias had almost no bounds. The militia epitomized both ancient and current republican virtue. "Native courage" substituted for money and career advancement. Americans even rejected standard training techniques as smacking of unrepublican professionalism. "Away then," said John Pickering, "with the trappings (as well as the tricks) of parade; *Americans* need them not: *their* eyes are not to be dazzled, nor their hearts awed into servility, by the splendour of equippage and dress; *their* minds are much too enlightened to be duped by a glittering outside." General Charles Lee accepted this notion of the militia as an anti-army army when he claimed that without drilling in "the tinsel and show of war" he could train a fighting force in three months.

Washington, of course, did not accept these assessments. He insisted that congressional fears of the "Evils" resulting from a standing army were "remote" and in the present case "not at all to be dreaded." Washington, in fact, came to see the concern about creating a national army as so unfounded that he attributed the fear to "narrow politics" and warned that an overzealous effort to subordinate military to civilian authority could produce "a contrary effect." For militias, he had almost complete disdain: "To place any dependence upon militia, is, assuredly, resting upon a broken staff," he told Congress. Near the end of the war, he insisted that the militia had not been helpful in a single battle. They were useful only as "light parties to skirmish the Woods, but incapable of making or sustaining a serious attack."

After the surrender at Yorktown, an event known as the "Newburg Conspiracy" provided Americans with another grateful remembrance of Washington's leadership. Frustrated by Congress's unwillingness to reinstate back pay, some officers met in secret. They planned to retreat and leave the citizens in the East prey to the remaining divisions of the British army. Upon learning about these plans, which were being distributed as a circular, Washington called a meeting with his officers. He acknowledged the soldiers' plight but reminded them that Congress moved slowly because "there is a variety of interests to reconcile." The army, however, was animated by other concerns. Its moral credit rested with a sense of honor which the author of the circular was certain to dissipate. Washington spoke of Congress as an honorable body which moved on a different moral plane than the military. Why, then, "distrust" civilian authority when it acted differently than the military, especially when the consequence of such distrust would be to "cast a shade over the glory which, has been so justly acquired?" No soldier who had a regard for the "Military and national character of America" would wish to "open the flood Gates of Civil discord, and deluge our rising Empire in Blood." Washington concluded the address by reading a letter as proof of Congress's good intentions. Reaching for his glasses, the General said: "Gentleman, you must pardon me. I have grown gray in your service and now I find myself going blind." Many officers wept.

Thus, while Washington believed that units led by career officers were much more effective than amateur forces like the revolutionary militias, he nevertheless was firmly committed to the proposition that all military organization should be under the authority of civilian elected bodies such as Congress. This firm commitment to civilian control of the military won the hearts of Americans in general, who were well aware that English civil war produced a military dictatorship under Oliver Cromwell in 1653. Months later, Washington added to this precedent of civilian authority by resigning as commander in chief. He explained his action in a "Circular to the States," which immediately became known as "Washington's legacy." In December of 1783, Washington stated his intention to resign and "return to that domestic retirement, which is well known, I left with the greatest reluctance, a Retirement for which I have never ceased to sigh through a long and painful absence."

The same general pattern (a reluctance to accept authority and careful execution of his agenda once in power) characterizes Washington's monumental leadership roles as the first United States president. His initial negative reactions to Madison's invitation to attend the Constitutional Convention in 1787, however, was not feigned. He insisted at first that he had already made commitments to attend a meeting of revolutionary war officers, the new Society of Cincinnatus. Then he complained about rheumatism in his shoulder. Although he was as concerned as others about the fragility of the Articles of Confederation, what really bothered Washington was his concern that his attendance would be "considered inconsistent" with his pledge upon retiring from the military "never more to intermeddle in public affairs." Finally, however, he accepted Madison's invitation, concluding that a refusal to attend might be considered a "dereliction to republicanism, nay more, whether other motives may not . . . be ascribed to me for not exerting myself on this occasion." As chair of the convention, Washington artfully maintained neutrality while at the same time supporting the positions of those delegates favoring a strong national government.

When the issue of the presidency was raised at the convention, delegates felt awkward in their discussions, since each knew Washington was the prohibitive favorite as the first occupant of the office. Still, as ratification by the states proceeded, he insisted that he was not interested. Washington held firm in his refusal to state whether he would serve if elected. Jefferson, however, like many of his contemporaries believed Washington would accept. He politely remarked that despite Washington's "vast reluctance" he "will undertake the presidency if called to it." When informed of the electoral college's choice, Washington replied: "I am so much affected by this fresh proof of my country's esteem and confidence, that silence can best explain my gratitude. . . ." Not until all the electoral votes were counted and Washington was informed of his victory did he leave Mt. Vernon to assume his presidential responsibilities.

It is difficult to underestimate the challenges that faced the first president. Washington was well aware that every action he undertook could set a precedent. There were innumerable decisions to be made about the office, including forming a cabinet, appointing staff, and forming relationships with members of Congress as well as making policy decisions about the revolutionary-war debt and financing the new government. In this context, Washington faced a political dilemma. Although he now epitomized the new nation's desire for a republican hero, his own political positions—while hardly counter-revolutionary—were not the same as those of many Americans. On many issues, including the need for a standing army, a more distant relationship with France, and a strengthened presidency itself, he agreed with the nationalist, conservative positions of the Federalists. Washington thus risked failure in two general ways: He could abandon his role as national icon and forcefully advocate his own positions, or he could retain his heroic nonpartisan role and let others run the government. For the most part, Washington successfully avoided either exclusive alternative, managing to retain his role as republican hero while working in various ways with others to promote those policies he thought were best for the new nation. His strategy had many important consequences for the presidency in general, and certainly for the founding presidents who followed him.

Although Washington studiously stood apart from the controversy in Congress over whether the president should be addressed as "His Highness the President of the United States and Protector of the Rights of the Same" or other monarchical titles, he assiduously promoted patterns of etiquette and ceremony for the office. He took the oath of office in the Senate chamber and offered a brief address, practices similar to those of the British monarchy. He made a tour of New England after the first session of Congress was over and held many balls and ceremonies. Forrest MacDonald (*The American Presidency*) reached these conclusions about Washington's efforts in this regard:

> Such concern can be regarded as trivial . . . but Washington did not so
> view them, and he was right. He fully understood, if only intuitively,
> that the presidency, if properly established, would be dual in nature,
> chief executive officer but also ritualistic and ceremonial head of
> state, and that the latter function was quite as vital as the more pro-
> saic administrative one.

This strategy did not please everyone. Jefferson, Washington's secretary
of state, complained privately that Washington had been seduced by
"Anglican monarchical aristocratical" views and was moving toward a
British model of governance. When Jefferson's comments were leaked to
the press, however, he was forced to contend that his remarks were taken
out of context.

In policymaking and administrative matters Washington delegated
an enormous amount of authority to his former aide-de-camp, Alexander
Hamilton. As secretary of treasury, Hamilton enjoyed large administrative support. Of the nearly 800 civil service federal employees in 1792,
about 660 worked in Treasury. In close collaboration with Washington,
Hamilton proposed to Congress a plan for the federal assumption of the
war debt and a national bank. Hamilton's prominent position created
open warfare with Jefferson, who opposed the bank as unconstitutional.
Despite Washington's efforts to mediate between the two cabinet members on the grounds that public disagreement would only cause "confusion and serious mischief" for the nation, he was ultimately unsuccessful.
With the support of Madison in the House of Representatives, Jefferson
formed an opposition political party in 1792 and left the administration.
Moreover, some members of Congress began to perceive Hamilton as the
real source of policymaking—a de facto prime minister—and Washington
as head of state.

Washington's relationship with Congress as described by Bryon W.
Daves was "semi-aloof." He was forthright in protecting what he determined as rightful executive authority and promoting initiatives through
his cabinet members but reluctant to provide a sustained leadership role.
In one minor incident, upon receipt of a letter from a foreign nation
addressed to both the president and Congress, Washington consulted
with congressional leaders over who should open the packet.

On more significant questions, Washington usually exhibited the
same reticence. In the first weeks of Congress, during the creation of executive departments, when some members argued that a president should
receive approval from the Senate before dismissing executive officials,
Washington let James Madison (then a House member) make the arguments against this view. Thus, the position that the president had the
right to fire his own officials, although vigorously challenged by Congress
later in the nineteenth century—and by implication the position that the
presidency contains powers unspecified in the Constitution by the vesting clause—was made by a member of Congress, not by the president.

Washington's view that the authority of Congress must be respected was challenged early in his first term. The president in general tended to be more solicitous of the Senate than of the House, in part because the Senate shared important powers with the executive branch and also because the Senate was the chamber most friendly to the president's policies. In this case, Washington asked the Senate for its advice on treaty negotiations with the Creek Indians. After debating for days over where the president should sit, the Senate welcomed Washington and his secretary of war designate. After a reading of a position paper handed to Senator John Adams, another member suggested that policies of previous Congresses should also be read. A lively discussion followed, and Washington became visibly agitated. After another fruitless session, Washington vowed never to ask the Senate as a body for advice again. In the short term, the decision pleased many groups, including anti-Federalists in the House who harbored suspicious of a cabal between the president and the Senate. For Federalists anxious to expand presidential power, Washington's decision to seek advice and consent from the Senate as a whole on treaties only after they were negotiated pleased them as well.

In areas Washington regarded as within his executive authority, he was energetic and innovative. He was actively involved in even minor appointments. As Leonard White has reported, "[No] collector of customs, captain of a cutter, keeper of a lighthouse, or surveyor of revenue was appointed except after specific consideration by the President." As to criteria, Washington refused to appoint former Tories or anyone with a record of opposition to the new Constitution. These were, of course, prudent standards for a new regime. Washington's policy also meant that the remaining pool of available talent consisted of Federalists. The president was careful to recommend active Federalists to the courts. His ten Supreme Court nominations (more than any other president) assured that the judicial branch would generally promote the Federalist agenda for many years to come.

Washington also took an active role in Indian policy. In the early days of the republic, tribal nationhood was not only a legal concept but also a political and military reality. Since Britain and Spain exercised influence over various tribes, relationships with Native Americans presented a complex foreign policy problem. As a former general, Washington assumed responsibility for the details of this frontier diplomacy. He met personally with the chief of the Senecas and held summit conferences with the leaders of the Six Nations in his first term. He determined where frontier troops would be stationed and even how they should be disciplined. His secretary of war attempted with some success to limit land speculation, which always created new pressures for Indian removal. Whenever Congress asked for information about executive policies in this area, Washington provided documentation (despite the concern of some cabinet officials about what would later be called executive privilege).

Nevertheless, what had been a congressional policy issue in the old constitution became primarily an executive issue in the new one.

The most decisive as well as the most controversial exercise of executive authority domestically was Washington's reaction to the so-called "Whiskey Rebellion." An important element of Washington's economic policies involved the creation of federal taxes. The excise tax on whiskey was enormously unpopular in western Pennsylvania, since farmers in the area used whiskey as a currency. In the summer of 1794 the protests against the tax became violent. There was an attack on the house of the excise inspector, tarring and feathering of tax collectors, and an angry march to Pittsburgh. Washington, no doubt influenced by the course of the French Revolution and even the recent formation of the Democratic-Republican Party, described the Whiskey Rebellion as the work of dangerous "self-created societies" which required forcible repression. He ordered Knox to request a federal judge to declare a state of emergency under the terms of the Militia Act of 1792 and wrote the governors of four states requesting them to provide armed forces.

Some leaders openly expressed suspicions of Washington's motives. Madison charged that the action was an excuse to create a standing army. The Pennsylvania governor insisted a militia call-up was unnecessary. Nevertheless, Washington personally led troops as far as Carlyle to confront the rebels. Jefferson facetiously concluded, "An insurrection was announced and proclaimed and armed against, but could never be found." Indeed, the army (which at 13,000 approached the size of the revolutionary Continental forces) encountered no resistance. However, Washington later told Congress that the rebellion threatened to "shake government to its foundation." On January 1, 1795, he declared a day of national thanksgiving. Whatever the real threat in western Pennsylvania, Washington had provided a vivid image of the military might of the federal government.

In foreign affairs, Washington faced more difficult problems. The new revolutionary government in France did not behave like the monarchy it replaced. The French regarded the United States as an ideological ally, since both nations now had republican governments and were also bound by the Treaty of Alliance of 1778. The revolutionaries sent Edmond Genet to the United States to help make these points. Genet was more than a visiting minister, becoming actively involved in domestic political disputes and encouraging Americans to take direct action in support of the French cause. Federalists regarded Genet in particular and the French in general as dangerous to the republic and feared that the terror of the revolution in France would be imported to the United States. The newly organized Democratic-Republicans, on the other hand, were more sympathetic to the French. To some of them (including Jefferson), even if their revolution had taken a particularly violent turn, the French were on the right track.

Washington himself was not sympathetic to the French. Moreover, he felt that closer ties with France would antagonize Great Britain. Washington knew how economically dependent the United States was upon Britain and also had great respect for its sea power, as the British possessed the most formidable navy in the world. Unlike some Federalists, however, Washington was not anxious to ally the new republic too closely with the British for fear of accentuating its former colonial status. Therefore, Washington issued what has come to be known as his "Proclamation of Neutrality." A debate ensued immediately over whether the action was constitutional. Madison, writing under the pseudonym Helvidius, contended that since the Constitution gave Congress the power to declare war, it followed that Congress—not the president—also had the power to declare neutrality. Hamilton, writing as Pacificus, argued that since the Constitution gave the president significant authority in foreign affairs, it was not wise—nor even constitutional—to begin making exceptions.

Washington's proclamation not only increased factional conflict domestically but also did not work as a foreign policy. The British seized American ships with impunity and the French, under the direction of Genet, continued to use American ports to outfit privateers. Washington was forced to enter into negotiations with the British, which led to the Jay Treaty of 1795. No one, including Washington, liked the treaty since it required the United States as the weaker party to accept significant concessions, including a restriction on the exportation of cotton. However, policies that are only marginally successful in the short term can nevertheless produce major long-term effects. The proclamation became an important precedent for presidential authority in foreign affairs.

By apparently giving it away, Washington's last acts as president were masterful examples of his strategy of achieving power. For once again, although the Constitution placed no limits on presidential terms, Washington resigned. He announced his resignation by releasing a farewell address. His decision not to seek a third term awed even Washington's critics. Jefferson was particularly impressed. Presidents followed Washington's precedent until 1940, when FDR sought and won a third term. The farewell address was a tradition less rigorously adopted by subsequent presidents, but the words of Washington himself have been carefully studied by later generations.

Washington began by informing his audience that he intended to retire and acknowledged a "debt of gratitude . . . for the many honors" his countrymen have bestowed upon him. "Here, perhaps I ought to stop," said Washington, but "a solicitude for your welfare" required that he continue, and the president offered his advice in terms of the "disinterested warnings of a parting friend who can possibly have no personal motive to bias his counsel." This self-description as a "parting friend" is repeated when Washington closes with a second reference to himself as an "old and affectionate friend." The farewell address thus has two parts: a short and very Washingtonian preamble in which he speaks as an American version of the Roman leader Cincinnatus (who turned in his sword for his plowshare) and a longer analysis in which he speaks as a departed figure, indeed as the lawgiver of antiquity. In a way, the shorter section is essential to the longer one, since the power of Washington's advice depends on his role as a reluctant and impartial leader.

Washington's specific counsel includes three basic pieces of advice. First, he warns against the pernicious consequences of faction. Men who are "cunning, unprincipled and impatient" will always appear, for the "love of power and proneness to abuse it . . . predominates in the human heart. . . ." Washington quite sternly urges citizens not to tolerate these "ambitious, corrupted and deluded citizens" and to follow only the "real patriots." Political parties "enfeebled" the government, promoted suspicion and jealousy among citizens that could lead to "riot and insurrection," opened "the door to corruption and foreign influence," and "encouraged citizens to pursue patronage rather than disinterested service." Second, he demands that Americans accept the Constitution as the "pillar," "prop," and "foundation" of American nationhood. As such, says Washington, it demands "respect for its authority, compliance with its laws, acquiesce in its measures." Finally, Washington warns Americans to avoid excessive affection or hatred toward other nations. Affection leads Americans to overlook the faults of other countries and antagonizes those not favored, and hatred blurs ability to see possible sources of common interest. Thus, Washington criticized those who looked to France and Great Britain as either allies or enemies and instead urged as the "great rule of conduct" the avoidance of strong political connections with foreign powers.

Washington's counsel has been selectively followed by subsequent presidents and Americans in general. His advice to treat the Constitution with reverence has, of course, been generally followed, although there have been periods in which the Constitution has been severely criticized. Some Americans portrayed it as a slaveholder's document in the 1850s, and as a tool of economic elites in the Progressive Era and in the 1930s. Despite Washington's warning about factions, political parties have become an essential mode of governance. His foreign policy advice has been taken quite seriously, and many Americans interpreted the "great rule of conduct" as an authorization for isolationism. Washington's reluctance to be involved in European affairs and his admonition to avoid excessive love or hate for certain nations did not prevent presidents from participating in two major European wars, nor did it stop Americans from harboring animosity to particular nations, however justifiable, as in the case of the Soviet Union during the Cold War.

JOHN ADAMS (1797–1801)

While Washington certainly had long-term goals in mind in his farewell address, he had short-term goals as well. He was genuinely concerned about the rise of political parties, and about the lasting authority of the new Constitution. After all, the first constitution, the Articles of Confederation, only lasted ten years. What might prevent support for yet another, with all the attendant crisis that would follow? Many Federalists regarded the Constitution as too democratic and longed for one more similar to the British model. Many Democratic-Republicans, on the other hand, thought the Constitution was not democratic enough. Washington also worried that European powers might take advantage of internal discord in order to bring the United States under their influences—either economically, politically, or both.

Each of these concerns continued to be serious problems after Washington left office. When the founders created the electoral college, they did not anticipate the existence of political parties. The most renowned figure in the republic was to be chosen by electors, and the one with the next highest number of votes would be vice president. Yet even in 1792, there was considerable political maneuvering. All public figures accepted the fact that Washington would be re-elected, but the Republicans decided they would support their own candidate for vice president. The Federalists supported John Adams. Washington was elected unanimously, but Adams barely had enough votes for second place.

In 1796, the Federalists supported Adams for president and Thomas Pinckney for vice president, and the Republicans Jefferson for president and Aaron Burr for vice president. Before the adoption of the Twelfth Amendment, electors had to decide whether to vote for both men on the party ticket or selectively leave a ballot blank to assure that one of their party's candidates would be vice president. However, if they left too many ballots blank, the candidate from the other party might come in second. The key figure in these behind-the-scene calculations was Alexander Hamilton, who first insisted that Federalists cast their ballots for both Adams and Pinckney. Some Federalist electors rejected Hamilton's advice, believing that Pinckney might pick up a few Republican ballots and win (which was Hamilton's very intention). However, too many Federalists left blank ballots. Adams won the presidency; Jefferson came in second and became vice president. Thus, Adams found himself president of an administration in which his party competitor was his own vice president! (Imagine, for example, that George W. Bush found that his vice president in 2000 was Joseph Lieberman.)

Despite these party intrigues, Adams followed the same general model of governance as Washington, seeing himself as the disinterested republican leader. In fact, as senator he wore a powdered wig and often carried a sword at his waist. Like Washington, he did not campaign for the presidency. Indeed, Adams was a highly regarded leader during the revolution and held important diplomatic posts. Newspapers referred to him as the "Atlas of Independence." On the other hand, Adams suffered greatly, as did many later presidents, from comparisons to popular predecessors. Adams himself once remarked that Washington was like "the sun setting in full orbit" and he was another rising, "though less splendid." Moreover, while some always suspected Washington's partisanship, Adams's was much easier to identify. After the revolution, Adams became decidedly more conservative. In 1799 his stubborn insistence in the Senate that the president be addressed in monarchical terms made him an easy target for Republicans. Perhaps Adams could have recovered from these charges had he made adjustments and/or had some good luck.

Thus, Adams governed both without the force of Washington's personality and in the context of a much more well-developed party system than in Washington's administrations. Adams could have attempted a degree of rapprochement with Jefferson to create some kind of coalition government in order to carry on the model of a nonpartisan administration, although such a tactic would have been quite difficult given the political differences between the two men. Instead, Adams moved in a different direction. He asked all the cabinet members in Washington's administration to continue to serve. No doubt Adams had in mind the notion that his action would be a signal of his intent to establish executive continuity. Unfortunately for Adams, most of these cabinet officers were loyal to Alexander Hamilton, who was now the major power in the Federalist Party and whose political views were even more conservative than Adams's. His center of support rested with the "High Federalists" who were very sympathetic to Great Britain. Some even regarded Jefferson as an agent of France, and some were openly opposed to expanding political participation in the states. Even Jefferson understood that these Federalists were "only a little less hostile" to Adams than to him. Later, Adams himself recognized that he had made a serious mistake in not appointing his own loyal cabinet.

The splits in Adams's own party, and the Republican opposition, immediately combined to reach a crisis over relations with France. Republicans had already made the Jay Treaty, which they interpreted as capitulation to Great Britain, a political issue in the 1796 elections. Now France argued that the United States had become too close to Great Britain and threatened retaliation. They began seizing American ships and warned that America would face all the "the power and violence" that France as a great nation could bring to bear. Adams called Congress into special session and asked for funds to prepare for war. When the French indicated that they were willing to negotiate, Adams sent a diplomatic mission to Paris. The French foreign minister, however, told the American delegation through emissaries that the United States would have to provide funds if the talks were to proceed. He demanded $10 million in loans in addition to $250,000 for himself. One American delegate, Charles Pinckney, is reported to have said the answer was "No, no! not a sixpence!" When Republicans in Congress requested information on the negotiations, Adams provided a complete account that identified the three French diplomats as "X," "Y," and "Z." The "XYZ" affair affronted Americans so much that war appeared to be inevitable.

Adams briefly became a popular figure with Americans as the "rally effect" took hold. Federalists were, of course, the most bellicose. Their slogan was "Millions for defense, not one penny for tribute." Republicans were suspicious, since they regarded the incident as a pretext for Federalist desires to raise federal taxes and create a large standing army. Adams effectively moderated Federalist demands. He was, however, forced to accept one more act of humiliation from Hamilton, at whose instigation George Washington reluctantly agreed to command the armed forces in the event of a French attack, with Hamilton as his second in command. Since the aged former president was unlikely to assume direct command, Hamilton, in effect, would be commanding general. Adams was furious at Hamilton's maneuvers but was unsuccessful at preventing him from assuming command. Upon hearing rumors that his Federalist rival intended to use his command to invade Spanish Florida and Louisiana with the aid of British troops, Adams told his wife, Abigail, that he must find a way to prevent Hamilton from acting upon his "mad" schemes since he could "become a Bonaparte."

For two years France and the United States fought an undeclared war (called the Quasi-War). The United States, in fact, captured over 80 French vessels. Although under severe pressure from Hamilton and other Federalists in the Senate to ask for a formal declaration of war, Adams secretly sent a second peace mission to France. Both sides were aware that recent defeats by the British had changed the power differential, and a treaty was reached acknowledging the rights of the United States as a neutral power and relieving it of obligations from the 1778 alliance.

One might conclude that Adams would be celebrated as a great peacemaker. Indeed, many historians now make this case. David McCullough (John Adams) concludes that the decision to send a second peace mission to France was the "perhaps the bravest act" of Adams's entire career, more so even than signing the Declaration of Independence. After his retirement, Adams described his efforts to avoid war as "the most disinterested and meritorious actions of my life." Several factors, however, intervened. The agreement with France announced in November 1800 came too late to alter the election. Also, Adams's own party resented his actions. During the Quasi-War he remained committed to increasing national defense, including the creation of the Department of the Navy, but to many Federalists Adams lacked the will to engage fully in a war with France. In the summer of 1800, when members of his own cabinet refused to support his peace initiative, he demanded their resignations.

In addition, Republicans could never forgive Adams for signing the Alien and Sedition acts passed by Federalist congressional majorities in 1798. Composed of four measures, the acts increased from five to fourteen years the period of residence required before one could apply for citizenship, gave the president authority to deport foreigners for a period of two years, and forbade "treasonable conspiracies" and criticism of Federal officials "with the intent to defame" or "to bring them into contempt or disrepute." Federalists argued that these were necessary wartime measures. There were, after all, over 25,000 French nationals living in America. Republicans, turning the tables on the conventional Federalist comparisons of their party to the French revolutionaries, called the acts the "Federalist reign of Terror." The Virginia and Kentucky state legislatures opposed these acts and declared them void in bills written by Madison and Jefferson.

THOMAS JEFFERSON (1801–1809)

The contest between Adams and Jefferson in 1800 was one of the most bitterly contested presidential elections in American history. Although the differences between their two political parties were significant, a major reason for the animosity surrounding this election was the fact that the model of the founding presidency did not acknowledge the validity of party competition. The more intense the competition, the more the participants concluded the political system was about to collapse. Hence, each side believed the 1800 election was likely to be the last one for Americans. Republicans were convinced that a monarchy would be instituted if the Federalists won, and Federalists were just as certain that Jefferson would carry the nation to a revolutionary reign of terror (as had happened in France) if he were elected. Thus, the excitement of the presidential contest, which Americans later came to accept (and even enjoy), was highly magnified. Both parties campaigned vigorously. Since electors were chosen by state legislatures in about two-thirds of the states, party activists worked to produce local party majorities. In states in which they were chosen by voters in each district, party regulars handed out circulars that provided party identification for each elector. Even John Adams made public appearances. Although Jefferson did not do so, he did circulate his "platform," the first for a presidential candidate.

Adams was still handicapped by factions within his own party. Hamilton in particular was determined to deny Adams a second term. When the Federalist congressional caucus met in May of 1800, they decided to support Adams and Charles Pinckney "without giving preference to the other." This overt statement of "equal" support meant that the caucus was not fully committed to returning Adams to office since, unless some electors withheld votes for Pinckney, it would be possible for Adams to be selected as vice president under either Pinckney or Jefferson.

This awkward scenario did not become a reality, but another one did. Jefferson and Burr received the same number of electoral votes. Under these circumstances, the selection of the president went to the House of

Representatives. As noted in chapter 1, the founders did not really see the House's selection of the president as a defect since, in a nonpartisan environment, electors might select several renowned men. In 1800, however, the House was composed not of independent members but of men under party discipline. Federalist state delegations continually voted for Aaron Burr for president, and Republicans for Jefferson. After 35 ballots, and with the date of the inaugural approaching, the situation reached the point of a constitutional crisis. Minimally, the Federalists hoped to extract concessions from Jefferson or perhaps even to reach a deal with Burr. Maximally, Federalists thought they could continue the deadlock until March and get the Senate to declare a president until 1804. The new chief justice of the Supreme Court, John Marshall, was discussed as a possible acting president.

Jefferson did not take these schemes lightly and began to threaten retaliation against the possibility of "usurpation." In a letter to Monroe and anticipating victory two days before he was elected by the House on the thirty-sixth ballot, Jefferson wrote that had the Federalists declared an interregnum "the middle states would arm, and that no such usurpation, even if for a single day, should be submitted to." His trump card, as he saw it was the threat of a constitutional convention. "The very word convention gives them the horrors," he told Monroe, "as in the present democratical spirit of America, they fear they should lose some of the favorite morsels of the Constitution." When the crisis was over, both parties insisted that no other outcome than the election of Jefferson was ever really considered. The contested election of 1800, however, did just miss a violent outcome.

Jefferson did much to calm nervous politicians and citizens by invoking the principles of the founding presidency in his inaugural address. A major portion of the speech was devoted to healing the wounds caused by the first openly partisan presidential election in America. Jefferson noted, "We have called by different names brethren of the same principle." By emphasizing that the two contesting parties, Federalists and Republicans, stood generally for two basic principles—federal union and a republican form of government—he declared, "we are all federalists, we are all republicans." Jefferson did acknowledge that an important transfer of power had occurred, but he favorably compared it to the "throes and convulsions of the ancient world" and the violence of the French Revolution that had even reached "this distant and peaceful shore."

Few contemporaries failed to note Jefferson's moderate tone. John Marshall, Federalist and justice of the Supreme Court, praised the speech as "conciliatory" and "giving the lie to the violent party declamation which has elected him." Jefferson later commented that his administration constituted a revolution, though not by the "sword," and that he was proud to be "the first republican president."

Nevertheless, Jefferson did regard his presidency less as the first partisan election than as the first election that would put America back on its true "republican tac." According to Ralph Ketcham *(Presidents Above Party)*, Jefferson was greatly influenced by the arguments of the British political philosopher and critic of the Tories, Viscount Bolingbroke. Although he himself had been a Tory, Bolingbroke developed a sustained critique of political corruption in his *The Idea of a Patriot King* (1738). Bolingbroke remained a monarchist throughout his career, but this work attracted many republicans because it detailed the ways in which a virtuous leader could reform a corrupt regime. Foremost in Bolingbroke's thought was the premise that factions are the result of the development of a "court party" that seeks the favors of a king who governs poorly. A "patriot king," however, could reverse these patterns of corruption that will ultimately lead to tyranny. Ketcham describes how Jefferson's policy agenda corresponds to Bolingbroke's:

> First, "purge the court" of the partisans and corrupt placemen, and second, replace them with a new class of men Jefferson would characterize as "an aristocracy of talent and virtue." The third measure of the patriot king was "to espouse no party, but to govern like the common Father of the people," an idea to which Jefferson aspired as he sought to triumph *over* party, rather than *through* party. Fourth, the patriot king would encourage a balanced economy (including commerce) that would insure the prosperity of the people, a conception not the least alien to one whose attention to practical improvements, profitable agriculture, and enlarged trade was as unceasing as Jefferson's. Finally, "the bearing of the patriot king constituted the fifth measure of his program." The leader, that is, had to be a moral guide for the people and in his bearing and manners a symbol of the best in the national heritage.

Ironically, a supporter of Washington might conclude he already embodied the principles of the "patriot king." Although he acknowledged that Washington was a "great man," Jefferson felt that he had not been fully committed to republicanism. Washington believed that the practicality of republican government was an open question which he was determined to give a "fair trial," but Washington's distrust of human nature led him to believe "we must at length end in something like a British constitution. . . ." This belief, Jefferson concluded, was the reason Washington had adopted so many "levees, birthdays, pompous meetings with Congress." These ceremonies were "calculated to prepare us for a change which he believed possible, and to let it come on with as little shock as might be to the public mind." "Federal monarchists" had poisoned Washington's mind against him, and Jefferson noted, "to this he listened the more easily."

As the "first republican president," Jefferson abandoned all the ceremonial practices of the presidency that Washington had instituted. He did not hold any balls or receptions. He refused to make any tours on the grounds that the president should not be the object of "public gaze." He did not appear before Congress. The State of the Union message was delivered to Congress in written form. When Jefferson met with diplomats, he used the forum of the small dinner party. Invitations were simply signed, "Th. Jefferson."

Jefferson also systematically sought to reduce the scope and size of the federal government. He decreased the size of the armed forces, and he supported the repeal of the Alien and Sedition Acts and the elimination of nearly all federal taxes. "We are hunting out and abolishing multitudes of offices . . . striking off jobs, lopping them off silently . . . ," he reported to his son-in-law in 1801. He even considered, then rejected, closing American embassies abroad. Despite this flurry of activity in support of the Republican platform, Jefferson himself remained publicly aloof. He did not, of course, take on the patriarchal persona of Washington or Adams. As Joseph J. Ellis *(The American Sphinx: The Character of Thomas Jefferson)* writes, "Political power, to fit the republican model, needed to be exercised unobtrusively, needed neither to feel or to look like power at all." Ellis calls this approach the "textual presidency" because Jefferson so excelled in "the art of making decisions . . . synonymous with the art of drafting and revising texts." The president would write a draft and then ask cabinet officers to comment. A consensus would emerge. (Jefferson preferred separate consultations in order to avoid "disagreeable collisions" at full cabinet meetings.) His private dinners with Republican congressmen were marvels of polite persuasion.

In one area in his first term, Jefferson did experience some resistance from his own party. Many Republicans were adamant in the demands that he remove federal officials whom they thought were not loyal to the cause. Jefferson was generally cautious on this matter, in part because he was concerned that the Republicans would be imitating the practices of Federalists. Jefferson did, however, refuse to acknowledge the "midnight appointments" of John Adams. After the election Adams appointed many Federalists to judicial offices, and Jefferson ordered his secretary of state, James Madison, not to sign the commissions.

One potential officeholder, William Marbury, filed suit in the Supreme Court. Republicans thought that they had before them a perfect "win–win" outcome to the conflict. Should the Court order that Marbury have the job, Jefferson could refuse to comply, with the argument that the judiciary was obviously a partisan, Federalist-controlled institution. Should the Court refuse to support Marbury, its authority over executive actions would be diminished. Republicans, who looked suspiciously upon the courts in general after their aggressive enforcement of the Alien and Sedition acts, would have been quite pleased with this scenario. John Marshall, the chief justice, however, avoided both outcomes. He concluded in *Marbury v. Madison* (1803) that the defendant did not have a right to the position, but only because the Judiciary Act of 1789 was unconstitutional, since it incorrectly granted courts original jurisdiction.

Thus, while Jefferson was able to thwart Adams's effort, the Supreme Court captured a much greater prize: judicial review, the right to declare acts of Congress unconstitutional.

Despite this huge victory for the courts, Jefferson was not deterred. He complained that the Federalists, defeated at the polls, "retired into the judiciary" like guerillas in order to beat back "all the works of republicanism." He supported the impeachment of Justice Samuel Chase, a devoted Federalist who delivered outrageous and inappropriate political diatribes from the bench. The House did, in fact, impeach Chase but the Senate did not convict him. Some Senate Republicans, though infuriated by Chase's behavior, did not believe his actions constituted "high crimes." No other Supreme Court justice has been impeached since this effort.

Two major unanticipated events challenged Jefferson's attempt to set forth a presidency that was nonpartisan but much more limited in scope than Washington's and Adams's. Preoccupied with European affairs and discouraged by the cost of quelling a slave rebellion in Santo Domingo, in 1803, Napoleon offered to sell the United States the Louisiana Territory. Later in the same year, as part of his objective to wage a "remorseless war against English merchandise," Napoleon ordered a naval blockade of Great Britain. Meanwhile, Great Britain intensified its practice of capturing American vessels and impressing American sailors into service in their navy. Jefferson's response to the first challenge was to purchase the Louisiana Territory. This decision greatly enhanced Jefferson's reputation, both in his own day and in later generations. In the other case, Jefferson supported an embargo of all American shipping in 1807. He argued that the action was "the last card we have to play, short of war." The British increased impressments of American sailors and the French continued their blockade of the continent. This decision, and Jefferson's attempts to enforce it, was so unpopular that it later led to secession efforts in New England. Just before he left office, Jefferson signed a bill repealing the embargo. According to Henry Adams, Jefferson endured a "mortification such as no other president suffered."

Earlier, when Spain handed over the territory to France, Jefferson realized that the most feared leader in the world now possessed land on America's western boundary. A French empire in the West "produced more uneasy sensations through the body of the nation" than any "since the revolutionary war." Jefferson concluded, "the day that France takes possession of New Orleans . . . we must marry ourselves to the British fleet and nation." Jefferson took swift and decisive action as soon as he learned of Napoleon's offer to sell the Louisiana Territory. He immediately sent a diplomatic envoy to try to negotiate the purchase of the port of New Orleans. Moreover, Jefferson considered the purchase of Louisiana a momentous opportunity to provide new land for settlement. As a republican, Jefferson worried that eventually America would become overcrowded and poverty-stricken like Europe. He later told Congress that "by enlarging the empire of liberty we multiply its auxiliaries, and provide new sources of renovation, should its principles, at any time, degenerate, in those portions of the country which gave them birth."

Americans certainly agreed. Some Federalists tried to raise objections, but to the great majority of the nation this was as great a cause for celebration as the adoption of the Constitution. Less than two years later celebrations of the formal transfer of authority in New Orleans began. The *National Intelligencer* announced that "an assemblage so numerous, to celebrate an event, at once so glorious and so happy, may not occur again for centuries to come."

Jefferson himself, however, had doubts. He harbored the "gagging conviction" that his action exceeded the limits of the Constitution. Every person he consulted about the constitutionality of the action assured him there were no difficulties, but Jefferson, seemingly alone, persisted. He drafted a constitutional amendment, which he intended to submit to Congress along with the treaty, and later he wrote new drafts. The international situation was still a fluid one, however. The president worried about the possibility of reneging on Napoleon's part and finally submitted the treaty to Congress "in silence" regarding any constitutional amendment. By August he had reached a personal philosophical accommodation concerning his action, which he now described as one that involved the "executive seizing the fugitive occurrence." Admitting he had engaged in an act "beyond the constitution" as would the Congress in its ratification, both parties would have to present their deed to future generations:

> The Legislature in casting behind them metaphysical subtleties, and risking themselves like faithful servants, must ratify and pay for it, and throw themselves on their country for doing them unauthorized, what we know they would have done for themselves had they been in a situation to do it. In the case of the guardian, investing the money of his ward in purchasing an important adjacent territory; and saying to him when of age, I did this for your good; I pretend to have no right to bind you; you may disavow me, and I must get out of the scrape as I can; I thought it my duty to risk myself for you. But we shall not be disavowed by the nation, and their act of indemnity will confirm and not weaken the Constitution, by more strongly marking out its lines.

While Jefferson had less misgivings about his other decision, the embargo, the public at large certainly had more. Very quickly, Jefferson requested a series of supplemental acts designed to close legislative and administrative loopholes and soon found himself personally licensing shipping and confronting problems such as the amount of flour permitted in the cargo holds of vessels. "I do not wish a single citizen to be deprived of bread," wrote the suspicious president, "but I set down the exercise of commerce, merely for profit, as nothing when it carries with it the danger of defeating the objects of the embargo."

His attempts to regulate domestic commerce were challenged by a Republican judge. The administration ignored the decision. Jefferson, who was critical of Washington's action in the Whiskey Rebellion, now declared the Champlain region of New York in a state of insurrection. The proclamation was designed to stop entrepreneurs from sending goods on rafts to Canada, but unfortunately (for Jefferson) it coincided with the anniversary of the first battle in the American Revolution. Charges during the election of 1800 that Jefferson was a radical began to reemerge. Federalists insinuated that the real purpose of the embargo was an attempt, revolutionary in its scope, to return America to a Spartan republic that forbade commerce and manufacture. One partisan charged that Jefferson planned a "Chinese" approach to political economy, shutting off America to foreign commerce in the mistaken belief the nation would "enjoy an eternal rusticity and live, forever, thus apathized and vulgar. . . ." Finally, just before the end of his second term, a Republican Congress repealed the Embargo Act. Jefferson quietly signed the measure, declaring he was now "but a spectator" in his own administration.

From the advantage of hindsight, one can see the challenges Jefferson faced in reaching both decisions. In the first, his desire for secure boundaries for the young nation and the prospect of creating an "empire of liberty" that would provide land for later generations trumped his concern about providing precedent for an imperial presidency. In the second, his desire for peace led him to undertake measures as president that he would have certainly adamantly opposed earlier in his career.

JAMES MADISON (1809–1817)

When Jefferson left office, he wrote his successor, James Madison, "Never did a prisoner, released from his chains feel such relief as I shall on shaking off the shackles of office." Although Madison was eminently qualified for the presidency, he too would experience the same feeling eight years later. Madison's close friendship with Jefferson, his long career of public service, and his position as secretary of state in Jefferson's administration were a mixed blessing. Jefferson's popularity was in decline, and a small group of strident critics within the Republican Party were determined to deny him the nomination. The charges that Madison was Jefferson's "monkey on a leash" and "crown prince" were taken up by Representative John Randolph, the leader of the "Tertium Quids." Republican Party dominance during the founding presidency was anchored by party majorities in Virginia and New York. As a fellow Virginian, Randolph appealed to James Monroe to stand for the presidency. He also gave encouragement to George Clinton of New York. Monroe was annoyed with both Jefferson and Madison for their failure to support the Pinckney-Monroe Treaty to the Senate. Clinton, at age 69, served six

terms as governor and was vice president in the second Jefferson administration. He desperately hoped to cap his career with the presidency. As a
result of the efforts of Randolph and others, supporters of Monroe and
Clinton boycotted the Republican congressional caucus. The rump group
voted for Madison for president and Clinton for vice president. Fortunately for the Republicans, the Federalists were unable to capitalize on
their opposition's disunity. Madison remained aloof from conflicts within
his own party and the Federalist opposition. Monroe remained convinced
he might win the support of Federalist electors, and Clinton even threatened to turn down the vice presidency. By the time balloting took place,
however, Republican electors rallied around Madison.

When Madison took the oath of office in March, he faced three
immediate problems: almost half of the Republican congressional caucus
did not vote for him; the economy was in disarray as a result of the
Embargo Act; and war with Great Britain seemed inevitable. Madison's
first inaugural address provides some insights into how he hoped his
presidency could meet these challenges. He noted how "under the
benign influence of our republican institutions" America had prospered
since the revolution. "In their rage against each other, or impelled by
more direct motives," however, foreign powers retaliated against the
United States and damaged the economy. Madison promised to work
unceasingly to seek peace in these difficult circumstances and "to maintain sincere neutrality toward belligerent powers." In other words, the
problems that faced America originated from abroad. His views on the
office itself during this difficult period represent the acme of the principles of the founding presidency as revised by Jefferson, whom Madison
acknowledged as his exemplar. He listed what he understood as the
major functions of the office:

> To respect the rights and authorities reserved to the states and to the
> people as equally incorporated with and essential to the success of the
> general system; to avoid the slightest interference with the right of
> conscience or the functions of religion . . . ; to preserve . . . the freedom
> of the press; to observe economy in public expenditures; to liberate
> the public resources by an honorable discharge of the public debts; to
> keep within the requisite limits a standing military force always
> remembering that without standing armies their liberty can never be
> in danger, nor with large ones safe; to provide by authorized means
> improvements friendly to agriculture, to manufactures, and to exter-
> nal as well as internal commerce to favor in like manner the advance-
> ment of science and the diffusion of information as the best ailment to
> true liberty; to carry on the benevolent plans which have been so mer-
> itoriously applied to the conversion of our aboriginal neighbors from
> the degradation and wretchedness of savage life. . . .

For Madison, Jefferson's reformation of the presidency along republican
lines was complete and now required consolidation.

While Madison recognized the challenge of foreign powers, important changes in American politics made Madison's effort to routinize a streamlined presidency very difficult. First, Congress had begun to develop as a policymaking institution with interests different from those of the presidency. In the early days of the republic, the Speaker of the House was a minor office. The House was organized by several party leaders. Now the position was consolidated and when Henry Clay assumed the post in 1811, he utilized standing committees to introduce legislation under his direction. Second, while Jefferson was always annoyed by a small group of dissidents in his own party, a new group of young representatives from the West and South known as the "War Hawks" effectively challenged Madison's policies. These young men (most were in their thirties) did not have the veneration for the founders that previous representatives did and they were high risk-takers, especially on foreign policy issues. Third, while Madison was a respected leader in Congress and in the eyes of the public at large, he did not possess Jefferson's personal magnetism.

Throughout his two administrations, it seemed as if every action Madison took was criticized from some quarter. When he proposed the nomination of Albert Gallatin for secretary of state, Senator William Giles, the leader of a faction of conservative Republicans who often voted with the Federalists, offered no less than nine objections to the appointment. Although Gallatin was an extremely talented administrator and a personal friend, Madison relented and reappointed him as secretary of treasury instead. When Madison sent troops into West Florida in 1810, Federalists loudly complained about the expansive use of presidential power. When Madison considered relieving General Wilkerson of his command for incompetence, he faced objections from Maryland Republicans and concerns about Jefferson's feelings since the former president was one of Wilkerson's supporters. He reluctantly decided to retain the troublesome general. When Madison sought diplomatic assurances of safe passage for American shipping from Great Britain, the War Hawks called him "whifflin' Jemmy."

These criticisms reached a crescendo during the War of 1812. The war was relatively short (30 months) and ended inclusively. The Treaty of Ghent (1814) left American boundaries intact and did not resolve the major cause of the war (the British policy of impressing American sailors into His Majesty's Navy). Yet today it is still remembered for the humiliations suffered by the United States. The White House and Capitol were burnt by British troops as Madison, in flight, watched from Virginia. An ill-conceived invasion of Canada by the United States was repulsed by a small contingent of British soldiers. Most significantly for Madison, the war engulfed the entire period of his presidency. As Richard J. Barnet has concluded, "His fate was to lead the nation into its most unpopular war until the twentieth-century debacle in Indochina. The War of 1812 was

'Mr. Madison's war' just as the war one hundred fifty years later was Lyndon Johnson's war."

From the moment Madison asked Congress for a declaration of war in June 1812, it seemed that Murphy's Law (if something bad can happen, it will) dominated the entire conflict. Although Madison's reasons for his request were not unreasonable (British impressment policies, blockades of American shipping, and their support of Indian attacks in the Northwest) and he was responding to demands for stronger action in his party to defend national honor, the vote was very close. The House passed the request on June 4 by a vote of 79–49 and the Senate on June 18, 19–13. Impressment, the major provocation on the part of the British, was actually rescinded but news of the change came too late to influence the debate. Initially, optimism ran high. There were some spectacular American naval victories, and many political observers believed that an invasion of Canada to bottle up British troops and to provide a negotiating chip could be easily achieved. Henry Clay announced that the Kentucky militia alone could complete the task, and even Jefferson said that capture was just a simple matter of marching. After the British effectively blockaded the American navy and the invasion failed, second thoughts quickly arose. Congress was reluctant to raise taxes for the war and governors refused to honor Madison's requests for troops. In New England, opposition reached the level of treason. The governor of Massachusetts entertained British feelers for a separate peace and twenty-six delegates from New England met in Hartford to consider secession.

Peace negotiations began in 1814, and initially British demands were severe. An early proposal called for the recognition of the Northwest Territory as a separate Indian nation, no American fishing rights in the Atlantic, a redrawn border favorable to the British in Canada, and British navigation rights on the Mississippi. Finally, Madison had a bit of good luck. The demands stiffened American resolve. New England leaders rallied around the president and Wellington, when offered the command in Canada, balked. A treaty was signed on Christmas Eve.

Scholars of the presidency still place a good deal of blame for the War of 1812 on Madison. Robert Rutland has concluded that Madison incorrectly anticipated that the war would be confined to a few naval skirmishes. Others have argued that Madison was an ineffective war leader. One biographer concludes:

> The hour had come but the man was wanting. Not a scholar in governments ancient and modern, not an unimpassioned writer of careful messages, but a robust leader to rally the people and unite them to fight was what the times needed and what it did not find in Madison.

Still others blame the difficulties in the war on republican policies themselves. Republican principles required a limited chief executive and republican principles required a minimal defense establishment. In a sense, however, there was realistically little more that Madison could have done. From the beginning, his administration was overwhelmed by both external forces (the Napoleonic Wars) and internal ones (changes in Congress and the Republican Party).

JAMES MONROE (1817–1825)

In the last two years of his administration, Madison did enjoy some respite from criticism. The influence of the Federalists was in rapid decline, due in part to their strident opposition efforts to the War of 1812. Madison himself made some accommodations to the "new" Republicans from the West in his support for rechartering the National Bank in 1816 and in his willingness to consider internal improvement programs such as building the Cumberland Road. When James Monroe took the oath of office in 1817, he reiterated this new consensus. The government of the United States had reached a stage of near "perfection." No "essential improvements" were necessary; his administration need simply occupy itself with "preserving the virtue" of the people. This "era of good feeling" represented, for Monroe and other Republicans, confirmation of the project initiated by Jefferson. The presidency was shorn of monarchical elements and the political system was finally free of party conflict. Indeed, when Federalists attempted to mount a campaign against Monroe in 1815, Rufus King wrote a party activist: "Federalists of our age must be content with the past." King did eventually lead the Federalist ticket but carried only three states. There was no Federalist candidate at all in 1820. The United States was a one-party political system, or, as Republicans preferred to think, a no-party system.

Monroe's political career was perfectly suited for the persona of a Republican version of George Washington. He was a revolutionary war hero who was seriously wounded in the battle of Trenton. Like many Republicans, he opposed the ratification of the Constitution. He was a loyal supporter of the Republican Party and of Jefferson in particular. Unlike both Jefferson and Madison, however, Monroe was not a person with a philosophical bent. Reactions to his first inaugural address indicate that the press was aware of Monroe's practical nature. The *National Register*, for example, said:

> As to the style of the speech, it is, like the suit of clothes which president Monroe wore on the occasion, very good home-spun, and quite fine enough. It forms no objection with us, there are no flowers of rhetoric scattered through it.

John Adams was less kind. He described the new president as "dull, heavy, and stupid." Monroe emphasized his image as a nonpartisan figure interested in compromise and unity throughout his presidency. He reinstituted tours of the nation to emphasize the presidency as a symbol of national identity. These trips to various sections of the country were elaborate public-relations events, replete with ceremonial speeches by the president and locals and with parades and entertainment. Like Washington, Monroe faced charges that he was indifferent or impotent in areas that required aggressive public leadership. Henry Clay, for example, declared after his oppositionless re-election that the president "has not the slightest influence on Congress." Despite these criticisms, Monroe could be quite adept at implementing his limited agenda in indirect ways.

One item on Monroe's agenda was the maintenance of this new one-party system. Appointments and policies too generous to the remnant of the Federalist Party might destroy the party discipline of the Republicans. On the other hand, if the Republicans pushed their hegemony too far, it was possible for the Federalists to make a comeback. In other words, Monroe planned to discourage factions within the Republican Party and, at the same time, isolate any remaining Federalists. Concerned that the "Virginia Dynasty" was a source of sectional resentment that might split the Republicans, Monroe sought to select a cabinet with members from each region of the country. He asked Henry Clay to be secretary of war but he declined. He considered Andrew Jackson but learned that he too was not interested. He finally settled on John C. Calhoun, who, while from the South, was closely identified with the "new" Republicans from the West.

Monroe's surprise appointment, however, was John Quincy Adams for secretary of state. Adams was the son of a Federalist president but moved toward the Republican Party in his support of Jefferson's embargo policies and had served in Madison's administration as a diplomat. But while Monroe had a New Englander in the prime cabinet post, he also paid a price. In the founding presidency the position of secretary of state was considered the stepping stone to the presidency. Monroe not only offered the position to a recent convert to the party but also overlooked a prominent Republican and westerner, William Crawford. Crawford had considerable support as a presidential candidate in 1812 but declined to pursue the office in deference to Monroe. Clearly, he felt Monroe owed him a political debt which now went unacknowledged. A sullen Crawford did accept the secretary of treasury appointment. Adams proved to be an adroit secretary of state and an able counselor to the president. Crawford, on the other hand, was an uncooperative cabinet officer who embarrassed Monroe on more than one occasion, including failing to inform the president that the government was running a deficit.

Another recalcitrant Republican also placed Monroe in a difficult situation. Like all Republican presidents, Monroe kept a close eye on Florida. During his administration, Spanish power was dramatically ebbing and the president waited for the appropriate moment to force Spain to secede the territory. Monroe was also concerned the British would fill the power vacuum before the United States did. In 1818, he sent General Jackson to Florida to restrain the Seminole Indians from their raids on American territory and to disperse pirates from St. Amelia Island. Jackson gladly assumed the command and urged the complete military occupation of Florida, which he thought could be achieved in sixty days. In pursuit of the Seminoles, Jackson seized Pensacola and hanged two British subjects there. It seemed that everyone was outraged. The British and Spanish demanded apologies; the cabinet and Congress were fiercely divided; Monroe was very annoyed with his runaway general; Jackson especially was furious that he would be subject to any second guessing.

Monroe refused to censure Jackson, who, after his victory in New Orleans, was extremely popular with the public at large; but neither would he apologize to the Spanish. Speaking before Congress, Monroe indicated that the captured territory was to be returned but criticized the Spanish for failing to control their own territory and warned them that if they did not review their responsibilities, the United States would be forced to undertake further action. He explained that Jackson had acted on his own (a point that the general denied) but that he had behaved reasonably given the situation in the field. Whether Jackson's actions and Monroe's threats were the primary reason for Spanish secession of Florida to the United States just months later is a difficult question to answer. Monroe, however, was certain that they were.

In a related area of foreign policy, Monroe acted with the same kind of deliberativeness and with the same success. As the Spanish empire crumbled, one South American country after another began to resist colonial rule. At first, Monroe took a Washingtonian position of neutrality. However, this diplomatic indifference to attempts to seek liberty from colonialism nagged at Monroe's republican conscience, and the imminent power vacuum in the whole hemisphere concerned him as well. Russia was asserting rights over portions of the Oregon Territory; France offered to aid the Spanish in putting down rebellions; and then, of course, there were always British imperial interests. When the British, in fact, started exploratory diplomatic discussions with the United States to issue a joint declaration of noninterference, Monroe systematically sought advice from former presidents Jefferson and Madison. While Jefferson admitted that he would prefer to see Cuba to be part of the United States someday, he concluded that a joint declaration would be a major victory for American interests. Madison agreed. Monroe's cabinet was uncharacteristically unanimous as well. Monroe, however, was concerned that the United States might appear to be seen a junior partner with the British if a declaration was issued.

Instead, he decided to act unilaterally. In December, 1823, Monroe's message, read before a joint session of Congress, included the statement that the United States would "consider any attempt" on the part of European powers "to extend their system to any part of this hemisphere as dangerous to our peace and safety." Monroe based his declaration on the exceptional nature of America itself. Since the "political system . . . [of Europe] is essentially different" from America, the United States had no interest in participating in their conflicts. America had won its liberty by the "loss of so much blood and treasure" and could not risk endangering this sacrifice by ignoring attempts to control governments in South America whose fates were "more immediately connected."

Of course, the enforcement of what later came to be called the "Monroe Doctrine" still depended on the might of the British navy. In fact, Monroe's declaration was made at a time when the United States could barely control its own immediate borders. Nevertheless, its issuance asserted presidential authority in foreign affairs and was an expression of American confidence in the moral, and eventual political and military, authority of its political system. Much later, in the twentieth century, critics argued that the Monroe doctrine provided a rationale for an American form of colonialism as the United States intervened in South American governments for economic reasons.

In other areas, including internal improvements, the issue of slavery and the economic crisis of 1819, Monroe's policies were less successful. In each, Monroe was never quite certain what direction to take. Although he professed heterodox views on the issue of the federal government's role in promoting economic development, Monroe vetoed congressional legislation providing for the repair of the Cumberland Road and the creation of tolls. Although the original bills establishing the link between Maryland and western Virginia were signed by Jefferson and Madison, Monroe vetoed the bill. In his mind, internal improvements were a valuable federal policy, but a constitutional amendment was required to authorize any legislation. In 1822, however, in his annual message to Congress, Monroe contended legislation to repair federal projects already built was constitutional. A year later he supported federal funds for building canals, as long as states could determine where they would be built.

Monroe's repeated insistence that internal improvements required a constitutional amendment appears to have been heartfelt. He even sent copies of his position papers on the subject to members of the Supreme Court for their comment. Monroe's major political problem as president, however, was the fact that Congress, and major portions of the public, did not have these scruples and had developed elaborate rationales for an extensive federal role in economic development. Henry Clay's "American system," for example, claimed that the federal government not only could significantly increase economic prosperity with these internal improvement projects but also could promote national unity as the East, North, South, and West came to be more connected economically with one another. There was a small contingent of orthodox Republicans in Congress who disagreed violently with these views, but they were annoyed almost as much by what they saw as Monroe's willingness to compromise on this question.

During Monroe's presidency five new states were admitted to the union. In 1818, Congress began to take up the petition of Missouri for statehood in a routine manner. During the proceedings, however, Congressman James Talmadge of New York proposed two amendments that were soon passed. One prohibited the further importation of slaves into the territory and another emancipated all slaves in Missouri when they reached the age of 25. These amendments created intense debate both within Congress and in the nation. Jefferson in retirement described the controversy as a "fire-bell in the night" that "awakened and filled me with terror." The House passed the Talmadge Amendments, but the Senate excised them from their bill. Even more intense debate continued through the next session of Congress in the fall of 1819. Petitions were sent to Congress, and numerous state legislatures passed resolutions of support or opposition. Henry Clay finally forged a compromise in March of 1820. Missouri would enter the union as a slave state (hence voiding the Talmadge Amendments), Maine would enter as a free state, and the rest of the Louisiana Territory north of 36° 30' would remain "forever free."

What were Monroe's actions during this crisis? He did not mention Missouri in his 1819 annual address to Congress. Privately, he opposed the amendments and urged friends to publish letters and articles opposing them. He wrote George Hay, his son-in-law and political confidant, that "a paper showing that Congress have no right to admit into the union any new state on a different footing from the old, written with ability and moderation, would be eminently useful." Monroe tended to blame the controversy on the "personal aggrandizement" of politicians in the Northeast who were stirring up the public. He composed a draft of a veto message but finally indicated that he would sign the Missouri Compromise. On this first national debate on slavery, Monroe stood on the sidelines. Part of his reticence to participate was the result of his own position as a slave owner (Monroe owned about 70 slaves), and part was the result of his own general views on the limitations of federal authority. Whatever his motives, he let leadership on this momentous issue come exclusively from Congress.

Monroe was also inactive in the face of the Panic of 1819. After a period of rapid growth, the economy took a serious downturn due in part to faulty investments, corruption by officials of the Bank of the United States, and a drought in the West. Cotton and rice were half their 1818 price and money in circulation was quite scarce, leading to numerous bank closures. Several prominent business people urged Monroe to call Congress into special session. Monroe refused. He did review the economic crisis in his annual address but left Congress to decide whether additional taxes and/or tariffs were necessary.

If Monroe's primary objective as president was to eliminate permanently what he called the "discord" of party division from the American political system, he failed to achieve his objective. Although his appointment of Adams as secretary of state and his other appointments were designed to broaden the Virginia base of the founding presidency, his actions only delayed the emergence of factions that led to a new party system. Actually, the elements that supported the era of good feelings were declining before Monroe's gaze. Virginia's population was being superseded by new concentrations in the lower South and West. The issues raised by the Federalists, particularly in regard to internal improvements, were now being raised by the Westerners. Moreover, other issues, particularly the question of slavery, moved to the center of the political agenda. Also, a new generation of political elites, who did not share the revulsion against partisanship felt by both the old Republicans and Federalists, rapidly entered the national arena in the 1820s. On the other hand, Monroe's presidency did illustrate the capacity of a determined leader to delay and moderate change, if only temporarily. Monroe's foreign policy was a skillful adaptation of the Republican agenda, and he was able to contain the ambitions of men like Clay and Jackson on his own watch.

John Quincy Adams (1825–1829)

Although the candidates did not fully realize that the election of 1824 represented the end of the founding presidency, there were enough signs to indicate some new system was emerging. First, there was no candidate from Virginia, the state that produced all previous presidents except for John Adams. Second, there were in 1822 no less than eight possible presidential candidates. The number declined to five two years later and then to four when Calhoun settled for the vice presidency. Third, each candidate for the first time clearly represented a region of the nation: Adams (New England), Crawford (the South), and Jackson and Clay (the West). Fourth, the Republican Caucus failed to effectively endorse a candidate. Crawford's supporters showed up and he received the nomination, but the other candidates sought nomination through caucuses in various states. Jackson's supporters, in particular, made special efforts to attack what they called "King Caucus" as a nominating procedure. The Tennessee General Assembly in 1823, for example, passed a resolution declaring the caucus system both unconstitutional and unfair. The caucus, they declared, not only violated the constitutional principle of the separation of powers but also gave an unfair advantage to the more populous states.

The 1824 election did not turn upon differing political platforms as much as it reflected personalities and sectional attachments. Adams carried New England and New York; Crawford, who suffered a stroke in September, carried only Virginia, Delaware, and his home state of Georgia (plus five electors in New York); Clay won Kentucky, Missouri, and Ohio (plus four electors in New York); and Jackson won the rest, including

Pennsylvania's 26 electoral votes. Although Jackson won the popular vote and the highest number of electors, he did not receive a majority. The election, by constitutional mandate, went to the House of Representatives. Jackson, following the precepts of the founding presidency, remained distant from the negotiations among House members who voted by state with one vote each. Adams, on the other hand, was more active. When the ballots were counted, he received the votes of thirteen states, four of which had been carried by Jackson and three by Clay in the general election. Jackson's and his supporters' primary complaint was not so much the disparity between the popular vote and the final one as it was the fact that Adams nominated Clay as secretary of state. Jackson referred to Clay as the "Judas of the West," and his supporters attacked the legitimacy of an election that was the result of the "corrupt bargain." In Adams's defense, some compromises and adjustments had to be made for a president to be elected, but the cabinet appointment did seem to be a flagrant one.

Adams worked very hard to heal the wounds from this unusual election. He closed his inaugural address with the admission that "the peculiar circumstances of the recent election" left him "less possessed of your confidence in advance than any of my predecessors." He attempted to form a cabinet that recognized the new party factions. He even offered Jackson a position in the new administration. In an effort to establish that his "intentions were pure and upright" despite the charges, he refused to fill federal positions with his political sympathizers.

Adams focused on new national institutions as well as internal improvements as the main goal of his administration, believing that a series of federal projects would serve as a basis for national unity. He proposed a naval academy, a national university in Washington, DC, and a national observatory. He claimed that the "magnificence and splendor of their public works are among the imperishable glories of the ancient republics." Acknowledging that internal improvements had been controversial, Adams asked, twenty years after the construction of the Cumberland Road: "To how many thousands of our countrymen has it proved a benefit? To what single individual has it ever proved an injury?"

Adams's inventive ideas, however, were never seriously considered by Congress. Adams did not enjoy the popularity of Jefferson, who was also elected by the House of Representatives. Adams, in fact, described himself as "a man of reserved, cold, austere, and forbidding manners." Nor did he have the political acumen of the third president. His decision not to employ patronage left him without friends in the executive branch and did not prevent his enemies from charging him with corruption anyway. His domestic proposals actually functioned as a red flag to his campaign opponents who, except for Clay, were suspicious of internal improvements. Almost immediately, Congress, led by the politically talented Martin Van Buren in the Senate, lined up against the president. After the congressional elections in 1826, the House and Senate were divided between those who called themselves "Adams men" and those who called themselves "Jackson men," with the former in a clear minority. Although Adams was able to make some contributions to American foreign policy, particularly in regard to commercial treaties with a dozen nations, his presidency overall was caught in a gridlock created by an emerging party system.

SUMMARY AND COMMENT

By 1828, the main features of the founding presidency disappeared. The primary means of presidential governance, the persona of the non-partisan republican hero, was gone—and not just on the temporary terms that the Republicans of 1800 envisioned. The early mode of presidential election also disappeared. The congressional caucus maintained the façade of disinterested citizens throughout the founding presidency. Now, as it fell into disuse, it came under attack. The great threat that the founding presidents faced, encirclement and dismemberment by European powers, faded. Some domestic issues remained on the political agenda, such as internal improvements and the Indian question, but a new one—slavery—eventually absorbed all other concerns.

How effective was this first presidential system in governing the nation? Except for the unfortunate John Quincy Adams, students of the institution rate the founding presidents as great (Washington and Jefferson) or above average (John Adams, Madison, and Monroe). Without attributing success in the early republic to presidents themselves, it is easy to see how these assessments were reached. While each of the founding presidents struggled with the limitations imposed on them by the "republican hero" model, most were quite agile in adapting the persona to fit their objectives. Washington, in particular, found ways to promote policies he thought were in the nation's best interest without openly identifying himself with the partisan conflicts that surrounded him. Through the use of his secretary of treasury as a point man and a well-defined agenda for strengthening the national government economically and politically, Washington placed the presidency at the center of the new political system. Jefferson also remodeled the presidency on republican lines by removing many of the precedents created by Washington. By insisting that partisan activity was temporary and by governing "textually" beneath the public eye, Jefferson altered the office without changing its broad outlines. Other presidents were less successful, of course. Madison found the Jeffersonian model of the republican hero a difficult one from which to lead a nation to war, and Monroe could do no more than contain the rising factions in his own party.

Each of these presidents often found themselves unable to respond effectively as new circumstances challenged their agenda. Washington's veil of nonpartisanship was rent late in his second term. When factions in his own party challenged him, John Adams found he could not govern as Washington did. Jefferson struggled with extending America's borders when they could be seized only by a more vigorous kind of presidential action than he approved. John Quincy Adams's attempts to assert that his actions were animated by disinterested service were treated with derision by those operating in the incipient party system.

All of the founding presidents believed Congress was an institution that required deference. Each, however, encountered occasions in which the boundaries were contested. Washington, originally anxious to consult the Senate in the area of treaty-making, gave up the practice of meeting with the Senate. He refused to provide the House with documents pertaining to Jay's Treaty and in the last months of his term lectured the House on his responsibilities. "Having been a member of the General convention and knowing the principles on which the Constitution was formed," he reminded the House that they were attempting to act beyond their constitutional authority. As Congress, however, became more organized, it was able to assert itself more and more effectively. Supreme Court Justice Joseph Story concluded in Monroe's first term that the House in particular "absorbed all the popular feeling and all the effective power in the country." The model of the nonpartisan president aloof from daily political conflict was a difficult base from which to challenge this ascendancy.

Despite the demise of the founding presidency, later presidents have sought to reclaim portions of its features. As we shall see, Dwight Eisenhower perceived the office as a relatively limited one in certain areas occupied by a figure above party politics. In fact, many of his tactics imitated Washington's.

Bibliographical Essay

Many scholars find Jefferson's departures from the practices of the first two presidential administrations so dramatic that they divide the period between "Federalist" and "Jeffersonian" visions of the office. Forrest MacDonald, for example, takes this approach in *The American Presidency: An Intellectual History* (Lawrence: University Press of Kansas, 1994). Ralph Ketcham, however, ably argues that there is far more in common among the first presidents than there are differences in *Presidents Above Party: The First American Presidency, 1789–1829* (Chapel Hill: University of North Carolina Press, 1984). Michael A. Genovese also categorizes this period as the "foundational stage" of the American presidency in his *The Power of the American Presidency, 1789–2000* (New York: Oxford University Press). In his study of early presidential electoral strategies, Richard McCormick in *The Presidential Game* (New York: Oxford University Press, 1982) calls the period from 1788 to 1820 the "Virginia game" in which politicians from that state used the principles of republicanism with "consummate skill" to advance their interests and those of their allies.

Washington's status as "republican hero" is explored by Barry Schwartz, *George Washington: The Making of an American Symbol* (Philadelphia: Temple University Press, 1976) and Garry Wills, *Cincinnatus: George Washington and the Enlightenment* (Garden City: Doubleday, 1984). Wills's work emphasizes Washington's strategy of gaining power by seeming to reject it, as does Glenn A. Phelps's *George Washington and American Constitutionalism* (Lawrence: University Press of Kansas, 1993). Two biographies of Washington examine the complex questions of his intent on issues ranging from his role at the constitutional convention to his actions in regard to the Whiskey Rebellion: John E. Ferling, *The First of Men: A Life of George Washington* (Knoxville: University of Tennessee Press, 1988) and Douglass Southall Freeman's five-volume study, *George Washington* (Boston: Scribner's 1948–57). Many of the works on Washington's presidency focus on precedents set in his administration. Glenn A. Phelps's *George Washington and American Constitutionalism* focuses on his contribution to constitutional precedent. Don Higginbotham discusses Washington's policies as both general and president and their impact on civil–military relations in *George Washington and the America Military Tradition* (Athens: University of Georgia Press, 1985). Henry J. Abraham and Barbara A. Perry examine the legacy of Washington's court appointments in "The Father of Our Country or Court Packer-in-Chief," Mark Rozell, et al., *George Washington and the American Presidency* (Westort, CT: Praeger, 2000). David K. Nichols argues that the Washington presidency was a model for the assertive modern presidencies of the twentieth century in *The Myth of the Modern Presidency* (University Park, PA: Penn State University Press, 1994). The legacy of the Farewell Address is explored in Matthew Spalding, *A Sacred Union of Citizens: George Washington's Farewell Address and the America Character* (Totowa, NJ: Roman and Littlefield, 1996).

John Adams has received extensive attention, especially for a one-term president who was not reelected. John R. Howe, Jr., *The Changing Political Thought of John Adams* (Princeton, NJ: Princeton University Press, 1966) is an analysis of his political thought. Manning Dauer offers an account of splits within the Federalist Party in *The Adams Federalists* (Baltimore, MD: Johns Hopkins University Press, 1955), as does Stephen G. Kurtz, *The Adams Presidency* (Philadelphia: University of Pennsylvania Press, 1957). Dauer places the cause primarily on economic factors while Kurtz emphasizes foreign policy differences. Adams is characterized as a moderate Federalist who, although plagued with party factionalism, still managed to achieve many of his goals, in Ralph Adams Brown, *The Presidency of John Adams* (Lawrence University Press of Kansas, 1975) and David McCullough, *John Adams* (New York: Simon and Schuster, 2001). Alexander DeConde offers a less enthusiastic conclusion in regard to Adam's foreign policy in *The Quasi-War: The Politics and Diplomacy of the Undeclared War with France, 1797–1801* (New York: Scribner's, 1966), as does James Morton Smith in regard to the Alien and Sedition Acts in *Freedom's Fetters: The Alien and Sedition Laws and American Civil Liberties* (Ithaca, NY: Cornell University Press, 1956).

As Merrill D. Peterson has ably illustrated in *The Jeffersonian Image in the American Mind* (New York: Oxford University Press, 1960) Jefferson's reputation as a statesman and president has fluctuated dramatically. At the moment, literature on Jefferson is experiencing a significant slump. Dumas Malone's six-volume biography is still a valuable work: *Jefferson and his Time* (Boston: Houghton-Mifflin, 1948–81). The essays in Peter S. Onuf, ed., *Jeffersonian Legacies* (Charlottesville: University Press of Virginia, 1993) are more critical. An early negative assessment that is still consulted is the first four volumes of Henry Adams's *History of the United States During the Presidencies of Thomas Jefferson and James Madison* (New

York: Scribner's, 1889–91). Forest McDonald's *The Presidency of Thomas Jefferson* (Lawrence: University Press of Kansas, 1976) effectively compares the successes of the first term and the failures of the second. Joseph J. Ellis, *The American Sphinx: The Character of Thomas Jefferson* (New York: Knopf, 1997) emphasizes Jefferson's strategy and tactics as president. Robert Tucker and David C. Hendrickson, *Empire of Liberty: The Statecraft of Thomas Jefferson* (New York, 1990) contend that Jefferson attempted to initiate a new American style of foreign affairs as president.

Henry Adams was as critical of James Madison as he was of Jefferson, concluding that Madison was "not only among the weakest of presidents but also among the dullest of men." Recent biographers, however, have emphasized the constraints he faced as president. See Robert Allen Rutland's *The Presidency of James Madison* (Lawrence: University Press of Kansas, 1990) and his *James Madison: The Founding Father* (New York: Macmillan, 1987), as well as Ralph Ketcham, "James Madison and the Presidency" in Thomas E. Cronin, ed., *Inventing the American Presidency* (Lawrence: University Press of Kansas, 1989). Lance Banning reviews Madison's pre-presidential career in *The Sacred Fire of Liberty* (Ithaca: Cornell University Press, 1995). John K. Mahon's *The War of 1812* (Gainesville: University of Florida Press, 1972) is a thorough review of "Mr. Madison's war." Richard J. Barnet's *The Rocket's Red Glare: War, Politics and the American Presidency* (New York: Simon and Schuster, 1990) attempts to assess the impact of the War of 1812 on Madison.

Noble E. Cunningham, Jr. emphasizes James Monroe's persona of republican hero and contains interesting comparisons to Jefferson's version of governance in *The Presidency of James Monroe* (Lawrence: University Press of Kansas, 1996). Also see Harry Ammon's biography, *James Monroe: The Quest for National Identity* (New York: McGraw-Hill, 1971). Ernest May reviews the Monroe Doctrine as a policy decision in *The Making of the Monroe Doctrine* (Cambridge: Harvard University Press, 1975).

The disputed election of 1824 and the rise of party factions is reviewed in Richard P. McCormick, *The Presidential Game* (New York: Oxford University Press, 1982). Stephen Skowronek explores the theme of the Adams's presidency as one of a "crisis of identity" and argues that his agenda of internal improvements was bold though futile in *The Politics Presidents Make* (Cambridge: Harvard University Press, 1993). Also see Mary W. M. Hargreaves, *The Presidency of John Quincy Adams* (Lawrence: University Press of Kansas, 1985).

THE PARTISAN PRESIDENCY

Partisan Presidents

President/ Political Party	Term of Office	Vice President	Percent Electoral Vote	Percent Popular Vote
Andrew Jackson (D)	1829–1833	John C. Calhoun	68	56
Andrew Jackson (D)	1833–1837	Martin Van Buren	76	54
Martin Van Buren (D)	1837–1841	Richard M. Johnson	58	51
William H. Harrison (W)	1841–1841	John Tyler	80	53
John Tyler (W)	1841–1845	—	—	—
James K. Polk (D)	1845–1849	George M. Dallas	62	49
Zachary Taylor (W)	1849–1850	Millard Fillmore	56	47
Millard Fillmore (W)	1850–1853	—	—	—
Franklin Pierce (D)	1853–1857	William R. King	86	51
James Buchanan (D)	1857–1861	John C. Breckenridge	59	45
Abraham Lincoln (R)	1861–1865	Hannibal Hamlin	59	40
Abraham Lincoln (R)	1865–1865	Andrew Johnson	91	55

When Andrew Jackson was elected president in 1828, few observers realized that his administration would initiate a new form of presidential governance, much less that the following years would be called the Age of Jackson. However, Jackson's supporters and critics did recognize certain novelties in his presidency. He was readily identified as the first "outsider" to hold the office. Jackson was the candidate of the "West," whose base was neither Massachusetts nor Virginia, and who had held no cabinet position in previous administrations. Moreover, Jackson seemed to reject all the constraints built into the founding presidency. He did not finesse party loyalty as president, as Jefferson did. In fact, Jackson openly defended the "spoils system" of appointing party regulars as a democratic practice. He did not accept the republican principle of a limited presidency but rather spoke of the office as the "tribune of the people," and he insisted on a liberal interpretation of his constitutional right to exercise his veto powers.

To his critics, Jackson represented a threat to the republic. Henry Clay called Jackson a "military chieftain" who would overtake the carefully calibrated system of checks and balances and replace them with executive power, much as Napoleon had done in France and Caesar in the Roman republic. Opponents to Jacksonian ideas organized themselves into the Whig Party. Although the Whigs were only able to elect two presidents (Harrison and Taylor) before their demise in 1852, they offered a very competitive challenge to the Democrats in general. After 1832, no Democratic candidate for the presidency received more than 51 percent of the vote.

The period between 1828 and 1864 is, then, primarily one of partisan rivalry. Every issue on the political agenda, from economic questions to Indian affairs to slavery, was interpreted through the lens of party politics. As the Whig Party declined in influence in the 1850s, a new party alignment emerged—Democrats and Republicans—that continued the struggle. In general, Whigs supported a role for the federal government in economic development. Democrats, for the most part, opposed federal funds for highways and canals. The cause célèbre of the Jacksonian Democrats was the Bank of the United States. Jackson regarded the Bank as a "hydra" of corruption and vetoed its recharter in 1832. Indeed, the Democratic presidents in this period defined themselves in large part by their vetoes. Jackson also vetoed congressional legislation for the Marysville Road, Polk vetoed harbor improvements, Pierce vetoed aid to mental institutions, and Buchanan vetoed the Homestead Act. Whigs, on the other hand, believed in a limited presidency while the Democrats, supporting Jackson's precedent, regarded the office as the agent of majority rule. On questions about the rights of Indian tribes and antislavery, many Democrats could be ruthlessly negative while many Whigs claimed to be the party of conscience.

In popular speech, Democrats regarded Whigs as rich elitists who only wanted to use government to advance their own interests and who opposed Jackson and his party successors because they feared the people. To Whigs, Democrats were destructive in their attacks on the federal government and who, in preying upon peoples' fears, elevated the power of the presidency to dangerous levels. As the Civil War approached, the new Republican Party depicted Democrats as willing to support any concessions to the South to maintain their power, and Democrats portrayed Republicans as radicals whose policies would lead to Southern secession.

In the period of the founding presidency, presidents struggled with the constraints imposed on them by the persona of the republican hero who remained above party politics. In this new period, presidents enjoyed greater freedom to advance their own agendas openly, but they also faced fierce criticism from the opposing party. Both political parties employed rough language, not only against their opponents but against one another as well. When Jackson announced his intention to veto the Bank charter, Nicholas Biddle replied: "When we begin, we shall crush [the Jacksonians] at once." Jackson's reaction was no less forthright. When asked if he would back down, he answered: "Were all the worshippers of the Golden Calf to memorialize me and request a restoration of deposits, I would cut my right hand from my body before I would do such an act." As the rivalry between Van Buren and Calhoun heated up in 1831, Calhoun openly remarked that he would: ". . . kill him dead, sir, kill him dead. He will never kick, sir, never kick." Here is Davy Crockett's description of Martin Van Buren: "He is laced up in corsets, such as women in town wear, and, if possible, tighter than the best of them. It would be difficult to say, from his personal appearance, whether he was a man or a woman, but for his large and gray whiskers." Abraham Lincoln (with some warrant) accused presidents Pierce and Buchanan of forming a massive conspiracy to extend slavery.

These partisan presidents were clearly engaged in battle and elections were compared to military campaigns. Voters were systematically mobilized. The percentage of those voting rose from 27 in 1824 to nearly 80 in 1840. Since elections were frequent, states staggered election days, and state legislatures took months to choose senators, "political agitation was more or less constant," according to Whig party historian Daniel Walker Howe. The wear on presidents was noticeable. Except for Jackson and Lincoln, none of the nine presidents in this period served more than a single term.

Unlike the founding presidency, the partisan presidency was focused almost exclusively on domestic policy. The great exception was the Mexican War (1846–1848), and that too was the subject of partisan conflict. The young Congressman Lincoln staked his reputation on his opposition to the conflict when he introduced his famous "spot resolutions." There were, of course, minor diplomatic initiatives, including Van Buren's negotiations in the Jackson administration to open the West Indies to American trade and the "Guano Wars" in Fillmore's administration to provide American businesses access to fertilizer in Peru. Until Lincoln faced the international implications of the Civil War, particularly in regard to possible British recognition of the Confederacy, presidents and the public did not look abroad.

At home, despite the contentiousness of issues such as slavery, America was on the verge of an economic takeoff (perhaps as an unanticipated consequence of the War of 1812). Forced to improvise as a result of import restrictions, American merchants brought the factory system home. The introduction of textile manufacturing to Lowell, Massachusetts, for example, awed Americans. Edward Everett wondered how "all the voices of successful industry—the abode of intelligent thousands"—could come into almost immediate existence except through the "work of enchantment." Jackson, too, was taken with the "experiment" at Lowell. Reviewing 2,500 young women employees in parade from his vantage point of a hotel balcony, he exclaimed, "Very pretty women, by the Eternal!" and left the town with "a more positive attitude toward manufacturing."

Many presidents and other officeholders, as well as the press, defended the new partisan politics as an effective mechanism for guaranteeing national unity in this period of conflict and rapid economic change. Despite the conflict they engendered, parties could overcome sectional loyalties. Partisan politics did not, of course, prevent civil war in 1861 but as the period began with one of the nation's most forceful presidents, Andrew Jackson, it ended with yet another, Abraham Lincoln.

ANDREW JACKSON (1829–1837)

There is an apparent paradox between Jackson's persona and the period that has become known as the Age of Jackson. Who could be more irrelevant in the dawn of America's first commercial age than an aged military man who forthrightly defended dueling, still harbored open hatred of the British for their actions in the Revolutionary War, openly admired Napoleon, and once asserted that his reputation was worth more to him than his life? But as Marvin Meyers concluded in *The Jacksonian Persuasion*, Americans were "venturesome conservatives" in this period. Excited by change and at the same time anxious to preserve republican tenets, Americans found in Jackson a formula that incorporated both. Jackson portrayed himself as both the legacy of past republican virtue and as the leader of the people, who would fight to open new economic opportunities for all under the principle, "equal rights for all, special privileges for none."

Jackson was born on the Carolina frontier in 1767. His family suffered disastrously from the revolution, which reached proportions of civil war in his part of the country. His father died shortly before his birth. The young Andrew's older brother died from fever early in the war. He and his other brother Robert were captured by the British; both were wounded by an insouciant British officer when they refused to shine his boots. Robert died from smallpox, and young Andrew barely survived. His mother died from cholera after attending two cousins interred on a British POW ship. Orphaned at 14, the young Jackson later insisted that while he was "amply repaid by living under the mild administration of a republican government," he swore enmity to the "tyranny of Britain," which had forced him to "struggle for our liberties" in his early youth and took "everything that was dear to me. . . ."

The Battle of New Orleans established Jackson's national reputation. Americans were so thrilled by the victory that they joyously attributed credit to many sources. They variously credited the victory to the sharp-shooting "Hunters of Old Kentucky," to the American "democratic spirit," to the courage of the "western farmer," and to American technology. But most of all they praised Jackson, the "king-breaker," the "man of iron" who freed the "infant" republic from colonial dependency and humiliation. One nineteenth-century account of Jackson's entry into the liberated city captures perfectly the equipoise of old/new as young/old that came to form Jackson's persona:

> [He] was a tall, gaunt man, of very erect carriage, with a countenance full of stern anxiety. His complexion was sallow and unhealthy; his hair was iron grey, and his body thin and emaciated . . . But the fierce glare of his bright and hawk-like grey eye, betrayed a soul and a spirit which triumphed over all the infirmities of the body.

As John William Ward more recently observed, the more infirm Jackson's body became, the more visible to his admirers became his iron will.

Jackson's own account of the significance of the victory also provided images of republican virtue. He used the multi-ethnic and racial composition of the American forces to give the battle a world historical significance that evened the score after centuries of British domination. To French soldiers, he spoke of the victory as one over "the hereditary, the eternal enemies of your ancient country." To the Spanish, he urged remembrance of past injury and "avenging the brutal injuries inflicted by men who dishonor the human race." He praised the heroism of "men of color," whom he had invited "to share in the perils" and now invited "to divide the glory of your white countrymen." To the regulars, he exclaimed: "This is the true military spirit! This is the true love of country!" Jackson's accolade to the people of New Orleans offered proof that virtue was sill alive:

> Inhabitants of an opulent and commercial town, you have by spontaneous effort shaken off the habits, which are created by wealth, and shown that you have resolved to deserve the blessings of fortune by bravely defending them.

Thus, in Jackson's mind, the people of New Orleans (and by implication, all Americans) were rejuvenated through the contagion of martial spirit. The city had become old and "weak," but this threat gave its inhabitants the knowledge that liberty is more dear than property, "dearer" even than "your wives and children."

Jackson's spiritedness did not go unnoticed, and he was forced early and often to respond to those who challenged its utility. His own actions gave his opponents plenty of ammunition. His unprecedented declaration of martial law in New Orleans later brought him before a federal court. In the Seminole campaign, some cabinet members in Monroe's administration saw Jackson as a renegade general seemingly uncontrollable by federal civilian authorities. His order to hang two British subjects for allegedly aiding the enemy and his attack upon a Spanish fort created an international incident and prompted a French governmental official to refer to Jackson as that "Napoleon des bois." As Jackson's presidential ambitions became clear, his opponents began "building ardently upon incidents of his military past" and "managed almost to read into the records of history a legend of his rude violence and uncontrolled irascibility."

Jackson, of course, always gave as good as he got. After his defeat in the presidential contest of 1824, he pointed to the fact that 99 electors had voted for him as proof of the inaccuracy of charges that he was a threat to the republic. He admitted spiritedness in his youthful opposition to the "yoke of tyranny" during the revolution and his defense of western citizens against "savages," concluding: "If this can constitute me as a Military Chieftain, I am one." He had been charged with "taking bold and high-handed measures," but none of them were designed for his "personal aggrandizement." Did the charge imply that "all our brave men in war, who go forth to defend their rights and the rights of their country . . . be termed Military Chieftains?" Under these definitions even Washington could be so considered, "because he dared to be a virtuous and successful soldier, an honest man, and a correct man." He might be a military chieftain, but at least he had not been part of plans to "impair the pure principles of our Republican institutions" or to frustrate the people's will. Jackson concluded that "demagogues . . . had done more injury to the cause of freedom and the rights of man, than ever did a 'Military Chieftain.'" He had been "a soldier for the good of my country," and now he would retire again to his farm. He would never be a "hanger on upon office and power." "If this makes me so, I am a 'Military Chieftain.'"

This image of Jackson as the epitome of military virtues was, however, only one part of his persona. Robert V. Remini (*The Legacy of Andrew Jackson*) notes:

> [t]he House election of 1825 that awarded the presidency to John Quincy Adams had a profound impact on Jackson's thinking. Unquestionably, it was the single event—if single events in history actually do determine actions by themselves—that converted him into a rabid Democrat. . . .

Jackson thus portrayed himself as a spokesperson, not only of traditional republican values but also of new ones.

The day after Adams's own inauguration, Jackson began his first use of Jefferson as the legitimizing device of his presidential campaign. While Jackson continued to employ Washington as a general symbol, it was henceforth Jefferson who became the great weapon of the Democratic Party. As Merrill Peterson observes, "so tight" were the Jacksonian symbols of Jefferson, democracy, and the Democratic Party that "one scarcely existed in the public mind apart from the others and attempts to disengage them met with fleeting success." Democratic politicians developed with unerring accuracy the tactic of disarming opponents "by squirting Jefferson's opinions in their eyes." Jackson thus began his own "inauguration" when he compared Adams's "pomp and ceremony" to the swearing-in twenty-four years earlier: ". . . when Mr. Jefferson was inducted into office, no such machinery was called in to give solemnity to the scene. He rode his own horse, and hitched him himself to the enclosure."

There are, of course, important differences between Jackson and his alleged mentor. It is true that Jefferson opposed the Bank of the United States as well as internal improvements and distrusted the courts, and that Jefferson too campaigned on the post-revolutionary emergence of an aristocracy. It is also true, of course, that Jefferson would never have conceived of the presidency as a tribune of the people, held the legislature in such low esteem, or harbored hatred for Indians. Nor would he have adopted the nationalist ethos that reached its apogee in Jackson's nullification crisis. However, the use of Jefferson did supply Jackson with an important linkage. Jefferson led a movement of democratic protest and attempted to accomplish his goal through the reduction of the scope of the federal government.

Jackson's inauguration in 1829 was itself a sign that he was the leader of a democratic movement. No doubt emboldened even more by the punch provided by the president, enthusiastic crowds surged through the White House, causing considerable damage to floors, fixtures and china. Jackson's critics saw this celebration as the beginning of the reign of "King Mob." To his supporters, however, the event was evidence that Jackson was the "people's president."

Jackson's inaugural address was moderate in tone. He even suggested that there was room for negotiation on the question of tariffs and internal improvements. He did indicate, however, that his administration would be committed to reform, particularly in terms of government offices that were in "unfaithful or incompetent hands." Jackson's opponents criticized his approach to public administration, but Jackson developed a powerful set of arguments as to why his administration—and others in the future—were entitled to replace federal bureaucrats. Jackson defended the extension of party loyalty to the bureaucracy in republican terms. Patronage, or the *spoils system* (from the adage, "to the victor belongs the spoils of the enemy")—the replacement of government personnel with individuals loyal to the winning candidate—was an implementation of the republican principle of rotation in office. Bureaucrats can come to think of their positions as their own exclusive "species of property." Jackson believed that after a few years an officeholder feels he has a "life estate" to his position, and after twenty years, he feels that the office is entitled to his children as well. Replacement would "destroy the idea of property so generally connected with official station." Besides, argued Jackson, "the duties of all public officers are . . . so plain and simple that men of intelligence may readily qualify themselves for their performance; and I cannot believe that more is lost by the long continuance of men in office than is generally gained by their experience."

The primary agency of public employment in a federal political system with a very small army and navy was the post office. These positions were passed out to party loyalists largely on the recommendation of local Democratic officials. Jackson, however, did offer other plans to democratize the federal government, although they were never enacted. He proposed to Congress an automatic term limit of four years for all federal employees and the direct election of federal judges, including Supreme Court justices. In addition, Jackson proposed abolishing the electoral college, reducing senatorial terms to four years, and restricting the presidency to one term (perhaps of six years). As Robert Remini writes in his assessment of Jackson, "his remarkably advanced views were far more democratic than the American people could tolerate at the time. Indeed, they are unacceptable even today."

The defining moment in Jackson's first term was his veto of legislation to recharter the Bank of the United States (BUS) in July of 1832. Remini has called this act the "most important veto ever issued by a president." The veto was indeed important for three reasons. First, while Jefferson opposed a national bank and Madison and Monroe also had deep reservations about its constitutionality, the Democrats had in practice acquiesced to its continued existence. Henry Clay, in fact, was so convinced of its usefulness as a campaign issue that he supported legislation to continue the bank four years before its charter expired. When Jackson responded with his famous veto message that the bank was an agency of the "rich and powerful" to "bend the acts of government to their selfish purposes," his opponents charged that it was his action that was unconstitutional. Before Jackson, presidents used the veto power sparingly, with only three significant vetoes signed by previous presidents. Now Jackson—who used the veto 12 times in eight years—was asserting, in effect, that the president could object to legislation on the grounds that it was unworthy in his mind. Both Webster and Clay saw the significance of this change in practice and called Jackson's use of the veto "a claim to despotic power" and a "perversion of the veto power," respectively. Despite these protestations Congress was unable to override the president's actions, and this expanded use of the veto became a significant power in the presidency's arsenal for all later occupants of the office.

The second reason that Jackson's decision to veto the BUS recharter was important was that it showed that a president was capable of successfully undertaking a project of mammoth proportions in peacetime. The description of his veto decision and his later actions to withdraw currency from the bank and place it in state chartered banks as the "Bank War" was an apt one. Jackson's attitude toward the bank was one of ferocious hostility, but so too were the attitudes of its defenders toward him. After Nicolas Biddle, the powerful head of the bank made his assertion that the Jacksonians would be crushed, Jackson would not budge when confronted by a delegation of terrified businessmen. "I am not in any panic," he said. If business needed relief, Jackson told them, "Go to the monster. Go to Nicholas Biddle."

It is difficult today to appreciate the significance of Jackson's project to destroy the BUS. The bank was in a position to bring the nation to economic ruin, when challenged (as Biddle attempted to do) and it was a national institution almost co-terminus with the founding. The decision to destroy the BUS was in many ways the equivalent of the nationalization of property in a socialist regime.

The third reason the "Bank War" was important was that it solidified Jackson's persona with the American people as both a former military hero and a defender of the people. The bank question was a major issue in the 1832 presidential election, and Jackson won 219 electoral votes to Clay's 49. Whigs bitterly opposed this interpretation of the presidency. Webster in particular was appalled by Jackson's argument that the presidency was the primary defender of the people's liberties. The entire history of the "spirit of liberty" was devoted to restraining executive prerogative, not expanding it.

> Crowned heads have been compelled to submit to the restraints of law, and the *people*, with that intelligence and that spirit which make their voice resistless, have been able to say to prerogative, "Thus far shalt thou come and no farther."

Nevertheless, Jackson's argument that the president was the "direct representative of the people" was firmly placed on the political agenda for others to follow. When Whigs contended that this interpretation of the office constituted an "elective despotism," Jackson replied, where would the "humble members of society—the farmers, mechanics and laborers"—turn without the "right to complain of the injustice of their government," if not to their president?

Jackson's affection for the humble members of society did not extend, however, to two of the most vulnerable groups in the nation: Native and African Americans. The Choctaw, Chickasaw, Cherokee, Creek, and Seminoles were named the "Five Civilized Tribes" because of their assimilation to white society. Many members of these tribes were prosperous farmers. The discovery of gold in Georgia added to the desire of whites for new land to settle. When the Cherokee appealed to the Supreme Court for relief from attempts to usurp their land, the justices responded that the

Cherokee were not in fact a sovereign nation. In a subsequent case in 1832 (*Worchester v. Georgia*), the Court also ruled that Georgia could not pass laws regarding Indian territory because Indian land was under federal supervision. At this point, Jackson actively entered the controversy. Jackson, who was long known as a ferocious "Indian fighter" (he was named "Sharp Knife" by the tribes), sided with Georgia and refused to support the Supreme Court's decision. In fact, he is reported to have said, "John Marshall has made his decision, now let him enforce it." Now being without support from the federal government, Georgia, and (in effect) the Supreme Court, the Cherokee acceded to Jackson's demand that they sell their lands and relocate to an area west of the Mississippi. In 1838, 18,000 Cherokee were moved, of whom 4,000 died en route in what has become known as the "Trail of Tears." Similar fates awaited the other tribes.

Put bluntly, Jackson and most Democrats did not see the inconsistency between their intense commitment to democratization and their denial of basic rights to Native Americans. Jackson simply contended that Native American tribes could not be permitted to exist as separate nations within existing state governments, because it violated national unity and because Native Americans were not capable of self-government. Nor could Native Americans continue to live next to whites since, in his view, Indians could not survive under these circumstances. As for African Americans, Jackson contended that slaves were a form of property that could not be taken away without the owner's consent. He regarded abolitionists, including that "arch fiend" John Quincy Adams, as wealthy "malcontents" who were using the slavery question to thwart the advances of democracy for white males. He did not find the "gag rule" adopted in 1836, which prevented Congress from debating or even printing abolitionist petitions over slavery, as inconsistent with democratic principles.

Jackson despised John C. Calhoun and regarded his 1833 attempt to encourage nullification of the tariff (as well as what he called other southern "theatricals") as a hypocritical political maneuver. When he issued his proclamation declaring the doctrine that a state had a right to selectively nullify an "impractical absurdity," he privately expressed concern that slavery would be the "next pretext" of Southern politicians to assert not only nullification but also open secession. Thus, Jackson could see the potential divisiveness of the slavery question but never could recognize the institution as a monstrous violation of human rights. While his position on these issues seems inexcusable in the twenty-first century, perhaps the kindest explanation for Jackson's indifference and even hostility to these minorities is that he saw any restriction on the right of the majority as a conspiracy to turn away from democracy. The fact that the Whigs took up the cause of both groups only fuelled his ire.

MARTIN VAN BUREN (1837–1841)

Martin Van Buren seemed to be everything that Andrew Jackson was not. He was short; Jackson was tall. He wore lace; Jackson dressed in simple garments. He was cunning; Jackson was direct. Van Buren did enjoy some significant advantages, however. He was an incredibly adept politician who rose to the leadership of "Regency," the New York state political machine known for its intricate system of rewards and favors. Although he had supported Crawford for president in 1824, Jackson appointed Van Buren as secretary of state, and thus began his long tenure as Jackson's closest confidant and ally in the president's battles with Calhoun. In fact, Calhoun prevented his appointment as ambassador in England only to find that the "little magician," as he was called, managed to secure a place on the 1832 ticket as Jackson's vice president. In 1836 Van Buren won the presidency, in part because he faced a divided Whig opposition.

In many respects, Van Buren saw the political future more clearly than his mentor, Jackson. Although Old Hickory was a stalwart Democrat, he tended to view the party he reformulated as an extension of his own personality (which to some degree it was). The success of future presidents depended on adaptation to the fact that the office was now inextricably connected to political parties as organizations. Since Van Buren did not have the forceful persona of Jackson, his accommodation to this new form no doubt also fit his own political agenda.

Van Buren offered several reasons for his defense of political parties. First, he contended that nonpartisanship could be a mask for the continuation of an elite in power. Free government requires a party opposition as "the vigilant watchman over the conduct of the people, and to compel their servants to act on principle." He even criticized the hope expressed in Monroe's second inaugural address that party organization might become extinct in America. Second, Van Buren defended parties as good in and of themselves. Party activity taught the values of discipline, loyalty, and devotion to a common cause. As one of Van Buren's friends concluded, "political consistency" is "as indispensable as any other moral qualification." Third, Van Buren asserted that party activity encouraged and assured mass political participation. Party competition serves to "rouse the sluggish to exertion, give increased energy to the most active intellect . . . [and] prevent that apathy which has proved the ruin of Republics."

Immediately upon assuming office, Van Buren faced an enormous challenge to his partisan approach that he never was quite able to meet. The nation fell into a terrible depression. A booming American economy created a large trade-balance deficit with Great Britain. This situation was not a danger in itself, since British bankers were heavy investors in new American manufacturing. When foreign investors, however, reacted by demanding payment, it soon became apparent that the Jacksonian financial system of state banks, many of which engaged in "creative" lending policies, was not able to respond.

The so-called Panic of 1837 was partly the result of Jackson's monetary policies, from which Van Buren had previously benefitted. Van Buren found it difficult to propose any policy that could be seen as a criticism of Jackson's policies. Recentralization of finance was a Whig idea and, moreover, the Democratic Party was strongly committed to "hard money" and a federal government that stayed out of the economy. Van Buren, therefore, understandably withstood pressure to reinstate the Bank of the United States and reaffirmed the party's commitment to a laissez-faire economy. "All communities,"he told Congress, are apt to look to government "for too much." He did propose a substitute policy, the formation of an independent subtreasury that would keep funds separate from state banks. The proposal, however, satisfied no one and, although Van Buren called Congress in special session in September of 1837, his bill did not pass.

Congress finally passed Van Buren's proposals to deal with the panic in 1840 and the economy appeared to briefly improve. However, poor economic conditions soon returned. This time, the Whigs benefited from the new partisan presidency. The energized Whig Party organized with surprising skill under an anti-Van Buren platform. They called the president "Martin Van Ruin" and accused him of aristocratic tastes, including his installation of a hot-water tank in the White House. The "end of the magic" (to use the phrase of Donald B. Cole, a Van Buren biographer) came in November of 1840, when Van Buren became the second U.S. president to fail to be reelected.

WILLIAM HENRY HARRISON (1841) AND JOHN TYLER (1841–1845)

The presidential election of 1840 was an important one in American history. Although no dramatic issues were presented to the American public, the election represented a significant shift in the character of party competition in America. Before 1840, the two party systems, Democratic-Republican/Federalists and Democrat/Whig, divided on the general question of how popular the political system should be. Federalists and Whigs openly championed the cause of elite leadership and limits on broader political participation.

In 1840, however, the Whigs openly abandoned this position. They nominated William Henry Harrison again, but this time with a new vigor. Harrison was a general, an Indian fighter, and a hero of the War of 1812— that is, he had the same bona fides as Jackson did in 1832. When a Democrat jokingly remarked, "Give him a barrel of hard cider" and a pension and Harrison "will sit the remainder of his days in a log cabin," Whigs adopted the symbols of cider barrels and log cabins. Whigs portrayed themselves as the party of the people and portrayed Democrats, led by Van Buren (who actually came from a very modest background), as the elitists. Democrats campaigned largely on organizational terms, abandoning Van Buren as the head of the ticket and urging voters to reject these newfound populists and stick to the party of Jefferson and Jackson. Harrison won in a close election (40, 000 votes with over 2.5 million cast), carrying the electoral college (234–60) and both houses of Congress.

Neither the triumphant Whigs nor the dispirited Democrats could have predicted the immediate future. Harrison died a month after his inauguration. John Tyler, a lifetime Southern Democrat who broke with Jackson over the nullification crisis in 1833, was selected for vice president on the Whig ticket in a bold effort to gain votes. Now, however, as soon as Tyler was sworn in on April 2, he immediately began by vetoing a Whig bill to reinstitute the Bank of the United States. Whigs were outraged. Threatening crowds demonstrated outside the White House. When Tyler vetoed another bank bill, Whig cabinet members resigned and the new president began to fill his cabinet with Democrats. A caucus of the Whig Party in Congress expelled Tyler from their party.

This crisis was in part the result of unforeseen circumstances. The death of Harrison was the first instance in which a vice president assumed office as president, but it is important to note that the event occurred in the context of the new partisan presidency. Henry Clay at first declared that Tyler would govern as a "regent," that is, in the same way a caretaker would rule when a child succeeded a king. When Tyler refused to play this role and behaved like a Democrat and former president Jackson weighed in by supporting Tyler's actions, Whigs argued that Tyler was actually only an "acting president," presumably with less power than a directly elected one. Moreover, since Tyler was in Clay's words a "president without a party," it was unclear how he could govern at all. Under Clay's leadership, the Whigs brought the nation to the point of a constitutional crisis by encouraging cabinet resignations. They planned to refuse to confirm Tyler's replacements, thus hoping to force the president to resign. When that plan failed because Daniel Webster, secretary of state, refused to participate in the strategy, impeachment proceedings were started in the House. They also failed.

Tyler managed to stay in power despite these challenges largely through his use of the veto. Whigs were not the only party concerned with Tyler's status. Democrats, defeated in the last election, worried that their party might meet the same fate as the Federalists had. In fact, Tyler threatened to form a third party of states'-rights Southern Democrats. The president effectively manipulated his delicate situation with the question of Texas, which became an independent republic in 1836 and voted to join the Union. Whigs were notably unenthusiastic, in part because the admission would alter the balance between slave and free states. Most Democrats were supportive, especially former president Jackson.

Tyler negotiated a treaty with Texas to join the Union in 1844 and sent troops to insure that Mexico would not react militarily. When the Whig-controlled Senate failed to confirm the treaty, Tyler devised an imaginative alternative. He sent the measure to both Houses and requested a joint resolution of annexation. The bill passed after a compromise was reached that authorized the formation of up to four states from the territory and guaranteed that no slavery would be permitted north of the 36° 30′ parallel. Tyler signed the bill two days before leaving office. On the last day of his administration, Congress was able to exercise its first override on one of Tyler's vetoes of a minor bill. Nevertheless, Tyler was jubilant. At a celebration, he exclaimed: "They cannot say now that I am a man without a party!"

JAMES POLK (1845–1849)

Tyler's acquisition of Texas was, nevertheless, not enough to get him reelected in 1844. No Whig would vote for him, and the annexation raised suspicions among many Northern Democrats, who questioned his commitment to the Union. Tyler did attempt to form another party and even had some support among delegates at the regular party convention. Jackson, however, convinced him to end his third-party quest and support the Democratic nominee. Tyler's Texas initiative did, however, greatly alter the election. Since Van Buren, who was the party favorite, did not support annexation, he so angered Jackson that he was not able to gain the necessary two-thirds of the convention delegates. On the ninth ballot James Polk, the House organizer of the Texas bill, was selected by the party.

Polk won a very close election against Henry Clay, the Whig party candidate. In fact, while the election of 1844 can be seen as one which, according to Richard P. McCormick, "brought the party game to maturity," it also revealed the first signs of the impact the slavery question would have on the partisan presidency. The Liberty Party, a protest group started by abolitionists, ran James G. Birney for president. Birney received only 2 percent of the vote, but it was enough to give the election to Polk.

Although he was a one-term president, James Polk frequently receives high marks from presidential experts. Part of the reason for this assessment is based on the fact that Polk successfully reinvigorated the aging Jacksonian coalition. Known as "Young Hickory," Polk represented much the same persona as Jackson. He was an assertive Tennessean who believed in strong presidential leadership. In addition, Polk did what he said he would do as president. In a conversation with George Bancroft at his inauguration, Polk declared with great specificity his goals as president. According to Bancroft, Polk "raised his hand in the air and bringing it down with force on his thigh" announced four measures for his administration: tariff reduction, an independent treasury, settlement of the Oregon boundaries and the acquisition of California. Since he completed each—and more, in terms of territory—it is natural to ask why Polk did not become a presidential icon. Three years later when the boast was reality, the young Polk himself frequently complained that he was unappreciated. "With me, it is emphatically true that the Presidency is no bed of roses."

Part of the reason for Polk's early success is the fact that he fully adapted to the contours of the partisan presidency. In fact, his inaugural address was the first recognition of the new environment. Polk said, ". . . the Chief Magistrate must almost of necessity be chosen by a party. . . ." He used the patronage system effectively, replacing three-fourths of the postmasters, and vigorously withdrew patronage for Democrats who challenged his policies. As a former Speaker of the House, Polk knew intimately how legislation was passed and, most importantly, he knew how to obtain votes. The passage of a major bill lowering tariffs (a traditional Jacksonian pledge) was approved by a margin of a single vote.

Polk supplemented his role as strong party leader with that of a strong president. If he was a man of telescopic vision, Polk was also what today would be called a micro-manager on those issues he sought to promote. Fiscal austerity was a central Jacksonian tenet, but presidents before Polk exercised only episodic control over their own executive departments, and this supervision was achieved largely through their treasury secretaries. Polk, on the other hand, insisted on reviewing the budget of each cabinet member and requested revisions.

It is with territorial expansion, however, that Polk was most forceful. The Democratic Party had always supported an extended republic, and the 1844 platform included the demand that the British settle boundary disputes in the Oregon Territory. The slogan "54° 40' or fight!" claimed that nearly the entire Northwest coastline was American territory. In his first annual message to Congress, Polk presented a dire picture of negotiations with Britain, invoked the Monroe Doctrine, and hinted at stronger U.S. measures. Meanwhile, Polk privately authorized negotiators to take a more moderate position that received the support of Southern Whigs. The treaty divided the territory at the 49th parallel, which was about where both sides expected negotiations to end. The Senate approved the agreement, 38–12.

In regard to Mexico, Polk had broader goals. At a minimum he planned to add the New Mexico and California territories to the United States, and at a maximum he planned to occupy Mexico itself. Polk first offered to buy New Mexico and California. When the Mexicans rejected the offer, he sent troops to the Texas border. Mexico claimed that the southern border of the United States was the Nueces River; Polk claimed it was the Rio Grande, which was further south. Polk already had a declaration of war drafted and when, as expected, Mexican troops attacked, he presented it to Congress.

Although Polk did achieve his minimum objective, the war created significant problems that help explain his relatively obscure historical status. First, victories by Whig generals Zachary Taylor and Winfield Scott politicized the conflict. Polk was suspicious of his generals' own political ambitions. When Taylor unilaterally issued an armistice with Mexican forces, Polk was furious at the man who was "giddy" at the thought of becoming president and demanded that Taylor turn a large part of his command over to Scott, whom he later dismissed. Second, the war was extremely controversial. Whigs took up the opposition and gained control of the House in 1848. Third, and most important, the rapid addition of new states exacerbated the slavery question. Would the new states permit slavery or ban it? Whigs claimed that Polk was willing to avoid war in Oregon, which would be free territory, and was anxious to provoke it with Mexico, which would add slave states to the Union. Polk's offer to purchase Cuba, an island that slaveholders desired for many years, was treated as further proof of Polk's agenda.

Whether Polk's actual plan was to add slave states to the Union in order to strengthen Southern power or, more likely, a desire to be an agent of America's "manifest destiny" to extend the republic from the Atlantic to the Pacific coast, he did not clearly see the consequences of his own actions. The controversy over the slave question overshadowed the fact that Polk had added more than a million square miles of land to the United States.

ZACHARY TAYLOR (1849–1850) AND MILLARD FILLMORE (1850–1853)

The Whigs were interested in Zachary Taylor as a presidential candidate even before his military victory at Buena Vista, Mexico, in February of 1847. If Harrison was successful in 1836, why not another general? The fact that Taylor had absolutely no political experience was yet another attraction to many Whig leaders, since they were struggling to expand their base as waves of immigrants were tilting the electoral balance against them. Additionally, Taylor had taken no position on slavery and the new territories. Southern Whigs were satisfied that Taylor was a Virginia slaveholder, and Northern Whigs accepted Taylor's vagueness in their desire for the patronage that came with the victor.

Democrats too thought they found the key to victory in their candidate, Lewis Cass, a senator from Michigan. Originally Cass was a supporter of the Wilmot Proviso, a piece of legislation repeatedly tacked on to appropriation bills that forbade slavery in any of the territory ceded by Mexico, which passed the House twice (in 1846 and 1847) but was blocked in the Senate. Cass, however, concluded that the most effective resolution to the problem should be a policy that permitted each territory to decide for itself whether it would permit slavery. The doctrine of "popular sovereignty" was adopted by Stephen Douglas in the 1850s in his debates with Abraham Lincoln. Popular sovereignty seemed like a dream policy for the Democrats, since it took the slavery issue off the federal agenda and Southerners generally favored it.

The election of 1848 was another close election. Crucial to Taylor's victory was the formation of the new Free Soil Party led by Martin Van Buren. The ex-president attracted a large portion of a faction of the Democratic Party opposed to slavery, the "Barn Burners" (named after farmers who burned down their barns to rid them of rats), and the electoral votes of New York went to Taylor.

As president, Taylor behaved quite differently than the Whigs anticipated. He generally followed the Whig commitment to a limited presidency and vigorously exercised his patronage powers, but Taylor also used the power of his office to prevent attempts to compromise on the question of slavery in the territories. Taylor himself favored admitting California with its slave-free constitution, opposed Texas's claim to the New Mexico Territory, and was sympathetic to admitting the Mormon Territory (now the state of Utah). Southerners were aghast at Taylor's positions, since the result would be the addition of more free states to the Union.

What neither party realized was that Taylor was an ardent unionist. When Southerners threatened to force federal troops out of the New Mexico Territory, Taylor responded, "I will command the army in person and hang any man taken in treason." Thus, when Henry Clay began creating a congressional coalition in support of a compromise as Southern threats of secession and unilateral action were rising, Taylor stated his adamant opposition and threatened to veto the bill. Just as the confrontation was reaching a climax, Taylor died. Vice President Millard Fillmore assumed the presidency a day later on July 10, 1850.

Although Fillmore was personally opposed to slavery, he swiftly sought support for what became known as the Compromise of 1850. He sought and accepted the resignations of his entire cabinet and managed to swing enough Whig votes in Congress in support of the bill. The legislation, crafted by Clay with the support of Webster and Douglas, admitted California as a free state and denied Texas's claims but permitted no restrictions on slavery in New Mexico and Utah. The complex legislation also ended the slave trade in Washington, DC (although not slavery itself) and promised severe sanctions for those who protected fugitive slaves. Fillmore praised the compromise as the "final settlement" of the slavery question, but, as the implications of compromise became clearer, it seemed to satisfy no one. Northern abolitionists opposed the Fugitive Slave Act and began organized resistance. The Whig Party was so divided over the compromise that it took 54 ballots to select a nominee in

1852. Fillmore was dumped as the Whig Party candidate and Winfield Scott, yet another general, was selected. Although their fate was not clear in 1852, the Whig Party never recovered.

FRANKLIN PIERCE (1853–1857)

Franklin Pierce was chosen as a compromise candidate by a party that was also racked by faction and conflict. The Democrats, who once again hoped to revive the Jacksonian coalition, portrayed him as the "Young Hickory of Granite Hill." Pierce is almost universally portrayed as a terrible president who had the last chance to avoid civil war and failed miserably. He has been depicted alternately as weak and indecisive (Harry Truman once said that Pierce was a complete "fizzle" who "didn't know what was going on, and even if he had, he wouldn't have known what to do about it") and as a conscious agent of Southern interests (a "Doughface," in the slang of the time).

These assessments, while not inaccurate, need some revision. Pierce was in many ways a Byronic figure. Though blessed with a comfortable family background (his father was governor of New Hampshire) and a handsome bearing, Pierce was a reformed alcoholic. Tragedy struck his family shortly after he was elected president. His eleven-year-old son was killed in a train accident. Pierce's deeply religious wife interpreted the death as a sign from God that Pierce should not be distracted from the duties of his office. Guilt-ridden by the accident, Pierce returned to drink. In the context of this event, he threw himself into the affairs of state, working twelve-hour days. His plan was to invigorate the Democratic Party by appointing young cabinet members, distributing patronage to all the party factions, strengthening public support for the Compromise of 1850, expanding American territory, and reducing the budget.

Pierce did, in fact, reduce the national debt from $60 million to $11 million, and he did add to territorial expansion in the Southwest through the Gadsen Purchase (of land from Mexico). However, policies that solidified the party in 1828 tore it apart in 1852. In his inaugural, Pierce attempted to seal the Compromise of 1850 as a pillar of national accommodation. He announced,

> I believe that involuntary servitude is recognized by the Constitution. I believe that it stands like any other admitted right, and that the States where it exists are entitled to efficient remedies to enforce the constitutional provisions. I hold that the laws of 1850, commonly called the "compromise measures," are strictly constitutional and to be unhesitatingly carried into effect.... I fervently hope that the question is at rest....

The slavery question, of course, was not laid to rest. As Pierce strove to add new territory and reduce the budget, Congress began to take up the admission of the Nebraska Territory. Stephen Douglas, a Democrat with presidential ambitions, hoped to bring this new territory into the Union quickly. In order to obtain Southern support, Douglas proposed that the settlers determine for themselves whether slavery would be permitted in the new states. "Popular sovereignty" was the policy principle employed in the 1850 compromise, but this effort effectively repealed the Missouri Compromise of 1820. To Douglas, the risk of creating a new crisis was worth the effort. He hoped to have his name attached to legislation that added new states; he hoped the admission of new states would bring to fruition his project of a railroad from Chicago to the West Coast; and he hoped that the legislation would sharpen differences between Democrats and Whigs, to the benefit of the latter.

But why did Pierce actively support the bill? It is true that he already had claimed the 1850 compromise made the 1820 settlement of the issue "inoperative and void" and, like Douglas, he was anxious to court Southern Democrats. On the other hand, Pierce might have concluded that the initiative was too high-risk or that he should not support a project that would aid a party rival. Thus the president could have remained neutral or mildly supportive and reserved his options for later developments.

After three months of debate, the Kansas-Nebraska Act was passed in May of 1854. Pierce signed the legislation and declared that the slavery question was now finally settled. The results were disastrous for the Democratic Party, Pierce, and the nation as a whole. Civil war broke out in the territories as slaveholders rushed to secure a stronghold. Democrats lost seats in the mid-term elections. In a disputed election that included ballot stuffing and physical intimidation, pro-slavery forces gained control of the territorial legislature. Anti-slavery settlers reacted by declaring their own government in Topeka.

Pierce responded by sending in federal troops, declaring the pro-slavery government in Lecompton the legal one and the Topeka free-soilers as "traitors." He attempted to forge a coalition with the new American ("Know Nothing") Party recently formed in opposition to immigration. This new party, however, split in 1855 into Northern and Southern factions, and Pierce was denied renomination by his own divided party. Out of office, Pierce continued to believe opposition to slavery was an issue fostered by ambitious Northern politicians. Although he supported the North in the Civil War, he opposed the Emancipation Proclamation as a measure foisted on Lincoln by abolitionists. Though Pierce was not a Southern sympathizer and he did have an agenda that he thought would defuse the slavery question, he never appreciated the moral or political power of the anti-slavery cause.

JAMES BUCHANAN (1857–1861)

James Buchanan was an experienced politician who served as U.S. senator from Pennsylvania for 11 years and served as secretary of state under Polk. He was a presidential candidate for the Democratic Party nomination in 1848 and 1852. In 1856, Buchanan was finally selected at age 65, partly because he was not associated with the Kansas crisis since he was serving as ambassador to Great Britain, and partly because he was acceptable to Southerners. The devastation the slavery question wreaked on the party system was clear in the presidential election. Buchanan's main competitor was Fremont, the candidate of the new Republican Party. Millard Fillmore, who ran on the Whig and American party tickets, won only eight electoral votes.

Buchanan pursued essentially the same policies as Pierce: he attempted to reduce the budget, heal Democratic Party factions, extend American territory, and resolve the slavery question. In each case, Buchanan failed even more spectacularly than Pierce. A financial panic in 1857 wiped out the government surplus. Buchanan was in open war with Stephen Douglas, his rival for the nomination and the most powerful Democrat other than himself. His designs on the annexation of Cuba and parts of Mexico were blocked by the Senate.

His treatment of the issue of the terms for the admission of Kansas as a new state was a complete disaster. At the urging of Douglas, Pierce appointed Robert J. Walker, a Mississippi Democrat, as governor of the territory. When Walker certified an election of anti-slavery legislators, Buchanan refused to support his decision and succumbed to the demands from pro-slavery Lecompton delegates that Walker be dismissed. At this point Douglas, who was up for election himself in Illinois, decided to side with Walker and oppose the government in Lecompton. When Pierce threatened him by reminding Douglas how Jackson destroyed Democrats who opposed him, the senator replied, "Sir, General Jackson is dead." After elections on the state constitution that were boycotted by both sides, Kansas applied for statehood allowing for slavery. Pierce used massive pressure (including cash bribes) to force the Senate to assent. Douglas, however, used his personal influence to kill the House bill. In a sense, everyone lost except the new Republican Party. There was no swift admission of the territory, and the region suffered from terrible violence, becoming known as "bleeding Kansas." Douglas was regarded as untrustworthy by Southerners and opportunistic by Northerners.

On the Kansas question and other issues, Buchanan used a common tactic. He argued, for example, that it was beyond the power of the president to interfere with the electoral process in a territory—but, of course, interfere he did, in this case and others, despite his arguments about the limitations of executive power. When the Utah Territory, under the leadership of Brigham Young, threatened rebellion, Pierce used all the powers of the office, including the use of federal troops, to restore order. In his inaugural address, Pierce announced his unqualified submission to judicial review and declared that he would support the position of the Supreme Court on the pending decision of the rights of slaves in free states. Pierce, however, privately urged a broad judicial response by the court in the Dred Scott case and actually knew the results of the decision when he delivered his address. Anti-slavery activists were immediately suspicious, and Lincoln himself suggested the existence of a conspiracy.

Perhaps Buchanan's most unusual tactic was his response to those states who began seceding from the union soon after Lincoln's presidential victory in 1860. Buchanan contended in his final message to Congress that while there was no constitutional right to secession, neither the president nor Congress was constitutionally authorized to prevent exits from the Union. He concluded, "The Executive has no authority to decide what shall be the relations between the Federal government and South Carolina. . . . "

ABRAHAM LINCOLN (1861–1865)

Andrew Jackson began the partisan presidency by creating a new political party that mobilized the electorate. It cannot be said that Lincoln was the founder of the Republican Party that replaced the Whigs as the major competitor to the Democrats, but his interpretation of the Republican cause was so significant that he not only transformed the party system but also dramatically altered the presidency itself, and even the conception of American identity.

By the 1850s the Democratic Party was reduced to a series of factions in addition to the North–South split. In the North, more conservative Democrats were called the Hunkers; anti-slavery Democrats were called Barn Burners. Among the former, there were "soft-shell" Democrats willing to accept the Van Buren supporters who bolted in 1848, and "hard-shell" Democrats who weren't. The Whigs were even worse off. The party had split into Northern and Southern factions as well, but it began to experience defections in serious numbers as anti-slavery "Conscience Whigs" drifted toward the Free Soil Party and conservative Whigs toward the Know Nothing Party. Moreover, Whigs were troubled by the rise of new immigrant voters who tended to vote Democratic, thus threatening to relegate them to the status of a permanent losing party.

Both Democrats and Whigs also expressed concern that the party system itself was disintegrating. Both parties were having difficulties distinguishing between themselves, as each sought to avoid the slavery question in efforts to keep their respective factions together. Third-party movements like the Republican Party faced another dilemma. They could attract attention and gain votes by developing a clear position, but in the volatile political situation events could make their own uniqueness obsolete. Thus the Free Soil Party faced a loss of growth after the Compromise of 1850. The Know Nothing Party was poised to become a major party in 1856 but instead split into Northern and Southern factions. The Republican Party had found a distinctive claim for voters with its pledge to prevent the extension of slavery, particularly after the Kansas-Nebraska Act; but when the Supreme Court declared restrictions on slavery unconstitutional, many Republicans felt that their platform was moot.

Abraham Lincoln's own career illustrates the way this explosive political environment, in which voters could no longer be counted on to stay with their party, effected politicians. Lincoln began his career as a Whig who won election to the state legislature in 1834 and the House of Representatives in 1846. He retired from politics two years later. As he explained in a campaign biography: ". . . I was losing interest in politics, when the repeal of the Missouri Compromise aroused me again." Two years after his return to politics, Lincoln left the Whigs for the new Republican Party. Lincoln's decision to join the Republicans was less risky than the choice faced by other politicians, since he was unknown outside of Illinois. When he learned his name had been placed in nomination as vice president on the Republican ticket in 1856 (the eventual choice was William L. Dayton), he was astounded and thought the reporter mistakenly confused him with Levi Lincoln, a Massachusetts politician.

The political deftness as well as the moral insight of Lincoln can be seen by briefly reviewing his pre-presidential political positions. The young Lincoln argued as early as 1838 that the key document of nationhood was the Declaration of Independence and, implicitly, not the Constitution. In the Lyceum address Lincoln emphasized the fragility of the Union, whose fate now rested with the second generation of Americans. He warned that the edifice created by the fathers of the republic "must fade, is fading and has faded. . . ." However, unlike Washington, who in his farewell address urged Americans to pledge fidelity to the Constitution when tempted by the sirens of faction and designing politicians, Lincoln's demand for filial piety centered upon pledging obedience to the "patriots of seventy-six."

Lincoln's success in galvanizing support for the Republican Party rested on a set of arguments that responded to two core propositions repeatedly made by Southerners in the 1850s: (1) The institution of slavery was not inconsistent with democratic society; and (2) the United States as a political unit contained the implicit right of secession on the part of one or more states. For the most part, the Democrats and the Whigs in the North were not happy to accept either proposition but seemed incapable of effectively refuting either.

Indeed, as Lincoln developed his positions after the deepening crisis created by the Kansas-Nebraska Act of 1854, he too found that neither of the Southern propositions was easily refutable through a simple appeal to the American Revolution. There was a gaping hole, of course, in the Southern recourse to liberal contractarian arguments on the one hand and the defense of slavery on the other. But Lincoln faced his own contradictions as well. If he used the Declaration as the ballast for his central antisecessionist support, focusing on its assertion of equality ("all men are created equal"), then he must also confront the Declaration's seeming support for rebellion ("the right of the People to alter or abolish" governments). In more immediate political terms, Lincoln faced marginalization if he adopted an abolitionist position that centered on the former part of the text at the expense of the latter, and he faced indistinguishability from his rivals in both parties if he accepted various kinds of accommodations that would satisfy the Southerners enough to keep them from exercising their alleged right to separate.

In his Springfield speech accepting his party's nomination for U.S. Senate, Lincoln moved dramatically away from the latter alternative by employing the biblical metaphor of a house divided to predict that the Union "cannot endure, permanently half-slave and half-free." This symbolism was not lost on the biblically oriented nineteenth-century audience. The phrase Lincoln employed is derived from Matthew's account of the questioning by the Pharisees of Jesus' healing power. Jesus' response, "Every kingdom divided against itself is brought to desolation; and every city or house divided against itself shall not stand," is an extremely complex statement that explores the nature of belief, faith, and motivation. Simply summarized, the "house divided" metaphor seeks to show the confusion and desperation that accompany actions undertaken in absence of divine guidance. Lincoln, by employing the phrase, was contending that people will pay a price for ignoring "ancient truths" in their common heritage and for tolerating evil. "Satan cannot cast out Satan" was part of Jesus defense of his divine powers, and Lincoln was applying this New Testament lesson to those who would accommodate the spread of slavery. Thus, Lincoln linked the slavery crisis to an ancient biblical narrative, in which division is not a natural right but a certain sign of descent into perdition. He also linked those like Douglas, who apparently sought compromise, to a conspiracy which amounted to complicity with evil.

The house-divided position still provided Lincoln with some wiggle room, however. In the debates with Douglas, he variously contended that his comment was simple prediction and that he never advocated political or social equality for African Americans. Nevertheless, the critique of Douglas's doctrine of popular sovereignty from which Lincoln drew the house-divided position, along with the vividness of the metaphor, placed him in a position where the Declaration suitably reread became the central framework from which he attacked the legitimacy of secession.

As Lincoln moved into the national arena, he boldly chose Jefferson—the joint author of the Virginia–Kentucky resolutions, advocate of states rights, and slave owner—as his exemplar. In Ottawa, Douglas leveled the charge of the "newness" of Lincoln's reading of the Declaration. He raised the question of why the Union could not endure "in the same relative condition that our fathers made it." Lincoln responded that he based his position on the "original principles" in Jeffersonian "fashion."

However, Lincoln's Jefferson was quite different from the Southern hero, as this commemoration offered a year after the debates indicates:

> All honor to Jefferson—to the man who, in the concrete pressure of a struggle for national independence by a single people, had the coolness, forecast, and capacity to introduce into a merely revolutionary document, an abstract truth, and so embalm it there, that today and in all coming days, it shall be a rebuke and a stumbling block to the very harbingers of reappearing tyranny and oppression.

The Declaration could have been "merely a revolutionary document" had not Jefferson the foresight to introduce the idea of an "abstract truth."

Freed of his own stumbling block in terms of opposing secession, Lincoln was able to move in two directions. One involved his insistence that once the eternal meaning of the Declaration had been brought to life, it would be a tragedy to restrict its application to white males of English descent. Douglas's arguments about what the signers historically meant carried little weight under Lincoln's reading of the Declaration. The document was adopted by "iron men" when we were a "very small people." But what was the connection between the "old Declaration of Independence" and these "old men"? If ancestry by blood was the nature of the historical connection, these "new" Americans have none. If, however, the connection could be traced to moral principle (". . . all men are created equal"), a kind of moral paternity could be established, since its sentiment could be recognized as "the father of all moral principle in them, and that they have the right to claim it as though they were the blood of the blood, and the flesh of the flesh, of the men who wrote the Declaration, and so they are." To read the document in Douglas's terms now would be to cut "the electric cord" (the connection between the old and new) that "links the hearts" of patriots.

Moreover, Lincoln was not adverse to laying the more practical arguments alongside his mythic one. In a multi-ethnic society Lincoln knew the import of his assertion that any restriction of equality in the Declaration challenged the rights of Germans, Irish, French, and Scandinavians: "If one man says it does not mean the Negro, why not another say it does not mean another man?" Thus *new* Americans should see the import of dedicating themselves to this *old* document.

The other direction Lincoln took involved pursuit of the implications of a founding that occurred in 1776 committed to the proposition of equality. Having erased from the Declaration the reading that it contained the right to revolution on the part of its constituent units, and having emphasized its "embalmed" message now brought to life, Lincoln turned to the Southern secessionist statements and their new constitution. He noted the recurrent citations of the Declaration but asked why "unlike the good old one, penned by Jefferson, they omit the words 'all men are created equal?'" When he examined the preamble to the constitution of the CSA (Confederate Sates of America), Lincoln pointed out that "unlike our good, old one, signed by Washington," it did not begin with "We the people" but instead substituted "We the deputies of the sovereign and independent states." "Why," Lincoln asked, "this deliberate pressing out of view, the rights of men, and the authority of the people?"

Although Lincoln argued that the Union had not originated in a contract among the states, nor was it dependent on the performance of mutual obligations among them, he never denied the contractual trope per se. In his Lyceum address, he responded to the problem of civil unrest with a call for reaffirmation of the American social contract that emphasized obedience to the law:

> Let every American, every lover of liberty, every well-wisher to his posterity swear by the blood of the Revolution never to violate in the least particular the laws of the country, and never to tolerate their violation by others. As the patriots of seventy-six did to the support of the Declaration of Independence, so to the support of the constitution and laws let every man remember to violate the law is to trample on the blood of his father, and to tear the charter of his own and his children's liberty.

Consistent with his later positions, the young Lincoln's contractual thought took the citizen, not the state, as the contractual party and based the pledge on the "blood of the Revolution." So important is this pledge to the future of the republic that Lincoln insisted it must become the "political religion of the nation" taught by "every family, every school and college, every clergyman and legislator."

As Lincoln faced the prospect of civil war, his criticism of Southern actions borrowed on this expansive contract to deny the right of secession in terms of a threat to order in general. Southern ideas about secession were invidiously "new." "No government proper," he argued, "ever had a provision in its organic law for its own termination." Even if the United States were a compact among states, a unanimous vote would be necessary, for "plainly, the central idea of secession is anarchy." Standing alongside this argument, however, was one which grew more prominent as the Civil War progressed, finally subsuming the other. As Lincoln, however, re-read the Declaration as a document of a Union dedicated to equality, he began to transform the nature of the contract in several significant, even monumental, ways. The contract tied national identity to a commitment to the equality proposition in the Declaration. As long as slavery was a regional practice, Lincoln was willing to tolerate its existence (although the House Divided speech at the least pointed to eventual extinction, as Southerners were quick to remonstrate). However, as he showed in his debates with Douglas, any policy of popular sovereignty threatened to place the institution on "a new basis, which looks to the perpetuity and nationalization of slavery."

Lincoln used a wide variety of arguments to support this judgment that slavery was in danger of becoming a national institution and as such was eroding the principles of the republic. In Peoria, he presented an economic argument that slave and free labor could not coexist in the new territories: "Slave states are places for poor white people to remove from, not move to. New free states are the places for poor people to go to, and better their condition." The nation "needs these Territories," warned Lincoln, in order to maintain equality of opportunity.

Lincoln's primary supporting arguments rested on the assertion that nationalized slavery would require the repudiation of those central beliefs that made America a free nation. To Lincoln, this paring down of the shining abstract truth of the document represented a threat to everyone. He argued that the founding fathers who framed the principles that defined us as Americans had been uncomfortable with slavery and always meant slavery to be a local institution. The Declaration asserted the doctrine of self-government as an "absolute and eternal right." "If the Negro is a man, is it not to that extent a total destruction of self-government to say that he too shall not govern himself?" He closed his Ottawa, Illinois address in the debate with Douglas by quoting Henry Clay. Clay had once said that those who wished to repress liberty in America would have to "go back to the era of our independence, and muzzle the canon which thunders its annual joyous return; they must blow out the moral lights around us; they must penetrate the human soul, and eradicate there the love of liberty. . . ." Douglas, in his policy of caring not whether slavery was voted up or down, was of necessity attacking the "sacred right of self-government" itself. He was "blowing out the moral lights around us."

Even with these brilliant interpretations of the Declaration of Independence in regard to slavery and the alleged right of secession, Lincoln faced monumental problems as president. Though he won the election in 1860, he received less than 40 percent of the vote in a four-way race. Moreover, he did not win a single Southern state. Lincoln gained only 1 percent of the vote in Virginia and was not even on the ballot in several Southern states. When he took the oath of office, seven states had already seceded and rebels had seized numerous federal forts and buildings.

As president-elect, Lincoln refused to speak on the secession question. His first inaugural, while one of the most eloquent speeches ever delivered, was a carefully phrased message to the South. Lincoln assured the South that he had no intention of destroying slavery in places where it existed: "I have no purpose, directly or indirectly, to interfere with the institution of slavery in the States where it exists," said Lincoln. "I believe I have no lawful right to do so, and I have no inclination to do so." But he also was adamant that there was no right to secession, either constitutional or moral.

In the spring of 1861 Lincoln clearly distinguished himself from the abolitionists as well as those, like Buchanan, who asserted that the government had no right to forcibly resist secession. Lincoln, however, faced an immediate crisis. South Carolina had left the Union in December, and two federal forts were under its control. Fort Sumter, however, was occupied by federal troops and badly in need of provisions. The CSA demanded immediate withdrawal. At first, Lincoln was inclined to give up the fort. His problem was not only that the fort was militarily indefensible, but also that an aggressive Northern response might trigger further secession. The entire upper South, including Virginia, was still in the Union. Lincoln also realized that if the North fired the first shot, Southern resistance would be strengthened. He therefore began informal negotiations with South Carolina and even offered to surrender the fort if he had assurances that Virginia would not secede (claiming that he would trade a fort for a state any day). Lincoln then attempted to send a message of federal resolve by reinforcing federal troops at Fort Pickens, Florida. On April 6 he made his fateful decision. He announced he would send supplies to Fort Sumter. Six days later, state militia attacked the fort. Thirty hours later, Sumter surrendered and the Civil War began. It ended four years later, with more than 500,000 casualties.

Lincoln achieved some of his goals through his astute actions regarding Fort Sumter. The South did start the war. Lincoln is reported to have said, "The plan succeeded. They attacked Sumter—it fell, and thus, did more service than it otherwise could." Lincoln, however, was unable prevent the secession of more Southern states, and there were charges by Democrats that he maneuvered the South into the attack.

While Lincoln had proceeded very carefully up to the attack on Sumter, he acted with incredible speed afterwards. Between April and July of 1861, Lincoln unilaterally asserted a range of presidential powers previously unimaginable. Indeed, Clinton Rossiter (*Constitutional Dictatorship*) refers to Lincoln's actions as a "constitutional dictatorship," and Michael Riccards (*The Ferocious Engine of Democracy*) refers to the period as the "80-day dictatorship." Lincoln issued a proclamation calling up 75,000 state militia to federal service and added 40,000 volunteers; he ordered a naval blockade of the coast; he ordered his secretary of treasury to spend $2 million to buy military equipment; he suspended the writ of habeas corpus from Philadelphia to Washington, DC, permitting the imprisonment of individuals without warrant and trial in civilian courts; and he ordered the post offices closed to treasonable correspondence. Lincoln justified these measures in a variety of ways, both specific and general. He contended that Article I of the Militia Act of 1795 authorized him to call for federal troops in time of national peril and that Article I of the Constitution enabled him to suspend habeas corpus in an emergency. He claimed that his oath of office "to take care that the laws be faithfully executed" gave him authority for his actions and spoke of "the war powers of the government" as an overall grant of power.

Lincoln called Congress into session in July and asked for authorization for all these measures after the fact. Congress did approve the measures, although the courts were less agreeable. Justice Taney, chief justice of the Supreme Court, ruled that the suspension of habeas corpus was unconstitutional. Lincoln publicly disagreed and ignored the decision.

Throughout the Civil War, Lincoln continued to expand presidential powers without effective opposition from Congress and the courts. In 1862, for example, he issued an executive order that all persons encouraging draft evasion be tried in military courts. After the war was over the Court declared that this measure was unconstitutional, but the justices openly noted that they might have decided differently had the case been taken up during the war.

Perhaps the most far-reaching exercise of presidential power by Lincoln was his issuance of the Emancipation Proclamation in 1863. In this instance, Lincoln moved quite cautiously. On the one hand, Lincoln had stated very carefully in his inaugural that he had neither the power nor the desire to end slavery. He also was very concerned about keeping border slaveholding states in the Union and avoiding dissension in the North among those who supported the war but not emancipation. However, other considerations were becoming even more compelling. Congress, on its own initiative, passed a series of confiscation acts in 1861 and 1862, one of which declared that the slaves of any rebel were henceforth "forever free." Lincoln continued without success during this period to urge border states in the Union to pass emancipation legislation that was gradual and included compensation to slaveholders. Only a month before issuing the proclamation, Lincoln presented to Congress a complex plan for the South that included financial incentives for gradual emancipation that could be completed by 1900.

There were, however, strong moral and political arguments in favor of action to end slavery. Many Republicans were adamantly advising Lincoln to act. The war was dragging on and Democrats were beginning to formulate a peace policy. There was the threat that Great Britain might recognize the rebel government. The status of slaves in liberated territories was becoming a problem demanding a clear policy, and there was the issue of adding former slaves to the Union Army. Frustrated by these conflicting pressures, Lincoln wrote a letter for publication in the *New York Tribune* in which he said, "If I could save the Union without freeing any slave, I would do it; and if I could save it by freeing some and leaving others alone, I would also do that." One month later Lincoln issued the proclamation after the battle of Antietam. The order, however, was carefully justified on the grounds of "military necessity" and only provided for emancipation in those territories in rebellion.

Critics then and later noted the absence of moral argument in the proclamation as well as the fact that the order did not free a single slave under federal control. The proclamation, nevertheless, accomplished many important goals. It fortified international support for the North; it solidified domestic opinion; it ended the issue of compensation; and most importantly, it provided the groundwork for the Thirteenth Amendment that abolished slavery.

In 1863 in a speech commemorating the battle at Gettysburg, Lincoln stated war aims in terms so simple and eloquent that the address is regarded as a masterpiece of political discourse. Birth ("four score and seven years ago our fathers brought forth on this continent a new nation, conceived in liberty and dedicated to the proposition that all men are created equal"), trial ("Now we are engaged in a great civil war, testing whether that nation so conceived and dedicated can long endure"), and rebirth (". . . we here highly resolve that these dead shall not have died in vain; that this nation, under God, shall have a new birth of freedom . . .") were the symbols he used to describe the war. The address built on the theme of a "house divided" that Lincoln introduced nine years earlier and infused the legal language of the Emancipation Proclamation with a moral and religious significance. By announcing that the nation was based on the principle that all men are created equal, Lincoln not only identified the end of slavery as a war aim but also claimed that its destruction was essential to America's identity.

Indeed, by studying the address in terms of what it does *not* contain, one can see more clearly the brilliance of Lincoln's effort. There is mention of no soldier's or general's name, no mention of the enemy—there is not even a mention of slavery or of the Declaration itself. The reader of the address is rather propelled, in rising crescendos, to comprehend its messages: the war has a profound meaning; there is a national identity that has monumental historical meaning; there is a profound connection among generations of Americans. Each of these messages peel away to reveal yet higher levels of meaning: the dead can and must be honored; humans are capable of monumental projects; one generation can atone for the actions of another. What remains is a statement of the horror and hope of human existence itself, in which recognition of birth and death is consoled by the prospect of rebirth.

Despite the national drama that he provided in the address, Lincoln moved cautiously on Reconstruction issues. His plan to permit states back into the Union after 10 percent of the population signed loyalty oaths was regarded as too generous by Republican members of Congress. Representatives were also concerned that in his December 1863 message Lincoln offered few guarantees of freedom for former slaves. Salmon Chase, secretary of treasury, considered challenging Lincoln for the upcoming presidential nomination. When he withdrew, several prominent abolitionists supported Fremont. Meanwhile, Lincoln faced a formidable challenge from General George McClellan, whom Lincoln dismissed in 1862. The Democratic Party platform acknowledged the sacrifices of Union soldiers but urged negotiation to end the war.

Although Lincoln himself was pessimistic about his chances for reelection and even began preparations for a transition, several events balanced the scales in his favor. Fremont withdrew, and Atlanta fell to

Union forces in September. McClellan attempted to revise the proposal to start peace negotiations, but it was too late. Lincoln made some important decisions to help his cause. He took the chance that Union soldiers would support him and arranged furloughs to permit them to vote. Union commanders risked temporary depletion in their ranks to grant the president's request. Although the military vote alone did not determine the outcome of the election, the symbolism of servicemen returning to their communities to support Lincoln impressed civilians. Moreover, Lincoln used federal troops to oversee balloting.

Lincoln's victory was substantial. He won 55 percent of the vote, the largest margin of victory since Jackson's in 1828. A month after his second inauguration, Lincoln was assassinated. The future of the party he helped to form, the status of African Americans, and the future of the Union itself were questions that would now have to be answered by others. In this sense, Lincoln's legacy was incomplete. His second inaugural is generally regarded as a conciliatory document. The address closes with the biblical injunction to behave with "malice toward none and charity to all," but the body of the speech interprets the war as the result of divine retributive justice. Both sides had "read the same Bible" and prayed to the same God; both had invoked "his aid against the other." But Lincoln is clear about the righteousness of the Northern cause: "It may seem strange that any men should dare to ask a just God's assistance in wringing their bread from the sweat of other men's faces. . . . "

He also warned:

> [I]f God wills that it continue until all the wealth piled up by bondsman's two hundred and fifty years of unrequited toil shall be sunk, and until every drop of blood drawn with the lash shall be paid by another drawn with the sword, as was said three thousand years ago, so still it must be said, "The judgments of the Lord are true and righteous altogether."

The inaugural, as well as Lincoln's initial policies in regard to Reconstruction, thus provided others with some support for their postwar positions. Would Lincoln have been concerned primarily with rebuilding the Union? Or would he have focused upon redeeming the pledge that "all men are created equal"? Despite these profound ambiguities, Lincoln established many powerful precedents. He showed, for example, how the power of rhetoric can transform a nation, how a president can be alternately bold and cautious in his actions, and how the presidency itself can respond to crisis. As he himself said, shortly after the 1864 election:

> It has long been a grave question whether any government, not too strong for the liberties of the people, can be strong enough to maintain its own existence in great emergencies. . . . Until now it has not been known to the world that this was a possibility. It shows also how sound and strong we still are.

SUMMARY AND COMMENT

The period of the partisan presidency began and ended with two strong presidents, Andrew Jackson and Abraham Lincoln, who both masterfully changed the "rules of the game." Jackson defied the inhibitions of the founding presidency by creating a political party he led himself. He rejected the tradition of nonpartisanship and deference to Congress and replaced them with party discipline and the force of his personality. Moreover, Jackson revised and extended the tenets of Jeffersonian democracy by creating a "people's presidency" that sought to engage the support of people anxious to further their economic well-being through the principle of "equal rights for all, special privileges for none." Lincoln risked his political career by joining a new political party and led the Republicans to victory by challenging what had become an iron rule of politics in the period: Every president and presidential aspirant assumed that accommodation to the institution of slavery was an inevitable part of politics. Lincoln erased this political practice, even at the cost of civil war.

James M. McPherson *(Abraham Lincoln and the Second American Revolution)* has argued that the key to Lincoln's success lay in his "hedgehog" approach to politics. McPherson borrows upon Isaiah Berlin's famous distinction between political thinkers who approach tasks as either a hedgehog or a fox. The fox pursues many agendas "often unrelated and contradictory," while the hedgehog connects "everything to a single vision." More than any of his contemporaries, Lincoln, according to McPherson, pursued policies that were governed by a central vision, expressed in the Gettysburg Address, that this "nation, conceived in Liberty, and dedicated to the proposition that all men are created equal . . . shall not perish from the earth." To Lincoln, slavery violated this proposition, and secession meant an end to the American experiment in self-government. While he was quite willing to modify his tactics in his hedgehog pursuit, Lincoln always kept his focus on his goal.

In many ways, Jackson too was a hedgehog. He was absolutely convinced that smaller government was essential to the preservation of liberty for all, and he followed policies, such as the destruction of the Bank of the United States, that served his goal. James Polk followed Jackson's path as well in his single-minded pursuit of territorial expansion.

The other presidents in this period, however, were more like foxes. Martin Van Buren, the "Little Magician," was extremely adept at party politics. Pierce and Buchanan understood the intricacy of compromise though not, of course, the evil of slavery. Once Jackson created the partisan presidency, the political system generally rewarded those who could appreciate the complex terrain of party competition. The partisan presidency was a period of extremely even party competition nationally. Politicians who could figure out how to add small increments of votes to the Democratic or Republican base (or to avoid erosion) were valuable assets.

The problem, of course, was that the eradication of slavery demanded the sensibility of the hedgehog. Polk's approach of adding new states was not the right formula, since it only exacerbated conflict over slavery without offering a solution. Slavery was a mammoth institution in antebellum America. More than four million slaves composed about half the population of the deep South. Southerners were able to detect the most indirect possible challenge to the institution and threaten to vote accordingly. One only has to compare economic practices with far less impact than slavery (tobacco, for example) and examine the difficulties in restraining or eliminating them to see the magnitude of the challenge posed. Thus while the period of the partisan presidency was quite successful in managing most conflicts and even in producing talented presidents, it was unable to deal with the issue of slavery without the collapse of the two parties and their reformulation under conditions of civil war.

Bibliographic Essay

Richard McCormick, *The Second Party System* (Chapel Hill: University of North Carolina Press, 1966), and Everett Carl Ladd, *American Political Parties* (New York: W. W. Norton, 1970) provide overviews of party competition in general during this period. Michael F. Holt's *The Political Crises of the 1850s* (New York: Wiley, 1978) is a particularly helpful review of party strategies in the 1850s. Holt's "Another Look at the Election of 1856," in Michael J. Birkner, ed., *James Buchanan and the Political Crisis of the 1850s* (Selinsgrove: Susquehanna University Press, 1996), illustrates the electoral volatility of a disintegrating party system. The interaction between the moral and economic aspects of slavery and party competition is elegantly explored in J. David Greenstone, *The Lincoln Persuasion: Remaking American Liberalism* (Princeton, NJ: Princeton University Press, 1993). Although Greenstone focuses upon Lincoln's transformation of the party system, his chapter on Van Buren's strategies is particularly informative.

Marvin Meyers's creative interpretive synthesis, *The Jacksonian Persuasion* (Stanford, CA: Stanford University Press, 1957), is a masterpiece of ideological analysis that places Jackson at the center of the transformation of the founding presidency to a partisan one. Also see John William Ward, *Andrew Jackson: Symbol for an Age* (New York: Oxford University Press, 1962), for a fascinating attempt to ascertain what Jackson meant symbolically to American citizens. Robert V. Remini, *The Legacy of Andrew Jackson* (Baton Rouge: Louisiana State University Press, 1988) is an insightful, sympathetic attempt to assess Jackson while Michael Paul Rogin's *Fathers and Children: Andrew Jackson and the Subjugation of the American Indian* (New York: Vintage, 1975) is more critical.

Donald B. Cole presents a positive portrait of Van Buren in his *Martin Van Buren and the American Party System* (Princeton, NJ: Princeton University Press, 1984) that is very adept in placing his actions in the context of party politics in the period. Holman Hamilton's imaginative triple biography, *The Three Kentucky Presidents: Lincoln, Taylor and Davis* (Lexington: University of Kentucky Press, 1978) is also an excellent account of the parameters of the partisan presidency.

Also see Norma Lewis Peterson, *The Presidencies of William Henry Harrison and John Tyler* (Lawrence: University Press of Kansas, 1989). Polk's grand success (and failure) has attracted more attention than any other president in this period except, of course, Jackson and Lincoln. See Charles A. McCoy, *Polk and the Presidency* (Austin: University of Texas Press, 1960); Paul H. Bergeron, *The Presidency of James A. Polk* (Lawrence: University Press of Kansas, 1987); and Charles Sellers, *James K. Polk: Continentalist 1843–1846* (Princeton: Princeton University Press, 1966), p. 213.

There are many examinations of Lincoln's response to the partisan presidency. James M. Macpherson's *Abraham Lincoln and the Second American Revolution* (New York: Oxford University Press, 1990) emphasizes Lincoln's role as a revolutionary figure. William E. Gienapp's " 'No Bed of Roses': James Buchanan, Abraham Lincoln and Presidential Leadership in the Civil War Era," in Michael J. Birkner, ed., *James Buchanan and the Political Crisis of the 1850s* (Selinsgrove: Susquehanna University Press, 1996), compares the decisions of the two presidents. Michael Davis, in *The Image of Lincoln in the South* (Knoxville: University of Tennessee Press, 1971), reviews the various assessments of Lincoln in the region in the ante- and postbellum period. Roy P. Baster, *Lincoln Legend* (Boston: Houghton Mifflin, 1935), is an early attempt to trace the various "Lincolns" in American political culture. Examples of psychologically informed interpretations of Lincoln are Charles B. Strozier, *Lincoln's Quest for Union* (New York: Basic Books, 1982); and George B. Forgie, *Patricide and the House Divided* (New York: W. W. Norton, 1979). Forgie argues that Lincoln's career and political thought were the result of a politically induced Oedipal complex. His psychologically ambivalent relationship with the founding fathers led to the pursuit and "symbolic murder" of Douglas.

Harry Jaffa, in *The Crisis of the House Divided* (Garden City, NY: Doubleday, 1959), accepts some of the psychological implications of Lincoln's own quest for immortality in relation to the founders, but he forcefully argues that Lincoln's belief that the Kansas-Nebraska Act represented a real possibility of the nationalization of slavery was well founded and neither psychologically motivated nor the result of political opportunism. Don E. Fehrenbacher, *Prelude to Greatness: Lincoln in the 1850's* (Stanford, CA: Stanford University Press, 1962) and David Zarefsky, *Lincoln, Douglas and Slavery* (Chicago: University of Chicago Press, 1990) provide useful close readings of the issues discussed in the Lincoln-Douglas debates.

Douglas has not had many defenders since George Fort Milton's 1934 biography, but Robert W. Johannsen's *The Frontier, the Union, and Stephen A. Douglas* (Urbana: University of Illinois Press, 1989) contends that Douglas epitomized the new West more than Lincoln. Glen E. Throw's *Abraham Lincoln and American Political Religion* (Albany: SUNY Press, 1976) contains thoughtful analyses of the Lyceum speech, the Gettysburg Address, and the second inaugural. Many of these interpretations are defended and debated in Gabor S. Boritt and Norman O. Forness, eds., *The Historian's Lincoln* (Urbana: University of Illinois Press, 1988). Frank J. Williams and William D. Peterson have collected essays which examine Lincoln's influence today, particularly among U.S. presidents, in their *Abraham Lincoln: Contemporary* (Campbell, CA: Savas Woodbury Publishers, 1995). The case for Lincoln as an opportunistic politician is made in Hofstadter's *The American Political Tradition* (New York: Knopf, 1948), and accepted in part in Gore Vidal's novel, *Lincoln* (New York: Random House, 1984). Philip Abbott reviews Lincoln's arguments against secession in "The Lincoln Propositions and the Spirit of Secession," *Studies in American Political Development* (Spring, 1996), pp. 103–29. William L. Miller presents a detailed moral defense of Lincoln's major presidential decisions in *Lincoln's Virtues* (New York: Knopf, 2001).

THE ECLIPSED PRESIDENCY

Eclipsed Presidents

President/ Political Party	Term of Office	Vice President	Percent Electoral Vote	Percent Popular Vote
Andrew Johnson (R)	1865–1869	—	—	—
Ulysses S. Grant (R)	1869–1873	Schuyler Colfax	73	53
Ulysses S. Grant (R)	1873–1877	Henry Wilson	78	56
Rutherford B. Hayes (R)	1877–1881	William A. Wheeler	48	50
James A. Garfield (R)	1881–1881	Chester A. Arthur	58	48
Chester A. Arthur (R)	1881–1885	—	—	—
Grover Cleveland (D)	1885–1880	Thomas A. Hendricks	55	49
Benjamin Harrison (R)	1889–1893	Levi. P. Morton	58	48
Grover Cleveland (D)	1893–1897	Adlai E. Stevenson	55	49

When Lincoln was assassinated in 1866, the presidency had become the center of power in the American political system. Such a rapid concentration of power in the office was not replicated until the following century. Lincoln governed without Congress from the fall of Fort Sumter to July 4 on the grounds of "public necessity." Justice Taney challenged Lincoln's authority to suspend habeas corpus, but the president rejected his arguments. In 1863 in the Prize Cases, the Supreme Court supported Lincoln's decision to blockade Southern ports. Only the president, concluded the Court, can determine when to exercise his powers as commander in chief in time of insurrection. (Not until 1866 did the Supreme

Court challenge presidential authority in the *Ex Parte Milligan* decision.) When Congress was called into session on July 4, 1861, it approved all of Lincoln's unilateral actions, which he based on the commander-in-chief clause, his oath of office, and "war powers."

Under Lincoln's leadership, the thirty-seventh and thirty-eighth Congress (1861–1865) passed over 800 pieces of legislation, twice the number of any previous session. The thirty-eighth Congress spent more money than had been appropriated in the entire history of the republic. Lincoln financed the war through issuing "greenbacks" (legal tender backed by the government), bonds, and new taxes. Still, by the end of the war the United States was $2.8 billion in debt. Lincoln filled the federal government with members of the six-year-old Republican Party. In 1861 there were about 40,000 civilian federal jobs. By the war's end, the number had increased to nearly 200,000. Most of these positions were held by loyal Republicans.

Through the seven presidencies extending from 1866 to 1896, presidential powers were dramatically restricted or eliminated. The Senate asserted its right to control the president's replacement of cabinet members and other executive officials in the Tenure of Office Act. Andrew Johnson's refusal to comply constituted one of the articles of his impeachment. The legislation was not repealed until 1887 despite the objections of each subsequent president after Johnson. As party machines grew, the president's patronage authority shrank. Senator Roscoe Conkling of New York assumed control of all federal patronage for the New York Customs House in the Grant administration. Conkling's machine was tremendously lucrative. Clerks and assessors made handsome incomes through bribes and kickbacks from importers, and Conkling's machine raked in a portion of the take. It took two presidents (Hayes and Garfield), at the cost of considerable political capital, to dislodge Conkling.

Although the presidency was still a partisan institution in this period, political parties assumed new forms and characteristics. Initially, the Democrats were severely tainted by their opposition to the Civil War. Many "Union Democrats" were avid opponents to secession and slavery, and the party in general suffered from their demand for negotiations in the election of 1864. Republicans were adept at reminding voters of the recent past. During the war, the antiwar wing of the Democratic Party was called "Copperheads" by the press. These Democrats had indeed created a number of antiwar semi-secret societies in order to avoid prosecution by the administration. In 1869, Congressman Benjamin Butler, a Radical Republican, produced a bloody shirt during his speech against the Klan. Waving the "bloody shirt" to keep memories of Civil War sacrifices alive became a powerful electoral tactic. Grant, Hayes, and Garfield were all Civil War heroes, and their campaigns emphasized the recent rebellion. The Democrats survived, however, by focusing on local issues and building strong state and city political machines based in part on the support of new immigrants. By 1876, Democrats recovered and achieved national parity with the Republicans. A formidable coalition formed. Called the "Bourbon Democracy," it was composed of Northern businessmen and white Southerners.

Although in this period Republicans dominated the presidency (Grover Cleveland was the only Democrat elected between 1866 and 1896), they perceived themselves as quite vulnerable. They won presidential elections in 1860 and 1864—without any support from Southern voters. With the war over, Republicans envisioned a nightmare scenario: Former Confederates would return to political office; because of newly freed slaves who had no effective voting rights, Republicans would be a permanent minority party. Even worse, half a million casualties would be wasted as slavery in a new form returned to the South. Republicans fought desperately to enfranchise African Americans in hopes of preventing the return of the Southern slaveholding aristocracy to power. When the last federal troops were removed from the South in 1877, Republicans sought to expand their base in other ways.

Despite this competition, both political parties were prone to factionalism, perhaps in part because there were few strong presidents to hold their respective parties together. Republicans split between party regulars, "Stalwarts," and reformers. The latter actually supported the Democratic candidate in 1872. Democrats, too, split between their regulars and agrarian reformers.

One of the most remarkable elements of the eclipsed presidency is the fact that as both parties struggled with splits, and as Congress and the president fought battles over the Tenure of Office Act and civil service reform, the economic system was undergoing a transformation that changed the nation as much as the Civil War did. When Charles Francis Adams returned to the United States from Britain in 1871, he observed a silent revolution occurring in America after the Civil War. He was surprised to see "a greatly enlarged grasp of enterprise and increased facility of combination" in the country:

> The great operations of war, the handling of large masses of men, the influence of discipline, the lavish expenditure of unprecedented sums of money, the immense financial operations, the possibilities of cooperation were lessons not likely lost on men quick to receive and to apply all new ideas.

The changes in American society were sudden and drastic. The number of manufacturing jobs rose fourfold between 1859 and 1899; the number of factories doubled between 1879 and 1899. The number of people living in cities increased five times from 1860 to 1900. U.S. steel companies produced 200,000 tons of steel in 1867. By 1895 the steel output of 6 million tons surpassed that of the British, and 10 million tons a year were produced in America before the turn of the century. The roads, rails, and canals that had been part of the Whig political agenda of "internal improvements" now carried steel and coal to new manufacturing cities such as Fall River, Bridgeport, Paterson, Scranton, Troy, Youngstown, and Akron.

Presidents in this period bore the brunt of some of the negative consequences of industrialization. Scandals created by the new concentrations of wealth, financial panics, and actions in labor disputes threatened their administrations, but none was willing or able to attempt a direct confrontation of these issues. While presidents and the parties they represented ignored these developments at home, so too was participation in foreign affairs limited. Congress prevented Grant from annexing Santo Domingo (now the Dominican Republic). Hayes sought to promote American interests in South America. Not until McKinley, however, did foreign policy concerns have an impact on the presidency.

The period of the eclipsed presidency is often slighted by presidential scholars as one in which a series of weak presidents presided over what historian Mark Wahlgren Summers has called "the era of good stealings." Nevertheless, this period is instructive because it illustrates the capacity of institutions such as Congress and the courts to recapture powers ceded by them, and because it offers an opportunity to observe how presidents react to new circumstances unfavorable to the expansion of the office.

ANDREW JOHNSON (1865–1869)

Lincoln's interpretation in his second inaugural that the war was providentially willed did not prevent him from declaring lenient peace terms with the defeated Confederacy. Many Republicans in Congress, however, took Lincoln at his word. To them, the divine scourge that had greeted the South was the result of the region's defense and promotion of slavery. Now was the time to root out all vestiges of the economic system that rested on slavery. Thaddeus Stevens, the radical Republican leader in the Senate, declared in 1865 that "the whole fabric of Southern society must be changed. . . ." He asked:

> How can republican institutions, free schools, free churches, free social intercourse exist in a mingled community of nabobs and serfs; of the owners of 20,000 acre manors with lordly palaces, and the occupants of narrow huts inhabited by "low white trash"? If the South is ever to be made a safe republic let her lands be cultivated by the toil of the owners or the free labor of intelligent citizens.

Nevertheless, Lincoln himself moved slowly toward implementing emancipation, since preservation of the Union had always been his central political objective. With the war won and the South effectively without slaves, the president welcomed the rebels back into the Union. By 1865 three Southern states had accepted Lincoln's requirement that 10 percent of its citizens take an oath of loyalty and recognize the end of slavery as a condition for readmission. The assassination of Lincoln left open any link he might have planned to connect his apocalyptic interpretation of the Civil War to the problems of peace. It was left to others to attempt to interpret or revise Lincoln's vision. The surrender of Lee at Appomattox ended the fratricide but opened up staggering constitutional, economic, political, and moral problems.

What was the constitutional status of the states that had seceded? Were they still states, since the Confederate States of America (CSA) had never been recognized by the North, or had they forfeited their status as states and now assumed the role of conquered provinces? Who should decide this question as well as the terms of readmission—the president or Congress? In the Prize Cases (1862), the Supreme Court acknowledged the CSA as a belligerent power and described the Civil War as an insurrection. In subsequent cases regarding the status of property in the CSA, courts continued to accept a dual account of secession. In *White v. Bruffy* (1877), Justice Field contended that the recognition of the belligerent status of the CSA was a humanitarian gesture that was operational only during hostilities, and that the United States never acknowledged "in any form" the "lawfulness of the rebellious organization or the validity of any of its acts. . . ." Lincoln assumed that the initiatives would come from the office of the president, but Congress did not recognize his plan and offered its own, which Lincoln subjected to a pocket veto.

Whatever the legal status of the former CSA, the economic problems of the defeated South were enormous. When Carl Schurz, a Northern Republican, surveyed the region for the president immediately after the surrender, he was shocked by the effects of this new kind of war. Some parts of the South had escaped devastation, but in others the countryside

> . . . looked for many miles like a broad black streak of ruin and desolation—the fences were all gone; lonesome smoke stacks, surrounded by dark heaps of ashes and cinders, marking the spots where human habitations had stood; the fields a sickly patch of cotton or corn cultivated by Negro squatters.

Political problems involved in readmission were readily evident. The South had been soundly defeated, but the nationalism that emerged in the 1850s had not disintegrated. As historian W. J. Cash noted in *The Mind of the South*, the war had left the Southerners

> . . . far more aware of their differences and of the line which divided what was Southern from what was not. And upon that line all their intensified patriotism and love, all their high pride in the knowledge that they had fought the good fight and had yielded only to irresistible force, was concentrated, to issue in a determination . . . to hold fast to their own, to maintain their divergences, to remain what they had been.

Northern Republican politicians worried about the possibility of a resurgent Confederacy and even the possibility of the emergence of guerrilla warfare. They worried about the impact of Southern representation in Congress. Would readmitted Southern representatives again align with Northern Democrats, stronger in numbers if the black population were included as part of the census? Would black citizens, if enfranchised, vote at the bidding of their former masters?

Then there was the moral issue of slavery itself as well as the economic and legal status of black Americans. The abolitionist strategy eventually coincided with Lincoln's own goals, but the Emancipation Proclamation ended slavery only in the states in rebellion. Lincoln worked very diligently with Congress in the enactment of the Thirteenth Amendment, which abolished slavery. The South acquiesced in ratification, although several Southern states added codicils insisting that their accession did not foreclose in their minds the issue of compensation. Generally, emancipation created a panic in the South. Before the war, John C. Calhoun had warned that abolition would make "the last first" in the South. Southerners were adamant in rejecting the most minimal social and economic implications of abolition. Emerson Etheridge, a prominent Tennessee politician, said in 1865 that "negroes are no more free than they were 40 years ago, and if one goes about the country telling them that they are free, shoot him."

The series of policies that attempted to deal with these problems is referred to as Reconstruction. Briefly, Reconstruction can be divided into two policy experiments. Presidential Reconstruction, in which the executive branch assumed the initiative in policy formation, began under Lincoln and was revised by his successor, Andrew Johnson. Congressional Reconstruction can be said to have started in 1867 with the passage of the First Reconstruction Act, which divided the former CSA into five military districts and ended officially in 1877 when the last federal troops were removed from the South.

The central figure in the first, or presidential, Reconstruction was Andrew Johnson. In many ways Johnson's career was a replica of Lincoln's. The vice president had been raised in a border state in very modest circumstances. He was economically a self-made man and had taught himself to read as an adult. However, there was an essential difference between Johnson and Lincoln, aside from different political and intellectual talents and psychological proclivities. Lincoln had become a Whig and later a Republican. Johnson's party ideology was derived from a more conventional route given his economic background: He was a Jacksonian Democrat.

Lincoln's decision to join the new Republican Party placed him among the affluent elites of antebellum America. His ability to create ideological bridges between people of his own humble origins and the Whigs' agenda was part of his genius as a politician. Johnson, on the other hand, nurtured his personal class resentments. Early in his career, he announced his goal: "Some day I will show up the stuck-up aristocrats who are running this country."

The outbreak of the Civil War made Johnson an ideal vice presidential choice. Lincoln had complained in 1858 that "much of the plain old Democracy is with us, while nearly all the old exclusive silk-stocking Whiggery is against us." In 1864 he renamed the Republican Party the "National Union" Party in order to solidify bipartisan support for the war. When Tennessee joined the CSA, Johnson refused to give up his Senate seat and remained in the Union. In 1862 Lincoln appointed him military governor of the state. Johnson nursed an intense hatred of the Southern aristocracy, which he saw as a force with a political and economic stranglehold on the small farmer. Republicans eagerly looked forward to his leadership after Lincoln's assassination.

Johnson's plan for Reconstruction included an amnesty for those who had taken an oath of allegiance to the Union, as did Lincoln's proposal, but Johnson's plan also included an important revision. Confederates who owned more than $20,000 worth of property were ineligible for amnesty. Johnson explained to a Virginia delegation that the exceptioned class could appeal individually for special pardons to the president, but he reminded them, "You know full well it was the wealthy men of the South who dragooned the people into secession."

When various states began to hold constitutional conventions, however, voters elected as delegates members of the planter aristocracy whom Johnson so detested. His dream of a restored yeoman South shattered, Johnson seemed to move toward another ideological position. If the small farmers were unable or unwilling to wrest political control of their states from the old landed aristocracy, he would be certain that his beloved farmer would not be forced to share power and status with African Americans. He swiftly granted numerous pardons to the planter class. When the new state governments enacted a series of Black Codes that restricted freedmen's movement without permission of their employers and provided imprisonment for blacks who quit work before the expiration of their contracts, and when numerous terrorist groups such as the Klan emerged in the South, Johnson refused to act. He vetoed congressional legislation authorizing the formation of a federal Freeman's Bureau to provide education, protection, and economic assistance to former slaves. These actions precipitated congressional attempts at Reconstruction.

An acrimonious exchange between Frederick Douglass and Johnson in 1866 illustrates the president's position. In light of recent events in the former CSA, Douglass appealed to Johnson to support measures to give black Americans the right to vote. Johnson replied that slavery had been abolished with a "great national guarantee." He asked Douglass if it was not true that, as a black slave, he looked upon "a large family, struggling hard upon a poor piece of land" with less esteem than he did the large slave-owning planter. This in itself was a cruel question to ask a former slave, but Douglass politely but emphatically disagreed.

Johnson, insisting that such a situation was indeed the case in his experience in Tennessee, continued:

> The colored man went into this rebellion a slave; by the operation of the rebellion he came out a freeman. . . . The non-slaveholder who was forced into the rebellion, who was as loyal as those that lived beyond the limits of the State, but was carried into it, lost his property, and in a number of instances the lives of such were sacrificed, and he who has survived has come out of it with nothing gained, but a great deal lost. Now, upon what principle of justice, should they be placed in a condition different from what they were before? On the one hand, one has gained a great deal; on the other hand, one has lost a great deal, and in a political point of view, scarcely stands where he did before.

Douglass attempted to argue that the small white farmer and the new black freeman could use the ballot to overturn the plantation aristocrat, but Johnson found this scenario inconceivable and ended the exchange, shouting a racial epithet after Douglass left the room.

To Northern Republican representatives in Congress and many former abolitionists, it seemed as if Jefferson Davis had become president. Immediately after the war, the Republican Party was composed of two groups: the conservative or moderate Republicans who were willing to accept Lincoln's and Johnson's proposals in principle, and the radical Republicans who hoped for a more comprehensive Reconstruction. Johnson's emerging position drove the former into the radicals' camp. Enraged by Black Codes and the patterns of terror in the South, radicals proposed constitutional remedies. The Fourteenth Amendment, which guaranteed every citizen due process and equal protection under law, was designed to enable the federal courts to protect black Americans from injustices by the states. This nationalization of civil rights made legislators in Northern states skittish and would not have passed had it not been made a condition for readmission on the part of the Southern states.

After the congressional elections of 1866, congressional Republicans gained enough votes to pass veto-proof legislation. The First Reconstruction Act was passed in the spring over Johnson's veto. Republicans also passed two other pieces of legislation designed to reduce the president's power. One, the Tenure of Office Act, required the Senate's approval before the president could remove any executive official, and the other, contained in the Army Appropriations Act, stated that General Grant could not be reassigned without his own approval and that all orders to Grant must be subject to Grant's approval before taking effect. Congress, in effect, dramatically reduced the president's powers as executor of laws and commander in chief. It did not take Johnson long to take Congress's bait.

In the spring of 1867, the president fired Edwin Stanton as secretary of war. Stanton refused to leave and barricaded himself in his office. Very cleverly, he also appointed Grant, a national hero, as his successor. This ploy failed, however, when Grant, who had presidential ambitions of his own, privately warned senators that Johnson was a dangerous man who might even attempt to dissolve Congress. He subsequently returned to his headquarters. In January, by a vote of 35–6, the Senate refused to accept Stanton's removal. A month later the House impeached Johnson. In May, Johnson escaped impeachment by one vote short of the two-thirds required for conviction.

Johnson's fate—impeachment and near conviction—has been judged by later generations as a grave error. Chief Justice William H. Rehnquist, for example, concluded in 1992 that congressmen mistakenly followed the maxim that "the end justifies the means." Constitutional protections for an independent executive were regarded as "obstacles to the accomplishment of a greater good." Certainly, the Tenure of Office Act was itself of doubtful constitutionality. Lawyers for the president made this point during the impeachment proceedings. Moreover, it is questionable whether Johnson's action constituted an impeachable offense in itself, since the Constitution requires evidence of "high crimes and misdemeanors" for the removal of a president. Clearly, Congress had sought impeachment to remove, or at least punish, a recalcitrant president.

On the other hand, blame can certainly be assigned to all parties in the conflict. In terms of the immediate struggle, both Congress and the president were engaged in a complex game of "chicken." Congress, fearful that Johnson would fire their ally in the cabinet, sought to protect him and warned the president to modify his policies. Johnson, who normally acted like a lion, was almost too clever in this instance in responding like a fox. Technically, he said, he was only suspending the secretary of war, not firing him. Johnson thought that Congress would not dare deny Grant the post when it returned to meet. Upping the ante, in September Johnson pardoned all but the highest-ranking Confederates who swore an oath of allegiance to the Union.

When Congress threatened impeachment, Johnson went on a speaking tour defending his actions. One of the articles of impeachment actually quoted from these public addresses, charging him with attempting to bring Congress into "disgrace, ridicule, hatred, contempt and reproach." This article might seem strange today, but in the nineteenth century presidents rarely spoke about policy before crowds of people. Though not impeachable, Johnson's charges were irresponsible and slanderous. He contended, for example, that recent riots in New Orleans against African Americans were planned by members of Congress. It was in Johnson's interest, as he saw it, to goad Congress since he hoped at this point to gain the nomination of the Democratic Party for reelection for president.

In the end, neither Congress nor the president won. Radicals in Congress were unable to mount a continued consensus for Reconstruction. Johnson spent the remainder of his office stripped of many of his powers and didn't receive the presidential nomination anyway.

Ulysses S. Grant (1869–1877)

When Grant took office in 1869, the possibilities of a successful presidency appeared to be quite good. When he left office after two terms, however, Grant's popularity had experienced a dramatic decline. In his last State of the Union address, the outgoing president glumly recognized his failures, which he attributed in part to his lack of "any previous political training." Today, Grant is almost uniformly ranked as one of the nation's worst presidents.

Some aspects of this assessment can indeed be connected to his own political inexperience; other aspects were due to his own personality. Like many military men, Grant was a grand delegator and like some, he was also fiercely loyal to his associates. The consequence of this combination of traits was myriad scandals during his presidency. His administration became synonymous with political corruption. Indeed, the scandals in the Grant administration are almost too numerous to mention. His family and friends engaged in numerous get-rich-quick schemes at the public's expense. The most infamous, however, was the "Whiskey Ring," a cabal of distillers, politicians, and federal officials (including Orville Babcock, one of the president's close advisors) who defrauded the government of millions of dollars in tax revenue. When his young secretary of treasury, Benjamin Bristow, tried to break up the ring by seizing records, Grant dismissed him and defended Babcock by giving him another post, personally testifying at his trial, and obstructing a congressional investigation. Although Grant himself was scrupulously honest with federal funds, he appointed officials in Indian Affairs, the Freeman's Bureau, Customs, and the Department of War whose major goal was personal enrichment.

In some areas, however, Grant was quite attentive to detail and reasonably effective, especially given the challenges he faced. He won election and reelection by substantial margins, often receiving more votes than state Republicans. In a brilliant campaign speech accepting the nomination in 1868, Grant quietly concluded, "Let there be peace." These few words electrified the nation. Factions in both parties interpreted these sentiments differently. To former slaves and Radical Republicans, it meant an end to the congressional–presidential gridlock of the Johnson years. To white Southerners and Northern Democrats, it meant "local self-government" and a moderation of Reconstruction policy.

In fact, however, Grant's options were relatively limited. First, his major goals were contradictory. He sought to uphold the civil rights of freemen while at the same time offering conciliatory policies for Southern whites. Second, despite his popularity, he was largely unable to lead Congress, particularly the Senate, and unable to control the factions in his party. After the inauguration Grant could not force Congress to repeal the Tenure of Office Act. Instead, Senate Republicans offered a compromise, which he accepted. All but three Southern states had been readmitted to the Union when he took office and a few troops remained in the others, which limited his power to enforce civil rights. Many moderate Republicans were beginning to give up their project to base the Republican Party in the South with African-American voters and sought to attract white support instead. Republican reformers were so disgusted with Grant's record that they formed another party, the Liberal Republicans, in 1872 and supported Horace Greeley, who also became the Democratic candidate for president.

Nevertheless, Grant fought persistently to counteract the reign of terror against former slaves that spread throughout the South. Formed in 1866 in Tennessee by six Confederate veterans, the Ku Klux Klan spread rapidly. Acting secretly, often at night, Klansmen burned schools, beat and murdered anyone who challenged them, and intimidated former slaves to keep them from voting. In essence, the Klan acted as agents of local Democratic parties. These "redeemers," as they called themselves, won elections after Republican voters, black and white, were prevented from going to the polls.

Initially, Grant did not focus on the activities of the Klan, since he believed the Fifteenth Amendment would effectively solve the problem of racial conflict. When it was apparent that congressional legislation to deal with the problem would be defeated and Klan power rose, Grant threw all his influence behind the bill. Congress passed the Ku Klux Klan Act in April of 1871, the first of three enforcement acts designed to curb violence in the South. The bill authorized the president to suspend habeas corpus and to try terrorists in federal courts. Grant moved carefully in invoking his authority. In October, he declared nine counties in South Carolina to be in a "condition of lawlessness," and federal marshals made hundred of arrests. Federal grand juries brought over 3,000 indictments, although many of the Klansmen received light sentences. (The Supreme Court effectively invalidated the Klan Act and other enforcement acts in 1876. Grant's rehabilitation of presidential power thus proved to be short-lived.)

Grant's response to Indian policy was even more self-initiated. When he took office, the situation on the Western Plains had reached crisis proportions. Settlers poured into the region, and the Sioux and Cheyenne responded by raiding homesteads. The settlers demanded protection from the federal government. Philip Sheridan, the Civil War hero who commanded the Army of the Shenandoah, vigorously pursued the Cheyenne warriors. He wrote to his brother in 1868, "The more [Indians] we kill this year, the less we have to kill next year." Sheridan's efforts were enormously popular with Congress. Grant, on the other hand, included comments on the need for "proper treatment" of the "original occupants of this land" in his inaugural. In subsequent messages to Congress, the president was more direct. He warned that "wars of extermination . . . are demoralizing and wicked" and stated that previous dealings with Indians were "open to charges of cruelty and swindling."

Grant immediately announced his "peace policy" in Indian Affairs and sought congressional legislation to support his initiative. In broad terms, the policy called for the treatment of Indians as individuals rather than as tribes, the security of reservations from white settlements, educational aid, and eventually full citizenship. In order to reduce corruption in the Department of Indian Affairs, Grant relied on the advice of his former military secretary, Ely Parker, a Seneca chief. He appointed Quakers as Indian agents on the grounds that members of the sect were humane, dedicated reformers. By today's standards, objections could be raised to Grant's peace policy for its paternalism and commitment to assimilation. Nor was mismanagement eliminated. There were severe challenges to the policy, particularly after the attack on Custer at Little Big Horn. Nevertheless, Jean Edward Smith, a recent biographer, has concluded:

> A president less confident of his military judgment, or who stood more in awe of wartime heroes, would likely have given Sherman and Sheridan their head. The result would have been total war. The Indian tribes would have been driven mercilessly. Tens of thousands would have perished, and ethnic cleansing would have been the order of the day. Instead, Grant abruptly changed direction. Rather than fight, he chose to make peace with the Plains Indians. This was a surprise.

Despite mounting criticism of his presidency, Grant hoped to win nomination to a third term in 1876. While he had support from the Stalwarts, other Republicans were not anxious to return attention to his administration and Garfield received the nomination. Without a pension and as a result of bad investments, Grant was destitute. He had, nevertheless, one last and more positive legacy to offer. Wracked with pain from cancer, Grant worked on his memoirs day and night in order to provide income for his family. *The Personal Memoirs of U.S. Grant* was a great financial and literary success. Royalties provided his family with $450,000, and Mark Twain's initial assessment that the work was comparable to Julius Caesar's *Commentaries* has been confirmed by later generations.

RUTHERFORD B. HAYES (1877–1881)

The inauguration of Rutherford B. Hayes on March 5, 1877 was remarkable in that Hayes was the ultimate beneficiary of the most severely contested presidential election in American history. Contested presidential elections are not uncommon, but even the elections of 1800, 1824, and 2000 are less complex and turbulent than the events that occurred after election day in 1876. The resolution in Hayes's favor enveloped his entire presidency and further weakened the office.

In the wake of the scandals in the Grant administration, both parties nominated reformers with reputations for personal integrity. Hayes, governor of Ohio, was a former Whig, an anti-slavery and temperance activist who was wounded five times in the Civil War. Samuel S. Tilden, governor of New York, had been a Barn Burner (anti-slavery Democrat) before the war and was a major figure in the destruction of the Tweed political machine in New York City. Both parties expected a close election and poured all their resources, financial and rhetorical, into the campaign. Neither Hayes nor Tilden personally campaigned according to custom, but Hayes urged his supporters to wave the "bloody shirt," asking repeatedly, "shall the late rebels have the government?" Tilden used what was called the "perfect system," the identification of voter concerns followed by intense mailings and personal visits by party regulars. The national Republican Party spent $200,000 on the campaign (financed in large part by a two percent assessment on the salaries of civil servants.)

On election night, Hayes was prepared to concede the election to Tilden. Tilden had won New York and was ahead in the popular vote. By the next day, however, the situation became murky. The winner in three Southern states (Louisiana, Florida, and South Carolina) and Oregon was in doubt. Without all of them, Tilden would have 184 electoral votes to Hayes's 185. Republicans controlled the election boards in the three Southern states and insisted their candidate had actually won. (In Oregon, the Democratic governor declared one Republican elector ineligible since he was also a federal officeholder.) On December 6, the four contested states sent two sets of ballots to Congress. The question now was which electors should be counted. The Constitution was unclear as to whether the presiding officer of the Senate (a Republican) or the combined House or Senate (under Democratic control) should decide which votes to count.

The crisis was even more complex than this dispute, however. It was feared that Stalwart Republicans, led by Conkling, might prefer a Democrat over Hayes, the reformer. Meanwhile, Southern Democrats began negotiations through intermediaries to explore the price for their support of Hayes. Some Southern Democrats wanted commitment for federal support of a railroad and most of all wanted the last of federal troops withdrawn from their region and a commitment to home rule. To further complicate matters, Grant seemed convinced that Tilden had really won Louisiana and was reluctant to use his resources to aid Hayes.

At this point, the strategy of the candidates themselves was crucial. Tilden seemed reluctant to intervene, while Hayes actively pursued his cause behind the scenes. He sent a letter to Grant asking for his support. He let it be known he would consider the Southern proposals. Since both parties were not sure how their members would vote, they agreed to a compromise. An electoral commission would decide which electoral votes to count. The commission, composed of seven Democrats, seven Republicans, and Independent Judge David Davis, received the reluctant support of the Hayes forces. Davis resigned, however, to run for the Senate in Illinois as a Democrat, and Justice Joseph P. Bradley was selected to replace him. Northern Democrats threatened to filibuster past the inauguration date while Southerners posed the question again to Hayes: Would he support home rule? Hayes refused to answer directly. Bradley voted with the Republicans in each contested state. After hours of acrimonious debate, Congress accepted the commission's decisions at 4 A.M., two days before the scheduled inauguration. A month later, Hayes ordered the last federal troops out of the South.

Hayes's effectiveness throughout his career was based on his persona as an honest compromiser. The Compromise of 1877 was not regarded as fair by Democrats, despite the participation of some Southerners as well as some Republicans who despaired about the fate of African Americans. Hayes was repeatedly referred to as "His Fraudulency" and as Ruther-fraud B. Hayes. The highlight of his administration actually came in the very beginning of his presidency. The Stalwart wing of the party was so annoyed by Hayes's refusal to consult with them on his cabinet choices that they delayed the confirmation of his entire cabinet. The Senate even violated its own custom by refusing to confirm one of its own members, Senator John Sherman. The tactic was so blatant that public opinion turned in Hayes's favor. The Senate backed down and swiftly confirmed all the nominees in April of 1877.

Hayes won another battle with the Senate Republicans, though at considerable cost. In an effort to clean up the graft and corruption in the New York Customs Service he replaced three of its officers, including future president Chester Arthur. The Senate refused to accept his replacements. For eighteen months the president battled the Senate and finally won in 1879. Hayes attempted to use this victory to promote the creation of a civil service in which government positions would be based on performance in competitive examinations. However, as he complained to his friend George Curtis, there were "no champions of civil service reform" in Congress. There were those who "would float or lean that way," but there was "no earnest man to propose bills, to make the argument, and to champion the cause as a hobby."

In partisan politics, Hayes engaged in a futile effort to win over white Southerners to the Republican Party. Touring the South in the summer and fall of 1877, Hayes convinced himself that the civil rights of African Americans would be better protected if white Southerners joined the party. Politics in the South would be based less on race and, of course, the Republican Party would benefit. Hayes gave numerous patronage posts to Democrats in an attempt to wean them away from their party and promised Southern governors that he would never again resort to "bayonet rule." Despite Hayes's efforts, Southern Democrats did not join the Republican Party and the position of African Americans deteriorated even further.

JAMES A. GARFIELD (1881) AND CHESTER A. ARTHUR (1881–1885)

Hayes kept his promise to serve only a single term. Without an heir, the convention split into warring factions. The Stalwarts supported Grant and the reformers supported James G. Blaine. James A. Garfield allied himself with neither faction and instead supported his fellow Ohioan John Sherman, secretary of treasury in the Hayes administration. Grant led in the initial balloting, but the reformers effectively denied voting by the unit rule, a procedure in which each state delegation indicated their preference as a bloc. Grant was unable to pick up enough votes, and after 33 ballots some delegates began to shift to Garfield. Three ballots later, Garfield won the nomination. The Stalwart wing, however, exacted a price. They demanded and won the second place for Chester Arthur, the Custom House head removed by Hayes. The Democrats nominated Winfield Hancock, a Civil War hero whose regiment had fought bravely at Gettysburg. The decision to nominate a Civil War veteran was nearly successful. Garfield won by only .02 percent of the vote.

Garfield was an experienced politician who had served 17 years in Congress. Though he was tainted by the Credit Mobilier scandal during the Grant administration, Garfield moved swiftly. He insisted on his own cabinet choices despite pressure from the Stalwarts in the Senate. When he nominated William H. Robertson, a Republican reformer, to the coveted New York Port Authority position, Conkling and his Senate supporters announced they would approve all his choices but this one. Garfield responded in protest by announcing that he would withdraw *all* his nominations. As public support for the president rose, Conkling tried one more maneuver. He and fellow Senator Thomas C. Platt resigned in the hope that the New York state legislature would re-elect them. The legislature, however, chose two other men to fill their positions. Garfield wrote triumphantly to a friend that the battle had decided in his favor whether the president was the "registering clerk of the Senate or the Executive of the United States."

At the peak of his popularity, Garfield was assassinated by a Stalwart supporter in July of 1881. He struggled for his life for over three months. On September 19, Chester A. Arthur, the former Custom House chief and ally of the Stalwarts, became president. As president, however, Arthur moved in unexpected directions. Like Lyndon Johnson's support of civil rights after Kennedy's assassination, and like Richard Nixon's decision to open diplomatic relations with China, Arthur changed policies he supported through his entire career. The son of Irish immigrants, Arthur became a wealthy man at the public's expense. Even when he became president, he ordered a complete redecoration of the White House and hired Louis Tiffany, the New York designer, to convert his new home to the popular art nouveau style. In his inaugural address Arthur praised the slain president for his "unyielding fortitude." In his first message to Congress he also announced his support of civil service reform. Building on popular indignation over the assassination of Garfield, Arthur signed the Pendleton Act in 1883. The Act created a bipartisan Civil Service Commission, prevented federal employees from contributing percentages of their salaries to political parties, and set up competitive examinations for positions. The reform covered only about a tenth of the 130,000 federal employees, but it broke the log jam over the issue and provided the baseline for later reforms.

GROVER CLEVELAND (1885–1889)

Democrats were encouraged by the presidential elections of 1876 and 1880. In their minds, they actually won the former election and Hancock nearly defeated Garfield. The two parties were clearly now at parity, and Democrats craved the presidential prize that had been denied them for 28 years. The Republican Party was rent with factions and Arthur, who was in poor health, was hated by the Stalwart wing of the party. In fact, yet a new group of reformers called mugwumps (a derivative of an Indian term, "chief," designed to chide the group for its sense of self-importance) was ready to support a reform Democrat. Cleveland, elected mayor of Buffalo in 1881 and a year later elected governor of New York, had several attributes that suited the party. He had a reputation as a reformer, he was not involved with the bitter Reconstruction controversies, and he could attract Republican votes. Most of all, like Jimmy Carter in 1976, he was a new man on the national political scene.

The Republicans, however, nominated a strong insider as their candidate. James G. Blaine, who nearly won the nomination in 1876 and 1880, resigned from Arthur's administration as secretary of state and opposed his renomination. Blaine's national reputation was based in large part on his opposition to an 1876 Confederate amnesty bill. When a fellow Republican described his opposition as "like a plumed knight" who marched down the halls of the American Congress and "threw his shining lance full and fair against the brazen forehead of every traitor to his country," his reputation as an orator was enhanced. The "plumed knight," however, lost favor with reformers by 1884 and was never trusted by the Stalwarts.

Blaine ran a "bloody shirt" campaign that appeared to be leading him to victory, but both parties realized that the state of New York was the key to the election. Cleveland was vulnerable since he opposed the Tamany machine as governor. Blaine, however, made two serious mistakes. When a Protestant minister at a rally spoke of the Democrats as the party of "rum, Romanism and rebellion," Blaine sat silent. Irish voters turned out heavily for Cleveland. Also, during the campaign in New York, Blaine spoke in extremely positive terms about the contributions of new corporations at an extravagant fundraiser that included Jay Gould, Andrew Carnegie, and other powerful industrialists as honored guests. Democratic newspapers portrayed the dinner as a sellout to big business. Cleveland carried New York by less than 1,200 votes. A switch of 600 voters would have elected Blaine president.

Contemporary scholars are often puzzled by Cleveland's domination of national politics over the next twelve years. Although narrowly defeated by Benjamin Harrison in 1888, Cleveland won reelection by a large margin four years later. He is the only president to serve two non-consecutive terms and the only Democratic president in an era of Republican dominance. How was Cleveland able to make such an extraordinary comeback after his defeat in 1888? What explains the popularity of a president whose achievements were relatively limited?

Cleveland was not a good speaker, nor was he particularly imaginative as a politician. His legislative record was a mixed one. He represented no grand cause. Although known as a reformer, Cleveland's agenda was largely limited to administrative improvements. He presided during a serious economic depression. Cleveland was conservative politically and economically, so much so that by his second term the Democratic Party had moved in a dramatically different direction. Cleveland, however, did convey a very strong sense of character. He portrayed himself as an independent person who made judgments without apology, to the best of his ability. Two biographers provide a sample of conflicting conclusions about Cleveland's character. To Allan Nevins, whose 1932 biography is still widely cited, Cleveland showed a "courage that never yields an inch in the cause of truth, and that never surrenders an iota of principle to expediency." To Rexford Tugwell, however, Cleveland was a "narrow conservative." "Nothing," concluded Tugwell, could "cause him to lift his eyes to a larger future for the nation."

Cleveland carefully cultivated his persona as a man of character. He openly acknowledged the paternity of a child when rumors emerged during the 1884 campaign; he delivered his inaugural address without notes; he frequently indicated that he hated politics and regarded the office as a burden; and he often quoted Washington, angrily criticizing those who challenged the first president's reputation for honesty. This sense of independence, a variation on the theme of the founding presidency, gave Cleveland a great deal of leeway when he took positions, such as opposition to the free coinage of silver and his opposition to the Pullman strike, different from those of his party and of Congress. On the other hand, Cleveland's cultivation of character also isolated him from developments in the economy and made him vulnerable to criticism that he was failing to respond to the plight of farmers and workers.

In his first term, Cleveland's approach to government worked reasonably well. He was able to force Congress to repeal the Tenure of Office Act. He vetoed scores of private pension bills popular with voters, often with short ironic comments such as "It is stated that about five years ago, the claimant was gathering dandelions" when his leg broke but "it is not evident that the fracture had anything to do with military service." His opposition to coining silver, which farmers regarded as crucial to alleviating tight credit, was supported more by Republicans than by Democrats. He worked very hard to appoint qualified individuals to government employment, spending many evenings with his postmaster general reviewing applications over draughts of beer. Near the end of his term, Cleveland made an unprecedented decision to devote his annual message to Congress to a single topic—reducing tariffs—and made the issue the centerpiece of his reelection campaign.

BENJAMIN HARRISON (1889–1893)

Benjamin Harrison, the grandson of William Henry Harrison and a first-term senator from Indiana, won the Republican nomination as a dark-horse candidate in 1888. In some ways, Harrison's demeanor was a replica of Cleveland's. Harrison had prematurely grey hair and beard, steel blue eyes, and a reserved demeanor that unsettled his opponents. However, unlike Cleveland, Harrison was prone to withdraw from controversy. His campaign was largely managed by party regulars who focused on the tariff question raised by Cleveland. This time the Republicans won New York, and Harrison carried the North (except for New Jersey and Connecticut) and the West. Cleveland, however, won the popular vote by 100,000 votes.

Harrison's administration thus rested on a tenuous mandate. Grover Cleveland remained a favored figure with the public. Harrison's claim that "Providence gave us victory" was derided by party leaders who saw more practical reasons for his election. One Republican exclaimed, "Think of the man! He ought to know that Providence hadn't a damn thing to do with it!" With Republicans in control of both Houses of Congress, Harrison willingly let his party take the lead in legislative initiatives. Despite the close election, Congress swiftly and systematically reversed Cleveland's policies. A massive tariff bill was passed in 1890. In the same year, Congress passed the Dependent Pension Act that doubled the number of veterans' benefits to nearly $1 million at a cost of $60 million, nearly wiping out the federal surplus, and the Sherman Silver Purchase Act to placate Western miners. The McKinley Tariff Bill was so controversial the Democrats took control of the House in 1890 by a large margin. Harrison, who relied heavily on Republican congressional leadership, was unable to provide much direction in the last two years of his administration. He turned his attention to foreign policy, particularly in terms of rebuilding the navy and creating commercial trade agreements in Latin America. Harrison presented Congress with legislation to annex Hawaii late in his term (which Cleveland withdrew when he resumed office).

GROVER CLEVELAND (1893–1897)

Once he was out of office, Cleveland carefully followed national politics and, encouraged by Democratic congressional victories in 1890, declared his availability. While popular with Democrats at large, Cleveland nevertheless confronted two problems: He was opposed by David B. Hill, governor and head of the powerful party machine in New York; and he opposed the coinage of silver so important to Westerners. Hill overreached himself by calling New York Democrats to an early "snap" state convention, and Cleveland finessed the silver issue by focusing on the inadequacies of the Sherman Act. He won renomination on the first ballot. Republicans renominated Harrison despite attempts by some delegates to turn to another candidate. Cleveland easily won, although James B. Weaver's eight percent of the popular vote and 32 electoral votes as a third-party Populist candidate showed that the Democrats were in danger of splitting apart over the silver issue and farmer protest about high prices and tight credit.

Political and economic circumstances had changed significantly since Cleveland left office, although the returning president did not recognize it. Two months after Cleveland took office, stock prices fell unexpectedly and dramatically. The events of May 5, known as Industrial Black Friday, led to 15,000 bankruptcies and 600 bank failures. Unemployment rose to an estimated 20 percent. All groups suffered, but farmers bore the brunt of the panic. Prices for crops were already low, and now they plummeted. The depression lasted Cleveland's entire term.

Cleveland did actively seek to deal with the economic crisis. He believed the major cause of the depression was the coinage of silver, which frightened investors at home and abroad. Cleveland called Congress into special session in June and requested repeal of the Sherman Silver Purchase Act. Congress reluctantly agreed, but economic conditions did not change. Cleveland next asked Congress to reduce tariffs. After months of debate, Congress passed the Wilson-Gorman Bill, which only reduced tariffs slightly from 49 percent to 42 percent. Cleveland, in disgust, decided neither to sign the bill nor veto it, letting it become law without his support. However, Cleveland did have a point about the relationship between silver and the depression. Unlike in the 1930s, every nation at that time relied on the gold standard. Major coinage of silver made the United States an economic outlyer. Farmers, however, were convinced that the gold standard was the source of their plight, and Cleveland made no attempt to acknowledge their fears. The tariff bill satisfied no one.

In the spring of 1893, Cleveland made another decision that had wide ramifications. George Pullman, the owner of the Pullman Car Company, was well known for his innovative wage and labor policies, including the model town of Pullman that he built to provide housing for his employees. When the depression struck, Pullman reduced wages by 25 percent without lowering rent on his houses. When workers asked for an interview to explain their situation, he fired the delegation. A strike immediately followed, and the American Railway Union (ARU) led by Eugene Debs joined the work stoppage. The strike was very controversial, because Pullman was regarded as a model employer and workers were portrayed in newspapers as ingrates. Jane Addams, the Chicago reformer, however, argued that Pullman was more like King Lear, a man obsessed with the obedience of his workers, whom he treated like subjects in a monarchy. Cleveland's attorney general and former lawyer for several rail corporations, Richard Olney, obtained an injunction by a federal court to end the strike on any train carrying U.S. mail or engaging in interstate commerce. When workers ignored the order, Cleveland sent federal troops to Chicago to break the strike.

Although Hayes had used military force in 1877 to stop a strike, Cleveland's actions were unprecedented because they did not come at the request of state authorities. The governor of Illinois, John Altgeld, in fact, insisted he did not want federal troops in his state. Cleveland, however, was dismissive of Altgeld and answered his long legal memos with single-sentence replies. Later, Cleveland expressed no regrets about his action. "I woke up one morning and as I got out of bed I asked myself: 'Did the people elect Eugene Debs or Grover Cleveland President?' That settled it." Cleveland's decision was generally popular in the country at large, but it gained the enmity of significant elements in the Democratic Party. Farmers hated Cleveland for his monetary policies, and now workers and union leaders responded similarly.

The midterm elections in 1894 were a disaster for the Democrats, who lost 113 seats in the House and 5 in the Senate. Moreover, the surviving Democrats were almost exclusively from the South, a center of Populist protest, and thus critical of the president's economic policies. Cleveland became reclusive. The Democratic Party nominated William Jennings Bryan in 1896 and formally repudiated all of Cleveland's policies in their platform. In fact, speakers at the convention openly criticized the president. Senator Ben "Pitchfork" Tillman of South Carolina (so named because he campaigned on the pledge to "stick a pitchfork into the ribs of the president") told an appreciative audience that Cleveland was a traitor to his party.

SUMMARY AND COMMENT

The period of the eclipsed presidency (1865–1896) provides some answers to two important questions about the chief executive in the American political system. First, it suggests the features of the political system in general that must be in place for the presidency to "shrink" from the more central institution it had briefly become under Abraham Lincoln. Lincoln's transformation of the office occurred during a grave national emergency. The Civil War provided the environment for Lincoln to expand the powers of the office. Congress and the courts largely receded in the face of the crisis. The Democratic Party too briefly lost its capacity to effectively oppose the president.

When the emergency subsided after the defeat of Southern secession, each of these institutions regained their capacity to challenge the chief executive. Congress insisted it had the right and the capacity to deal with post–Civil War problems. The courts began to challenge the exercise of presidential power, and the Democratic Party resuscitated itself by 1876. Without a hostile international environment, there were few opportunities for presidents to exercise their powers. Moreover, both political parties were extremely well organized at the state and local levels and enjoyed a degree of independence from the president. Each party depended on patronage to sustain itself, so that while Republicans and Democrats were anxious to place a member of their own in the White House, they were not willing to permit any president to share in the distribution of jobs any more than minimally necessary. Presidents from Hayes to Cleveland struggled to control patronage, with some success but at considerable political cost.

Second, the eclipsed presidency allows us to raise the question of whether a chief executive with very limited powers is desirable. One can certainly make the case that serious problems in the political system, especially civil rights for African Americans and economic justice, were not addressed very effectively during this period. Presidents spent most of their political capital attempting to retrieve basic elements of their authority, such as the right to change officials in their own branch of government. On the other hand, the political system did function. There was no resurgence of Southern separatism, Western expansion proceeded at a rapid pace and, with the exception of the Panic of 1893, there was dramatic economic growth. Despite severe limits on their powers, presidents imaginatively sought to deal with problems they faced. Grant vigorously attacked the Klan and prevented a genocidal war with the Plains Indians, Garfield outfoxed the powerful Senator Conkling, Arthur changed his ways and successfully promoted civil-service reform, and Cleveland found a way to rally the public to his causes through the force of his personality.

Bibliographical Essay

Mark Wahlgren Summers emphasizes the limited hand of presidents in terms of the corruption issue in *The Era of Good Stealings* (New York: Oxford University Press, 1993), and John M. Dobson provides a helpful analysis of the development and structure of political parties after the Civil War as well as attacks by reformers in *Politics and the Gilded Age* (New York: Praeger, 1973). H. Wayne Morgan offers a review of presidential electoral strategies in *From Hayes to McKinley* (1969). For general studies that explore the impact of industrialization on economic and political institutions in international context, see Charles Moraze's *The Triumph of the Middle Classes* (Garden City, NY: Doubleday, 1961) and David S. Landes, *The Unbound Prometheus* (Cambridge: Cambridge University Press, 1969). Nell Irvin Painter's *Standing at Armageddon: The United States, 1877–1919* (New York: W.W. Norton, 1987), is a very readable synthesis of the efforts of social historians to assess the period, with an emphasis on political and social theory.

The most recent comprehensive analysis of Reconstruction as a policy problem is Eric Foner's *Reconstruction: America's Unfinished Revolution, 1863–1877* (New York: Harper & Row, 1988). Also see earlier works: John Hope Franklin, *Reconstruction: After the Civil War* (Chicago: University of Chicago Press, 1961), and Kenneth M. Stamp, *The Era of Reconstruction, 1865–1877* (New York: Vintage, 1965). David Donald's *The Politics of Reconstruction 1863–1867* (Baton Rouge: Louisiana State University Press, 1965) is an excellent analysis of the legislative dynamics of the reconstruction acts as both reactions and preemptive strategies in terms of the president's strategy. Brooks D. Simpson's *Reconstruction Presidents* (Lawrence: University Press of Kansas, 1998) analyses the policies and goals of Lincoln, Johnson, Grant, and Hayes. Simpson gives high marks to both Grant and Hayes for good intentions and places considerable blame for failures on the racism of Northern voters.

Hans L. Trefouse offers a balanced view of Andrew Johnson in *Andrew Johnson: A Biography* (New York: Harper & Row, 1989) which can be compared to James E. Sefton's *Andrew Johnson and the Uses of Constitutional Power* (Boston: Little, Brown, 1980). There are several studies of Johnson's impeachment, such as Michael Les Benedict, *The Impeachment and Trial of Andrew Johnson* (New York: W. W. Norton, 1973); and Hans L. Trefousse, *The Impeachment of a President* (Knoxville: University of Tennessee Press, 1975). William H. Rehnquist's *Grand Inquests* (New York: William Morrow, 1992) includes the impeachment of Andrew Johnson as well as Samuel Chase.

Jean Edward Smith, *Grant* (New York: Simon and Schuster, 2001) offers a vigorous defense of the eighteenth president that includes a challenge concerning the charges of extensive corruption in his administration. Also see Brooks D. Simpson's *Let Us Have Peace* (Chapel Hill: University of North Carolina Press, 1991) that includes an analysis of Grant's first presidential campaign. Although Grant's memoirs are available in many editions, it is interesting to note that his narrative ends before his presidency.

Ari Hoogenboom's *The Presidency of Rutherford B. Hayes* (Lawrence: University of Kansas Press, 1988) offers a positive review of his administration. Keith Ian Polakoff's *The Politics of Inertia: The Election of 1876 and the End of Reconstruction* (Baton: Rouge: Louisiana Sate University Press, 1973) treats charges of the "Compromise of 1877" with some skepticism. Allan Peskin's *Garfield* (Kent, OH: Kent State University Press, 1978) and Thomas C. Reeves's *Gentleman Boss: The*

Life of Chester Alan Arthur (New York: Knopf, 1975) present positive assessments within the context of the eclipsed presidency. Both works offer intricate accounts of the conflicts between Conkling and Garfield and Arthur. Reeves struggles, however, to find a satisfactory explanation for Arthur's transformation to reformer. For contrasting views on Cleveland, see Allan Nevins, *Grover Cleveland: A Study in Courage* (New York: Dodd, Mead, 1932) and Rexford Tugwell, *Grover Cleveland* (New York: Macmillan, 1968). Alyn Brodsky's recent biography, *Grover Cleveland* (New York: St. Martin's, 2000) elaborates upon Nevins's approach and is a useful treatment for those interested in pursuing the impact of character on presidential decision making.

CHAPTER 5

THE MODERN PRESIDENCY

Modern Presidents

President/ Political Party	Term of Office	Vice President	Percent Electoral Vote	Percent Popular Vote
William McKinley (R)	1897–1901	Garret A. Hobart	61	51
William McKinley (R)	1901–1901	Theodore Roosevelt	65	52
Theodore Roosevelt (R)	1901–1905	—	—	—
Theodore Roosevelt (R)	1905–1909	Charles W. Fairbanks	71	56
William H. Taft (R)	1909–1913	James S. Sherman	67	52
Woodrow Wilson (D)	1913–1917	Thomas R. Marshall	82	42
Woodrow Wilson (D)	1917–1921	Thomas R. Marshall	52	49
Warren G. Harding (R)	1921–1923	Calvin Coolidge	76	60
Calvin Coolidge (R)	1923–1925	—	—	—
Calvin Coolidge (R)	1925–1929	Charles G. Dawes	72	54
Herbert Hoover (R)	1929–1933	Charles Curtis	84	58
Franklin D. Roosevelt (D)	1933–1937	John N. Garner	89	57
Franklin D. Roosevelt (D)	1937–1941	John N. Garner	98	61
Franklin D. Roosevelt (D)	1941–1945	Henry A. Wallace	85	55
Franklin D. Roosevelt (D)	1945–1945	Harry S. Truman	81	53

The meaning of the term "modern" is a complex one. The concept is often contested because writers are frequently attempting to resist some of its features. Modern practices and institutions involve the readiness to change and experiment, the systematization of rules and procedures, and the application of scientific analysis to problems. Whether modernization is, on the whole, helpful and constitutes "progress" can be a difficult question. Obviously, modernization brings advantages and disadvantages. Modern technology, for example, permits us to travel rapidly and converse immediately across long distances, but it does create problems as well. Automobiles cause pollution, and computers reduce direct human contact. As we shall see, modernization of the presidency, which begins in 1896, is a mixed blessing to the public and to presidents themselves.

What made the presidency modern? Political and economic development varies in its pace and intensity across countries, as well as across institutions within countries. Great Britain was the first nation to experience the Industrial Revolution; the United States followed shortly thereafter. On the other hand, Great Britain still retains a monarchy and expanded its enfranchise to all males much later than the United States did. Until 1918, 40 percent of the males in Great Britain were ineligible to vote.

In the United States, Congress modernized as a political institution well before the presidency. Under Henry Clay's leadership, the House of Representatives expanded its committee structure and organized itself under party discipline. In the nineteenth century, the Senate added a complex system of patronage. Under Thomas Reed's leadership, the House routinized and streamlined its rules. Washington created three cabinet positions in 1789 (war, state, and treasury); only two more were added in the next 100 years. As we noted in the last chapter, the Senate very jealously guarded its role in appointing and firing cabinet members. While Lincoln created a makeshift administrative system to prosecute the Civil War, these structures were soon abandoned. The administrative agencies created by Congress at Wilson's request during World War I were dismantled by Congress over the president's objections. Not until the Harding presidency did the president receive an agency (Bureau of the Budget) to oversee the budget, and at the same time Congress established the General Accounting Office to audit executive expenditures. In 1937 a commission appointed by Franklin Roosevelt decided the "president needs help" and recommended hiring six personal advisors and creating the Executive Office of the President. Congress delayed acting upon the request for two years. Between 1896 and 1945, the presidency fitfully developed as a modern institution. By 1945 the president had a bureaucracy to give him advice and administer programs, although a new problem arose: Did the president control his own bureaucracy or did it control him?

The impetus for the development of the presidency as an institution came from the rapid the emergence of the United States as both a world economic power and a political power. By 1896 the United States was producing one-third of the world's economic goods. As Noel Jacob Kent observes, "No market seemed safe from Yankee invasion. . . . Massive, well financed U.S. corporations, operating out of continental bastions, seemed intent on seizing every overseas market in sight." Singer sewing machines captured 75 percent of the world market, and firms like General

Electric that had in-house scientists were revolutionizing production. Of course, during the Great Depression the United States suffered accordingly from the global economic collapse, but in 1945 it was indisputably the strongest economy in the world.

As the economy modernized, it placed terrible strains on the political system. The most disturbing aspect of these economic changes was the sheer size of new economic structures. The name *trust*, which had once connoted belief, faith, and reliability, now became the description of a new kind of industrial organization that challenged the very principle of democratic governance. Trusts were collections of businesses bound legally to one another that in their perfect form captured the entire market for a product through vertical controls on procuring, manufacturing, and retailing a product.

John D. Rockefeller's Standard Oil Company became for many Americans the archetypal model of the trust. When Rockefeller entered the oil business in the late 1860s, he found a highly volatile industry subject to booms and busts. The oil that sold for $20 a barrel in 1860 brought only 10 cents on the 1861 market. Starting with five small refineries, Rockefeller worked out arrangements with railroad companies to lower rates for long hauls. Companies with local markets now struggled with higher costs. To apply even more pressure, Rockefeller developed agreements, called *drawbacks*, with rail officials. Under these agreements, the railroad companies that moved oil for other businesses paid a portion of those rates to Standard Oil. Moving across the country like a conquering general, Rockefeller gobbled up his competitors state by state. Henry Demerest Lloyd wrote in the *Atlantic Monthly* in 1881, after Rockefeller had broken the resistance of independent drillers, that Standard Oil had "done everything with the Pennsylvania legislature but refine it."

Rockefeller's oil empire was not the only instance of successful trust building. Trusts were created in tobacco, sugar, steel, chemicals, and other products. *Holding companies,* a new economic structure that emerged in the late 1880s to avoid antitrust restrictions, continued these consolidations. Between 1895 and 1904 an average of 300 firms disappeared every year. As a result, a single business accounted for 60 percent of the production of a product in 50 different industries. Moreover, the trusts, holding companies, and mergers helped create a new set of huge national economic institutions. Bankers who profited from the sale or merger of business came to supervise this new surplus capital.

As the economy became more complex and global, the president increasingly became the spokesperson who interpreted these developments for Americans. As we shall see, McKinley was the first president to undertake the task of explaining the new economy to citizens. Presidents had always been involved in economic policy, but the modern presidents took on responsibility for a much more developed system. In fact, most presidents in this period identified their administrations in general with the policies they advocated: McKinley (the Progressive Society), Theodore Roosevelt (the Square Deal), Wilson (the New Freedom), and Franklin Roosevelt (the New Deal). Modern presidents had several different specific approaches to economic policy. McKinley and Hoover offered visions of economic performance in which the government would lightly supervise corporate activity. The Progressive presidents (Theodore Roosevelt, Taft, and Wilson) and Franklin Roosevelt were more concerned, though in different ways, with the ability of corporations to govern the economy by themselves.

If Americans were alternately thrilled and dismayed by global economic changes, they also experienced the same reactions to political developments. McKinley, who offered the first vision of the modern economy, also offered the first modern vision in terms of international politics. He announced in his second inaugural (1901):

> The American people, entrenched in freedom at home, take their love for it with them wherever they go, and they reject as mistaken and unworthy the doctrine that we lose our own liberties by securing the enduring foundations of liberty to others. Our institutions will not deteriorate by extension, and our sense of justice will not abate under tropic suns in distant seas.

McKinley justified this expansion of the American mission as the "path of progress," for "after 125 years . . . we will not surrender our equality with other powers . . . by no act of ours will we assign ourselves a subordinate rank in the family of nations." Americans have always seen their government as an exceptional one that was worthy of imitation. McKinley expanded upon this belief by dismissing the concern, common among the founding presidents in particular, that an expansive mission abroad would likely reduce liberties at home. He believed that modern America had progressed to an equality of power with other nations and could use its moral authority to create a better world. McKinley's perspective was reformulated by Woodrow Wilson as one in which America would make the world "safe for democracy," and by Franklin Roosevelt, who declared that the world should share in the four freedoms (discussed later in this chapter).

America accepted its role as a great world power very reluctantly, however. There was great disenchantment with Wilson's policy after World War I, and Franklin Roosevelt faced significant opposition for his support of opponents of fascist aggression in Europe and Asia until the attack on Pearl Harbor. A central task of modern presidents was convincing Americans that they had international obligations, and managing conflicts when they had been assumed. In broader terms, a world power, whether or not at war, requires a considerable degree of executive initiative. Economic and military treaties must be negotiated, conflicts between nations settled, and international investment promoted and protected.

The modern president assumed the roles of the nation's chief bureaucrat, economic manager, and diplomat. In addition, as a result of attempts to reform the modern economy, the process of presidential selection changed. The convention system begun by the Jacksonians had been the mode of presidential selection for almost a century. Progressive reformers argued that conventions were not always representative of voter preference and recommended that delegates be chosen by the party members directly, in elections called primaries. By 1916 over 50 percent of delegates in each party were chosen by voters. After World War I, however, primaries lost momentum. The reform movement had subsided, and party professionals had never liked the system. Nevertheless, primaries survived in many states and constituted over one-third of delegate selection (until the 1970s when primaries again became popular). No president during this period defeated an incumbent or even received the nomination primarily from victories in these elections. All presidents and presidential aspirants, however, now had to take the public at large into consideration when seeking the nomination. In 1912, for example, Theodore Roosevelt challenged Taft and won 10 of the 12 states holding primaries. He did not receive the nomination, although he badly divided the party and ran on a separate ticket.

Also, in 1936 the Democrats abandoned the requirement that two-thirds of the delegates agree on a nominee, reducing the power of Southern delegates to veto a candidate. When Roosevelt flew to Chicago in 1932 to deliver his acceptance address, he helped to personalize the convention system.

WILLIAM MCKINLEY (1897–1901)

The election of 1896 transformed both political parties. The dominant conservative, pro-business "Bourbon" wing of the Democratic Party centered in the East was discredited by the recent depression and gave way to a populist, pro-farmer wing centered in the West. William Jennings Bryan, a 36-year-old congressman from Nebraska, electrified the Democratic convention with his "Cross of Gold" address and was nominated for the presidency. Bryan began the speech with the assertion that there were those in the country who would give the definition of a businessman too limited an application:

> The man who is employed for wages is as much a businessman as his employer; the attorney in a country town is as much a businessman as the corporation counsel in a great metropolis; the merchant at the crossroads store is as much a businessman as the merchant of New York; the farmer who goes forth in the morning and toils all day—who begins in the spring and toils all summer—and who by the application of brain and muscle to the natural resources of this coun-

try creates wealth, is as much a businessman as the man who goes upon the board of trade and bets upon the price of grain. . . . We come to speak for this broader class of businessmen.

The "cross of gold" metaphor that closed his 1896 speech can be understood as a political symbol more complex than the demand for free silver. Bryan is often criticized today for emphasizing the silver issue at the expense of other portions of the populist program. However, in an important sense, the demand for an economy based on a silver standard represented something more than just a misplaced panacea for easy credit, inflated prices on the part of farmers, and greed on the part of western mining interests. To the populists, the gold standard represented the growth of finance capital as an economic structure beyond the influence or control of the average American. "Property is and will remain the stimulus for endeavor and the compensation for toil," insisted Bryan, but the Declaration of Independence had also declared that all men are created equal:

> Our ancestors, when but three millions in number, had the courage to declare the political independence of every other nation; shall we, their descendants, when we have grown to seventy millions, declare that we are less independent than our forefathers?

McKinley, too, had a plan for America. Guided by his brilliant campaign manager, Mark Hanna, he attracted an enormous amount of corporate contributions for his effort, but the candidate's message openly rejected class conflict (or conflict of any kind). America, argued McKinley, could create a "progressive society" (not to be confused with the Progressive Movement that was soon to emerge) in which both corporations and workers could live in harmony. Unlike many business leaders, McKinley and Hanna supported unionization as a legitimate avenue for stabilizing relations between capital and labor. McKinley largely ignored the image of society as the survival of the fittest and instead offered voters a vision of America as a society with a harmony of interests. Economic mobility was still possible in a corporate society through the careful supervision of the economy. "I believe," he told Pennsylvania miners, that "the business of this free government is to preserve the American market for the American producer, whether in the factory or the farm, and to preserve the American mines and the factories of the American workingmen."

Describing himself as the worker's best friend, McKinley attacked the Democrats' adoption of a silver standard by arguing that only "sound money" was in the interest of the worker: "When the miners of West Newton have dug their coal by their honest toil, they want to be paid in dollars that are equal to the best dollars of the world. . . ." The Republicans employed two symbols to counteract Bryan's cross of gold. One was the dinner pail to designate prosperity; thousands of replicas were passed out at campaign rallies. The other symbol was the American flag. McKinley remained at his home in Canton, Ohio, during the campaign, but Hanna had brigades of Civil War veterans travel throughout the country proclaiming that "1896 is as important as 1861." Distraught Democrats came to see the flag itself as a party banner and often ripped flags from the trains.

Both Bryan's and McKinley's contemporaries and today's commentators have generally underestimated both men. The "Great Commoner," as Bryan was frequently called, has been evaluated on the basis of views he took late in his life, such as his testimony at the Scopes trial in 1925, and McKinley has been overshadowed by the charm of his campaign manager, Mark Hanna. William White once cleverly described McKinley as "on the whole decent, on the whole dumb, who walked among men like a bronze statue determinedly looking for a pedestal." In reality, Bryan was not a country bumpkin, nor was McKinley a puppet of his campaign manager. Both men synthesized the views of their times and offered a vision of modern America. Bryan believed that America must somehow learn to treat small-town and rural perspectives fairly. He once said, "Burn down your cities and your cities will spring up again as if by magic; but destroy the farms and the grass will grow in the streets of every major city in the country." For McKinley, a prosperous America was the key to economic justice.

McKinley won the argument in 1896 and four years later as well. He received seven million votes to Bryan's 6.5 million and won the electoral college 271–176. Immediately, McKinley set out to distinguish his presidency from that of the reclusive Cleveland. He appeared at a series of dedications (including Grant's Tomb), reinstituted public receptions, and even encouraged the press to cover his vacations. Most significantly, he set up a large table in the White House at which the press could congregate. Hence, McKinley initiated what later became known as the White House press room. Using a sympathetic press as an anchor for his policy initiatives, McKinley proposed increased tariff rates that were passed as the Dingley Tariff in 1898, and he won congressional support for placing the United States on the gold standard.

In foreign policy, however, McKinley's reliance on the press became a doubled-edged sword. In 1895, a revolution broke out against Spanish rule in Cuba. Spanish authorities responded with great force. There were 300,000 troops in the country, and casualties were very high on both sides. McKinley faced a worrisome situation. Spain clearly was an empire on the verge of collapse. Even liberal Spanish governments were unable to reach the conclusion that independence was the best way to stop the bloodshed and loss of revenue. Americans in general were very sympathetic to the rebels for humanitarian reasons and the press, led by newspaper publishers Randolph Hearst and Joseph Pulitzer, ran daily stories about Spanish atrocities. Moreover, the rebellion depressed American investment in the island's economy.

McKinley carefully reversed Cleveland's pro-Spanish tilt and sought to convince the government in Madrid to institute reforms. On February 15, 1898, however, this diplomatic maneuvering came to a halt when the U.S. *Maine* blew up and sank in the Havana harbor. The press portrayed the sinking of the *Maine* as an undeclared act of war (although the Spanish denied responsibility) and demanded an immediate American response. McKinley's reactions, however, were cautious, since the Spanish denied responsibility for the incident. He appointed a board of inquiry and requested authorization from Congress to intervene in Cuba if necessary. When diplomatic efforts failed and the board declared that the Spanish were probably responsible for the attack, McKinley asked for a declaration of war on April 11.

The Spanish-American War lasted only three months. Admiral Dewey won a spectacular naval battle at Manila Bay in the Philippines on May 1, and American forces occupied Manila six weeks later. The Spanish army in Cuba surrendered in late July. Despite the short duration of the conflict, the war represented a major turning point in the presidency. McKinley was quite quick to employ modern technology to direct what Secretary of State John Hay called "a splendid little war." In a war room in the executive mansion, the president placed fifteen telephones that connected him to each of the cabinet officers. He also used the telegraph and an early version of a dictaphone to facilitate his administration and supervision of events. As Richard T. Loomis has noted, McKinley used "remote voice communication for the first time to project presidential presence into the battle zone on a near real-time basis."

While many Democrats in particular expressed concerns that America was taking on the role of an empire and perhaps beginning to head down a path fatal to republics in the past, McKinley insisted the founding fathers would have approved of America's new role as an international power. He announced:

> . . . hereafter will the nation demonstrate its fitness to administer any new estate which devolves upon it. . . . The path to progress is seldom smooth. New things are often hard to do. Our fathers found them so. We find them so. They are inconvenient. They cost us something. But are we not made better for the effort and sacrifice, and are not those we serve lifted up and blessed?

The president confessed that the decision to govern the Philippines—and Guam and Puerto Rico—was reached only after much prayer and only to save the Filipinos from "savage indolence and habits."

McKinley was easily reelected to a second term. The president added polling of swing groups (such as Catholics and organized labor) to his campaign tactics and sent millions of copies of campaign material to newspapers. McKinley himself sent personal letters to campaign workers. Bryan retained about 45 percent of the vote but lost six states he had won four years earlier. The Republicans controlled both Houses of Congress. A friendly press began to run stories about the rebirth of the presidency as the central institution of the federal government. McKinley planned a visit abroad, to become the first president to leave the country while in office. He undertook the first steps to reverse his own tariff policies by replacing them with "reciprocity" agreements with selected nations. In the spring of 1901, the president started a six-week tour of the South and West. The tour was a huge success and McKinley was at the height of his popularity. On September 6, he was shot and killed at a public reception in Buffalo, New York, thus ending a presidency that had surprised everyone. This former governor of Ohio, thought by many to be a creature of the public relations machine of Mark Hanna, was the first modern president.

THEODORE ROOSEVELT (1901–1909)

McKinley's innovations have been eclipsed by his successor. Theodore Roosevelt is frequently rated among the top ten presidents while McKinley ranks between 17 and 22. Part of the reason for this variation in ranking is that Roosevelt led one of the major reform movements in American history and benefited from some changes begun by McKinley. It is difficult, however, not to include the force of Roosevelt's personality on his own contemporaries and on later generations as a central factor. Being in his presence could be intimidating, indeed frightening. Here was a man who was little over 5' 8" tall but who seemed "palpably massive," with an enormous head, a frame of pure muscle, and shining teeth and glasses that cartoonists would employ alone to indicate his persona. When he spoke, one contemporary could think of nothing but "a man biting ten penny nails," yet his admirers often referred to Roosevelt's boyishness. "You must remember," said his friend Sir Cecil Spring-Rice, "that the President is about six." The public responded by sending him hundreds upon hundreds of "teddy bears." There were others, however, who were concerned about Roosevelt's boyish energy. To Mark Twain, the president was "clearly insane"; to Woodrow Wilson, he was "the most dangerous man of the age." Speaker of the House Joe Cannon, a man not adverse to the use of power, complained: "Roosevelt's all right but he's got no more use for the Constitution than a tom cat has for a marriage license."

To many, Roosevelt seemed a man nearly out of control, but he was an astute observer of politicians and political trends who could move like a lion as well as a fox. Roosevelt wrote biographies of several political figures, including Oliver Cromwell, the leader of the English Revolution. Roosevelt concluded that he was "not only one of the greatest generals of all time" but also "a great statesman who on the whole did marvelous work." He failed because he "lacked the power of self-repression possessed by Washington and Lincoln." "The more I have studied Cromwell," concluded Roosevelt, "the more I admire him, and yet the more I have felt that his making of himself a dictator was unnecessary and destroyed the possibility of making the effect of that particular revolution permanent."

Roosevelt was selected as vice president on the McKinley ticket because New York machine bosses hoped to remove him from state politics. Mark Hanna objected. He could not accept the fact that "that damn cowboy" would be a heartbeat from the presidency. But Hanna relented, and Roosevelt surprised party leaders by loyally following their instructions during the campaign. When McKinley was assassinated, Roosevelt immediately appreciated the significance of the president as a symbol of American democracy. Roosevelt's estimates of McKinley were always polite, but it had also always been clear that he regarded the president as a mediocre person. Nevertheless, in his first annual message to Congress as president, Roosevelt compared the fallen president to Lincoln and praised McKinley for "the grand heroism with which he met his death." The assassination of McKinley represented an attack not only on "this President, but all Presidents," even "the very symbol of government." McKinley had so embodied the will of the people that the effect of his assassination was as if an entire New England town meeting had been stuck down.

Roosevelt could also behave like Machiavelli's fox in advancing what he regarded as the natural expansion of the office. In 1905 he became convinced that legislation was needed to regulate railroad rates, since the difference between prices charged for large shippers and small ones was enormous. In addition, he believed in legislation that would enable the government to "take control over corporations" in general if they behaved contrary to the public interest. After Roosevelt convinced the Speaker that he intended to send legislation to the House to lower tariffs (although he really had much less interest in the issue), a trade was brokered. When the House passed the Hepburn Act, which gave the Interstate Commerce Commission (ICC) greater authority to deal with the problem, Roosevelt withdrew his alleged tariff proposal. When the Senate, which was much more under the influence of state legislators, balked, Roosevelt feigned defeat and left for a vacation in the West. The vacation, however, turned out to be a speaking tour against the Senate delay on his proposed legislation. Senators felt the heat of Roosevelt's rhetoric and passed the Hepburn Act overwhelmingly in 1906.

In foreign policy, Roosevelt could be equally crafty. He watched developments in the Far East closely, and he privately expressed concern that Russia was gaining too much influence in the region. When war broke out between Russia and Japan, he quickly sided with the latter and even considered sending token military support. The swiftness of the Japanese victory, however, made him reconsider, since he did not want any single power to dominate the area. Roosevelt offered to mediate and proposed the terms for a settlement of the conflict at a peace conference in Portsmouth, New Hampshire. The Japanese had their suspicions about the president's motive but signed the treaty. As an unanticipated bonus, Roosevelt won the Nobel Peace Prize for his efforts, and his own authority as president was enhanced. Influence in China remained divided, and a serious international conflict was settled among major powers.

Theodore Roosevelt could also act like a lion. In fact, forceful and direct action was probably his natural inclination. He readily grasped the notion that presidential power under modern conditions rested on the force of rhetoric. Roosevelt contended that the president was "a steward of the people bound actively and affirmatively to do all he could do for the people, and not content himself with the negative merit of keeping his talents undamaged in a napkin." Since his relationship with his own party was often strained and there was no great international emergency to galvanize the public, Roosevelt offered the view that the office functioned most effectively as a "bully pulpit."

When Roosevelt took office in 1901 after McKinley's assassination, the reform movement known as Progressivism was well under way at the state level. Many of the same figures who were appalled by Populist protests a generation earlier now concluded that modern capitalism did require reformation. Middle-class reformers were determined to restrain the trusts, expand democratic procedures (including direct election of senators), and provide protection to consumers and workers. Roosevelt was generally conservative, but as a member of an old, privileged family he was hostile to "new wealth." He seized the Progressive agenda and carried it into the national arena. In February, he brought an antitrust lawsuit against the Northern Securities Company, a railway conglomerate. Despite falling stock prices and criticism in financial circles, he prevailed. The Supreme Court validated his action a year later.

In May of 1902, a strike by coal miners threatened the economy. Unlike previous presidents, Roosevelt was not particularly sympathetic to the mine owners. He criticized both the "speculator" and the "demagogue" as social types and noted that the spirit of class had been the downfall of republics in the past. He expressed his determination that America would become neither a "government by a plutocracy" nor a "government by a mob." Roosevelt regarded both labor and capital as lacking in discipline and vision. Capitalists could show a "hard indifference to suffering," a "greedy disregard of every moral restraint which interferes with the accumulation of wealth, and cold-blooded exploitation of the weak." Laborers were guilty of "laziness, of sullen envy of the more fortunate, and of willingness to perform deeds of murderous violence." When the mine owners refused to accept his proposal for a settlement, he threatened to use federal troops to take over the mines. The horrified owners gave way, and a compromise settlement was reached that was generally favorable to the unions.

Roosevelt contended that he did not "usurp power" as president, but "I did greatly broaden the use of executive power." In no case is this approach more evident than in the Panama Canal project. Several previous administrations offered proposals to Congress for a canal through Central America, and each faced insurmountable obstacles: Would all international shipping have guaranteed passage? Where would the canal be built? What would be the cost? In 1901 Roosevelt quickly settled the first problem. He announced the right of all ships to pass through a canal, provided the United States owned it. The British immediately agreed, and French investors in an earlier project were persuaded. The Senate approved the treaty and authorized Roosevelt to negotiate for rights to a canal with Colombia. Unfortunately for Roosevelt, the Colombian government demanded more money than was initially agreed upon. The furious Roosevelt warned the Colombian officials, who he called "foolish and homicidal corruptionists," that he would have the canal one way or another. There was still the possibility that arrangements could be made with Nicaragua.

Many contemporaries charged that Roosevelt insisted on the Colombian passage in deference to American investors, but it is possible that the president's wounded pride was justification enough for him to take unilateral action. The United States immediately encouraged the Panamanians to revolt against the Colombian government. When the conflict began, Roosevelt sent a warship to the area to prevent the Colombian army from sending in reinforcements. Roosevelt's determination to build the canal was so great that he threatened to take the canal by force if the revolution was unsuccessful. In fact, he even included such a reference in his 1903 annual message to Congress (although it should be noted that the president used the same tactic of circulating possible drafts in the case of the Hepburn Act). This alternative was not necessary, since the Panamanians gained control and immediately signed a treaty with the United States for the construction of a canal under American sovereignty.

Although the cost was high in terms of lives sacrificed from disease and accidents, the canal was completed on schedule in 1914 and was even under budget at $367 million. During his administration and later, Roosevelt personally identified himself with the project and identified the project with American determination and ingenuity. He described building the canal as "the greatest task of its own kind that has ever been performed in the world at all." Amazed sightseers returned to report their experiences in newspapers. Later, Roosevelt expressed great satisfaction about his own daring. "I took Panama without consulting the cabinet," he told one audience, and to another he said: "I took the canal zone and let Congress debate, and while the debate goes on the canal does also."

The Panama Canal project was one of the most successful initiatives begun by Roosevelt, but there were several others in which he would use the "bully pulpit" to galvanize public support for a policy. Although big game hunting and environmentalism are at odds with one another today, the two pursuits were intertwined for the president. Roosevelt and Gifford Pinchot, his head of the Forest Service, developed the concept of "conservation" (a term used by British colonial administrators in India) as a set of policies designed to protect the environment. Previous presidents had set aside forests as public lands to be protected from development, but Roosevelt increased the acreage dramatically and created a national movement. The 1902 Newlands Reclamation Act reserved 150 million acres of timberland and created the U.S. Park Service.

Despite his actions in Panama and in the Russo-Japanese War, Roosevelt was frustrated by his inability to convince Americans to accept their role as a great world power as fully as he would have liked. In 1903 he compared America's new international role to its own Westward expansion. Just as Americans once had trodden "the rugged ways that lead to honor and success" as pioneers, they now stood on the verge of becoming one of the "great expanding nations" in world history. The power and authority of all such nations was eventually destined to decline, but the opportunity now existed for Americans to leave "indelibly their impress on the centuries."

Roosevelt was able to assert American influence in Latin America, not only in the case of the canal but also during a financial crisis in Santo Domingo. The island dictatorship was unable to pay its foreign debts, and some European powers threatened to intervene. Roosevelt objected, citing the Monroe Doctrine. He also added a codicil that became known as the Roosevelt Corollary: Should any Latin American nation engage in "wrongdoing" or be unable to run its affairs with "reasonable efficiency," the United States would intervene. In Santo Domingo, Roosevelt worked out an agreement in which the U.S. would be the customs agent for the country and send 55 percent of its revenues to European creditors until its loans were paid off. When the Senate refused to sign the treaty, Roosevelt announced that he regarded the arrangement as an executive agreement, which didn't require Senate approval. Two years later the Senate finally approved the treaty, although Roosevelt insisted that he had the authority to do so without Senate support.

Aside from these efforts in Latin America, Roosevelt's global goals for America were limited to symbolic measures. In his 1913 *Autobiography*, he described sending an American fleet around the world as his greatest achievement in foreign policy. He was certain that this decision was "essential" for "our own people especially, but also by other peoples, that the Pacific was as much our home waters as the Atlantic, and that our fleet could and would at will pass from one to the other of the two great oceans." After his term was over, Roosevelt strongly criticized Woodrow Wilson for failing to act more aggressively toward German actions, and he was a leader of the Preparedness Movement that objected to American neutrality in 1914. When America entered the war, Roosevelt volunteered to raise and lead a division of troops. He was bitterly resentful when Wilson denied his request.

Few presidents have enjoyed their term in office as much as Theodore Roosevelt, who once said no one ever had as "good a time" as he did. In a sense, his exuberance was the key to his successes. His enthusiasm overcame conventional views of the presidency and the exercise of presidential power. Roosevelt ignored the rules developed in the founding presidency that discouraged direct communication with the public at large, and he rejected congressional prerogatives asserted during the eclipsed presidency. His ebullience also enabled him to pursue new policies with self-confidence, as in his actions during the miners strike and his formulation of the conservation movement. Roosevelt's power, on the other hand, was limited to the force of his own personality. As expansive as it was, Roosevelt's persona nevertheless still had to confront Congress, the courts, and his own party. When he decided to return from retirement in 1912 and run again for the presidency, these forces finally hemmed him in. Although he was at his rhetorical height in 1912, Roosevelt could not convince his party to renominate him, nor could he obtain the support of enough voters. Perhaps more than any other president, Roosevelt illustrates the power that personality can exert in the office as well as its limitations.

WILLIAM HOWARD TAFT (1909–1913)

Like the successors to many other strong presidents, William Howard Taft suffered by comparison. His role in Roosevelt's administration was in some ways like that of Van Buren in Jackson's. Though not as close an advisor to Roosevelt as Van Buren was to Jackson, Taft nevertheless performed well as one who smoothed out and implemented Roosevelt's grand projects. As secretary of war, he supervised the construction of the Panama Canal and went to Japan to personally encourage mediation of the war with Russia. In 1907 Roosevelt sent him on a diplomatic tour of the world. Although quite different men (Taft once said he wished the president wouldn't "think aloud" so much), the relationship suited both parties, and Roosevelt hand-picked his secretary of war as his successor. Taft easily defeated Bryan in his last run for the presidency, and Roosevelt left the country on a big-game hunting expedition.

Taft's talents as a modern president rested more in his ability to routinize reforms rather than in experimenting with new projects. His cabinet, composed of wealthy lawyers and businessmen, better fit his inclinations than one filled with policy entrepreneurs. Taft's greatest achievements came with his bureaucratization of Progressive reforms. He brought assistant postmasters and consular officials into the civil service, supported a postal banking system for small depositors, and established a court of commerce to decide cases arising from the Interstate Commerce

Act. He even tried to establish a procedure for submission of international disputes to The Hague.

With larger, more contentious issues Taft was less adept. His first initiative was tariff reform. When Congress was uncooperative, he refused to involve himself in particulars, declaring, "I have no disposition to exert any other influence than that which it is my function under the Constitution to exercise." Consequently, Republicans added 800 amendments and Democrats proposed an income tax proposal with the bill. When Taft reluctantly signed the Payne-Aldrich tariff, he lost support of Progressives in his party who became convinced he was a tool of conservatives. Taft's deference to conservative congressional leaders was all the more unfortunate for him, since reformers were about to succeed in restricting their power. After 1910, the Speaker of the House no longer had the power to appoint committee chairs.

While Taft was as supportive of conservation policy as Roosevelt, he was uncomfortable with Roosevelt's reliance on executive order to create federal reserves and sought congressional authorization instead. Progressives were suspicious of Taft's motives, and the controversy came to a head when a government official accused Taft's Secretary of Interior Richard A. Ballinger of collusion with private developers. Taft rejected the charge but Gifford Pinchot, Roosevelt's forestry head and a Taft holdover, did not, and he secretly helped the accusing official write an article about corruption in the administration. Pinchot was fired, and while both Taft and Ballinger were exonerated by Congress, the incident was one of the reasons for Roosevelt's break with the president.

By 1912, Taft found himself surrounded by opponents. After his election in 1904 Roosevelt had pledged not to run again, although another term would not have violated Washington's precedent. He said:

> I regard the memories of Washington and Lincoln as priceless heritages for our people, just because they are the memories of strong men, of men who cannot be accused of weakness or timidity . . . who, nevertheless, led careers marked by disinterestedness just as much as by strength. . . .

Roosevelt concluded, "It is a very unhealthy thing that any man should be considered necessary to the people as a whole, save in the way of meeting some crisis." Clearly, in 1912 Roosevelt thought that Taft was frittering away his achievements as president. Roosevelt's estimation of Taft cascaded in a matter of months—from an opinion that Taft was not a "bad president" and certainly a better one than McKinley to the assessment that he was a "flub-dub with a streak of the second rate and the common in him." One of Roosevelt's biographers, William H. Harbaugh, captures the former president's dilemma regarding the upcoming election. Roosevelt could wait until 1916, but:

> Could he avoid stumbling over himself? Could he for five years do and say the contradictory things necessary to the preservation of his

hold on both the right and left? Could he accept the inevitable even after he had convinced himself that Taft's nomination in 1912 was, in fact, inevitable?

Harbaugh concludes that Roosevelt did not act until he was reasonably certain he could win renomination by his party.

Roosevelt was very successful in utilizing the new system of presidential primaries. He won ten of the twelve state primary elections and piled up over a million votes to Taft's 766,000. The former president also moved sharply to the left. In a February speech in Columbus, Ohio, he affirmed the Progressive agenda with such vigor that he snapped the strained relationship with moderates and conservatives. Roosevelt supported control of monopoly prices and initiative, referendum and recall, and he also attacked the Supreme Court. Old Guard Republicans regarded the address as a "charter of demagoguery" and "the craziest proposal" that ever came from Roosevelt "or from any other statesman." On the other hand, Roosevelt's enthusiastic adoption of even the most controversial elements of Progressivism won over many others. William Allen White, a well-known Kansas newspaper editor, said: "I put his heel on my neck and I became his man." Most of the convention delegates, however, were chosen by state party organizations, and when it was clear that he would lose the Republican nomination, Roosevelt and his delegates walked out of the convention hall. In August, the dissidents formed a new Progressive Party and held another convention in August that nominated Roosevelt.

Meanwhile, the Democrats were undergoing a transformation of their own. Since 1896 they had flourished at the local and state levels, but their commitment to rural and Southern interests was not enough to win the presidency. At their convention in Baltimore, Democrats understood that they finally had a chance to win the office, since the Republicans were divided. The delegates were deadlocked, however, between Speaker of the House Champ Clark of Missouri, House Majority Leader Oscar Underwood of Alabama, and Woodrow Wilson, governor of New Jersey. Underwood, Clark, and Wilson split the primaries they entered, and Southerners continued to support Underwood. Ironically, Wilson, who made his reputation as a reformer, won the nomination on the forty-sixth ballot by seeking the support of party machines in Illinois and Indiana after criticizing Clark's acceptance of delegate support from Tammany Hall.

In the general election Wilson called his agenda the New Freedom in contrast to Roosevelt's New Nationalism. Wilson attacked the New Nationalism as a form of paternalism. He believed that trusts should be dismantled rather than supervised by big government. "Free men need no guardians" was Wilson's campaign theme. However, the split in the Republican Party was most responsible for the first Democratic presidential victory since 1892. Roosevelt received over 4 million votes and Taft 3.5 million to Wilson's 6.3 million.

WOODROW WILSON (1913–1921)

Although Wilson was not widely known as a national figure before 1912 and received less than a majority of the popular vote (41.8 percent in 1912 and 49.2 percent in 1916), no president had a more thorough plan for how the office should be managed and how his agenda should be implemented. Wilson is primarily remembered for his failure to win Senate support for the League of Nations in World War I. Later presidents frequently have regarded Wilson as a tragic figure. His failure was a major factor in the pre- and post-war policies of FDR, who sought to learn from his mistakes, and Herbert Hoover and Richard Nixon wrote extensively about Wilson. His failure, though significant, must be placed in the context of his other projects. Wilson sought to modernize not only the presidency and the American political and economic system but also world politics in general. In these terms, Wilson was remarkably successful overall. Although he could be amenable to compromise (as in the case of passage of the Federal Reserve Act), he often framed his objectives in moral terms and was not very generous in regard to the motives of his opponents. For example, when he opposed Victoriano Huerta's coup d'état in Mexico, Wilson announced he would "teach the South American republics to elect good men." To many, Wilson brought a sense of idealism to the office, but to others he was doctrinaire and self-righteous.

In a series of articles and books written before he was president, Wilson offered brilliant analyses of the American political system. The general thrust of these works was that while the Constitution was a magnificent framework in its day, political developments required significant changes. In other words, the American political system needed to be modernized. In *Congressional Government* (1884), Wilson reviewed the founders' plan:

> The makers of the federal Constitution followed the scheme as they found it expounded in Montesquieu, followed it with genuine scientific enthusiasm. The admirable expositions of the *Federalist* read like thoughtful applications of Montesquieu to the political needs and circumstances of America. They are full of the theory of checks and balances.

But while Congress was supposed to check the president and the president to check Congress, much like the "theory of gravitation," the founders failed to realize that government was not a "machine but a living thing" and is "accountable to Darwin, not to Newton." The rise of political parties and political machines had transformed Congress into the dominant institution of the federal government.

Wilson was not in principle opposed to legislatures, but he was opposed to the way the American Congress governed. He described the intricate system of lawmaking in *Congressional Government*: the power of committee chairs; the dependence of legislators on state and local parties; and the absence of a national vision, debate, and policy coordination. As a result, Wilson concluded, there is no "responsible" government in America: "A dozen men originate [legislation]; a dozen compromises twist and alter it; a dozen offices whose names are scarcely known outside Washington put it into execution." Of course, the president was supposed to be a counterweight to Congress, but its power was so supreme that the presidency had become an office of "mere administration, mere obedience of directions from the masters of policy, the Standing Committees." Wilson regarded the veto as the only significant power left for the president, but even here its exercise was negative: "The President obstructs by means of his 'No'; the houses govern by means of their 'Yes'." At best the president could "tire the Senate by dogged persistence," but he no longer dealt with it "upon a ground of real equality."

Congressional Government was written at the height of the eclipsed presidency. Wilson continued to argue that his basic diagnosis was valid, although he acknowledged that Cleveland, "direct, fearless and somewhat unsophisticated," revealed the potential for a revitalized presidency. He also noted that the war with Spain was indicative of a stronger presidency in an era in which the United States took on a major international role. For Wilson, however, only a major change in the political system could produce the necessary elements of "responsible government." He advocated abandoning the "radical" defect of the separation of powers and replacing it with by a parliamentary system, in which the chief executive would be the party leader who worked with Congress to pass legislation that was "national and liberal" and not "sectional and selfish."

When Wilson took office in 1913, he knew, of course, that there was no possibility of an immediate conversion to a parliamentary system. He did, however, initiate a series of changes he regarded as the first steps on the road to the transformation from president to prime minister. First, he developed a series of legislative proposals and only presented a new one when the previous bill was nearly ready to be passed. Second, he went before Congress personally to present his case for his first proposal, tariff reform. Wilson was the first president to make such an appearance since John Adams, and when reporters asked about the nature of the perceived crisis Wilson informed them that this practice was designed to be routine. Third, Wilson relied exclusively on Democratic majorities to fashion the bills themselves and politely ignored the tactic of bipartisan participation, even with Progressive Republicans. Fourth, the president spoke to the public at large when the tariff bill was delayed in the Senate, charging that lobbyists were swarming throughout the Senate chambers and spending money "without limit." Pro-tariff legislators challenged the president on this point and set up a committee to investigate. When the committee in fact reported that many senators did indeed hold stocks in companies adversely affected by tariff reform, opposition to his legislation dissipated.

The Underwood Tariff Act is still regarded today as a textbook case of successful presidential leadership. Tariffs were reduced by 25 percent, and many products (especially those in which American companies were dominant) were placed on a tariff-free list. For Wilson, these tactics were also designed to show how a president could govern in a system with less separation of powers. The president proposed legislation that was endorsed by the legislative majority party, and if passage was threatened the president would take his program to the people.

Wilson used fundamentally the same approach to other legislation in his first term. Along with other Progressives and even many conservatives, Wilson believed the banking system was antiquated and in need of modernization. Since each bank was currently responsible for providing its own flow of currency, any shock to the system could create a "panic" in which large numbers of investors demanded their cash. In order to avoid this possibility, banks tended to restrict credit, which acted as a brake on economic development. Wilson believed that financial interests required a centralized banking system that was privately controlled, while many Democrats led by Bryan strongly favored a government-managed system. In addition, Carter Glass, chair of the House Banking Committee, and William McAdoo, secretary of treasury, both had their own plans.

In this case, Wilson acted as an honest broker with Democratic Party leaders. He proposed a hybrid alternative that included a system of private banks supervised by a Federal Reserve Board appointed by the president. The Federal Reserve Act passed in December of 1913, with every Democratic legislator supporting the bill. The following year, the Federal Trade Commission (FTC) was established by Congress with help from the president at crucial legislative junctures. Wilson had largely given up on his campaign pledges of trust-busting and accepted an approach similar to the one advocated by Roosevelt. The FTC was granted investigative authority and the power to order corporations to stop unfair practices.

In a period of two years Wilson had significantly altered presidential–congressional relations and created a new federal bureaucratic infrastructure to regulate the economy. In 1914, the president met with congressional leaders to discuss formulation of his plan to institute a national primary to elect presidential candidates. To Wilson, a national primary would take presidential nominations out of the hands of party leaders and also establish the president as the leader of national trends in public opinion. In addition, Wilson hoped that a major party realignment would take place in the 1916 elections. To that end he supported social legislation that he opposed in the past, including federal restrictions on child labor, an eight-hour day for rail workers, and loans for farmers. In his optimum scenario, a new Democratic Party shorn of its old Bourbon and Populist elements would produce large majorities in both Houses. Led by the president, it was conceivable that America could move to a parliamentary system in fact, if not in name.

Wilson's plan, although carefully conceived and executed, did not take certain factors into consideration. One, of course, was the impact of foreign policy. Wilson issued a neutrality proclamation when war broke out in Europe. While neutrality was initially a popular policy, it proved difficult to implement. Should American ships from neutral ports honor British blockades of German cities? Could American bankers provide loans to the Allied governments? Were German submarines entitled to attack ships that entered their waters? German Americans and Irish Americans suspected Wilson was really pro-British. Pacifists and isolationists feared Wilson's call for a military buildup was a prelude to American entry into the war. Interventionists concluded that Wilson was indecisive and mocked his statement that "there is such a thing as a man being too proud to fight." Another factor was the unexpected resilience of party machines. Many voters who supported Wilson supported local politicians as well. After the election, Wilson himself admitted that the "rigidity of party association" made the question of fundamental change "one of the most puzzling questions" he faced. As a result of these and others factors Wilson barely won the election, which was in doubt for several days. Moreover, Democrats lost control of the House. No realignment occurred. Wilson was still a minority president, and he no longer enjoyed the legislative majorities necessary for carrying out his agenda.

After the election, Wilson hoped the United States could mediate an armistice on the principle of "peace without victory." In fact, he responded to some German peace overtures. The Allies were, however, in danger of losing the war. The revolution in Russia complicated matters further, and Wilson expressed concern that the whole structure of European colonization might disintegrate. In January, the German government made a fateful decision to reopen unrestricted submarine warfare in the Atlantic in an effort to force British capitulation before America entered the war. In an intercepted and decoded telegram, which Wilson made public in February, a German official offered an alliance with Mexico if it declared war on the United States.

On April 2, 1917, Wilson asked Congress for a declaration of war. Although previously he had portrayed the conflict as a struggle for influence among great powers, he now declared Germany a rogue state engaging in a "warfare against mankind." It was the task of America to make the world "safe for democracy" and, in paraphrase of the Declaration of Independence, he pledged "our lives and our fortunes" to win the struggle.

When America entered the war, the number of European casualties was already staggering. Russia and Germany lost 2 million men, France 1.3 million, and the British 750,000. Most military experts felt the United States, with an armed force of only 125,000, would have little more than a symbolic impact on the war. Within a year, however, the U.S. put 2.8 million men in uniform and was a decisive force in the Allied victory. American convoys carried supplies and soldiers to Europe and helped repulse a massive German advance that had reached the suburbs of Paris.

Even before the Central Powers signed an armistice in November of 1918, Wilson decided he would personally lead the American treaty delegation in Paris. The decision was an extremely bold one. No president had ever undertaken such an effort (in fact, no president before Roosevelt had ever left American soil). Given the loss in blood and treasure, it was unlikely that the Allies would permit a latecomer to dictate peace terms. In January of 1918, Wilson presented to Congress his peace plan, known as the Fourteen Points Address. These included general principles such as arbitration of colonial disputes, self-determination for all nationalities, freedom of the seas, arms reductions, removal of trade barriers, "open covenants openly arrived at," and an "association of nations" (later known as the League of Nations), as well as specific recommendations on national boundaries. European delegates were more than skeptical; they were hostile. French Prime Minister George Clemenceau remarked that God gave the world ten commandments, which people broke; now Wilson gave the world fourteen points, and "we shall see their fate."

Wilson was forced to accede to almost all of the Allied objections to his points. He was able, however, to gain agreement to a system of "mandates" for former German colonies and, of course, to a League of Nations. In retrospect, Wilson's goals were enormously optimistic ones. Not only were the European allies in a mood for retribution but the president also was, in effect, demanding that they construct an entirely new international system.

When Wilson returned to the United States in July he knew he faced significant opposition to the one part of the Fourteen Points that he managed to retain, and he planned a tour of the country to gain support. In the months that followed, Wilson suffered one of the most devastating defeats ever endured by a president. Twice the Senate rejected the treaty. Wilson appeared to have made some progress in changing public opinion as a result of his speeches, but thirty-seven addresses in twenty-two days exacted a terrible toll on the president's health. On September 25, Wilson suffered a stroke. For four weeks he received no visitors except his wife and never regained his health for the rest of his term. Despite his limited capacities, Wilson still spoke of running for a third term and even suggested that all Republican opponents to the treaty should resign and run for reelection on the question. He promised, if an unspecified number were reelected, that he would appoint a Republican secretary of state and that he and the vice president would themselves resign.

The great question posed by all Wilson biographers and presidential scholars in general is why the president didn't seek a compromise with his opponents. Although there was a relatively small group of opponents called the "Irreconcilables" in the Senate, others who had more moderate concerns might have been won over. The focus of the opposition rested upon Article X of the League, which stated that all members were obligated to defend the territorial integrity of one another. To League opponents, led by Senator Henry Cabot Lodge of Massachusetts, signing the treaty was unconstitutional, since Congress was the only body authorized to declare war; and it was politically unwise, since it would force America into participation in any number of foreign conflicts. Wilson responded to the first concern by reminding his audiences that action required unanimous support by the League, and to the second by arguing that American participation in this new international organization would actually reduce the chances of war.

One interpretation argues that Wilson's whole personality had great difficulty with compromise. Since Wilson thought that he was both morally and politically correct, why should he compromise with those who held wrong positions? Another view contends that Wilson would have offered a compromise (had he not suffered a stroke) after he softened up the opposition in his speaking tour. Thomas A. Bailey (*Woodrow Wilson and the Great Betrayal*) writes: "The obvious course was for him to seem unyielding, drive as hard a bargain as he could, and then at the last moment, when there was no danger of more reservations being added, make a grand gesture of accepting." Yet another contends that Wilson felt the stakes were simply too high to compromise. The choices before him were to: (1) accept reservations and risk the collapse of the League, since other necessary signatories might withdraw and/or offer their own codicils; (2) refuse reservations and risk American absence from the League, thus reducing its effectiveness; or (3) insist on full acceptance, creating a strong international order that could maintain world peace. Since, for Wilson, the first and second options led to unacceptable consequences, why not risk all with the third?

A final interpretation traces Wilson's decision to his mode of governance, outlined as early as *Congressional Government* in 1884. Wilson based his entire presidency on a model of leadership that relied on party majorities, executive-sponsored legislation, and occasional appeals to the public at large. In fact, Wilson urged voters to elect Democrats to Congress in 1918 "not for my sake or for the sake of a political party, but for the sake of the nation itself." The president's open return to partisanship in the midst of a war after he declared that "politics is adjourned" for the duration of the conflict may not have cost him majorities in both the House and Senate, since losses are routine in mid-term elections, but it does indicate his effort to return to his original model of leadership. Thus, when Wilson began his tour of the West and Midwest in defense of the League treaty, he was operating on a strategy that did not have all the pieces in place. The battle centered in the Senate, which was more resistant to presidential party leadership than the House; the Democrats were a legislative minority; and the foreign-policy crisis had subsided. Nevertheless, as the saying goes, generals fight the last wars. So, perhaps, do presidents. Wilson seemed to be attempting to salvage the strategy that was so successful in 1913–1915 and determined not to let his administration regress into the eclipsed period in which the Senate harassed and dominated presidents. As president, Wilson's strength lies less in his ability to improvise than in his talent to pursue a line of thought rigorously. In this sense, Wilson was actually playing to his strength.

WARREN G. HARDING (1921–1923)

Sometimes the difference of just a year or two in politics can be enormous. America in 1918, or even in 1919, was vastly different than America in 1920. Although Wilson hoped the presidential election of 1920 would finally be an opportunity for a referendum on the League, the Democratic candidate, James M. Cox, refused to take a clear position on the issue. Warren Harding, on the other hand, reiterated Republican opposition to American entry. Moreover, Wilson, unlike Lincoln, scrupulously avoided resting wartime presidential powers upon the Constitution and requested statutory authority from Congress for all his actions. With the war over, Congress rescinded the administrative structures it authorized. Post-war unemployment, labor strikes, a concern about communist influence that led to deportations of aliens under Wilson's attorney general, and a terrible influenza epidemic that killed over a half million Americans contributed to a weariness in public opinion on political issues. Harding captured this sentiment in an address in May of 1920 when he said, "America's present need is not heroes, but healing; not nostrums but normalcy; not revolution but restoration . . . not surgery but serenity." The presidency, however, did not cease to modernize, but the process now took different forms.

In nearly every poll rating presidential performance, Warren G. Harding finishes at the very bottom. This assessment is based in part on the major scandals that occurred in his administration that were uncovered shortly before his death on August 2, 1923. Harding is portrayed as a figure who *looked* more like a president than one who *performed* like one. Charles R. Forbes, the head of the Veterans Bureau and a member of Harding's group of poker-playing friends (called the "Ohio Gang"), was caught selling war surplus material to companies below cost in return for kickbacks. The attorney for the agency committed suicide when the scandal broke. Secretary of Interior Albert B. Fall was later discovered to have sold government leases to oil reserves at Teapot Dome, Wyoming, and Elk Hills, California, for kickbacks of over $400,000 (known as the Teapot Dome scandal). Although Harding was not personally implicated in this or other scandals, the trials and congressional investigations extended until 1929, and the connection between the administration and corruption became firm in the public mind.

On these terms Harding is rated as an incompetent president who, like Grant, was unable or unwilling to control voracious subordinates. Unlike Grant, however, Harding was an experienced politician who served as a state and U.S. senator. Part of the harsh assessment of Harding rests on the fact that after the stock market crash in the 1920s, Harding's clear preference for business interests (an orientation shared by Coolidge and Hoover) was regarded as irresponsible. In some ways Harding became identified with the "Jazz Age" more than even Herbert Hoover. He drank when liquor consumption was illegal, he was an avid poker player, and he had a mistress.

Despite these considerable shortcomings, Harding did initiate several significant features of the modern presidency. In fact, one of his defenders, Robert K. Murray *(The Harding Era)*, contends that Harding should be credited for advancing a political philosophy and agenda that was followed for an entire decade: ". . . his 882 days in office were more significant than all but a few similar periods in the nation's experience." Harding frequently spoke of a return to "normalcy," but his philosophy required significant innovation. Shortly after assuming office in 1921, he explained his agenda to Congress as one in which there would be "less government in business as well as more business in government." Harding appointed business leaders to regulatory commissions created by Progressives to supervise the economy. His secretary of treasury, Andrew Mellon, proposed an end to the wartime excess profits tax, reduced the top tax rates, and raised rates for low-income families. The administration supported emergency tariff legislation to alleviate falling farm prices, but the subsequent Fordney-McCumber Tariff bill restored Wilson's cuts and was one of the highest in American history.

Harding intervened in two major strikes—one by coal miners and another by rail workers—on the side of employers. In the case of the rail strike, he authorized his attorney general to request one of the most sweeping injunctions ever issued in a labor dispute. Union officials were forbidden not only from picketing but also from communicating with workers about the strike by telephone or "word of mouth." When several of Harding's cabinet members, including Herbert Hoover, strongly objected, Harding ordered his attorney general to restrict enforcement of some of the provisions.

Harding systematically focused on the revolution in communication and transportation that was underway. At his urging, In 1921 Congress passed the Highway Act, which provided federal funds for road construction that tripled in two years to $88 million. He also created a conference on commercial aviation and requested that Congress establish a federal agency to provide rules for flight routes and airports. In addition, Harding established a system of voluntary radio licensing supervised by the Department of Commerce and supported legislation to give the department authority to regulate airwaves. Many of Harding's proposals were eventually passed by Congress in Coolidge's administration, but it was Harding who foresaw the need for a government infrastructure to promote these technological developments.

As to the issue of "business in government," two major national conferences were held during the Harding administration, one on problems in agriculture and one on unemployment. Although neither conference produced major legislation, the practice of bringing experts together led to two major innovations for the modern presidency: It placed the office of the president at the center of policy evaluation, and it gave a role to professionals in solving policy problems. When FDR formed his "Brain Trust" in 1932 he adopted these principles, although their prescriptions were, of course, very different from those in Harding's administration.

In addition, Congress passed the Budget and Accounting Act in June of 1921. The concept of a federal budget was actually part of the Progressive agenda but it also fit well with Harding's proposal for economy in government. The legislation created a Bureau of the Budget to aid the president, who was now given authority to estimate expenditures and revenues for each fiscal year. The director reported directly to the president. (Congress also created in the act the General Accounting Office in order to oversee expenditures.) Harding appointed Charles G. Dawes as the first director. Dawes approached the position with religious fervor. He gathered federal bureaucrats together in a series of meetings in which he stood next to two brooms. One, he said, represented the Army allocation and the other the Navy. Dawes complained that when the Navy needed brooms it sought funds to buy them from outside contractors, even though the Army had plenty. With the image of the two brooms on the door to his office, Dawes saved the government over $1 billion in 1922. Although "business in government" was Harding's primary concern, the creation of the Bureau of the Budget placed the president at the center of budgetary policy and provided the president with the administrative structure to shape his programs.

Harding's cabinet was a curious combination of the "Ohio Gang," whose interests were primarily in patronage and self-promotion, and "modernizers" such as Herbert Hoover (Department of Commerce) and Andrew Mellon (Department of Treasury) who sought to promote economic growth and efficiency in government. For secretary of state Harding chose Charles Evans Hughes, over the objections of party regulars. Harding opposed American entry to the League of Nations in the 1920 campaign, and Americans in general were not anxious to assume any new international commitments. It was Hughes's task to negotiate peace treaties in the absence of Senate approval of Wilson's proposals. With Harding's support, Hughes also convened an international conference on arms limitations. Harding opened the conference on Armistice Day at the Tomb of the Unknown Soldier with a passionate plea for world peace so that "the millions dead shall not be in vain." Hughes followed the next day with a surprisingly dramatic proposal for naval reductions. The delegates agreed to several treaties, including a ban on poisonous gas in warfare, arms reduction and, in the Four Power Treaty (U.S., Great Britain,

Japan, and France), a mutual defense pact. The Senate reluctantly approved the agreements in April of 1922 with significant reservations.

When Americans learned of Harding's death on August 2, 1923, thousands of mourners stood by to watch the funeral train on its way to Washington. Revelations of scandals soon followed, however, and Harding immediately lost the affection of the public. Some scholars contend that Harding had actually experienced a learning curve and may have been able to weather the scandals and modify some of his policies. He informed Secretary Mellon in 1923, for example, that he would not support any more tax breaks for the wealthy. In any case, the Harding administration illustrates how modernization proceeded, even in the context of a president officially committed to returning to normalcy.

CALVIN COOLIDGE (1923–1929)

When President Harding died, Vice President Coolidge was visiting the family farm in Vermont. Since there was no telephone, a post office official knocked on the door at midnight carrying two messages: a notification of the death of the president, and a note from the attorney general informing Coolidge that he must take the oath of office to become president. By the light of a kerosene lamp, since there was no electricity at the farm, Coolidge took the oath before his father (a notary public), using the family Bible. This image of the simplicity of rural New England translated into Coolidge's primary mode of governance for the next six years. The persona of "Silent Cal" produced numerous anecdotes. For example, when a woman at a party told Coolidge she had made a bet that she could get more than two words from him, he replied, "You lose." During the 1924 election campaign Coolidge said, "I don't recall any candidate for president that ever injured himself very much by not talking." Some observers, of course, could interpret this style harshly. Theodore Roosevelt's daughter once said that the president "looked like he had been weaned on a pickle," and humorist Dorothy Parker reputedly remarked, when she heard of Coolidge's death, "How can you tell?"

There is no question that Coolidge was in fact a quiet man. When William Allen White asked him what was behind the mask, he replied that maybe there wasn't one. On the other hand, Coolidge's brevity provided a beneficial contrast to the expansiveness of Harding whose legacy was rapidly unraveling after his death. Upon taking office, the new president had virtually no national political base. When confronted with congressional investigations of Teapot Dome he moved carefully, announcing that he would retain Harding's cabinet, appointing special prosecutors, and finally asking for the attorney general's resignation on the grounds that a cabinet official could not defend himself and run a department at the same time. Asked about the scandal at a press conference, Coolidge replied, "Let the guilty be punished."

If his verbal economy served him well in the transition, Coolidge also was innovative in his approach to the election in 1924. The convention itself was broadcast by radio, and he clearly saw the implications of new communications technology. In fact, one could argue that Coolidge actually anticipated the development of "verbal overload" that characterizes the presidency today. In his autobiography Coolidge observed, "It is so often that the President is on the air that almost anyone who wishes has ample opportunity to hear his voice." He then explained that there was a kind of novelty in the personal appearance:

> It has seemed more appropriate for Mrs. Coolidge and me to appear at the rear of the train where people could see us. About the only time that I have spoken was at Bennington in September of 1928, where I expressed my affection and respect for the people of Vermont, as I was passing through that town on my way back to Washington. I found that the love I had for the hills where I was born touched a responsive chord in the heart of the whole nation.

Coolidge's limited campaign speechmaking was replaced by what is now called the photo-op. In the 1920s, as more and more consumer products were developed, advertising was a growth industry. Coolidge retained Edward L. Bernays, a public-relations expert, with effective results. One event sponsored by the Republican Party was a breakfast meeting at the White House attended by New York theatre actors. The highlight of the event was a song sung by the guests and led by Al Jolson. The lyrics of "Keep Coolidge" included refrains such as "without a lot of fuss/he did a lot for us" and "he's never asleep/still waters run deep."

Very quickly the image of "Silent Cal," the president who carried New England values to the White House, captured the public imagination. After a huge election victory over the divided Democrats, who took 100 ballots to nominate their candidate, Coolidge faced the task of governing as what Paul Johnson has called a "minimalist politician." Coolidge, of course, did not have the casual relationship with the press that Harding did. For example, when he decided not to run for reelection in 1928, he entered the press room and quietly distributed a page to each reporter that contained the single sentence, "I do not choose to run for president in 1928," refusing to add to the press release. This minimalist strategy actually enhanced his reputation with the press. As correspondent Tom Stokes wrote in his memoirs (*Chips Off My Shoulder*), "It was really a miracle. He said nothing. Newspapers must have copy. So we grasped little incidents . . . and created . . . a character who spoke sparingly and acted economically."

Although Coolidge spoke less than his predecessor, he did not reject rhetoric as an important mode of governance. He believed that an "unfortunate phrase in an address might not only become "magnified into the sensation of the hour," but if repeated frequently could also "create an atmosphere of distraction that might seriously interfere with the conduct of public business." Coolidge's rhetoric was well designed for the upcoming era of the "sound byte." When Boston police went on strike, as governor of Massachusetts he sent out the state militia with the justification, "There is no right to strike against the public safety by anybody, anywhere, anytime." Other statements that became aphorisms are: "The business of America is business"; "Under this republic the rewards of industry belong to those who earn them"; "Economy is idealism in its most practical form"; "America must be kept American"; and "I am for economy. After that I am for more economy."

As a minimalist politician, Coolidge had a limited agenda. With the end of the war, he announced in his inaugural address that the collection of taxes—necessary "beyond reasonable doubt" for securing the public welfare—was "only a species of legalized larceny." But how could taxes and the war debt be lowered at the same time? Coolidge argued that economies in government plus additional revenue from consumer buying assured the success of his plan. Some representatives, such as Senator George Norris, thought "good businessmen" would never chance Coolidge's "supply-side" strategy because it was too radical. Nevertheless, the Coolidge-Mellon tax plan was passed by Congress in 1924. Two years later another tax cut was passed by Congress at the president's urging; the Revenue Act of 1926 eliminated the gift tax, reduced the estate tax by 50 percent, and lowered the income tax.

On other issues, Coolidge carefully followed congressional wishes. For example, he signed the National Origins Act of 1924, which severely reduced immigration from southern Europe and stopped it altogether from Japan on the grounds that these limitations, like the tariff, "save American jobs for American workmen." Farmers were one group that noticeably did not benefit from the "Coolidge prosperity." Congress, led by Midwestern Republicans, attempted to alleviate their suffering by establishing a system of cooperatives that would sell surplus crops to the government, who would then place them on the world market at discount prices. Coolidge, however, vigorously opposed the legislation as a "cruelly deceptive" price fixing scheme that would create a "bureaucratic tyranny of unprecedented propositions." He vetoed the McNary-Haugen Act twice.

In foreign affairs, Coolidge relied heavily on the State Department. As he stated in his autobiography,

> . . . the ideal way. . . is to assign to the various positions men of sufficient ability so that they can solve all the problems that arise under their jurisdiction. If there is a troublesome situation in Nicaragua, a General McCoy can manage it. If we have differences with Mexico, a Morrow can compose them. If there is unrest in the Philippines, a Stimson can quiet them.

Coolidge remained largely indifferent to the rise of fascism in Europe. When asked if Germany could be permitted to delay or cancel war debts, Coolidge refused with the reply: "They hired the money, didn't they?" Almost by accident, the administration successfully negotiated the Kellogg-Briand Pact that outlawed war as a solution to problems and was ultimately signed by 62 nations. The French foreign minister originally proposed the idea as a bilateral agreement between the United States and France. Secretary of State Frank B. Kellogg initially was not willing to be involved in the effort, but in an attempt to mollify public demands for peace efforts he proposed a wider agreement. Coolidge was won over by Kellogg and later came to believe that the treaty was a highlight of his administration.

Of course, shortly after the noble effort to outlaw war, Germany, Italy, and Japan engaged in aggressive acts against other nations. As the Kellogg-Briand Pact came to be regarded as a chimera of peace, so did Coolidge's economic policies come to be seen in terms of prosperity. Within 10 years, Coolidge's minimalism was uniformly discredited.

HERBERT HOOVER (1929–1933)

Beginning with the stock market crash in 1929, the nation's economy underwent a series of startling crises. In October of 1929, the market stood at 485. By 1932, it was at 85. Banks closed (10,000 of them between 1929 and 1934); drought conditions were reported in 300 counties in 30 states; 12 million people were unemployed by May of 1932; and farmers lost their land to banks and/or tax collectors. In a single day in April of 1932, one-fourth of the entire area of the state of Mississippi went under the hammer of auctioneers. Perhaps as many as a million men and boys left their homes to wander the country, looking for work. By January of 1931 New York City operated 82 bread lines feeding 85,000 people a day. Farm income plummeted as corn prices fell to pre-Civil War levels. Many schools closed for lack of public funds. The Great Depression had begun.

Since Herbert Hoover was the president of the United States during this collapse, he became for generations of Americans the figure who, if not responsible for the Depression, was unable to cope with it. In the words of historian Carl Degler: "[H]is administration is usually depicted as cold hearted, when not pictured as totally devoid of heart, inept, or actionless in the face of the Great Depression." Degler himself demurs from this assessment, but others confirm the generalization. Elliot Rosen writes:

> [Hoover's] American system [was] intended to preserve individualism and nineteenth century anti-statist, laissez-faire attitudes. His policies as Secretary of Commerce, then as President contributed substantially and directly to the Great Depression.

It is indeed an ironic turn of history that Hoover should be discussed in such terms. For whatever Hoover's failures were in dealing with the

Depression (he spent the remainder of his life justifying the actions he took in 1929–1933), his political persona before the Crash of 1929 was quite different. In 1928 he was known as the "Great Engineer," and *The New York Times* said his "office looked more like a machine shop than a room, in whose mind commanded all experience and whose wave of hand organized fleets of rescue vessels and millions of contributions." As secretary of commerce in the Harding and Coolidge administrations, he was one of the most conspicuous modernizers in the cabinet. It was Hoover who worked hardest for a rationalization of the executive branch and who convinced Harding of the need for a national conference on unemployment. Coolidge found Hoover's incessant stream of reform proposals annoying and derisively referred to him as the "wondah boy." Because of his successful activities as an administrator of relief in Europe after World War I, to the press his name had come "to mean food for the starving and medicine for the sick." The man who in 1932 was said to have a face that would wither a flower was four years earlier "an idealist representing enlightened individualism, humanitarianism, harmony, liberty. . . ." Hoover was so committed to an "open presidency" that he created a New Year's Day open house and shook the hands of 6,000 of his fellow Americans at the 1930 event.

Historians who have studied both the pre- and post-Depression Hoover have attempted to reevaluate his ideological reputation. For instance, Martin Fausold, a Hoover biographer, has concluded that Secretary of Commerce Hoover was "the more liberal and progressive candidate in 1928." He received the support of Jane Addams, the Chicago reformer who had voted for Eugene Debs in 1920 and Robert H. La Follette in 1924. She endorsed Hoover's farm policy and his positions on collective bargaining. (Hoover had gone on record as favoring the curtailment of "excessive use" of injunctions in labor disputes.) Addams also admired his concern for the poor. Similarly, Joan Hoff Wilson concluded in her biography that "the great engineer and humanitarian still lived beneath the new mantle of the Great Depression president," and that Hoover was a "forgotten progressive and a remembered conservative."

Some historians believe they have detected in Hoover a political philosophy that was neither liberal nor conservative. William Appleman Williams describes Hoover as "the keystone in the arch that leads from Mark Hanna and Herbert Croly to such later figures as Nelson Rockefeller and Adolph Berle." For Williams, Hoover was one of the first American leaders to see that the competitive capitalism characterizing much of American history was operationally obsolete and needed to be replaced by a cooperative system of both labor and capital led by a "class conscious industrial gentry." Ellis Hawley, a historian of both the twenties and the New Deal, has taken Williams's observation one step further. Hawley calls Hoover's philosophy *corporativism.* Hawley is careful to point out that Hoover was not influenced by the "fascist perversion of the corporate ideal" but, like his counterparts in Europe, he was concerned about the "destructive competition" and "social anarchy" in capitalism and envisioned a new order through "scientific coordination and moral regeneration."

Hawley concludes that the dividing line between Hoover and FDR is not one of laissez-faire and a managed economy, as proposed by those who see Hoover as a conservative, but rather "one attempt at management, through informal private and public cooperation to other more formal and coercive yet also limited attempts." Murray N. Rothbard, the libertarian economist, concurs with this assessment. In *America's Great Depression* he argues that in such parts of Hoover's program as the Reconstruction Finance Corporation, which provided loans to banks and businesses, "laissez-faire was boldly thrown overboard and every governmental weapon thrown into the breach."

Was Hoover, who refused to use the full weight of the government to deal with social and economic problems, a believer in laissez-faire? Was he really a progressive caught in the storm of the Depression? Was he a *corporativist* seeking new kinds of partnership between government and business? An examination of Hoover's major theoretical work, *American Individualism*, suggests that in varying degrees all these contradictory assessments are correct.

Published in 1922, when Hoover was secretary of commerce in the Harding administration, *American Individualism* is a remarkable book. In fact, it is a neglected classic of American political thought. Hoover began his essay by outlining his understanding of American exceptionalism. In his seven years of service overseas, he had seen nations "burned in revolution." These ideologies may have been "clothed by the demagogue" in "the terms of political idealism," but they unleashed the "bestial instincts of hate, murder and destruction." America, too, had an ideology, one which "partisans of some of these other schemes" insisted was exhausted. Hoover defined this ideology as *individualism* but insisted that "our individualism differs from all others" and is "not the individualism of other countries." The remainder of the book is an attempt on Hoover's part to define the historical development of this ideology in America and to explain how much it contributes to America's political stability and economic well-being.

Hoover, who described himself as an "unashamed individualist," divided his discussion of individualism into four aspects: philosophical, spiritual, economic, and political. The philosophical grounding of individualism is based on the recognition of two basic instincts: selfishness and altruism. For Hoover, the dominant human instincts are selfish, and "the problem of the world is to restrain the destructive instincts while strengthening and enlarging those of altruistic character and constructive impulse." The "will-o'-the-wisp of all breeds of socialism" is that it asserts "motivation of human animals by altruism alone." In order to achieve a surface resemblance to other-regarding behavior, socialists find that they must create a "bureaucracy of the entire population." Similarly, autocracies, in which Hoover includes all forms of class rule, even unrestrained capitalism, suppose that "the good Lord endowed a special few with all the divine attributes." Autocrats treat others only as means. The proof of the futility of this idea lay with the "grim failure of Germany" and those in America "who have sought economic domination."

To date, according to Hoover, Americans had rejected both of these faulty conceptions of human nature. They rejected the "clap-trap of the French Revolution," and they rejected the idea of the "frozen strata of classes." As proof of the latter, Hoover cited the twelve men comprising the presidency, vice presidency, and cabinet, nine of whom "earned their own way in life without economic inheritance, and eight of them started with manual labor."

The second aspect of individualism, the spiritual, assumes there is a "divine spark" that can "be awakened in every heart." Hoover noted the impact of the religious origins of America in maintaining this idea. In this section of the book he outlined his conception of what can best be called *service individualism* as the key element in the American individualism that "differs from all others." Proof of this spiritual spark was the "vast multiplication of voluntary organizations for altruistic purposes" in America. According to Hoover:

> These associations for the advancement of public welfare improvements, morals, charity, public opinion, health, the clubs and societies for recreation and intellectual advancement, represent something moving at a far greater depth than "joining." They represent the widespread aspiration for mutual advancement, self expression, and neighborly helpfulness.

The essence of American individualism, then, was service. Hoover stated that "when we rehearse our own individual memories of success, we find that none gives us such comfort as the memory of service given. Do we not refer to our veterans as service men? Do not merchants and business men pride themselves in something of service given beyond the price of their goods?"

In his section on the economic aspects of individualism, Hoover completed his definition of the businessperson as one engaged in the provision of a service. The principle of "every man for himself and the devil take the hindmost" may have been a code of conduct in the American past, but

> . . . our development of individualism shows an increasing tendency to regard right of property not as an object in itself but in light of a useful and necessary instrument in stimulation of initiative to the individual. . . .

The goal of economic activity was not "the acquisition and preservation of private property—the selfish snatching and hoarding of the common product." As a form of "self expression" it was an activity designed to produce "a high and growing standard of living for all the people, not for a single class. . . ." Hoover listed the "comforts" (electric lights, plumbing, telephones, gramophones, and automobiles) that had begun as luxuries but now had become so commonplace that 70 or 80 percent of the population could afford them.

Hoover admitted that when private property became concentrated in the hands of the few, "the individual begins to feel capital as an oppressor," but American individualism had devised a variety of mechanisms to prevent this occurrence. One was the "American demand for equality of opportunity" as "a constant militant check upon capital." Hoover cited the income tax as a means by which the "surplus" from profits could be shared. He also supported regulation to prevent economic domination and unfair practices. In his chapter on the political aspects of American individualism, Hoover discussed the faults in the American system. He was careful to point out that the achievements far outweigh the shortcomings, but nevertheless his list was not a short one:

> [T]he spirit of lawlessness; the uncertainty of unemployment in some callings; the deadening effect of certain repetitive processes of manufacture; the twelve hour day in a few industries; unequal voice in bargaining for wage in some employment; arrogant domination by some employers and some labor leaders; child labor in some states; inadequate instruction in some areas; unfair competition in some industries; some fortunes excessive far beyond the needs of stimulation to initiative; survivals of religious intolerance; political debauchery of some cities; weakness in our governmental structure.

One can see, even from this brief summary of a brief book, how commentators can draw different conclusions from Hoover's political philosophy. An emphasis on his interpretation of American exceptionalism serves to underline the limits to governmental intervention in the economy. Hoover was so impressed by the failure of European governments and so impressed with the success of the American system that any measure which borrowed from socialism was to be rejected. There is a "deadline between our system and socialism," he wrote in *American Individualism*. "Regulation to prevent domination and unfair practices, yet preserving rightful initiative are in keeping with our social foundations. Nationalization of industry or business is their negation." It is often noted that Hoover in 1932 insisted that grass would grow in the streets of New York if FDR's programs were enacted. But in 1928, against the counsel of his advisers, Hoover accused Al Smith, the Democratic presidential candidate, of promoting socialism by his support of state purchase and sale of liquor. "Shall we depart from the principle of our American system," Hoover asked a crowd at Madison Square Garden, "upon which we have advanced beyond all the rest of the world, in order to adopt methods based on principles destructive of its very foundation?"

Yet, despite Hoover's claim of having discovered the essence of the American system in the concept of individualism, there clearly is a collectivist strain in his thought. He warmly embraced the corporation as a new form of economic organization that was more efficient, more rational, more innovative, and even more public-spirited than the small farm or firm. In 1928, for instance, he told residents of his home town of West Branch, Iowa, that despite the bravery and kindness of the early settlers we "must avoid becoming homesick for the ways of those self-contained farm houses of 40 years ago." These yeomen had "lower standards of living, greater toil, less opportunity for leisure and recreation, less of the comforts of home, less of the joy of living." Besides, there was no way to go back to simpler times. It was no more possible to "revive those old conditions than it was to summon back the relatives in the cemetery yonder." Farming was now a business with 80 percent of production for market use. Once self-sufficiency was transcended through improved feed and livestock and a "long list of mechanical inventions for saving labor," the economy of scale changed and the farmer joined an "economic system vastly more intricate and delicately adjusted than before."

Hoover's model envisioned groups of farmers, labor unions, corporations, chambers of commerce, and bankers, all nationally organized and motivated, as he said in *American Individualism*, by a mixture of self-interest and altruism. The government would foster the conditions for their cooperation. In this aspect we can see the elements of progressivism in Hoover's political thought. He never advocated a "greed is good" ideology. In fact, his central defense of capitalism was always based on its ability as a system to promote a sense of service to the community. He mirrored the progressive's commitment to discovering ways to promote the public good through a rational approach to solving social problems. No fault in the American system was not potentially remediable for Hoover. Even poverty could be abolished through a general increase in the standard of living and volunteer efforts of communities. The list of social problems he drew up in 1922 was "becoming steadily more local." "That they are recognized and condemned is a long way on the road to progress."

Seen from different angles, Hoover's American system was laissez-faire liberal, progressive, *and* corporativist. Hoover was a determined modernist who was searching for ways to meld the various strains of American political culture into a new, more rational system.

Of course, Hoover's synthesis was short-lived. He barely had a moment to implement his ideas when the Crash of 1929 and the Great Depression seven months after he took office smashed the American system as he understood it. The very aspects of his thought that had looked so irresistible in 1928 seemed limited and inflexible by 1930. Despite Hoover's famous dictum after the Crash that the economy was fundamentally sound, he expressed belief that the downturn would be a long, hard one. He refused to accept his treasury secretary's view that the

Crash provided social Darwinist opportunities for the elimination of inefficient business and the liquidation of unnecessary labor. Wages must remain stable and the unemployed provided for, according to Hoover. Business must accept some of the responsibility for the Depression because of "over-optimism as to profits."

Hoover believed the cause of the Great Depression rested with the unstable economies of Europe; hence, to copy measures undertaken in Germany and France or Britain would only compound America's problems. His approach to relief for the unemployed paralleled his approach as a relief administrator after World War I. In both cases he saw the government's role as one in which private relief funds were coordinated. When a Democratic Congress demanded direct relief monies for the unemployed, Hoover admitted that the impulse came from a "natural anxiety for the people of their states," but he insisted that direct appropriations would "break down" the "sense of responsibility and mutual help." The issue was not one of financial integrity, but Hoover feared that the "cost of a few score millions" would create "an abyss of reliance in the future upon charity in some form or another." Only the mobilization and organization of "the infinite number of agencies of self help in the community" could be the basis of "successful relief in national distress."

In 1932, however, Hoover had acted more boldly in dealing with what he called the "temporary mobilization of timid capital." The Reconstruction Finance Corporation, initially capitalized at $500 million by the federal government, was created to lend funds to railroads, banks, insurance companies, building firms, and loan associations. However, the administrators of the program tended to be overly cautious in their lending policies, at least in terms of the emergency at hand, and the public at large began to perceive the program as money spent on "plutocrats." By late spring Hoover seemed almost to have given up on the plan.

Hoover was now confronted with sporadic incidents of protest and violence. Farmers blocked sheriffs' sales of homes by placing logs across highways and smashing the car windshields and flattening tires of potential buyers. In Nebraska farmers carried signs that read "Be Pickets or Peasants" and commandeered a carload of cattle from a train. In cities there were hunger strikes, often organized by communists; miners demanded at gunpoint food from the company stores; angry crowds began appearing on streets in attempts to prevent the eviction of tenants from apartments. Perhaps the most dramatic example of protest, and one that received the most national attention, was the encampment of the "Bonus Army" in Washington, DC. When the petitions of veterans of World War I for a bonus were denied by Congress in 1932, the former soldiers built makeshift shelters outside the capital and even slept in unused government buildings on Pennsylvania Avenue. On July 28, 1932, Hoover ordered their eviction. General Douglas MacArthur used cavalry to chase the protesters away and burned the shacks. Hoover justified his action by emphasizing that no one was killed, and that the veterans had been duped by "communists and persons with criminal records."

The problem with Hoover's American system was that after 1929 its major premises no longer seemed operational. Local communities and volunteer organizations had nothing more to give. The vision of prosperity that Hoover had guaranteed would be the inevitable result of the growth of the corporation had been reduced to a memory. The divine spark seemed to have flickered and gone out. Still Hoover believed the country would have pulled out of the crisis if European banks had not defaulted in 1931. Then he blamed the persistence of the Depression on Roosevelt's policies. In fact, in spite of his unpopularity, the former president continued to advance his belief in the verities of the American system throughout the 1930s.

A typical formulation of Hoover's argument can be seen in a speech he delivered to the Colorado Young Republican League in 1936. According to Hoover, in Europe after World War I and at this very moment, "Liberty has been dethroned and dictatorship erected by men greedy for power." These leaders (whom Hoover leaves unnamed) blamed the "tragic miseries of the times" on "some party or class":

> They made great promises. They demanded violent action against human ills that are only slowly curable. They claimed that sporadic wickedness in high places had permeated the whole system of liberty. They shouted new destructive slogans and phrases day by day to inflame the people. They implanted hates in the souls of men. They first grasped at power through elections which Liberty provided. Then began most of the emergency instruments of power to "save the nation." The first demands were powers of dictation over industry and agriculture and finance and labor. Legislatures were reduced to rubber stamps. Honest debate was shut off in the halls of deliberation . . . these men insisted the civilization had begun all over again when they came to power.

Finally, Hoover argued, "Liberty died," and men were "goosestepped in a march back to the Middle Ages." The New Deal "has imitated the intellectual and vocal technique of typical European revolution." The National Industrial Recovery Act (NIRA) and Agricultural Adjustment Act (AAA) were the first steps in this process. What angered Hoover most of all was the New Deal's claim that it was now the party of liberalism. He urged youth to reject this "false liberalism":

> The spirit of liberalism is to create free men. It is not the regimentation of men. It is not the extension of bureaucracy. You cannot extend mastery of government over the daily life of people without somewhere making it master of people's souls and thoughts.

FRANKLIN D. ROOSEVELT (1933–1944)

If Hoover's reputation in regard to the Depression emphasizes his ideological rigidity, Franklin Delano Roosevelt's reputation rests largely on his opportunism and an almost uncanny knack at improvisation. Although he served two terms as an innovative governor of New York, he was regarded by many in 1932 as a candidate who was little more than a Democratic Harding. Walter Lippman described FDR as "a pleasant man who, without any important qualifications for the office, would very much like to be President." Hoover, who later would see Roosevelt in demonic terms, emphasized his vacillations and inconsistencies in 1932. According to Hoover, Roosevelt was a "chameleon in plaid." The Communist Party, which later made an uneasy peace with the New Deal, saw him as the last American president before a revolution, an American Kerensky. Roosevelt himself did little to dispel assessments about his ideological sophistication. When a reporter once asked him to what ideology he was committed, he hesitated a moment and said, "I am a Christian and a Democrat."

After his election in 1932 and throughout the New Deal, although FDR came to be credited as a strategic genius, he was also perceived as lacking any sustained political vision. Even the famous sympathetic assessment by Arthur Schlesinger, Jr., that the New Deal was an exercise in experimentation and a middle course between fascism and communism, is based on the premise that the president had no "rigid ideology." Schlesinger did admit that Roosevelt might hire "bold and imaginative subordinates," but he did so in order to "balance the right and the left."

All of these assessments, however, have difficulty in reconciling the major accomplishments of Franklin Roosevelt with the president's alleged opportunism. Although many of FDR's policies are still controversial today, his list of achievements suggests some leadership pattern beyond strategical talent. He extricated the nation from the most harrowing crisis (save that of the Civil War) in its history. He was the architect of the American welfare state. He guided America toward confrontation and victory against two brutal powers who were on the verge of bringing the world to its knees. Rexford Tugwell, a New Deal official who could sometimes be quite critical of the president, concluded on the basis of these accomplishments:

> We are a lucky people. We have had leaders when the national life was at stake. If it had not been for Washington we might not have become a nation; if it had not been for Lincoln we might have been split in two; if it had not been for this later democrat we might have succumbed to dictatorship.

Roosevelt openly stressed his willingness to improvise. One pertinent example is the Oglethorpe University campaign speech, in which he said that the Depression could only be defeated through "bold, persistent experimentation." On the other hand, while Roosevelt had many counselors (his "Brain Trust" was a systematic effort to utilize intellectuals in policy formation), he never brought any of them into his confidence. Schlesinger concluded that "no one could guess" what Roosevelt really thought in his "rare moments of solitude, when he could not evade the ultimates." Washington, too, hid his own feelings behind the reserve of the republican hero, as did Lincoln, even as he brooded about the purpose of the Civil War. Roosevelt, however, projected an image of neither sternness nor tragedy. His was the face of geniality. FDR could, of course, project anger and resolve but his most dominant persona was one of the "happy warrior," a term he helped invent for his mentor, Al Smith, governor of New York and presidential candidate in 1928. His campaign song was "Happy Days Are Here Again," and in 1932 Roosevelt's jaunty smile was a stark contrast to Hoover's glumness.

Like Coolidge with his silent demeanor, in all probability FDR really *was* a cheerful person. Nonetheless, FDR's persona of the genial country squire often led his adversaries to underestimate his abilities while at the same time giving hope to Americans, who were struggling with the economic crisis. Another aspect of Roosevelt's approach to leadership helps explain his successes. His air of supreme confidence was supplemented by an extremely adept use of previous presidents to justify and explain his policies. As we have seen, many presidents sought to use Jefferson in support of their policies. FDR employed not only the symbol of Jefferson but also those of Jackson and even Abraham Lincoln. This is not to say that FDR's readings of these presidents were not themselves opportunistic and inaccurate. However, this systematic and serial use of presidential exemplars kept FDR in close touch with the parameters of American political culture. While many were more interested in imitating policies from abroad, FDR's attention to these former presidents in the 1930s provided an anchor for his improvisational talents.

The basic outlines of Roosevelt's approach can be found in his first speech in the contest for the presidential nomination. The address is quite brief and was delivered nationally on radio. Raymond Moley, an early trusted adviser in the candidate's Brain Trust who broke with FDR in 1936, composed the draft for the speech, which was organized around the theme of the "forgotten man." The candidate argued that Americans had experience with crisis and experience with planning that could be used to fight the current Depression. In World War I, America had faced a challenge and responded to it by a national commitment to planning for war production. But Hoover had "either forgotten or does not want to remember" the success of this effort. In that war the United States had had a "great plan" because it was built "from the bottom to top and not from the top to bottom." Hoover had begun to plan for the "big banks, the railroads and the corporations," but, FDR asked, "How much do the shallow thinkers realize that approximately one-half of our population, 50 or 60 million people, earn a living by farming or in small towns . . . ?" Roosevelt did not say exactly what kind of plan he had in mind, but he assured his radio audience that it would focus on and include the participation of "Main Street," "farm owners," "little local banks," and "local loan companies."

The themes intimated in the Forgotten Man speech—the American precedent for planning, the need for democratic action, the focus on problems facing the middle class, the charge that the Depression was being prolonged (if not precipitated) by elites—all these themes were drawn upon in the 1932 campaign and, indeed, throughout the entire New Deal. In a Jefferson Day address in St. Paul, Minnesota, FDR spoke of the role of the federal government in promoting economic policy. He described the men he called two great planners, Jefferson and Hamilton, and their respective approaches. Hamilton, though a "financial genius," believed that only certain sections of the country and certain individuals were fit to conduct government. Jefferson, on the other hand, rode across the young country on horseback, "slowly and laboriously accumulating an understanding of the people in this country." He learned of the "yearnings and lack of opportunity, the hopes and fears of millions" of Americans and built a political party in support of the common principles of the people.

Roosevelt then briefly described the conflicts between Hamiltonian and Jeffersonian approaches throughout American history. He called for a "new concert of interests" based on "imaginative and purposeful planning" in accord with the model provided by Jefferson. The speech contained few examples of just what was to be planned, although FDR mentioned his policies as governor on the use of public power on the St. Lawrence River. He went on to assure his audience that he did not have in mind an "economic life completely planned and regimented."

The Concert of Interest address was a brilliant speech, even if Roosevelt's reading of history may have been suspect. Aside from articulating the themes mentioned above, he outlined a general approach to the Depression that was different from Hoover's in terms of American political thought. A new administration would resemble more the revolution of 1800 than the Russian model that was of increasing interest to the early Depression writers. FDR had appropriated the Jeffersonian symbol, one of the most powerful in American political culture, as a model for national reform. The conservative opposition within the Democratic Party had come to regard themselves as "Jefferson Democrats," and Hoover himself had cited Jefferson as proof of the need for local governments to solve problems. But Roosevelt asserted that Jefferson was "no local American." Jefferson had galvanized a whole people under threat of domination by aristocrats; he had been "willing to stake his fortunes on the stroke of a pen" when he purchased Louisiana, which "trebled the size of the nation over night." Not so subtly Roosevelt intimated that Hoover was the modern-day Hamilton.

In his speeches Roosevelt suggested the solution to the problem of the Great Depression could be found within the symbols and methods already embodied within the American political tradition. He also "Americanized" the sources of the Depression. It would have been surprising, indeed, in an election campaign if FDR had not blamed the Depression on Hoover. FDR used Hoover's own analogy of the Depression as a storm sweeping across American shores from Europe to attack the Hoover administration's competence: "[T]here are glimpses through the clouds, of troubled officers pacing the deck wondering what to do. . . ." But the candidate's critique quickly broadened not only to include Hoover and the Republicans but also the entire corporate business elite.

Roosevelt's Oglethorpe University address, which is famous for its injunction that the country required "bold, persistent experimentation," also recalled the "rose-colored days" of the 1920s when Americans were told they "could sit back and read in comfort the hieroglyphics called stock quotations which proclaimed that their wealth was mounting miraculously without any work on their part." This prosperity, said Roosevelt, was a "mirage" fostered by financial leaders and men in high public office. Corporate leaders had engaged in "gigantic waste," "superfluous duplication," "questionable methods of raising capital," "continual scrapping of useful equipment," and the depression of wages despite huge profits. They were "selfish" and "opportunist." In his nomination acceptance speech, FDR described the 1920s as a "period of loose thinking, descending morals, and an era of selfishness." "Let us be frank to admit," he told the delegates, "many of us too have made obeisance to Mammon."

Late in the 1932 campaign, Roosevelt gave a speech to a group of business leaders in San Francisco and pulled all these elements into a general philosophical approach to government. The Commonwealth Club address has been treated skeptically by historians. Arthur Schlesinger, Jr., for instance, admits it was a powerful speech but believes it represented speechwriter Adolph Berle's thinking more than it did Roosevelt's. Yet there is evidence that FDR encouraged his speechwriters to draft an address that would directly refute Hoover's philosophical understanding of individualism. The original title of the address was "Individualism: Romantic and Realistic."

The speech is structured around sets of pairs. Roosevelt compares the growth of central governments to that of centralized industry. He compares the rise of European monarchies to the new "princes of property." He compares Jefferson to Hamilton. He compares the needs of a country with a frontier to those of one whose "plant is built." The theme of the essay deals with one of the central preoccupations of political philosophy: How are rights preserved and exploitation avoided across time?

Often overlooked in analyses of the address is Roosevelt's presentation of great leaders. They are portrayed here in ambivalent terms, not unlike in Lincoln's Lyceum address. Lincoln had spoken of the need for men of great ambition at the time of the founding and of the threat they posed in an established republic. Roosevelt recounts the contributions of the "creators of national government" in Europe. "The people preferred the master far away to the exploitation and cruelty of the smaller master near at hand." The people, by and large, wanted "a strong stable state to keep the peace, to put the unruly nobleman in his place, and to permit the bulk of individuals to live safely." There were, however, "ruthless" men, and when there came a growing feeling that "ambition and ruthlessness" had "served their term," the people sought a "balancing—a limiting force." Roosevelt describes the new institutional forms created for this purpose—town councils, trade guilds, national parliaments, constitutions, and elections—as well as the formulation of the tenet that rulers bore a responsibility to their subjects.

America had come into existence as part of this struggle. Our own institutions reflected this concern with the oppressive consequences of centralized political power. But new kinds of creators came to fulfill a similar role in this country. Roosevelt traces their emergence to the Industrial Revolution and the "new dream" it created:

> The dream was the dream of an economic machine, able to raise the standard of living for everyone; to bring luxury within the reach of the humblest; to annihilate distance by steam power and later by electricity, and to release everyone from the drudgery of the heaviest manual toil.

But there was a "shadow over the dream." "To be made real, it required use of the talents of men of tremendous will and tremendous ambition. . . ." The American people accepted these men "fearlessly" and "cheerfully." "It was thought that no price was too high to pay for the advantages which we could draw from a finished industrial system." The methods of these men were "not scrutinized with too much care." The "financial Titans" were "always ruthless, often wasteful, and frequently corrupt." FDR estimates that investors paid for railroads three times over, but the railroads were built and "we still have them today." With this task now completed, however, these American creators threaten the people like the old feudal barons: "great uncontrolled and irresponsible units of power within the State" are a danger to everyone's ability to earn a living.

As in all of Roosevelt's speeches, he turned to Jefferson for a solution. Jefferson had beaten back the Hamiltonian challenge that only a "great and strong group of central institutions" led by "a small group of able and public spirited citizens" could best govern. In its place Jefferson had devised two sets of rights. Those of "personal competency," such as freedom of speech, required limitations on governmental power. Property rights, so argues Roosevelt, are historically variable in their implementation: "But even Jefferson realized that the exercise of the property rights might so interfere with the rights of the individual that the Government,

without whose assistance the property rights could not exist, must intervene, not to destroy individualism, but to protect it." Now a "re-appraisal
of values" was necessary. FDR's solution is presented in Jeffersonian
terms. A new "social contract" is required. "Every man has a right to life;
and this means that he has also a right to make a comfortable living."
"Every man has a right to his own property; which means a right to be
assured, to the fullest extent available, in the safety of his savings." If the
economic elite cannot meet these requirements, the "Government must
be swift to enter and protect the public interest." The "apparent Utopia
which Jefferson imagined for us in 1776" was still obtainable.

Despite the philosophical smoothness of Roosevelt's transition from
the rights of competency to the new social contract, the New Deal in practice struggled mightily in implementing the new order. Emergency legislation stabilizing the financial sector lessened panic. The attempt to form
a "concert of interests" in the form of the National Recovery Administration (NRA), however, proved to be a failure. Roosevelt seems to have
abandoned this approach even before it was declared unconstitutional by
the Supreme Court in 1935. The idea had been to reach an accord with
corporations in which wage-and-price agreements would be set by the
government in exchange for exemption from anti-monopoly restrictions.
Aid to farmers in the form of the Agricultural Adjustment Administration (AAA) was more successful, but critics were often astounded by the
policy of reducing food production in such a time of need. The president
spent millions of dollars on various relief projects. Its participants almost
uniformly agreed that such projects saved the lives of their families, and
the range of public works was quite impressive. Unemployed individuals
hired by the government built medical centers, water supply systems,
amphitheaters, bridges, and airfields; they also performed plays and
wrote books. FDR always regarded these programs as temporary, twice
reducing funding for them before they were all eventually dismantled by
more conservative Congresses in the late 1930s.

The new rights to make a living and to have safe savings accounts
were not pursued until 1935. Roosevelt was now faced with significant
challenges from both the right and the left. Huey Long, Democratic senator and former governor of Louisiana, complained that the NRA was not
Jeffersonian at all but rather a scheme to regulate small business. Although
Long insisted that he had "never read a line of Marx or Henry George or
any of them economists," the plan showed an amazing ideological ingenuity. Like all political panaceas, its attraction lay in its apparent practicality
and simplicity. Long proposed a tax on all income over $1 million that
would be used to finance what we would call today a negative income tax
(Long called it a homestead allowance) of $5,000 and an annual income of
$2,000. Long spoke in great detail about this capital endowment and the
benefits it could provide. A radio, washing machine, and automobile
could be in every home. The plan had certain ideological affinities to the

Jeffersonian idea of property for every American and plans in the Jacksonian era for redistributing private wealth. There was no hint of public ownership in the plan. Hence "Share the Wealth" steered away from conventional socialism, and there was the beauty of the absence of bureaucratic structure. At least as Long saw it, checks were to be sent to the government by the wealthy and mailed out to millions of Americans.

When Long died at the hands of an assassin in 1935, FDR was spared the prospect of him as a presidential candidate. But FDR still borrowed heavily from aspects of Long's program through his focus on the maldistribution of wealth in America. In his 1935 annual address to Congress, the president spoke of "weeding out" the "over-privileged" and shortly later proposed his own "soak-the-rich" tax plan. FDR also redefined the goals of the New Deal in response to a reporter's question as a way of providing people with "more of the good things of life, to give them a greater distribution not only of wealth in the narrow terms" but also of "places to go in the summertime recreation; to give them assurance that they are not going to starve in their old age. . . ."

In regard to the last objective cited by Roosevelt, a major challenge to the New Deal emerged. Dr. Francis E. Townsend led a movement for a national pension plan that attracted widespread support, not only among the elderly but also among those that saw it as a wedge to end the Depression. Townsend, unlike Long, was a man of quiet, even scholarly, presence. (E. B. White uncharitably described him as a "skinny bespectacled little savior, with a big jaw, like the Tin Woodman.") Townsend proposed a monthly pension of $200 to all Americans over the age of sixty to be financed by a 2 percent business tax. The only catch was that each retiree must spend the money within the month. "And mind you," the doctor told his audiences, "we don't care a rap what you spend it for!" The idea, of course, was to provide care for the elderly while at the same time creating consumer spending and a demand for business activity. This was a principle that many New Deal economists from Gardiner Means to Rexford Tugwell championed in general terms. But the attraction of the Townsend plan rested on the same basic ideological terms as the proposals of Long and others: the redistribution of wealth without nationalization and bureaucratic planning.

As with so many New Deal critics, FDR outflanked the Townsend movement with his own plan. It was to be financed by a tax on the first $3,000 of workers' incomes, not solely from taxes on business; it exempted from coverage large groups of workers, including farm laborers and domestics. Initially, only 60 percent of the workforce was eligible for coverage. In fact, William E. Leuchtenberg, a sympathetic Roosevelt biographer, described it as an "astonishingly inept and conservative piece of legislation." But it was more than enough to derail the Townsendites, who tried to create a third-party movement in 1936, failed, and then disintegrated as a result of bickering and scandal among their leaders.

Roosevelt's efforts to defuse his critics were based less on Jefferson than on another presidential exemplar, Andrew Jackson. To FDR, Jackson was a man who the "average American deeply and fundamentally understood." The American people "loved him well because they understood him well." Yet, Jackson seemed to be hated—by the "great media," by "haughty and sterile" intellectuals, by "musty" reactionaries, by "hollow and outworn" traditionalists. Indeed, it "seemed that all were against him—all but the people of the United States." Roosevelt argued that the same kind of elites (whom he called "economic royalists") who had attacked Jackson in the 1830s were now ready to "gang up against the people's liberties" one hundred years later. If, like Jackson, FDR had become the symbol of those who would attempt to stop their effort to "regiment people, their labor and their property," he "welcomed their hatred."

In Little Rock, Arkansas, Roosevelt added the theme of youthful vigor to his passionate devotion to Jackson. He reminded his audience that it was Jefferson who had "the courage, the backbone" to purchase the Louisiana Territory so that it might be peopled by "hardy pioneers." But it was from their "contemporary and counselor" Jackson that Arkansasians understood that their "fellow frontiersman" made "possible the first truly democratic Administration in our history." Arkansas, which became a state in the last year of Jackson's presidency, represented a Westward expansion that flowed "with the vigor of a living stream" through the "stagnant marshes" of a seaboard oligarchy. Prior to this movement West, power in America with rare exception rested "in the hands of men who, by birth or education, belonged to a comparatively small group." Jackson, as the epitome of the frontier spirit that brought men into the "Arkansas wilderness," inaugurated "an era of truer democracy" much to the "widespread apprehension" of the "so-called guardians of the Republic." The "spirit of the frontier hushing bee" is found today in carefully constructed statutes of the welfare state that protected American citizens from rapacious "economic royalists."

After winning reelection in 1936 by a record 523 electoral votes to Republican Al Landon's 8, Roosevelt made one of his few strategical errors. He proposed legislation that would permit the president to add a Supreme Court justice for each one over the age of 70. Roosevelt's rationale was that new jurists were necessary in an age of rapid change. However, everyone knew that the real reason for the president's proposal was because the Supreme Court had declared several New Deal bills unconstitutional. The president also suggested that conservative Democrats be replaced by liberals in the upcoming 1938 primary race. Roosevelt was frustrated by those Democrats who failed to support his "uncompromisingly liberal" 1936 platform. This attempt at party realignment was a major departure for the president whose recently hugely successful "New Deal Coalition" was based on an open-tent strategy that encouraged many disparate groups, from intellectuals to city machine bosses, from rural farmers to urban ethnic union members, and from African Americans to white Southerners, to vote Democratic.

In these cases, exemplars not of Roosevelt's choosing foiled his efforts. To Republicans and even some Democrats, his efforts were reminiscent of the behavior of European dictators. The Court Reorganization Bill came to be called the "court packing" plan, and FDR's efforts at party realignment were considered "party purges." Roosevelt was not completely unsuccessful in either effort, however. Although a Democratic Congress never passed his court plan, one justice, Owen Roberts, who previously voted with the conservative court majority, switched to support the liberals. Through subsequent retirements, Roosevelt ended up appointing nine new justices. Some liberals did win in Democratic primaries with FDR's support (including Representative Lyndon Johnson), but in others conservatives held on (including Tydings of Maryland, against whom the president personally campaigned). Roosevelt spent huge amounts of political capital in these efforts. He used the rhetorical device of calling Jackson on the phone. "Old Hickory" advised Roosevelt to fight on and not to get "scared . . . because you don't have majorities so big that you can go to sleep without sentries." By 1938, however, the New Deal was, for all practical purposes, dead. The media began to speculate about new candidates for the 1940 presidential election.

The rise of fascism, however, provided the president with a new political arena as he began to focus on international issues. In the early 1930s Roosevelt's interests were almost entirely domestic, although he did promote the Good Neighbor policy for Latin America. He was an internationalist early in his career but did not actively oppose the Neutrality Act of 1935, which required an arms embargo when states of belligerency occurred, despite objections from Secretary of State Cordell Hull. Roosevelt's Chautauqua address of 1936, in which he warned of pursuing "fool's gold" in seeking to trade with belligerents and described "men coughing out their gassed lungs," is one of the strongest antiwar speeches ever delivered by a U.S. president.

In October of 1937, however, the president spoke of the "breakdown of all international law and order" and suggested the possibility that collective action might be necessary to "quarantine" aggressors. In his controversial decision to seek reelection to a third term, Roosevelt warned that the world crisis involved an ethical choice of "moral decency versus the firing squad" and compared the crisis he faced to the one faced by Abraham Lincoln in 1860. Roosevelt began to cite Lincoln as a supplement to his Jacksonian references as early as 1936 when he began to emphasize Lincoln's modest class origins. Lincoln could not have come from "any class that did not know, through daily struggle, the grim realities of life." In his 1938 Jackson Day address, Roosevelt spoke of Lincoln as a man "scorned for his uncouthness, his simplicity, his homely stories and his solicitude for the little man." Lincoln's enemies were the same as Jackson's (and by analogy to FDR's own). "Gold speculators in Wall Street," a "minority unwilling to support people and their government unless the government would leave them free to pursue their private gains," were the declared enemies of Jackson/Lincoln/FDR. Had Lincoln lived, there would not have been the "uninspired commercial era" that followed the Civil War.

In 1940, Roosevelt hired Robert Sherwood, the author of a Broadway play about Lincoln, as a speechwriter and encouraged the press to follow up his analogy that, just as Lincoln had faced a nation half slave and half free, so the president now faced a world similarly divided. In August, the president paused in the middle of a press conference. He pulled out Sandburg's *Lincoln: The War Years* and read two passages. One passage included a quote by Lincoln from 1862, complaining that "the people have not yet made up their minds that we are at war with the South." The other, which was reported to have taken place a year later, was a complaint directed toward Union General George B. McClellan, whom Lincoln fired, and his supporters: "They have no idea that the War is to be carried on and put through by hard, tough fighting, that it will hurt somebody; and no headway is going to be made while this delusion lasts." Roosevelt noted what he called an "interesting parallel . . . Lincoln's belief that this country hadn't waked up to the fact that they had a war to win, and Lincoln saw what was going on." When a reporter asked how his lead ought to read, the president answered, "I'd say, 'President quotes Lincoln—And Draws Parallel.'"

His Republican opponent, Wendell Wilkie, rejected these comparisons to Lincoln and compared Roosevelt's ambitions to those of European dictators. He focused particularly on Roosevelt's decision to break the two-term restriction that had been observed since the time of Washington. The highlight of Wilkie's rhetoric was a speech made in his home town of Coffeeville, Kansas. For Wilkie, the small town was the repository of "freedom," "equality," and "democracy." The philosophy of democracy was nurtured and taught and preserved across generations at this level. "Our mothers taught us to be honest, polite, to be pleasant and kind . . . our fathers to be brave. . . ." The New Dealers spoke in the language of democracy and portrayed themselves as "great 'defenders' of democracy," but they are all "cynics who scoff at our simple virtues . . . and govern us with catchphrases." They have used relief money to manipulate votes; they "terrorize" their opponents by leaking untruths to newspapers; they "purge and purge" those who try to be independent of the "New Deal machine." Because they do not trust in a philosophy of democracy they "have concentrated power in their own hands." Roosevelt "may not want dictatorship," but "in his hands our traditions are not safe." He had "declared forty emergencies in the past seven years." Put on the defensive by Wilkie's charge that his reelection would mean that the United States would be at war in six months, Roosevelt pledged that "your boys are not going to be sent into any foreign wars."

Roosevelt won the election by a large margin, despite concerns about breaking the two-term tradition. After his reelection, however, in a series of measured steps, the president prepared the people for war. To defend nations fighting the Nazis in Europe, Roosevelt had extracted commitments from a reluctant Congress and an isolationist public in the six months before Pearl Harbor. He told the people in a fireside chat that the lend-lease arrangement with Britain was necessary to prevent its fall to the Nazis. FDR admitted that the United States risked war as it prepared to become the "arsenal for democracy." In his annual message to Congress the president repeated his argument that the threat of war now facing the country was unlike any other except the Civil War. Roosevelt said that even in World War I there was "only a small threat of danger to our own American future," but today "the future of all the American Republics is in danger." Without the protection of the British Navy the United States would not immediately be subject to invasion, but only because strategic bases would be required to facilitate troop landings. Thus, the first phase of an invasion would occur in Latin America through the activities of "secret agents and their dupes," just as it had already occurred in Norway. No negotiation is possible, despite those who "with sounding brass and tinkling cymbal preach the 'ism' of appeasement," for "no realistic American can expect from a dictator's peace international generosity. . . ."

So imminent was the crisis, in Roosevelt's review of the world situation, that he also declared what amounted to war aims:

The first is freedom of speech and expression—everywhere in the world.

The second is freedom of every person to worship God in his own way—everywhere in the world.

The third is freedom from want . . . everywhere in the world.

The fourth is freedom from fear . . . everywhere in the world.

The "four freedoms," included in the Atlantic charter and repeated throughout the war, are often interpreted as part of Roosevelt's progressive heritage. According to James McGregor Burns (*Soldier of Freedom*), the president had "picked up Woodrow Wilson's fallen banner, fashioned new symbols and programs to realize old ideals of peace and democracy. . . ." Indeed, FDR had already begun to elaborate a defense of America's participation in the World War as part of his attack on the isolationists and the charge that America had been drawn into the conflict by munitions dealers. But the four freedoms owed much to the Lincoln exemplar. In his debates with Douglas, Lincoln had insisted that the principles of Jefferson's Declaration of Independence applied to African Americans over his opponent's objections that he was extending the meaning of the document. Roosevelt's Jeffersonian-inspired freedoms not only were overlaid with Progressive and New Deal understandings but also involved a globalization of the Declaration—"everywhere in the world." Roosevelt declared in 1941 that he was now "Dr. Win the War" instead of "Dr. New Deal." That August, with British leader Winston Churchill, he defined Allied war aims in the Atlantic Charter in terms roughly equivalent to the four freedoms outlined in his address.

In his prosecution of the war, Roosevelt tended to follow the same honest-broker strategy he had undertaken in rebuilding the Democratic Party. In fact, he compared his role as commander in chief during the war to that of a "juggler" who "never let my right hand know what my left does. . . ." In a cryptic comment reminiscent of Lincoln's remarks to Horace Greeley about slavery and the Civil War, Roosevelt said: "I may have one policy for Europe and one diametrically opposite for North and South America. I may be entirely inconsistent, and furthermore I am perfectly willing to mislead and tell untruths if it will help win the war." He extended lend-lease aid to the Soviet Union when it was invaded by Germany and added the Soviets to an Allied coalition with the British, gave assurances to the Soviets that the Allies would open a second front against Germany in 1942, and generally refused to deal with divisive questions during the war such as territorial disputes or questions of colonial independence. FDR envisioned a post-war world built on cooperation between the great powers. This would be the animating idea behind the creation of the United Nations.

During the war Roosevelt's opponents found it almost impossible to challenge his domination of the political agenda, despite some regrettable policies and dangerous threats. In 1942, by executive order, he incarcerated U.S. citizens of Japanese descent and told Congress that should they fail to pass economic stabilization legislation he would act himself. Although reelected to a fourth term in 1944, Roosevelt was seriously ill, and he died on April 12, 1945, shortly after attending a meeting with Allied leaders at Yalta. Although there was initial congressional support for these accords, the almost immediate advent of the Cold War led to a reevaluation of the utility and wisdom of FDR's policy of cooperation and compromise with the Soviet Union.

Although Roosevelt is rated along with Washington and Lincoln as the greatest of presidents, his legacy is still a controversial one, owing in large part to the fact that two major initiatives of his administrations—the welfare sate and international intervention—remain contested policies to Americans. Certainly, Americans readily accept the need for emergency economic measures in the Depression, as well as some other programs such as Social Security, and they are prepared to justify the "Good War" against fascism. Nevertheless, Roosevelt pushed against certain tendencies in American political culture that celebrate economic individualism and isolationism. He successfully inoculated himself against these sensibilities, reassuring Americans during this time in office through his genial persona and his improvisational use of past presidents. Presidents without these talents and/or without the crises FDR faced have difficulty imitating FDR's successes.

SUMMARY AND COMMENT

When Franklin Roosevelt died suddenly in April of 1945, the presidency had been transformed once again. There were now 1.4 million federal employees in a variety of new agencies and commissions. (As late as 1931 there were only 600,000.) Grover Cleveland issued an average of 35 executive orders a year; FDR issued 285. Nineteenth-century presidents rarely spoke directly to the public; FDR initiated a series of "fireside chats" in which he addressed the public at large on policy issues ranging from unemployment to the situation in Europe. The presidency was now the center of legislative initiatives. Roosevelt's "first one hundred days," in which a record number of his recommendations were passed by Congress, became the benchmark of success or failure for later presidents. From 1933 to 1944 Roosevelt signed 369 executive agreements (commitments made by the president with another nation that do not require Senate approval). By contrast, in the 100-year period from 1789 to 1889 there were only 265. Perhaps the most dramatic example of the exercise of the president's power in foreign affairs was the Lend-Lease Act passed in 1941, which gave Roosevelt the authority to sell, lease, or exchange articles to any country he deemed vital to American security. Most of the $20 billion in funds expended went to Great Britain, but 38 countries received money over the next four years.

Although some scholars credit Roosevelt as the "first modern president," numerous features of modernization are evident in each of his predecessors since McKinley. War and industrialization steadily pushed federal personnel upward. McKinley used the tactic of "going public" on tariff legislation, as did Theodore Roosevelt on the Hepburn Act, and Wilson dramatized the State of the Union Address by delivering the speech in person. Wilson systematically attempted to place the president at the center of legislation through his efforts to move the political system toward a parliamentary model. McKinley attempted to prepare America for its role as a great power in his takeover of the Philippines, Teddy Roosevelt with his diplomatic initiatives, and Wilson with his failed effort to convince the Senate to enter the League of Nations. The Lever Act for a short time gave Wilson authority to regulate aspects of the economy that the president deemed necessary to the war effort. A major reorganization of the executive branch took place during the Harding administration. Although their visions varied from Coolidge's supply-side theories to FDR's New Deal, most presidents from McKinley onward accepted the role of the nation's chief economic planner.

Perhaps most significantly, the modern presidents approached the challenge of the presidency with a spirit of innovation that was lacking, or at least less pronounced, in other periods. Each embraced new technological advances, particularly in communications, with imaginative responses; and each was even willing to methodically craft their public personalities to advance their agenda, whether it be the image of the "Bull Moose," "Silent Cal," or the genial and confident FDR. When modern presidents failed, the causes could often be traced to their inability to respond quickly to changes in the office, the economy, or the world, as was the case with Wilson and Hoover.

On the other hand, it is important to note that modernization was never completely or willingly accepted by other institutions and/or the public. When Congress approved the recommendations of the Brownlow Commission, which acknowledged that the president needed help in governing the federal bureaucracy, it insisted that the Civil Service Commission and several other agencies remain independent from the new Executive Office of the President. Congress also limited the president's authority to reorganize to two years. Despite his best efforts, Woodrow Wilson was never able to shift the American political system to what he regarded as a more rational parliamentary model, nor was Hoover able to successfully apply the methods he used to feed starving Europeans to the problems of the Depression. Even FDR was unable to persuade Congress to bring the Supreme Court out of the "horse and buggy" age, much as he was unable to persuade the American public to purge conservatives from the Democratic Party in order to produce a more rational party system.

One of the major features of modernity in general is the paradoxical position in which we all find ourselves: There is a sense of individual freedom to experiment, find rational solutions to problems free of tradition and even reconstruct our own personas; yet on the other hand, we often find ourselves trapped by large, impersonal political and economic forces that Max Weber called an "iron cage." The modern presidents often seem to exhibit this contradiction. Largely freed from the restrictions of the founding, partisan, and eclipsed presidencies, they frequently still found themselves trapped by new forces and sometimes even by old ones.

Bibliographic Essay

For general accounts of modernity and modernization, see: Frederick R. Paul, *Modern and Modernism* (New York: Atheneum, 1988) and Paul Johnson, *The Birth of the Modern: World Society 1815–1830* (New York: Harper Collins, 1991). Fred I. Greenstein's discusses FDR's the transformation of the presidency into its "modern" form: "In Search of the Modern Presidency," in Greenstein, ed., *Leadership in the Modern Presidency* (Cambridge: Harvard University Press, 1988), pp. 296–352. Noel Jacob Kent presents a fascinating analysis of *fin de siecle* America, including a review of the presidential election of 1900, in *America in 1900* (London: M. E. Sharpe, 2000).

Leroy Ashby's *William Jennings Bryan* (Boston: Twayne Publishers, 1987) is a sympathetic account of the Great Commoner. A convenient collection of Bryan's speeches appears in Ray Ginger, ed., *William Jennings Bryan: Selections* (Indianapolis, IN.: Bobbs-Merrill, 1967). Paul Glad's *McKinley, Bryan and the People* (Philadelphia: J. B. Lippincott, 1964) is a fascinating analysis of the 1896 election that can be read along with Bryan's own account, *The First Battle* (Chicago: W. B. Conkey, 1896). Lewis L. Gould offers the view that McKinley was the first modern president in his *The Presidency of William McKinley* (Lawrence: University of Kansas Press, 1980). Richard Loomis discusses McKinley's use of telephone as an instrument of command in "The White House Telephone and Crisis Management," *U.S. Naval Institute Proceedings* 45 (1969). Gerald F. Linderman's *The Mirror of War* (Ann Arbor: University of Michigan Press, 1974) attempts to place the Spanish-American War in the context of changing American values. Also see David F. Healy, *U.S. Expansionism: The Imperialist Urge in the 1890s* (Madison: University of Wisconsin Press, 1970).

The fascination with Theodore Roosevelt's persona has led to many excellent studies. A few are: H. W. Brands, *The Last Romantic* (New York: Basic Books, 1997); William Henry Harbaugh, *Power and Responsibility: The Life and Times of Theodore Roosevelt* (New York: Farrar, Straus, 1961); Edmund Morgan, *The Rise of Theodore Roosevelt* (New York: William Morrow, 1992) and *Theodore Rex* (New York: Morrow, 2001); and Louis Achincloss, *Theodore Roosevelt* (New York: Times Books, 2001). Harbaugh is willing to offer criticism of Roosevelt's impetuousness and Achincloss emphasizes what he regards as the datedness of Roosevelt's values. John Milton Cooper, Jr.'s *The Warrior and the Priest* (New York: Reynal, 1963) examines the TR–Wilson rivalry with special emphasis upon their contrasting political styles. William Manners's *TR and Will: A Friendship that Split the Republican Party* (New York: Harcourt, Brace and World, 1969) examines another of Roosevelt's contested relationships. Taft offers his own views on the constitutional limitations of office in *The President and his Powers* (New York Columbia University Press, 1916). Also see Henry F. Pringle's thorough and sympathetic *The Life and Times of William Howard Taft*, 2 vols. (Hamden, CT: Archon Books, 1964).

Presidential scholars have been fascinated with both Wilson's successes and failures. Neils Aage Thorsen provides extremely astute analyses of Wilson's early views in *The Political Thought of Woodrow Wilson, 1875–1910* (Princeton: Princeton University Press, 1988). Daniel D. Stid also focuses on Wilson's political thought in *The President as Statesman* (Lawrence: University Press of Kansas, 1998) and provides a sympathetic account of Wilson's ideas on parliamentary democracy and party responsibility. Also see Kendrick A. Clemens's *Woodrow Wilson: World Statesman* (Boston: Twayne, 1987). For differing views on Wilson's great failure, see Thomas A. Bailey, *Woodrow Wilson and the Great Betrayal* (New York: Macmillan, 1945) and Herbert F. Margulies, *The Mild Reservationists and the League of Nations Controversy in the Senate* (Columbia: University of Missouri Press, 1989). Herbert Hoover's conclusions are also interesting: *The Ordeal of Woodrow Wilson* (Washington, DC: Woodrow Wilson Center, 1958).

The Great Depression has provided a noticeable negative background to the study of each of the New Era presidents. Robert K. Murray's *Warren G. Harding and His Times* (New York: McGraw-Hill, 1968) is one exception. He makes the argument for emergence of a "new" Harding before his death. His assessment can be compared with the more negative views offered by Eugene P. Trani and David L. Wilson, *The Presidency of Warren G. Harding* (Lawrence: University Press of Kansas, 1977). John Earl Jones has presented an excellent collection of essays on

Coolidge: Calvin Coolidge and the Coolidge Era (Washington, DC: Library of Congress, 1998). The essays by Robert H. Ferrell ("Calvin Coolidge, the Man and President") and George H. Nash ("The 'Great Enigma' and the 'Great Engineer'") are particularly insightful. Paul Johnson provides the astute characterization of Coolidge as the ultimate "minimalist" politician in his essay, "Calvin Coolidge and the Last Arcadia" in the same volume. Donald L. McCoy explores Coolidge's political style in *Calvin Coolidge: The Quiet President* (Lawrence: University Press of Kansas, 1977) Coolidge's post-presidential memoir, *The Autobiography of Calvin Coolidge* (New York: Cosmopolitan Book Corporation, 1931), is a perfect illustration of his "silent" persona.

Herbert Hoover's major speeches are available in a reprint of a 1934 edition: *State Papers and Other Public Writings of Herbert Hoover*, 2 vols. (White Plains, NY: Kraus International Publications, 1970). Also see Hoover's *The New Day* (Stanford, CA: Stanford University Press, 1928) for speeches in his 1928 presidential campaign. For Hoover as a laissez-faire conservative, see Arthur Schlesinger, Jr., *The Crisis of the Old Order* (Boston: Houghton Mifflin, 1955); John Kenneth Galbraith, *The Great Crash* (Boston: Houghton Mifflin, 1955); and Elliot Rosen, *Hoover, Roosevelt and the Brain Trust* (New York: Columbia University Press, 1977). Reevaluations include Carl Degler, "The Ordeal of Herbert Hoover," *Yale Review* 52 (summer 1963); Ellis W. Hawley, "Herbert Hoover and American Corporativism, 1929–1933," in Martin L. Fausold and George T. Mazuzan, eds., *The Hoover Presidency: A Reappraisal* (Albany: State University of New York Press, 1974); William Appleman Williams, *The Contours of American History* (Cleveland, OH: World Publishing, 1961); Joan Hoff Wilson, *Herbert Hoover: Forgotten Progressive* (Prospect Heights, IL: Waveland Press, 1992); and Martin L. Fausold, *The Presidency of Herbert Hoover* (Lawrence: University of Kansas Press, 1985).

There are some extraordinary biographies of Roosevelt and the New Deal: Arthur Schlesinger, Jr., *The Age of Roosevelt*, 3 vols. (Boston: Houghton Mifflin, 1957–1960); Frank Friedel's *Franklin Roosevelt*, 3 vols. (Boston: Little, Brown, 1973); James McGregor Burns's *Roosevelt: The Lion and the Fox* and *Roosevelt: The Soldier of Freedom* (New York: Harcourt Brace Jovanovich, 1956, 1970). The best one-volume accounts are William E. Leuchtenburg's *Franklin Roosevelt and the New Deal* (New York: Harper & Brothers, 1963), and Robert J. McElvaine, *The Great Depression* (New York: Times Books, 1984), although Rexford Tugwell's *The Democratic Roosevelt* (Garden City, NY: Doubleday, 1957) is full of insights. Bruce Miroff in his *Icons of Democracy* (New York: Basic Books, 1993) also has an interpretation of FDR as a leader who typifies "the possibilities and paradoxes in modern democratic leadership" which is well worth reading. Philip Abbott, *The Exemplary Presidency: FDR and the American Political Tradition* (Amherst: University of Massachusetts Press, 1991) focuses on Roosevelt's use of Jefferson, Jackson, and Lincoln in his numerous policy turns.

For assessments of the New Deal and FDR from theoretical perspectives, see Arthur Ekirk, Jr., *Ideologies and Utopias: The Impact of the New Deal in American Thought* (Chicago: University of Chicago Press, 1969); Paul Conkin, *The New Deal* (New York: Crowell, 1967); Harvard Sitkoff, ed., *Fifty Years Later: The New Deal Evaluated* (Philadelphia: Temple University Press, 1985); Morton Frisch, Jr., *Franklin D. Roosevelt* (Boston: Twayne Publishers, 1975); and Steve Fraser and Gary Gerstle, eds., *The Rise and Fall of the New Deal Order* (Princeton: Princeton University Press, 1989). Michael Szalay's *New Deal Modernism* (Durham, NC: Duke University Press, 2000) is an imaginative effort to assess the interaction between literary modernism and the New Deal. Also see "The New Deal Experiments," in Allan Brinkley's *Liberalism and Its Discontents* (Cambridge: Harvard University Press, 1998). One can also discern ideological tensions within the New Deal as well as the enigmatic role of FDR by reading accounts of its participants. Most revealing are Hugh Johnson, *The Blue Eagle from Egg to Earth* (Westport, CT: Greenwood Press, 1968); Rexford Tugwell, *The Brain Trust* (New York: Viking, 1968); Frances Perkins, *The Roosevelt I Knew* (New York: Viking, 1946); and Raymond Moley, *The First New Deal* (New York: Harcourt Brace Jovanovich, 1966).

Warren F. Kimball emphasizes FDR's eclecticism in his approach as commander in chief and as post-war planner. *The Juggler: Franklin Roosevelt as Wartime Statesman* (Princeton: Princeton University Press, 1991). Also see Eric Larrabee, *Commander in Chief: Franklin Delano Roosevelt, His Lieutenants and Their War* (New York: Harper and Row, 1987).

THE COLD WAR PRESIDENCY

Cold War Presidents

President/ Political Party	Term of Office	Vice President	Percent Electoral Vote	Percent Popular Vote
Harry S. Truman (D)	1945–1949	—	—	—
Harry S. Truman (D)	1949–1953	Alben W. Barley	57	50
Dwight D. Eisenhower (R)	1953–1957	Richard M. Nixon	83	55
Dwight D. Eisenhower (R)	1957–1961	Richard M. Nixon	86	57
John F. Kennedy (D)	1961–1963	Lyndon B. Johnson	56	50
Lyndon B. Johnson (D)	1963–1965	—	—	—
Lyndon B. Johnson (D)	1965–1969	Hubert H. Humphrey	90	61
Richard M. Nixon (R)	1969–1973	Spiro T. Agnew	56	43
Richard M. Nixon (R)	1973–1974	Spiro T. Agnew	97	61
Gerald R. Ford (R)	1974–1977	Nelson A. Rockefeller	—	—
Jimmy Carter (D)	1977–1981	Walter F. Mondale	55	50
Ronald Reagan (R)	1981–1985	George H. W. Bush	91	51
Ronald Reagan (R)	1985–1989	George H. W. Bush	98	59
George H. W. Bush (R)	1989–1993	Dan Quayle	69	53

As the Allied forces neared victory, Roosevelt began planning a new international order for the post-war world. To FDR, the peace in 1917 failed because the great world powers failed to act in concerted fashion. Roosevelt led the planning for a more effective world organization than the old League of Nations. The United Nations, created in a series of meetings beginning with the 1944 Dumbarton Oaks Conference, was predicated on the cooperation of the great powers. A Security Council was formed that included five permanent members (Britain, the United States, the Soviet Union, France, and China), each with a veto power. Smaller nations were assigned a subordinate role in the organization through participation in a General Assembly.

By the time of Roosevelt's death in 1945, this design for a new international system based on cooperation of the great powers was seriously disintegrating, and a new international system was emerging far different from the one FDR envisioned. Serious conflicts appeared at the Yalta Conference of the Allied powers in February. Churchill was distrustful of Stalin's motives in Eastern Europe, especially in Poland. Roosevelt acted in the role of mediator. A generally worded communiqué promised interim governments "broadly representative of all democratic elements," followed by "free elections" throughout Eastern Europe (although the Soviets refused to recognize the non-communist Polish government in exile).

At the Potsdam Conference in July, President Harry S. Truman complained publicly about the failure of the Soviets to respect the Yalta accords with regard to Eastern Europe. Stalin's reply to these kinds of objections was that "whoever occupies a territory also imposes his own social system . . . as far as his army can reach. It cannot be otherwise." In March of 1946 Winston Churchill delivered a speech at Westminster College in Fulton, Missouri. He declared: "From Stettin in the Baltic to Trieste in the Adriatic, an iron curtain has descended across Europe."

The first crisis resulting from the antagonism between the United States/Britain and the USSR occurred in Iran. Soviet troops refused to withdraw from northern Iran as scheduled in March. Truman sent an ultimatum to the Soviets, urged Iran to take its case to the United Nations, and informed the press of his actions before he received a response. A week later a troop withdrawal agreement with Iran was announced by the Soviets. American–Soviet disagreements, conflicts, and competition seemed to appear everywhere and on every issue. No agreement on German reparations could be reached. Truman said that the Russians could take what they wanted only from their zone of occupation. Action on a Soviet request for loans from the United States was delayed. Truman refused to permit the Soviets to share in the Allied occupation of Japan. The Red Army's grip on Eastern Europe tightened; there were daily conflicts between the Western Allied forces and Soviet occupation troops in Berlin.

Open war between the Americans and the Soviets seemed imminent. Fortunately, war never did break out, the Soviet Union and its empire dramatically collapsed in 1989–1990, and once again a new international system began to develop. However, for over forty years, with brief periods of limited cooperation, the United States and the Soviet Union fought a "cold war." The international system that emerged from the devastation of World War II created a new world for Americans. The United States, of course, had engaged in international conflicts throughout its history, but participation was sporadic and usually limited to the Western Hemisphere. America had clearly attained great power status as a result of World War I, but it largely refused to accept that role. In the words of John G. Stoessinger (*Crusaders and Pragmatists*), "[O]nce the sinner was punished and evil was purged, the United States could once more withdraw into itself, certain in the knowledge that force had been used in the cause of righteousness. The 'city on the hill' was once again secure." World War II produced an international system that sheared away the competitive multipolar dominance of European powers. Germany was in ruins. Britain and France could no longer maintain their colonial empires. The international system had become bipolar. "Not since Rome and Carthage," concluded Dean Acheson, secretary of state in the Truman administration, "had there been such a polarization of power on this earth."

Multipolar international relations can certainly lead to war (as they did in 1914) and harsh treatment of lesser states, but the number of great powers can also lead to shifting alliances and some political maneuverability through attempts to maintain a "balance of power" among participants. A bipolar system, however, is much more intense and limiting since it leads to the perception on the part of both parties that conflict is a zero-sum game in which one side must win and the other must suffer defeat. In 1947 President Truman outlined the nature of the new struggle in his request to Congress to aid Greece in its fight against communist guerrillas. He announced that "at the present moment in world history nearly every nation must choose between alternative ways of life." One way of life "is based upon the will of the majority, and is distinguished by free institutions . . . the second way of life is based upon the will of the minority . . . terror and oppression."

Bipolarity was not the only feature of this new international system. Air warfare had already revolutionized international politics by making any nation vulnerable to some kind of attack. According to John H. Herz, with the perfected level of airborne destruction reached in World War II, "the roof blew off the territorial state." The development of the atomic bomb radically altered international politics. The United States held a brief monopoly on the weapon. When the Soviets produced their own bomb in 1949, Harold Lasswell, a political scientist, concluded that a U.S.–USSR war at that time "might not end with one Rome but with two Carthages."

Strategists disagree about the extent to which nuclear weapons prevented a war between the new superpowers in the late 1940s and early 1950s, but this much is more certain: For nuclear weapons to function as deterrents against war, neither side could enjoy dramatic advantages in its arsenal or delivery systems. Such a lead might encourage one power to engage in nuclear blackmail (that is, the other side must accede to certain demands or face destruction). Alternatively, one of the powers might risk a "first strike." Only two basic alternatives are available in this dilemma: a mutual arms reduction, or a race on each side to match the perceived future advantages on the other side. The first alternative was largely impossible to achieve throughout most periods of the Cold War. The second led to the creation of what was called a *"mutually assured destruction"* (MAD) strategy—that is, the building of huge arsenals and extensive delivery systems to guarantee a "balance of terror" that would guarantee protection against the temptation to initiate a first strike on both sides.

Another aspect of this new bipolar international system was its pronounced tendency to produce crises. In a two-party conflict, particularly in the nuclear age, miscalculation of the will or strength of the other party creates almost immediately a destabilization of the system. The Cold War is strewn with serious international crises. Stalin miscalculated the West's resolve when he ordered a blockade of Berlin in 1948, and again when he accepted North Korea's plan to militarily unite Korea in 1950. The United States miscalculated the chances of China's entry into the war in Korea. Frequently, conflicts in the Third World would not bend to bipolar resolution, as the United States learned in Vietnam and the USSR in Afghanistan. In one instance, the Cuban Missile Crisis of 1962, the two superpowers came to the brink of nuclear war.

Nine presidents served during the Cold War. There were significant differences among them in terms of personality, ideology, and party, as well as variations in strategy. Eisenhower and Reagan preferred to delegate policy implementation to subordinates, while Kennedy and Carter managed affairs more closely. Truman, Kennedy, and Johnson pursued liberal domestic agendas during the Cold War, and Eisenhower, Nixon, and Reagan conservative ones. Four were Democrats, and four Republicans. Many developed major policy initiatives toward the Soviet Union. The Truman Doctrine, which declared support for anti-communist governments worldwide in order to contain Soviet advances, was the first such effort. Eisenhower offered the strategy of "brinkmanship" and "massive retaliation," Nixon of "détente," and Reagan announced support for anti-communist insurgent movements. No Cold War president, however, questioned the moral and political objectives of the struggle, and each vowed to continue the general policies of their predecessors.

How did this long conflict effect the American presidency? Certainly, the office itself expanded dramatically. The need to respond to a permanent military threat led to the creation of a much larger executive branch. New agencies were added, such as the Central Intelligence Agency (CIA) and the National Security Council. Presidents during past periods certainly confronted their share of crises, but the nature of the Cold War required presidents to adapt to the role of permanent crisis manager. Each knew that he must be prepared to deal with an international crisis, including the prospect of nuclear war, at any moment. Even sympathetic commentators wondered whether any one person could bear such a burden. The crisis-prone nature of the new international system also elevated the presidency to a position of heightened power in relation to Congress. The need for decisive action in the national interest shrunk the arena of congressional authority. Although there were scores of U.S. military actions during the Cold War, including two major conflicts in Korea and Vietnam, Congress declared war in none of these cases. After the Watergate scandal, some scholars questioned whether the Cold War had made the office so powerful that it had become an "imperial presidency," isolated from congressional checks and even to a certain extent from public opinion. During this period, in fact, presidents were granted considerable leeway in foreign policy. Until questions were raised about the war in Vietnam, presidents enjoyed so much authority that Clinton Rossiter spoke about a new kind of presidency that he called, without criticism, "constitutional dictatorship."

The power of Cold War presidents in foreign affairs, however, did not automatically extend to domestic policy. Although presidents could rely on a "rally effect" whenever they faced a crisis, their support in domestic affairs was more limited. Aaron Wildavsky, in fact, referred to the phenomenon of "two presidencies," a powerful one in international relations and a much more limited one domestically. On issues of domestic policy, presidents faced the same obstacles (the opposition party, strong congressional committee chairs, press oversight) that presidents in previous periods confronted. Nevertheless, there were some limited periods in which presidents enjoyed the levels of support necessary for legislative victories. The first two years after Johnson's landslide in 1964 was one such period and, to a somewhat lesser extent, Eisenhower's and Reagan's first two years as well. Many Cold War presidents, however, faced low "opportunity levels" for chances of congressional approval of their domestic agendas throughout their terms of office. Close election victories and/or control of one or more branches of Congress by the opposition party significantly diminished the opportunities for Truman, Kennedy, Nixon, Carter, and Bush throughout their terms of office.

Perhaps the most important change Cold War presidents faced domestically was in the area of civil rights. When Truman was elected in 1948, America was a severely segregated society with very limited economic and enfranchisement opportunities for African Americans. In 1950, in the American South there were fourteen medical schools open to whites, but none to African Americans; there were sixteen law schools for whites, but none for African Americans; there were fifteen engineering schools for whites, but none for African Americans; and there were five dentistry schools for whites, but none for African Americans. In the Jim Crow system in the American South, African Americans were confronted with the daily humiliation of conforming to laws requiring separate seating in restaurants and on buses. Of course, separate schools aggravated these conditions.

In the 1950s and 1960s protests against discrimination on the part of African Americans and resistance on the part of many white Americans formed the basis for a domestic crisis that some writers called the "Second Reconstruction." The spark that initiated the modern civil rights movement is generally traced to the refusal of Rosa Parks, a worker for the National Association for the Advancement of Colored People (NAACP), to move to the "colored" section of a Montgomery, Alabama bus in 1955. A boycott of public transportation was soon organized to protest the racial segregation of public municipal facilities. A leader in this project was the Reverend Martin Luther King, Jr., a young pastor of a Baptist church in Montgomery. King formed a new organization, the Southern Christian Leadership Conference (SCLC), to protest segregation throughout the South. A year later a similar boycott was launched in Tallahassee, Florida.

In 1960 a new strategy of protest was initiated by college students in North Carolina when they engaged in a sit-in in a restaurant when the owner refused to serve them. Sit-ins began in cities and towns throughout both the South and the North. The Supreme Court had declared segregated public school systems unconstitutional in 1954, but Southern resistance to integrated education was so adamant that there were several national crises. In 1957, President Dwight D. Eisenhower reluctantly sent federal troops to Little Rock, Arkansas, when Governor Orville Faubus refused to obey a court order. (Subsequently Faubus closed all the high schools in the state rather than accept racial integration.) In 1962 President John F. Kennedy sent federal marshals to protect James Meredith, a black man who wished to register as a student at the University of Mississippi.

As the civil rights movement gained momentum throughout the South, white resistance became more and more violent. Protesters were beaten by angry mobs. Churches and schools were bombed. In Birmingham, Alabama, local police used fire hoses and dogs to disperse protesters. Medgar Evers, a black civil rights worker, was assassinated, as was Viola Luizzo, a white civil rights volunteer. The bodies of three missing northern civil rights workers (James Chancy, Michael Schwerner, and Andrew Goodman) were discovered by agents of the Federal Bureau of Investigation after a massive search in Oxford, Mississippi. Civil rights leaders throughout the South, King preeminent among them, were committed to nonviolence both in principle and as a tactic, but as the conflict escalated other black leaders began to reevaluate this policy. Robert F. Williams, head of a local NAACP chapter in Monroe, North Carolina, organized members into rifle clubs and claimed the right of self-defense in the event of attack. New groups such as the Black Panthers and the Nation of Islam questioned the utility of nonviolence as well as the value of integration. Riots broke out in northern cities in the late 1960s.

Cold War presidents responded to this crisis at the same time that they were attempting to manage the Cold War. John Kennedy, in fact, contended that the Cold War could not continue to be effectively fought when democracy was denied at home to American citizens. A variety of legislation was passed to confront this challenge, including the Civil Rights Acts of 1964 and 1965 as well as a series of executive orders that came to be known collectively as "affirmative action." While the crisis subsided after the Jim Crow system was dismantled and African Americans secured voting rights, the issue of civil rights remained on the agenda. One of the most important consequences of this struggle was the change that it caused in the American party system. Democratic presidents could no longer rely on the "solid South" to help pile up votes in the electoral college, since white Southerners moved rapidly to the Republican Party. The New Deal Coalition, fashioned by FDR, became more and more frayed until it collapsed in 1968.

Finally, later Cold War presidents found that they could no longer rely on the convention system in order to secure party nomination. Hubert Humphrey was the last president to win nomination without winning primaries. In 1971, the Democratic Party completely changed its system of presidential nomination by requiring all delegates to be chosen by primaries. Republicans soon largely imitated this practice.

HARRY S. TRUMAN (1945–1953)

William Leuchtenburg has written that all presidents have suffered from the shadow of FDR. Whether they hoped to extend or restrict the welfare state Roosevelt created and/or to galvanize international support against aggression, the American public invariably compared the current officeholder to FDR. No president governed more under this shadow than did Harry S. Truman.

Truman was selected as vice president in 1944 when FDR decided to replace Henry Wallace and when other more visible candidates were rejected by factions in the Democratic Party. Truman was a competent border-state senator who was a loyal New Dealer. He had a close relationship with the powerful Pendergast machine of Missouri but nevertheless had a reputation as an honest politician. While few Democrats were ever able to compete with FDR's popularity in his lifetime, Truman was clearly a second- or even third-tier political figure.

When Truman was informed of Roosevelt's death, he was stunned. He exclaimed to the White House press corps: "Boys, if you ever pray, pray for me now. I don't know whether you fellows ever had a load of hay fall on you, but when they told me yesterday what had happened, I felt like the moon, the stars, and all the planets had fallen on me." The new president initially was popular as the nation rallied around the new wartime leader. It soon became apparent, however, that Truman needed his own persona. He was not an effective speaker, his intellectual scope appeared to be provincial, and he did not have the confidence of FDR's cabinet. As post-war transition problems mounted and the tensions of the Cold War caught public attention, Truman was criticized as an incompetent president. The phrase, "To err is Truman," was commonly used to describe his presidency. In 1948, many Democratic leaders were anxious to dump Truman and replace him with the popular World War II general, Dwight Eisenhower, on the presidential ticket.

While Truman certainly knew that he would always live in the shadow of Roosevelt, he sought a voice of his own. Gradually, he did develop one that, for the most part, was successful. FDR was a master of indirection in terms of his relation to the public, Congress, and his own cabinet. While he certainly could undertake bold decisions (such as when he took the United States off the gold standard in 1933 and when he took his "left turn" in 1936), for the most part he proceeded experimentally and thus nearly always kept his opponents and even his cabinet members off guard. Truman replaced this strategy of indirection with one of directness and "plain speaking." While he projected neither the caginess nor the eloquence of Roosevelt, he did emphasize his own talents: decisiveness and connection to the "common man."

In a sense, Truman modeled his presidency on the populist model of Andrew Jackson much more than his predecessor did, despite FDR's momentary adoption of the general's persona in 1936. For several years, the plain speaker from Missouri found an effective mode of governance. However, later in his second term Truman's "plain speaking" wore thin with the public, and he came to be seen as a stubborn and willful man. His popularity dropped even below 1947 levels. During this period, almost any leadership style was bound to fail in some respects, for Truman faced a series of truly monumental challenges in his seven years in office. He was confronted with the problems of bringing the war to a close. He faced serious issues relating to the transition from a wartime to a peacetime economy. He encountered a divided party and a strong Republican challenger for reelection, and he was forced to design the first set of strategies in dealing with the Cold War.

When Truman assumed the office of president, his military advisors predicted that the war in Europe would be over in six months but that the defeat of Japan would take longer, perhaps eighteen months or even more. While Japan was now completely vulnerable to U.S. air strikes, the task of invading the island nation was daunting, especially if one calculated that Japanese resistance would be as ferocious as it was at Iwo Jima. Moreover, the question of Soviet support loomed before policymakers. It was already clear that whatever territory the Red Army "liberated" would remain in their control. Stalin was anxious to send troops to the Pacific theatre, and the prospect of a new opportunity for Soviet expansion in Japan and China seemed inevitable.

Ironically, although the Russians were aware of the effort, Truman did not know about the Manhattan Project, the secret plan to build an atomic bomb at Los Alamos, New Mexico, before he became president. When the new president learned of the existence of the bomb, he appointed an ad hoc committee chaired by Secretary of War Henry Stimson to make recommendations. The committee decided that the bomb should be dropped after the Japanese were presented with a warning. Other options, such as a demonstration of the weapon, were rejected on the grounds that only two bombs were available and a dud might prolong the war. Thus, only months after he was in office, Truman made the most momentous decision of his presidency and also perhaps the most momentous of any Cold War president. On August 6 he ordered the use of an atomic bomb on Hiroshima, and another three days later on Nagasaki. Japan surrendered unconditionally on August 14, 1945. Truman years later insisted that his decision, while terrifying, was not a difficult one: "It occurred to me that a quarter million of the flower of our young manhood were worth a couple of Japanese cities, and I think they were and are."

Truman's decision was enormously popular at the time (and is still supported today by a large majority of Americans). His decisions, however, concerning the conversion to a peacetime economy were not well received. Although war production reduced unemployment to record low levels (1.2 percent in 1944), both Americans in general and policymakers in particular were concerned that the Depression would return once the war ended. Indeed, almost two million Americans lost their jobs in the ten months after V-E Day. Moreover, while wage and price controls and rationing were instituted during the war, prices were inching up much faster than wages. Unable to strike during the war, labor unions, which were better organized and more numerous than at any time in American history, were determined to recoup income lost during the war and the Depression. Although some planning had been done as early as 1943 to reconvert the economy to peacetime production, the precipitant close of hostilities left the government unprepared.

Happily, the economy rebounded surprisingly well. Unemployment stabilized; industrial plants rapidly converted to production of consumer goods; the GI Bill of Rights helped veterans resume their studies and reduced the job pool. Inflation was the administration's major concern. Truman dramatically reduced the federal budget from nearly $100 billion to $60 billion. Congress reluctantly gave him authority to enact new price-control measures, but union leaders were deeply resentful of the administration's efforts to convince them to continue their wartime no-strike pledges. Over four million workers went on strike in 1946. Truman called a Labor-Management Conference in November, but the meeting seemed to worsen the situation. As Donald R. McCoy has reported, "The proceedings of the conference resembled less a Quaker meeting than the shootout at the OK Corral."

While Truman was certainly sympathetic to union demands, he also was determined not to let inflation spiral out of control and destabilize the new chance for prosperity. When Congress refused to grant him authority to appoint fact-finding boards in troubled industries, he intervened personally to settle strikes. During a railway strike, he announced a plan to draft the strikers and order them back to work as federal employees. The threat worked. Truman proudly announced an agreement when he was handed the news in the middle of an address to Congress. Mine workers under the leadership of John L. Lewis went on strike in November of 1946, despite Truman's efforts to help reach a fair settlement. The president took Lewis to court, where he received an injunction to force workers to return or face a $3.5 million fine. Lewis, a man who stood up to the formidable FDR during the war, gave in and called off the strike.

Actions such as these made Truman very unpopular with labor, which was now a major part of the New Deal Coalition. Ironically, Truman was helped by Republicans in Congress who attempted to cash in on public resentment against strikes by passing the Taft-Hartley Act in June of 1947. The bill banned union shops and provided the president with authority to declare an 80-day "cooling-off" period should a strike occur. Labor unions were outraged. Truman vetoed the measure in strong terms, and Congress overrode his veto. At least in the short term, Truman enjoyed the best of both worlds. He established a reputation for standing up to unions and, at the same time, his veto of Taft-Hartley galvanized unions to support him in 1948 in hopes of repealing the act.

The tactic of intervening boldly in major strikes backfired, however, in Truman's second administration. During a particularly difficult period of the Korean War, steel-industry union leaders called a strike. Although Truman could have used the provision in the Taft-Hartley Act to delay the strike for 80 days, he chose instead to issue an executive order seizing the steel mills. Naturally, the president wanted to avoid utilizing legislation that he was on record as opposing. The argument he used instead for seizing the mills, however, quickly came before the Supreme Court. Truman claimed he had exercised his constitutional authority as commander in chief in a national emergency. Was he correct? Three members of court agreed with him—but six did not.

Youngstown Sheet and Tube Co. v. Sawyer is a complicated decision, since each of the six justices in the majority wrote separate concurring positions. Justice Hugo Black, who wrote the majority opinion, rejected outright Truman's claim that there were emergency constitutional powers inherent in the executive office. He argued that while past presidents may have made command decisions in "day-to-day fighting in the theater of war," and even though the "theater of war" might be "an expanding concept, we cannot with faithfulness to our constitutional system hold that the Commander in Chief of the Armed Forces has the ultimate power as such to take possession of property in order to keep labor disputes from stopping production." This, he concluded, "is a job for the Nation's lawmakers, not for its military authorities." Justice Jackson, while concurring, took a more restrained position. He, in effect, constructed a three-tier standard for assessing the constitutionality of executive power. If Congress authorizes, expressly or by implication, presidential actions, "his authority is at its maximum." If Congress does not act, either by inertia or indifference, the president's actions are in a "zone of twilight" in which the courts must reach judgments on the "imperatives of events." If, however, the president acts in express contradiction to Congress's wishes (as apparently Truman did in this case, since he ignored existing legislation), "his power is at its lowest ebb."

At the close of his argument, Justice Jackson poignantly stated the dilemma of the judicial branch in the age of the Cold War presidency. He noted that the Constitution was an

> . . . Eighteenth-Century sketch of a government hoped for, not a blueprint of the Government that is. Vast accretions of federal power, eroded from that reserved by the States, have magnified the scope of presidential activity. Subtle shifts take place in the centers of real power that do not show on the facade of the Constitution.

Jackson continued by describing the new presidency:

> Executive power has the advantage of concentration in a single head in whose choice the whole Nation has a part, making him the focus of public hopes and expectations. In drama, magnitude and finality his decisions so far overshadow any others that almost alone he fills the public eye and ear. No other personality in public life can begin to compete with him in access to the public mind through modern methods of communication. By his prestige as head of state and his influence upon public opinion he exerts a leverage upon those who are supposed to check and balance his power which often cancels their effectiveness.

Was Jackson referring to the capacity of the Supreme Court itself to restrain Cold War presidents? He seemed to be suggesting so in the final paragraph of his opinion: "Such institutions may be destined to pass away. But it is the duty of the Court to be the last, not first, to give them up."

Truman bitterly complained that the court decision was based on obsolete premises. He did, nevertheless, give back control of the steel mills. The president did not give up the fight, however. He asked Congress to give him authority to re-seize the mills. Congress refused to do so and the Senate, by a vote of 49–30, actually requested that he invoke the Taft-Hartley Act. Truman refused. A settlement was reached six weeks later that led to increased wages and prices. The Youngstown case did not have much direct impact on Truman's presidency since he was near the end of his second term. It did, however, serve as an illustration of the limits of presidential power, even in the Cold War period, and it was an apt illustration of the gambles that the plain-speaking president undertook.

Truman's battles with both unions and management severely damaged his popularity. An election that looked difficult to win became known as the "Impossible Campaign" when the Democratic Party split in three in 1948. A right-wing faction left the party over opposition to the national organization's platform statement on civil rights. A left wing abandoned the party in opposition to Truman's foreign policy of containment. This latter group called itself the Progressive Party and nominated Henry Wallace, former vice president under FDR and secretary of commerce in the Truman administration, as its candidate. Wallace insisted there were no differences between the United States and the USSR which could not be settled "by peaceful, hopeful negotiation." The Progressive Party opposed the Marshall Plan, the Truman Doctrine, and the draft. It denounced what it called "anti-Soviet hysteria," which was "a mask for monopoly, militarism, and reaction."

Faced with this dissension and Truman's own unpopularity, most observers thought that the president's chances for reelection were very slim. Truman, however, developed an almost perfect strategy and was helped by the tactics of Thomas Dewey, his Republican opponent. Truman was faced with a very uncooperative Congress after the 1946 elections. The president himself criticized some aspects of the New Deal. He attacked what he called its "lunatic fringe" and "crackpot professional liberals" and said that America needed a "rest from experiments." Nevertheless, Truman did propose the extension of Roosevelt's policies. He particularly emphasized the construction of new housing and public healthcare. The Eightieth Congress largely ignored these proposals. Truman called Congress in special session in July of 1948 and challenged members to act on his plans. He knew full well that the Republican-controlled Congress was even less likely to support his proposals in an election year. Truman, however, used this failure to attack what he called the "do nothing" Republican Congress in a series of "whistlestop" train tours from Labor Day to Election Day. These short, taunting speeches became more and more popular with voters. People in the crowds often responded with the shout, "Give 'em hell, Harry!"

Truman largely ignored the Southern-based "Dixiecrat" Party, but he did systematically attack the Progressives. In his famous "red herring" press conference, Truman implied that the domestic communist threat was a diversionary tactic of Republicans. With the aid of his advisor Clark Clifford, he also devised a strategy for attacking Wallace. In his St. Patrick's Day speech in 1948, Truman declared that he would never accept the support of Wallace "and his communists" even it meant his own defeat. In Los Angeles, he urged Wallace to reject communist support and "go to the country he loves so well and help them against his own country if that's the way he feels." The approach was designed to force liberal Democrats to attack Wallace as pro-communist, and at the same time to solidify support for Truman as the only "responsible" agent for continuing the domestic programs of the New Deal of the 1930s. The tactic worked. The Americans for Democratic Action (ADA), a group of liberal

Democrats formed in 1947 who did not initially think Truman could be relied on to the continue the New Deal, attacked Wallace for his refusal to renounce communist support of his campaign and supported Truman.

Dewey, on the other hand, fearful that any specific statements might erode his large lead in the polls, spoke only in generalities. On election night, many newspapers were so convinced of a Republican victory that they printed "Dewey Defeats Truman" headlines for the morning edition. Truman gleefully held up the headline of the *Chicago Tribune* when the results of his victory were reported. The "man from Missouri" defeated not only the Republicans but also members of his own party who doubted him. The president won 303 electoral votes and lost only four Southern states. The Progressives received only 2.38 percent of the popular vote. The New Deal coalition survived its first challenge of the Cold War presidency.

The foreign-policy decisions Truman faced both before and after the election were numerous and daunting. In the seven years of his presidency he was confronted with a Soviet roadblock of Berlin, a war that followed the creation of Israel, the development of an A-bomb by the Soviets, a communist coup in Czechoslovakia, the fall of China to the communists, the rise of the Communist Party in Western Europe, the invasion of South Korea by the North Koreans, and later the entry of the communist Chinese into the war. The governing approach Truman created to deal with these crises was the policy of containment.

At the close of World War II the United States was clearly the strongest economic power in the world. War production had increased the Gross National Product to $135 million, and the United States controlled two-thirds of the world's gold reserves. Although the United States had suffered half a million casualties, Soviet losses were monumental (perhaps as many as 15–20 million). However, Soviet military power was the greatest in the world. The Soviets had 175 divisions in the field at the time the United States was demobilizing its armed forces to pre-war levels. The United States, of course, had a monopoly on nuclear weapons, but that advantage was eliminated in 1949. It would be difficult, though not impossible, for the United States to win a war against the Soviets and, of course, after the "balance of terror" was achieved in nuclear weaponry, such a conflict could well produce an atomic holocaust.

Since direct military conflict was increasingly unthinkable, and since gradual surrender was unacceptable, what strategy should the United States pursue? A young Soviet expert in the State Department provided an answer that Truman quickly adopted. George Kennan was asked by the secretary of defense to respond to a paper on Soviet international objectives written by a government official. Portions of Kennan's critique of this internal document were presented to the Council on Foreign Relations, an influential organization of experts in international politics, in January of 1947. The enthusiastic reception by the council resulted in the publication of a version of the memorandum to the secretary in its journal, *Foreign Affairs*, as "The Sources of Soviet Conduct." Since Kennan was a State Department official and his position was not a settled government policy, the authorship was designated as "Mr. X." Kennan argued that the Soviets had plans for world domination. Fortunately, however, their Marxist framework led them to believe, unlike the Nazis, that time was on their side and that they could afford to pursue a policy of gradual conquest. He also argued, however, that the Soviet system, based on economic collectivization and terror, was in the long-term an unstable one. If the United States could "contain" the Soviets by resisting military aggression, the empire would eventually collapse by itself.

The first application of the containment policy came in 1946, when Truman asked Congress to support aid to the Greek government against local communist forces. The Truman Doctrine, as it was called, committed the United States to aid "free peoples who are resisting subjugation by armed minorities or by outside pressure." Two months later, Secretary of State George Marshall announced a proposal for a program to aid Europeans in their "struggle against hunger, poverty, desperation and chaos." The Marshall Plan was designed to give containment an economic as well as a military focus. Concerned that poverty bred support for communism, Truman proposed an initial appropriation of $17 million in support. Together, the Truman Doctrine and the Marshall Plan, both for which the president sought and received bipartisan support, helped stabilize the Cold War.

However, containment was never an easy policy to implement. In 1947, the Soviets blockaded all traffic to the French, British, and American occupation zones of Berlin, which was located deep in the Soviet sector. Were the Russians preparing for an invasion of Western Europe? Should the United States, French, and British send armed convoys to Berlin and risk World War III? Should they do nothing and give up the largely indefensible Berlin zones? After receiving conflicting advice, Truman decided on the option of airlifting supplies to the German city. After eleven months the Soviets lifted the blockade, and travel to Berlin continued throughout the Cold War.

The most difficult challenge to containment policy in the Truman administration occurred when North Korean troops attacked South Korea in June of 1950. Two days later the president pledged the defense of South Korea. The United Nations, with the Russian delegate curiously absent, asked all nations to resist the aggression. Within a week, however, U.N. forces were in complete retreat. Only with great effort was a stable position established around Pusan at the very southern tip of the country. Truman's commanding general, Douglas MacArthur, then engineered one of the most daring and successful counterstrikes in modern history. He struck North Korean forces behind their lines at Inchon. Now the aggressors were in full retreat. Rather than stop at the 38th parallel, the division of Korea agreed upon at Yalta, MacArthur continued to advance northward toward the Chinese border.

Truman and State Department officials warned the general about his movements, but MacArthur was adamant that he could successfully continue with victory by Christmas and even hinted about liberating communist China. With the 1950 election only weeks away, Truman was reluctant to publicly confront the popular general. The president paid a price. Chinese forces entered the war with 200,000 soldiers and drove U.N. forces back again, south of the 38th parallel. U.N. forces regrouped and reached the dividing line between the two countries. Meanwhile, MacArthur told congressional leaders that the U.S. forces should attack China, declaring that "in war, there is no substitute for victory." Truman warned MacArthur against making personal public-policy statements. When he was ignored, the president fired MacArthur on April 12, 1951. The action was in keeping with Truman's persona of directness but certainly was the most unpopular decision of his administration. Only 25 percent of the public supported the president, and some members of Congress demanded that Truman retract MacArthur's termination.

Truman's action, though late in reigning in MacArthur, was an extremely important one. It established the principle of civilian control of the military in the Cold War. MacArthur even refused to meet with the president when he returned to the United States, as tradition required. Instead, he spoke before a joint session of Congress. As Congressman Joseph Martin reported somewhat indelicately, when MacArthur ended his speech, there wasn't a "dry eye on the Republican side nor a dry seat on the Democratic." Despite the intensity of the debate over the firing, Truman kept a low profile and quietly leaked details of MacArthur's insubordination to the press. He also reiterated the principle of containment. U.S. objectives, he repeatedly said, were to engage in a limited war, not a total one. Such a policy was a frustrating one for policymakers and the public at large, and the war dragged on through the 1952 presidential elections.

The termination of MacArthur was, of course, only one of Truman's many controversial decisions. Even today, debate continues: Should Truman have ordered the dropping of the A-bomb on Japan? Should Truman have worked harder to sustain Soviet cooperation after the war such as, for example, delaying cancellation of lend-lease funds to their wartime ally? Should Truman have seized the steel mills in 1952? Truman's retrospective popularity among Republicans as well as Democrats thus seems more related to his style of directness and plain speaking than to his particular actions.

DWIGHT D. EISENHOWER (1953–1961)

Although Truman could have run for reelection in 1952, both his own unpopularity (his approval ratings hovered in the 30 percent range) and his fatigue led him to support Adlai Stevenson, governor of Illinois, for president. Truman believed that the Republicans would nominate Senator Robert Taft, but General Eisenhower was rapidly gaining party support. Eisenhower, an aide to MacArthur in the Philippines in the 1930s, was selected in 1941 by FDR (over hundreds of other more senior officers) to assume the position of commanding general of the U.S. forces. Eisenhower was soon chosen by the president as supreme commander of all Allied forces in 1943, and he led the D-Day invasion against the Nazis on June 6, 1944. In 1948 Eisenhower was clearly the most popular figure in America. His memoir, *Crusade in Europe,* was a best seller. Although Eisenhower refused overtures by Democrats to run for president, in January of 1952 he announced that he was a Republican. He easily defeated Taft on the first ballot at the Republican Convention in August and won a landslide victory against Stevenson in November.

Eisenhower's rise, first to military leadership and then to the presidency, was all the more remarkable because he assumed a role not undertaken since the founding presidency. Eisenhower's hope was that he would be drafted by the Republican Party and would arrive victoriously at the convention without ever having to deal for delegate votes. "He wanted," as Robert F. Burk concludes, "to be seen as, and sought as, a twentieth-century George Washington."

Throughout his two terms, Eisenhower crafted the persona of a leader who governed above partisan conflicts and who deferred to Congress on many issues. This approach to presidential power, like those of his founding predecessors, had both advantages and liabilities. On one hand, the public and many commentators found Eisenhower's approach a refreshing one, particularly after years of activist and partisan presidents. To Arthur Larson (*A Republican Looks at his Party*), for example, Eisenhower showed Americans a new way to think about themselves: "The bane of American political thought for many years has been an inclination to be ashamed of homespun American principles of the kind we hear orated on the Fourth of July." Those who "tried to escape this homely line of thought" moved in two directions. Some went "aristocratic" and others went "pseudo-intellectual." Eisenhower offered a "more sophisticated and advanced" response.

> He has dared to be obvious when the obvious was right. He has dared to exalt the local product and ignore the glamour of the imported idea. He has had the wisdom and the courage to steer us at last out of a twenty-year period in which much of our political thought, especially among university people, writers and journalists, was essentially Europe-based, and he has brought us back to our own traditions.

In short, Eisenhower had brought America out of its European thrall with all its "staleness of Marxian dialectic, the tiredness of Socialist clichés that sounded so smart during the thirties. . . ." For Larson, although Eisenhower risked ridicule with his homely speech and hid his sophistication, he nevertheless sharply turned the citizenry away from the New Deal by creating a center of executive power that had been obliterated in the 1930s.

To others, however, Eisenhower fit the image of the "captive hero," and his detachment was regarded by others as a sign of incompetence. To Marquis Child, for example, Eisenhower "betrayed a seeming indifference to the office he held." He "appeared more and more as a prisoner of his office, a captive of his own indecisiveness, a captive of the hero-worshipping public, a captive of the agonizing dilemma of an era of nuclear annihilation in which man's old savage instincts lay close to the fragile surface of law and order." Childs concluded that Eisenhower's performance was not only a personal tragedy but also a national one, "because the American people had romantically, impetuously, frivolously almost, invested so much of the future in a dream of the past." To William V. Shannon, Eisenhower was at best a transitional figure who lived off the accomplishments of his predecessors, and the 1950s would be regarded as the "time of great postponement." Eisenhower may have been an affable president, but he left his successors with a "black heritage of time lost and opportunities wasted." Irving Howe even gave Eisenhower's administration an ideological name which was the opposite of Larson's New Republicanism. "Ikieism" stood for a "sublime faith in the powers of drift," since it believed the nation's affluence was "eternal and ordained."

Perhaps as a result of Eisenhower's adoption of the founding presidency's strategy of governance, his reputation has continued to veer wildly from that of a prescient leader to that of "Grandpa Ike." More recently some commentators have sought to redeem Eisenhower's leadership style. In 1980 Fred Greenstein argued along the lines that Larson did in 1956 that Ike fashioned a "hidden-hand presidency," in which he exercised power behind the scenes while he preserved the role of patriot in public.

It was possible to discern Eisenhower's agenda, although it was certainly veiled through his own leadership style. Eisenhower had grave doubts about the impact of the New Deal on later generations. In 1949 he told a Texas audience that "if all Americans want is security they can go to prison." Eisenhower implied the war had taught Americans higher values than mere economic well-being. Those who died in World War II "believed in something more than trying to be sure they would not be hungry when they were sixty-seven." Writing in retirement, Eisenhower said that if in the future the nation rejected the "statist" legacy of the New Deal, his presidency would be remembered in heroic terms as "the first great break with the political philosophy of the decade beginning in 1933." If the nation did not, "the growth of paternalism to the point of virtual regimentation would so condition the attitude of future historians that our time would be represented as only a slight impediment to the trend begun in 1933 under the New Deal." One way of describing his position is "paternal anti-paternalism."

Yet Eisenhower, over the objections of many Republicans, never advocated dismantling New Deal programs. He apparently saw the reliance on the national government as a bad habit that could be broken. His views on the New Deal were never as negative as those of Ronald Reagan. Eisenhower believed in balanced budgets, supported the Tenth Amendment as a sacred statement of federal/state relationships, opposed agricultural price supports and the TVA, and favored a business-centered government. Yet he supported some massive federal projects, such as the St. Lawrence Seaway, and the creation of an interstate highway system. He also acceded to increases in the minimum wage and Social Security, as well as presiding over the creation of the Department of Health, Education, and Welfare.

Eisenhower's approach to the Cold War was similar to his approach to the New Deal in the sense that he rarely advocated dramatic departures from existing policies. In fact, especially in the early period of the Cold War, Eisenhower emphasized repeatedly that the Cold War could be won as long as Americans avoided panic and hysteria. Nowhere is this effort to reassure more evident than in his 1954 address before the nation on the hydrogen bomb. Eisenhower's authority as a military man gave his review of the history of weaponry an authenticity: "Now, this transfer of power, this increase of power from a single musket and a little canon, all the way to the hydrogen bomb in a single lifetime, is indicative of the things that have happened to us." But our real concern should focus on the fact that "advances in science have outraced our social consciousness, how much more we have developed scientifically than we are capable of handling emotionally and intellectually." The bomb was "merely a dramatic symbol" of our worries. In other words, our focus should rest with our own abilities to cope with change and risk—not the H-bombs, which were "not in themselves a threat to us." He admitted that "we can be excused for getting a bit hysterical" because "these dangers come from so many angles, and they are of such different kinds, and no matter what we do they seem to still exist." Rather, if Americans concentrated on the real source of our fears—"aggressive communism"—which was "from without," we could overcome our hysteria.

Then Eisenhower undertook a major conceptual transition. The H-bomb and its possible use were really no different than other problems faced in everyday life by all Americans:

> This is not greatly different from what the American family does. It has the problems of meeting the payments on the mortgage, paying for the family car, educating the children, laying aside some money for use in case of unexpected illness. It meets these problems courageously. It doesn't get panicky. It solves these problems with what I call courage and faith, but above all by cooperation, by discussing the problem among the different members of the family and then saying: this is what we can do, this is what we will do, and reaching a satisfactory answer.

This reduction of the threat of nuclear war and possible human extinction to the status of domestic problems facing American families, to the extent to which it was subsequently accepted, represents an acme of confidence in the power of reassurance on Eisenhower's part.

Eisenhower also promoted domestic tranquility in the midst of the Cold War by emphasizing the religious commitments of Americans. According to R. Gordon Hoxie, Eisenhower marked the "total restoration of American Messianism," and "with the exception of Lincoln" he "conveyed his views in moral and spiritual terms" more than any other president did. Some aspects of Eisenhower's religious focus were symbolically concrete. He initiated the White House Prayer Breakfast, established a national day of prayer, and supported "under God" in the pledge of allegiance and "In God We Trust" as an official motto. More generally, he reintroduced religion as a central aspect of national identity. Indifferent to particular sects, Eisenhower was adamant about the relationship between religious faith and the polity: "Our government makes no sense unless it is founded in a deeply felt religious faith—and I don't care what it is." He connected certain basic beliefs with citizenship: ". . . recognition of the Supreme Being is the first, the most basic form of Americanism. Without God, there could be no American form of government, nor an American way of life."

This restatement of civil religion was connected to the value of tranquility in two ways: religious faith provided Americans with the resources to remain calm in the midst of danger, and it provided a demarcation between America and "atheist" communism. "Our enemies of this faith know no god but force, no devotion but its use," said Eisenhower in his first inaugural. This "atheistic imperialism" of the Soviet Union was paired against the goals of the United States, which desired not "one acre" of territory and where "faith rules our whole way of life."

Despite these rhetorical efforts, however, Eisenhower was faced with many crises in his two terms in office. In an apparent contradiction to his commitment to reduce tensions and to prepare Americans for a long struggle, he unveiled his "New Look" in foreign policy shortly after his first inaugural. In an effort to control military spending, which had risen to 70 percent of the federal budget, Eisenhower and his secretary of state, John Foster Dulles, reduced conventional forces and increased funding for missile development and the air force. As a result, the United States enjoyed an enormous nuclear advantage over the Soviets, in terms of both missile and delivery systems, but could not compete with its armed forces, which outnumbered United States forces by almost two to one. The strategy of "massive retaliation" in case of acts of aggression was formulated to play to U.S. strength.

Often, Eisenhower resorted to nuclear threat in a crisis. During the 1952 election campaign, he made a very politically effective pledge, "I will go to Korea," and once in office threatened the Chinese with nuclear weapons to reach an agreement to end the war. In 1954, when French forces were surrounded at Dien Bien Phu in Indochina, some of Eisenhower's advisors recommended the use of nuclear weapons. The president refused: "You boys must be crazy. We can't use those awful things against Asians for the second time in less than ten years." On the other hand, Eisenhower believed that the loss of Vietnam would produce a "falling domino" effect. Nation after nation would fall under communist domination if Ho Chi Minh gained control. After a brief attempt to gain international support for the French, Eisenhower nevertheless decided against the use of American forces. Later in 1963 he said that jungle warfare would have "swallowed division after division of U.S. troops." The United States reached an accord in Geneva that partitioned Vietnam, and Eisenhower and Dulles negotiated a military pact (SEATO) with noncommunist regimes in the area.

When Soviet forces invaded Hungary in 1956 after a reform government took power, Eisenhower refused to authorize the use of émigré forces that had been covertly set up by the CIA on the grounds they would be quickly demolished by massive numbers of Soviet troops and the action might precipitate nuclear war. Sadly, Eisenhower concluded, Hungary was "as inaccessible as Tibet."

Eisenhower reduced American troop levels, in part due to his belief in balanced budgets and partly because he was concerned that continued high levels of military spending would eventually convert America into a garrison state. Ironically, these concerns led him to rely increasingly on covert operations by the CIA as an arm of foreign policy. The CIA engineered a coup in Iran that replaced its leader with the pro-American Shah Mohammad Reza Pahlavi. The Shah quickly rewarded the United States and Britain with 40 percent control of its oil assets that his predecessor had threatened to nationalize. In 1954 the CIA engineered a coup in Guatemala as well.

Throughout the Cold War Eisenhower forthrightly opposed congressional attempts to limit his authority, particularly in the area of foreign policy. He vigorously objected to the Bricker Amendment, which would have required congressional approval of executive agreements, and he refused to hand over State Department documents pertaining to communist subversion. In the area of civil rights, however, Eisenhower was much more reticent to exercise leadership. When the Supreme Court declared that school segregation was unconstitutional in *Brown v. Topeka Board of Education*, the president declined to give his endorsement, declaring only that "The Supreme Court has spoken, and I am sworn to uphold the constitutional processes of this country." Privately, he opposed the decision and said that he regretted appointing that "son of a bitch" Chief Justice Warren to the court. Some commentators note that Eisenhower was concerned that desegregation would actually erode racial progress in civil rights, but many others note that a more positive response on the part of the president may have reduced the violent resistance that followed the decision.

Eisenhower did, however, submit civil rights legislation that attempted to insure voting rights for African Americans to Congress in 1956 and 1957. When Senate Majority Leader Lyndon Johnson of Texas declared support for the legislation, the Civil Rights Bill, the first since Reconstruction, passed. The president's support was lukewarm, and he announced after its passage that "I can't imagine any set of circumstances that would ever induce me to send Federal troops . . . into any area to enforce the orders of a Federal court." Perhaps emboldened by this statement, Governor Orville Faubus of Arkansas refused to comply with a federal court order to admit nine African-American students to the Little Rock High School. After an attempt to convince Faubus to change his mind, and after an angry mob surrounded the school, Eisenhower issued an executive order directing his secretary of defense to federalize the Arkansas National Guard and send 1,000 army paratroopers to Little Rock. The crowds dispersed and the students were admitted. Eisenhower deeply resented being forced to make this decision since he believed the governor had reneged on a pledge to provide safe passage for the students. He blamed the crisis on "disorderly mobs" and "demagogic extremists," complaining that "our enemies are gloating over this incident and using it everywhere to misrepresent our whole nation."

During his term of office, Eisenhower suffered three health problems, two of which were quite serious. He recovered from a heart attack in 1955 and a mild stroke in 1957. At the end of his term he hoped to make a grand gesture for world peace. In 1955 the president held the first summit since the Yalta meetings and offered several major proposals designed to reduce the likelihood of nuclear war. One, "Atoms for Peace" (1953), proposed international control of nuclear energy for peaceful uses and another, "Open Skies" (1955), called for aerial inspection of nuclear disarmament. Both were rejected by the Soviets. Now Eisenhower proposed a new summit in Paris that hopefully would produce a permanent agreement on a nuclear test ban and make progress on other issues. He was also scheduled to travel to the Soviet Union and make a broadcast to the Soviet people.

Fate intervened. The United States had been surveying Soviet territory through the use of small U-2 planes that flew beyond the reach of Soviet anti-aircraft. U.S. Intelligence agencies found the information gathered very valuable and convinced the president to continue the surveillance, even though each flight involved substantial risk. Just before the summit, however, Premier Khrushchev cagily announced that a U-2 plane had been shot down by the Soviets. Since Eisenhower had been advised that even in the event of a crash the pilot and the instrument panels were certain to be destroyed, he authorized a cover story that the plane was only on a weather reconnaissance mission. Khrushchev then divulged that remnants of the plane were intact and that "we also have the pilot, who is quite alive and kicking!" He demanded an apology, or else Eisenhower's upcoming visit would be canceled. Naturally, Eisenhower refused. Although the Cold War was fought through many deceptions, the president, who based his reputation in large part on his status as a war hero, was caught in a lie. Although the American public rallied around the president when he returned from the Paris summit after repeated insults from the Soviet premier, chances for détente were dead and the Cold War once again escalated. Congress, in response, raised the military budget to higher levels. Eisenhower dutifully completed his term by substituting the trip to Moscow with a tour of Asia, but he wistfully told Charles de Gaulle: "What a splendid exit it would be for me to end up . . . with an agreement between East and West."

Eisenhower's adoption of the discarded republican persona has produced strikingly different assessments. Some commentators, such as William L. O'Neill, contend that the Eisenhower years were a "golden age" of American power and affluence and that "we would give almost anything if only they could be recovered." But to others, such as Eric Goldman, they were "the dullest and dreariest in all our history."

JOHN F. KENNEDY (1961–1963)

For an administration that lasted only a thousand days, the presidency of John F. Kennedy has received an extraordinary degree of attention. Historians and political scientists do not rate JFK in the top ranks, but the public certainly does. For example, in a recent Harris poll, Kennedy scored higher marks on domestic policy from the public than FDR, despite the former's very limited legislative achievements. Although students of the presidency might see Kennedy differently than the public in terms of achievements, he remains the focus of intense scholarly attention. Since the first evaluations by members of his administration, there have been waves of reassessments. Some writers, such as Garry Wills and Nigel Hamilton, have been quite critical of the president's policies and personal life while others, including biographers Richard Reeves and Irving Bernstein, have attempted to defend JFK from these attacks.

Part of the reason for this continuing interest is the fact that this brief presidency represented a large number of "firsts." Kennedy was the first Catholic president. Al Smith, a Catholic, ran for president on the Democratic ticket in 1928. His loss to Herbert Hoover cannot be traced primarily to his religion, but many party regulars believed that, particularly in a close election, religious affiliation is an important factor for many voters. Kennedy's confrontation with this issue created another first for his presidency. To show that he could attract Protestant voters, Kennedy entered

as many primaries as possible. The key state in 1960 was the highly religious and predominantly Protestant state of West Virginia. Kennedy
defeated Hubert Humphrey with 60 percent of the vote and removed a
major obstacle to his nomination. Kennedy thus became the first presidential candidate who won the nomination largely as a result of his primary victories. (JFK still had to defeat Lyndon Johnson, who entered no
primaries, at the Democratic Convention).

Kennedy was also the youngest elected president. He found ways to
use his youth as an asset rather than a liability. JFK's campaign speeches
were filled references to the need for "vigor" in the White House (a veiled
critique of the aging Eisenhower) as well as the responsibility of a "new
generation" to "get the country moving again." Kennedy effectively used
television to convey his persona of energy. Norman Mailer, like many
Americans, was captivated by his television image:

> His personal quality had a subtle, not quite describable intensity, a
> suggestion of dry pent heat perhaps, his eyes large, the pupils gray,
> the whites prominent, almost shocking, his most forceful feature; he
> had the eyes of a mountaineer. His appearance changed with his
> mood, strikingly so, and this made him always more interesting than
> what he was saying. He would seem at one moment older than his
> age, forty-eight or fifty, a tall slim, sunburned professor with a pleas-
> ant weathered face, not even particularly handsome; five minutes
> later, talking at a press conference on his lawn, three microphones
> before him, a television camera turning, his appearance would have
> gone through a metamorphosis, he would look again like a movie
> star, his coloring vivid, his manner rich, his gestures strong and
> quick, alive with that concentration of vitality a successful actor
> always seems to radiate.

While some scholars insist that Eisenhower employed the new
medium very effectively, many classify JFK as the "first TV president."
Marshall McLuhan, a media theorist, contended that Kennedy was an
ideal politician for the "cool" requirements of television. Kennedy's performances in the first televised presidential debate seemed to confirm this
assessment. At his press conferences, Kennedy spoke more directly to the
television audience, who were captivated by his wit and elegance, than to
the press corps who asked him questions.

Some of the other Kennedy firsts were more problematic. His victory
in 1960 over Richard Nixon was the smallest in history. He won the popular vote by only 0.2 percent of the votes cast. This slim margin, also
marred by charges of vote fraud in Illinois and Texas, severely inhibited
his authority over Congress. Kennedy also was the first—and to date the
only—president to confront the imminent possibility of nuclear war. In
October of 1962, in response to Soviet installation of missiles in Cuba,
Kennedy announced a quarantine of Russian shipping to the island.
Speaking to the public on television, he explained that "the 1930s taught

us a clear lesson: aggressive conduct, if allowed to go unchecked and unchallenged, ultimately leads to war." He continued: "We will not prematurely or unnecessarily risk the costs of worldwide nuclear war in which the fruits of victory would be ashes in our mouth, but neither will we shrink from the risk at any time it must be faced." Finally, Kennedy also was the first president since Reconstruction to recommend to Congress large-scale civil rights legislation. Although throughout his term the president took a cautious position in terms of protests in the South, in June of 1963 he called for an end to segregation and federal guarantees of voting rights for African Americans.

Kennedy's assassination on November 23, 1963, stunned Americans. As William G. Carleton noted in 1964, assessments of the slain president were mixed with the "mystic, the tragic." Kennedy was "surely one favored by the gods, one possessed of power, wealth, youth, the aura of manly war heroism, zest for living, personal charm and beauty, glamour, imagination, keen insight, intelligence, immense popularity, the adoring love of family and friends." But he was also one "cut down in a flash" in the "fullness of his strength." Would Kennedy have committed large numbers of troops to Vietnam? Would he have moderated the Cold War? Would he have been able to effectively lead the civil rights movement? Since there are no definitive answers to these questions, scholars and the public interpret the promise of the Kennedy years differently. To some, Kennedy's reputation as a "Cold Warrior" is certain proof that he would have vigorously pursued a war in Vietnam. Others, however, argue that the president developed a deep skepticism about military solutions after his experience in the 1961 Bay of Pigs incident. Arthur Schlesinger, Jr. once responded to charges of Kennedy's modest achievements and Cold War orthodoxy by contending that any assessment of JFK was like examining Jackson's presidency before the nullification crisis and the war on the Bank, or Lincoln's presidency if he had been killed six months after Gettysburg, or FDR's presidency if he had died in 1935.

What is certain about Kennedy is that he was well aware of the global and domestic changes that were imminent in 1960 and was prepared to respond to them. Two advisors to the candidate (Arthur Schlesinger, Jr. and Chester Bowles) emphasized to JFK that the presidency in 1960 would be a special prize, since the moment was ripe for a new period of reform. Schlesinger's memo to the president, "The Shape of National Politics to Come," was based on his father's theory of cyclical patterns in American politics. He predicted that the "approaching liberal epoch" would resemble the Progressive Era more than it would the New Deal.

How did John F. Kennedy react to changes when he assumed office? Before becoming president, as a congressman JFK had been a supporter of the New Deal in domestic programs. He energetically supported national medical care and other liberal causes. He was, however, generally hesitant to call himself a liberal, a word whose current definition had been created by Roosevelt. He offered this explanation in 1956 in response to a questioner who had spoken of the "somewhat emotionless quality" of his liberalism:

> In 1946 I really knew nothing about these things. I had no background particularly; in my family we were interested not so much in the ideas of politics as in the mechanics of the whole process. Then I found myself in Congress representing the poorest district in Massachusetts. Naturally, the interests of my constituents led me to take the liberal line; all the pressures converged to that end.

In foreign policy, however, JFK took positions to the right of even Cold War liberals. As a congressman he criticized the Yalta agreement (negotiated by a "sick Roosevelt") and voted to limit presidential terms. He declared that Russia was a "slave state . . . embarked upon a program of world domination." Kennedy supported the "get tough with Russia policy . . . most vigorously." His general relationship with the liberal wing of the party, led by Eleanor Roosevelt and Adlai Stevenson, was correct but cool.

In Kennedy's acceptance speech for the Democratic nomination, he described his programs as a "New Frontier." In particular, he was anxious to distinguish his form of liberalism from FDR's. In 1961, Kennedy told the president of Harvard: ". . . when Franklin had this job, it was a cinch. He didn't have all these world problems. He had only to cope with poverty in the United States, but look what I've got." Kennedy thought that the federal government ought to focus on areas of the country that suffered from pockets of poverty and stimulate economic growth in general, especially in terms of coping with new technological advances. The president was able to secure passage of some aspects of his program, including a tax cut, a slight increase in the minimum wage, funding for economic development in Appalachia, and job training for workers displaced by automation. He was unable, however, to obtain congressional passage for medical care for the aged, or aid to education and civil rights.

In Kennedy's inaugural address, he spoke of the Cold War as a "long twilight struggle." He held out the possibility of negotiation with the Soviets, but emphasized that Americans would "pay any price, bear any burden, meet any hardship" for freedom. The president thus proceeded on a dual tract in regard to the Cold War. He was extremely interested in covert military action as a strategy to aid containment and committed the United States to increasing its already considerable advantage in terms of nuclear missiles. At the same time, he was also interested in addressing the problem of poverty in the Third World, which he saw as the primary reason for the attractiveness of communism. In addition, he was interested in reaching agreements on specific issues, such as nuclear testing, with the Soviets. Unfortunately, his administration careened from one Cold War crisis to another with such rapidity from 1961 through 1963 that it is difficult to detect any policy distinct from that of previous Cold War presidents.

Clearly, Kennedy's most dramatic foreign policy failure was the April, 1961 invasion by Cuban exiles at the Bay of Pigs. Indeed, the administration's actions are now treated as a textbook case of poor decision making. CIA planning for this operation began in the Eisenhower administration, and JFK gave his approval without much discussion with his advisors. The plan involved recruiting and training 1,500 Cuban exiles, who would establish a beachhead in Cuba. From this point on, however, the goals of the operation became very vague. Apparently, CIA planners felt that the landing would produce a general uprising against Castro or that the Cuban leader would flee, as Arbenz did in the CIA Guatemalan coup in 1954.

Castro agents, however, easily infiltrated the exile organizations. When the exiles were trapped, the president faced a serious decision. American B-26 bombers strafed Cuban airfields prior to the landing. Should they now be used to provide cover for the beleaguered exiles? The decision was made more difficult, because in the 1960 campaign JFK had criticized the Eisenhower administration for failing to confront communism when it was only 90 miles away from the United States. The president decided not to provide air cover. The invasion failed. Four days later most of the troops surrendered. Kennedy admitted the existence of the covert operation to the public and took full responsibility for the action. Privately, he was angry at himself for failing to consider fully the risks of the operation and furious at the CIA for presenting him with such a flawed plan.

Two months later, Kennedy met Khrushchev at a summit conference in Vienna. Perhaps because he was inexperienced, or because he was under the influence of painkilling drugs for his back, Kennedy did not respond well to the demands of the Soviet premier. Khrushchev was particularly bellicose. While he agreed to a coalition government in Laos, he actually shouted at the young president, demanding a formal peace treaty with Germany. Either solve the German issue, Khrushchev threatened, or he would take actions on his own, including making Berlin a "free city." A shaken Kennedy returned home and a month later asked Congress for a major increase in defense spending, including a call-up of reserve units and plans for fallout shelters in the event of nuclear war.

In August of 1961 Khrushchev sealed the border between East and West Berlin, first with barbed wire and then with a concrete wall. Kennedy attempted to minimize the significance of the act by refusing to cut short his Cape Cod vacation. Once he was convinced that the Soviets intended neither to invade West Berlin nor to prevent allied traffic (as Stalin had done), Kennedy let the wall stand. Weeks before, he had told an advisor, "This is unbearable to Khrushchev. East Germany is hemorrhaging to death. The entire East bloc is in danger. He has to do something to stop this. Perhaps a wall. . . . And there's not a damn thing we can do about it." Indeed, more than four million East Germans had fled the communist regime (most of them doctors, teachers, and scientists) through Berlin since the end of the war. No doubt sensing a crisis, the number of refugees rose to one thousand a day in the period before the wall was built. Opening the borders in Eastern Europe in 1989 vividly illustrated the consequences of free movement from the Soviet bloc.

Kennedy and his advisors were convinced that they avoided a direct confrontation with the Soviets as well as nuclear war by acquiescing to the building of the Berlin Wall. War was averted, and Western rights to West Berlin were still protected. Nevertheless, JFK paid a large political price for his decision. Cold War presidents were always anxious to stabilize relations with the Soviets, but at the same time they always risked charges of abandoning containment policy, or even of appeasement.

Just weeks after the Berlin Crisis, Kennedy learned that Khrushchev had resumed above-ground nuclear testing. The president shouted: "F—d again! The bastards! That f—g liar!" When Adlai Stevenson, ambassador to the U.N., urged JFK not to resume testing as well, for the sake of world public opinion, he rejected the advice:

> I have no choice. They spit in our eye three times. We have to do this. . . . All this makes Khrushchev look pretty tough. He has had a succession of apparent victories—space, Cuba, the Thirteenth of August in Berlin, though I don't regard that as a Soviet victory. He wants to give out the feeling that he has us on the run. . . .

By the following fall, when the Cold War was at its most intense point since the late 1940s, Kennedy was presented with aerial evidence that the Soviets were installing ballistic missiles in Cuba. For weeks, the president denied allegations from Senator Keating, a Republican from New York, that a Soviet military buildup was underway. Keating provided an incredible amount of detail, derived in part from CIA leaks. Clearly, from the president's view and that of his advisors, he could not withstand another defeat at the hands of Khrushchev. JFK called together a special advisory group called EXCOMM (executive committee) that met secretly for thirteen days to review their options. Initially, EXCOMM decided to plan for an air strike followed by an invasion of the island. Chastened by his experience with the Bay of Pigs failure, Kennedy insisted on a through exploration of all options. It quickly became obvious there was no guarantee that all the missiles could be destroyed, and a nuclear retaliation from the Soviets was likely. In fact, preparations were made for government officials to retreat to underground bunkers in the event of a nuclear attack. Instead, the president decided to blockade Soviet ships around Cuba and to demand the withdrawal of the missiles.

The plan was still not without risk. It was possible that Soviet naval commanders might attempt to break the blockade and that the Soviets might delay long enough for the missiles to be fully operational. Yet the plan did work. On October 26, Soviet ships halted their advance to the island and an offer was made through back channels that the Soviets would be willing to withdraw the missiles if the United States declared that it would never invade Cuba. At a key moment in the crisis, Kennedy received a long cable from Khrushchev confirming the proposal, followed hours later by another much more bellicose one. On the advice of his brother, Attorney General Robert F. Kennedy, the president ignored the later correspondence and responded positively to the first. On October 28 an agreement was reached. The missiles would be withdrawn under U.N. supervision in return for the American promise. (A secret protocol included an agreement that the United States would withdraw its own missiles from Turkey.)

Scholars are continually fascinated by the Cuban Missile Crisis. Ted Sorensen, for example, has connected the president's failure in the Bay of Pigs Crisis to his success in the missile crisis. The former showed that Kennedy's "luck and his judgment had human limitations," and the experience "taught him invaluable lessons for the future." Proof of the maturity lies in the Cuban Missile Crisis a year and a half later in which the president "dazzled the world" with his "combination of toughness and restraint, of will, nerve and wisdom, so brilliantly controlled, so matchlessly calibrated. . . ." Thus, the Bay of Pigs had been a small price to pay for the leadership that emerged in the second crisis. Others, such as Garry Wills, insist the president "learned nothing from the first crisis." He writes:

> . . . [Kennedy] wanted to remove the missiles provided he did not appear forced to bargain with the Soviets to accomplish this. He must deliver the ultimatum, make demands that made Russia act submissively. He would not, as he put it, let Khrushchev rub his nose in the dirt. Which meant that he had to rub Khrushchev's nose in the dirt; and that Khrushchev had to put up with it. Kennedy would even risk nuclear war rather than admit that a trade of useless missiles near each other's countries was eminently fair. The restraint, then, was not shown by Kennedy, but by Khrushchev. He was the one who had to back down, admit his maneuver failed, take the heat from internal critics for his policy.

Similarly, Robert Thomson Smith (*The Missiles of October*) concludes that despite all the bravado JFK got the worst part of the bargain, as he had done at the Bay of Pigs, in Berlin, and in Laos. The pledge to never invade Cuba placed the island in the communist orbit for the foreseeable future, and Khrushchev received private assurances about removing the missiles in Turkey. He concludes:

> The more appropriate lesson of the missile crisis might be in the ancient idea of hubris, pride, arrogance, and that these qualities lead to a fall. As sure that they could control the Caribbean and indeed the world as they controlled their own campaign, the Kennedys found themselves, in the end, faced down by that stubby little peasant, Nikita Khrushchev.

Whatever position one takes on Kennedy's performance, the Cuban Missile Crisis illustrated some basic features of the Cold War presidency in stark terms. First, although the United States came perilously close to nuclear war, neither the public nor Congress was included or even informed about the crisis until the president made his October 22 speech announcing the blockade. On that day, the *San Francisco Examiner* headline read: "A Day of Mystery in D.C.!" Second, the crisis illustrated the importance of the perceptions of world leaders in making decisions in the Cold War. While the president regarded strong action as absolutely essential after what he saw as a string of serious foreign policy defeats, the Soviet premier precipitated the crisis from what he regarded as his own position of weakness. Concerned that the United States enjoyed overwhelming nuclear superiority and fearful that a U.S. invasion of Cuba was imminent, he placed missiles on the island as a quick fix to obtain a balance of power. Ironically, despite increased American involvement in Vietnam, the missile crisis did, in fact, produce a new awareness of the need for better communications between Cold War leaders. A "hot line" was installed between Washington, DC, and Moscow to permit instant contact in the event of future crises. Kennedy was felled by an assassin's bullet in November of 1963.

LYNDON B. JOHNSON (1963–1969)

As Americans mourned the death of John Kennedy, his successor, Lyndon Baines Johnson, confronted succession problems similar to others who had assumed the office in the wake of the assassination of a popular president. Like Andrew Johnson, the new president was a Southerner who had been placed on the Democratic ticket primarily for strategic electoral reasons. Although Kennedy had defeated Lyndon Johnson, Senate Majority Leader, on the first ballot, he knew that the South was crucial to his election. The decision to ask Johnson to run as Kennedy's vice president was a controversial one for Kennedy's advisors. His brother, Robert F. Kennedy, had unsuccessfully attempted to withdraw the offer. Johnson was an effective campaigner in 1960 and, although he was isolated from Kennedy's inner circle, he was a dutiful vice president. Neither of these performances, however, allayed suspicions of the liberal wing of the party after the assassination in 1963 that Johnson was too conservative, especially on civil rights.

Like Theodore Roosevelt, Lyndon Johnson was an ambitious politician who spent his career under the influence of others. As a congressman, he was a reliable New Dealer who caught the eye of FDR. He carefully cultivated close relationships with senior senators like Sam Rayburn to rise to the position of party leader, the youngest person ever to attain the post. As minority leader, he undertook what he called the "politics of responsibility" in attempting to form bipartisan support on some issues with President Eisenhower. Then in 1960, he accepted the vice presidency despite the fact that he regarded Kennedy as the less experienced politician. Johnson, like Teddy Roosevelt, yearned to make his mark, both on the presidency and on the nation.

Johnson set out to achieve this goal by promoting programs as homage to the slain president. He took the oath of office aboard Air Force One with the president's widow at his side and retained Kennedy's entire cabinet, despite his distance from Kennedy and the animosity between himself and Robert Kennedy. Five days after the assassination, he spoke before a special joint session of Congress and urged the passage of JFK's civil rights bill. He paraphrased Lincoln's Gettysburg Address: "Let us here highly resolve that John Fitzgerald Kennedy did not live—or die—in vain." Congress passed the civil rights legislation in February of 1964, wiping out the elaborate system of segregation implemented in the South after the Civil War. Wayne Matusow (The Unraveling of America) has called the act the "great liberal achievement of the decade."

In the spring of 1964, Johnson proposed a major expansion of the goals of the New Frontier. Although Kennedy had been concerned about the existence of poverty in an affluent society, his programs tended to be cautious and experimental. Johnson, however, proposed a "war on poverty." He called the programs he intended to submit to Congress the "Great Society" and described them in utopian terms:

> The Great Society is a place where every child can find knowledge to enrich his mind and to enlarge his talents. It is a place where leisure is a welcome chance to build and reflect, not a feared cause of boredom and restlessness. It is a place where the city of man serves not only the needs of the body and the demands of commerce but the desire for beauty and the hunger for community.

Privately, LBJ said he hoped to surpass not only Kennedy's agenda but FDR's as well. After JFK's assassination, Johnson told his advisors, "Every issue that is on my desk tonight was on my desk when I came to Congress in 1937." Johnson was even confident that he would defeat "hard core" poverty:

> The people I want to help are the ones who've never held real jobs and aren't able to handle them. Most never had enough money and don't know how to spend it. They were born to parents who gave up hoping long ago. They have no motivation to reach for something better because the sum total of their lives is losing.

Even a confident and adept president could not seriously expect to persuade Congress to pass more than a small part of his program. Eisenhower's success rate with Congress on domestic issues was 37 percent in 1957, and Kennedy's was only 27 percent in 1963. Significant changes, however, were occurring in the Republican Party which aided Johnson.

New patterns of wealth were emerging, particularly in the West and South. While many of these new entrepreneurs were Republican, many were also more conservative than others in the party. In 1960 Richard Nixon, who was acceptable to conservatives, reached a compromise with the liberal wing of the party by adopting platform recommendations offered by Nelson Rockefeller, governor of New York. Many conservatives regarded the "pact" as evidence they needed to capture control of the party in order to stop the pattern of "me-too-ism" with Democrats. Barry Goldwater, an Arizonian senator, was their candidate. Offering a "choice, not an echo," he won a majority of the eleven primaries he entered and won the party nomination at a divided convention.

Goldwater's positions on Social Security, civil rights, and world politics were pointedly controversial. Although many of his views gained support years later, voters overwhelmingly voted for Democrats. Johnson won 61 percent of the vote, and Democrats won large majorities in Congress. Armed with tremendous tactical legislative skills and now with a mandate and firm congressional control, Johnson was able to compile an astounding 69 percent success rate in Congress. As Eric Goldman observed, "Working in the White House during this period produced on occasion an almost eerie feeling. The legislation rolled through the House and Senate in such profusion and so methodically that you seemed part of a vast, overpowering machinery, oiled to purr."

Johnson, of course, knew intimately the bottlenecks in the House of Representatives. He convinced members to limit the power of the Rules Committee and add new members to the Appropriations and Ways and Means committees. The eighty-ninth Congress passed over sixty major pieces of legislation that included aid to poor students (Elementary and Secondary Education Act, Higher Education Act), environmental restrictions (highway beautification, air and water pollution standards), Medicare, changes in immigration restrictions, and creation of arts and humanities foundations. Johnson also obtained congressional approval for two new cabinet offices (Transportation, and Housing and Urban Affairs). The Great Society constituted the greatest amount of legislation since the New Deal. Johnson effectively functioned as a prime minister who could pass legislation with a stable party majority, and many journalists were predicting that the Republican Party would meet the same fate as the Whigs.

Johnson, however, also chose to continue and extend Kennedy's policies internationally. "I believe that we can continue the Great Society while we fight in Vietnam," he told Congress in 1966. Eventually the set of decisions to escalate American commitments in Vietnam not only ended many of the Great Society initiatives but also ended his presidency. LBJ noted Truman's struggle to defend his policies against the charge that he was "soft on communism" and that China was "lost" to the communists in the struggle under his watch. He felt that he could not risk the loss of Vietnam. In 1970, Johnson described with a gender metaphor his decision to escalate the war:

> I knew from the start that I was bound to be crucified either way I moved. If I left the woman I really loved—the Great Society—in order to get involved with that bitch of a war on the other side of the world, then I would lose everything at home. . . . But if I left that war and let the communists take over South Vietnam, then I would be seen as a coward and my nation would be seen as an appeaser and we would both find it impossible to accomplish anything for anybody anywhere on the entire globe.

Johnson, like Eisenhower and Kennedy, accepted the domino theory in Southeast Asia. Unlike these presidents, however, Johnson could not avoid a major military commitment. Eisenhower had refused to send American troops to the region after the defeat of the French forces and instead accepted the division of Vietnam into two regimes. (Partition, a common method of dispute resolution in the Cold War, had been previously utilized in Germany and Korea.) Eisenhower had supported the anti-communist government led by Ngo Dinh Diem in South Vietnam with economic and military aid. Kennedy had resisted pressures to approve of a coalition government in the South as communist guerilla forces gained momentum. He did, however, increase the number of military advisors from under 1,000 to over 16,000 and became intimately involved in Vietnamese politics. Richard Reeves *(President Kennedy)* reports a Soviet official casually noting that U.S. Ambassador Henry Cabot Lodge acted very much like a Russian official in an East European country. South Vietnam was rapidly becoming a client state that depended on the United States for its very existence. Three weeks before his assassination, Kennedy engineered a coup against Diem in an attempt to provide the country with a more popular leader. It is difficult to determine which direction Kennedy would have pursued in Vietnam. Although he strongly believed a non-communist South Vietnam was essential to the maintenance of a non-communist Asia, he also was clearly concerned about the prospects for nation building in South Vietnam and very suspicious of the projections of military advisors.

The day after the assassination, Johnson told Ambassador Lodge that he would not be the president who lost Vietnam. In August of 1964 the president made his first major decision about the conflict. A U.S. destroyer was fired upon by Vietnamese torpedo boats in the Gulf of Tonkin. Although communications were murky, two days later another destroyer reported hostile fire. Johnson immediately sent 64 bombers to North Vietnam and requested from Congress authorization to "take all necessary measures to protect American troops and prevent further aggression in Vietnam." Congress immediately passed the resolution. The vote was unanimous in the House and 88–2 in the Senate. Although the conflict quickly escalated into a major war, many members of Congress deeply resented the administration's claim that the resolution was the "functional equivalent of war."

During the 1964 campaign, Johnson rarely discussed Vietnam and referred to Goldwater's call for military escalation as "reckless." In February of 1965 Johnson responded to an attack on the American base at Pleiku with more retaliatory raids on North Vietnam. The president expanded these raids to a permanent policy of air raids called "Rolling Thunder." He also added 50,000 more U.S. forces and expanded their mission. Both policies were initiated without public disclosure. In June, and again in July, both political and military advisors informed Johnson that without the introduction of massive American ground troops, the war would be lost in months. The president expressed his concerns that the communists would match American troop increases and force him to escalate constantly. In a July meeting, he worried about the costs of the war and asked: "Are we starting something that in two or three years we simply can't finish?" His advisors, many of whom were Kennedy appointees, acknowledged his concerns but insisted that the war was winnable and that withdrawals would constitute an abandonment of the containment policy that had been an American hallmark for the past twenty years. The lone dissenter was Under Secretary of State George Ball, who made an impassioned plea for "cutting our losses" since Vietnam was the wrong place to take a stand.

By 1967 over 500,000 troops were stationed in Vietnam. The inability to convincingly establish progress in winning the war, coupled with disturbing moral issues in its prosecution, led to the formation of a large peace movement initially led by college students and subsequently joined by major segments of the most influential elements of American society, including the media and politicians. Protestors blamed the Americanization of the war in 1965 on the president and shouted outside the White House and anywhere the president traveled: "Hey! Hey! LBJ! how many kids did you kill today!" Johnson was angered and hurt by these attacks. He told Doris Kearns in 1970 that the students simply didn't understand him ("I always hated cops when I was a kid. . . . I'm not some conformist middle-class personality."), nor did they understand the communist threat, since they had not lived through World War II and Korea.

By 1968 Johnson had become more and more isolated. He refused to listen to critics in his administration. He felt that members of Congress who questioned his policies had betrayed him. He could not appear in public except under controlled circumstances without protesters taunting him. He began to worry about his own legacy:

> I felt that I was being chased on all sides by a giant stampede coming at me from all directions. On the one side, the American people were stampeding me to do something about Vietnam. On the other side, the inflationary economy was booming out of control. Up ahead were doz-

ens of danger signs pointing to another summer of riots in the cities. I was being forced over the edge by rioting blacks, demonstrating students, marching welfare mothers, and hysterical reporters. And then the final straw. The thing I feared from the first day of my Presidency was actually coming true. Robert Kennedy had openly announced his decision to reclaim the throne in the name of his brother and the American people, swayed by the magic of the name, were dancing in the streets. The whole situation was unbearable to me.

Johnson was challenged in the New Hampshire primary by Eugene McCarthy, senator from Minnesota, who was a critic of the war. Johnson won the primary, but his relatively slight margin (50 percent to 42 percent) showed that the once masterful president was in trouble with his own party. Robert Kennedy entered the race shortly thereafter. On March 31, the president appeared on television with two surprise announcements. He indicated that he had called a partial halt to bombing in North Vietnam and that because he planned to devote all his energies to a peace agreement, he would not be a candidate for reelection.

Johnson, who hoped to be the greatest of the "accidental" presidents, followed the path of others who were not elected to second terms. Both of Johnson's great initiatives remain controversial. Some writers argue the Great Society itself was a failure because it was either too cautious or too radical. Some also blame Johnson for Americanizing the war in Vietnam, while others blame him for not prosecuting it more effectively. Clearly, Johnson was able to anticipate some changes in America and reacted to them effectively. Yet in other ways, Johnson remained a figure bound by the politics of previous periods, when deals were struck by the individual with the most personal clout. According to Joseph Califano, Johnson was initially so stunned by urban riots that he was immobilized: "He just wouldn't accept it. He refused to look at the cables from Los Angeles describing the situation. . . . We needed decisions from him but he simply wouldn't respond." Soon Johnson became resentful: "A few hoodlums . . . moved from city to city making trouble. Spoiling all the progress I've made in these last few years." Charles de Gaulle once said that Americans were unable to come to terms with LBJ because he exhibited so clearly the generosity as well as the faults of the nation itself. "This man Kennedy," he concluded, "is America's mask. But this man Johnson, he is the country's real face."

RICHARD M. NIXON (1969–1974)

When Richard Milhous Nixon assumed office in 1969 after defeating Hubert Humphrey, the nation was undergoing a series of traumatic changes. The consensus on strategies to fight the Cold War was rapidly unraveling. Lyndon Johnson's efforts to create a significant movement toward a settlement in Vietnam before the election did not materialize. The Vietnam War so frustrated just about every segment of the population that the policy of containment itself was under challenge. Was it possible, and even desirable, for the United States to be the "world's policeman"? Criticism of the war extended to domestic policy. Some Americans complained that the War on Poverty was far too cautious; others complained that it had gone too far. One consequence of Johnson's reforms was a severe backlash among white voters. George Wallace, the segregationist governor of Alabama who defied federal orders to desegregate the University of Alabama, ran for president in 1968 on a third-party ticket. Wallace won 13.5 percent of the popular vote (compared to Thurmond's 2.4 percent in 1948), including 10 percent of the votes in the states of New Jersey, Ohio, and Michigan.

In his first inaugural address Nixon acknowledged the significance of these developments. He compared the problems America faced in 1969 to those of a "third of a century ago." When FDR surveyed the effects of the Great Depression, he had concluded, "They concern, thank God, only material things." But now, according to Nixon, the crisis was "in reverse": "We find ourselves rich in goods but ragged in spirit; reaching with magnificent precision for the moon but falling into raucous discord on earth."

Nixon's responses to these changes were often dramatic, complex, and puzzling. He developed what was called a "Southern strategy" to entice white Southerners into the Republican Party. Although he supported attempts to delay desegregation, he also supported the "Philadelphia Plan," a quota system to force unions to include African-American workers, and a "negative income tax" to replace welfare. He favored a general reduction of federal programs and dismantled many features of the Great Society but also proposed sweeping environmental legislation, in 1971 instituting wage and price controls.

In foreign policy, Nixon refused to support demands for an immediate end to the war in Vietnam. (A peace agreement was not reached until 1973.) Yet he also developed a policy of détente with the Soviet Union and, in one of his most surprising moves, personally visited communist China. In all these initiatives, the president was preoccupied—even obsessed—with secrecy. Of course, the most troubling secrets in the aftermath of the Watergate incident led to his resignation after impeachment by the House of Representatives.

There are numerous attempts to find a key that would explain Nixon's overall actions. When Garry Wills interviewed him in 1968, Nixon spoke of his admiration for Woodrow Wilson. Some commentators had already concluded that Nixon's "Wilsonizing" was just another feint, but Wills found this identification fitting despite his reputation as a conservative. For Wills, Nixon represented "all the liberal things we believed in once, now grown unbelievable," and he connected Nixon to Wilson in particular since both believed in "the self-made man at home," believed in self-determination abroad, and "gave an evangelical flavor to their exhortations for an 'open world' of peaceful competition between such nations." Wills, however, ignored a major revision on Nixon's part. In his interview, Nixon continued:

> Wilson had the greatest vision of America's world role. But he wasn't practical enough. Take his "open agreements openly arrived at." That is no way diplomacy is conducted. The Vietnamese war, for instance, will be settled at secret high level negotiations.

During his presidency, one of Nixon's advisors, Patrick Moynihan, told him that he was much like British Prime Minister Benjamin Disraeli, who frequently employed liberal policies for conservative ends. Nixon liked this analogy, although he was certainly aware that Moynihan was using the flattering reference to gain support for welfare reform. Henry Kissinger, Nixon's powerful national security advisor, compared himself to Metternich, the architect of the nineteenth-century "concert of Europe" international system that preserved traditional states against the challenge of socialism. By implication, he also compared Nixon to Emperor Francis I, Metternich's head of state. The analogy was always a self-serving one for Kissinger since Emperor Francis I was "dour and suspicious, unimaginative and pedantic." Like Nixon, Francis spied on his enemies and reveled in "getting even," while his talented counselor steadfastly developed farsighted policies in his name. The analogy also indirectly compares Austria in 1809 to the United States in 1968—not only flattering Kissinger but also allowing Nixon more credit. As Kissinger also remarked, after the Napoleonic Wars the Austrian government had lost "its élan and its self confidence." Moreover, since the government "could not draw its strength from the inspiration of its people, it had to achieve aims by the tenacity and subtlety of its diplomacy."

In 1973, Arthur Schlesinger, Jr. attempted to shift the focus away from Nixon's personality toward institutional concerns. In *The Imperial Presidency*, he described a new institution that was inadvertently created by the years of the Cold War. This new presidency was "born in the 1940s and 1950s" to deal with the demands of the Cold War and by the 1960s and 1970s began "to find nurture at home." The decline of the party system and the Keynesian revolution in economics created an "extraordinary historical moment" in which future presidents could resist or ride the "new tendencies of power." Before Nixon, the personalities of presidents functioned as a barrier to the imperial presidency. From Roosevelt through Johnson, presidents had been gregarious people. FDR's "delight in power" was balanced by his delight in recruiting "obstinate and opinionated men" who questioned his decisions. Truman was a direct and affectionless man. Eisenhower harbored "royal elements," but his "Whiggishness" restrained this inclination. Kennedy did create a court-like atmosphere in the White House, but his "ironic and skeptical intelligence customarily kept the Presidency in healthy perspective."

To Schlesinger, however, Nixon was truly a revolutionary figure. Nixon was consciously moving toward a "plebiscitary presidency" along the lines of Louis Napoleon and, more recently, Charles De Gaulle:

> A plebiscitary presidency, unlike a parliamentary regime, would not require a new Constitution; presidential acts, confirmed by a Supreme Court of his own appointment, could put a new gloss on the old one.

Nixon cut himself loose from his party and announced that his electoral mandate entitled him to undertake any action he deemed necessary.

> Nixon was carrying the imperial presidency toward its ultimate form in the plebiscitary Presidency with the President accountable only once every four years, shielded in the years in between elections from congressional and public harassment, empowered by his mandate to make war or to make peace, to spend or to impound, to give information out or to hold it back, superseding congressional legislation by executive order, all in the name of a majority. . . .

Was Nixon like Woodrow Wilson, Benjamin Disraeli, Emperor Francis, or Louis Napoleon? Each of these analogies captures aspects of Nixon's agenda—his efforts to recast the international system, to support surprisingly liberal policies, to concentrate power systemically—but none seems to capture his presidency as a whole. Perhaps the most useful characterization is a revision of the original assessment, offered by Gary Wills in 1993, that Nixon "survived by keeping all sides off balance—which makes it hard for a consensus to be reached among people so often inspired and disgusted by his acts (often in swift succession)."

Nixon's ability to respond to rapid change through unexpected innovations, often devised in secret, worked well for him until the Watergate scandal. His political position, even after his landslide reelection victory in 1972, was always precarious. He was never personally popular with voters. He was not an effective speaker. He was the first president elected since Zachary Taylor without a party majority in either the House or the Senate. He was despised by liberals for what they regarded as dirty campaign tactics extending back to his defeat of Jerry Voorhis for the House in 1946 and Helen Douglas for the Senate in 1950. He was mistrusted by conservatives who remembered his famous New York meeting with liberal Republican Nelson Rockefeller in 1960. Although he was often a tactical genius, Nixon was always personally insecure.

In domestic policy, Nixon used every conceivable strategy to promote his agenda. Distrustful of career bureaucrats as well as many of his own cabinet members, Nixon doubled the size of his White House staff; created a Domestic Council chaired by one of his advisors, John Erlichman; and gave the Office of Management and Budget increased authority to supervise the administration of programs. The ostensible purpose of his approach was to create a more coordinated administration but, as Robert

P. Nathan noted, his real purpose was to create a "counterbureaucracy." In the words of H. R. Haldeman, his chief of staff, ". . . 96 percent of the bureaucracy are against us, they're bastards who are here to screw us." When he was reelected in 1972, one of Nixon's first acts was to present each cabinet officer with an undated resignation to sign. Reversing his earlier plans, he announced massive reductions in the Executive Office of the President and elevated several cabinet members to the new title of "super-secretaries" since they were also to be "Counselors to the President."

Nixon used his veto powers liberally, but what most annoyed Congress was his expansion of the use of impoundment. Modern presidents regularly refused to spend money on selected projects appropriated by Congress. Nixon, however, impounded greater amounts of money than any other president (almost 20 percent of controllable expenses in the budget) and actually attempted to eliminate entire programs. The courts did not look favorably on this assertion of constitutional power on Nixon's part, but judicial remedies were slow. Meanwhile, representatives voiced their concern that the president was in effect exercising an absolute veto over legislation.

Nixon was reasonably successful, especially in his first term, as a legislative leader despite his position as minority president and his strategy of "taking on" Congress. One of his few specific campaign pledges was a promise to appoint a new attorney general to "launch a war" against criminal elements throughout the land. Three major bills dealing with crime control were passed in 1970. This legislation provided for a witness protection program, mandatory sentencing, and new drug-control measures. Nixon's revenue-sharing plan represented an entirely new agenda and was reluctantly approved by Congress. Nixon contended that the federal government was too large and that the states could better administer programs if they had access to federal funds. The proposal also fit well with his criticism of the Great Society, since it would reduce the number of categorical grants that required states to spend money as determined by Congress. Surprisingly, Nixon was receptive to environmental issues and highlighted his proposals in his first State of the Union message declaring "clean air, clean water, open spaces" were a "birthright of every American." Congress passed the National Environmental Protection Act in 1969 and the Clean Water Act and Water Pollution Control Act in 1970, and established the Occupational Safety and Health Administration in the same year.

Nixon was less successful in other areas. He failed to gain congressional approval for welfare reform. His plan was quite radical since it replaced welfare with a system of cash payments, established work requirements, increased allowances for food stamps, and committed the federal government to enforcement of national standards. Although the Family Assistance Act passed the House, Nixon seemed to lose interest in the legislation when criticism about its cost mounted, and the Senate only passed some portions of the bill. No doubt in part because of the president's often adversarial relationship with Congress, the Senate also refused to confirm two Southern jurists to the Supreme Court. Nixon was furious and publicly stated that no Southerner could be confirmed by the Senate.

While Nixon fought tenaciously for his legislation, he himself admitted his real interests were in foreign policy. Throughout his administrations the president's most pressing concern was the war in Vietnam, although he did not permit this problem to distract him from his effort to envision larger strategies. During the 1968 presidential campaign, Nixon refused to talk about specific alternatives in Vietnam but did emphasize that he indeed had a secret plan to end the war. Hubert Humphrey, on the other hand, felt bound to support Johnson's policies until October when he announced that he supported a conditional end to the bombing in North Vietnam. Faced with a choice between a candidate who seemed to be committed to following current policy and one who promised a new initiative, many voters chose the latter.

Once elected, Nixon initiated what he called his "madman" strategy. He instructed his national security advisor, Henry Kissinger, to convey through diplomatic as well as back channels that the new president was a reckless man who would risk anything, including major escalation, to end the war. The threat apparently did not work, since Ho Chi Minh refused to meet important elements of Nixon's peace terms, especially one requiring North Vietnamese withdrawal from the South. Publicly, Nixon advanced a gradual plan of American troop withdrawals as an alternative to a quick settlement. He insisted that "Vietnamization" of the war would insure "peace with honor."

Secretly, Nixon engaged in bold actions that escalated the conflict. He ordered the bombing of Cambodia in order to cut enemy supply lines. The covert bombing even involved forged air force flight records. In the spring of 1970, Nixon announced he was sending American ground troops into Cambodia. Although he insisted that the mission would end in two months, the public was now skeptical about such assurances after years of war. War critics in Congress claimed that in effect the president had declared war on another country without their authorization. Student protests spread across campuses, and at Kent State University four students were killed by National Guard troops. In an odd attempt to express his concern, Nixon visited student protestors at the Lincoln Memorial in the middle of the night.

The troops sent to Cambodia were withdrawn on schedule, but Nixon still was unable to reach a settlement as he faced reelection. The following year he undertook another gamble. He blockaded Vietnamese ports, mined harbors, and played what he called his "hole card"—the Christmas bombing of North Vietnam, which Michael A. Genovese (*The Nixon Presidency*) has described as "one of the most brutal examples of force in history." Still, these measures did not alter the terms the North Vietnamese had offered in 1969. During the 1972 presidential election, Nixon announced that "peace was at hand" and in January of 1973 a peace agreement was signed.

Critics contend that Nixon was forced to accept the same terms offered by the North Vietnamese in 1969 (American withdrawal of troops and a prisoner-of-war exchange) at the cost of many lives on both sides and turmoil at home. Nixon, however, believed that Vietnam was only one part (although an unexpectedly recalcitrant one) of a plan to alter Cold War policies. When Nixon escalated the war in 1972, many observers believed that tensions with the Soviet Union would rise. On the contrary, Nixon visited Moscow in the spring and spoke before the Russian people on television. He signed nine major agreements, including the SALT I accords that limited or froze antiballistic defense sites, ICBM launchers, and submarines carrying nuclear weapons. (In 1960, Eisenhower had hoped to achieve precisely these results but failed as a result of the U-2 incident. Nixon ignored advice from Kissinger that the same scenario would occur when he increased bombing in Vietnam.)

Nixon felt that significant changes were developing in the international system that permitted new initiatives. He arranged secret meetings between Kissinger and Chinese officials and in 1971 issued the surprise announcement that he was going to China. Although no major agreements were reached at the Chinese summit, the eight-day visit was extensively covered by the press through new satellite hookups. Americans knew even less about China's role in the Cold War than they did about the Soviet Union's. This extended view behind the "Bamboo Curtain" arranged by a president known primarily for his anti-communist views fascinated the public.

In these two initiatives as well as those involving the war in Vietnam, Nixon acted even more secretly than he did on domestic issues. He expanded the authority of the National Security Council and effectively froze out the State Department, including his own secretary of state, William Rodgers, from participating on many issues. In fact, this penchant for secrecy was so great that it is difficult to discern exactly what was Nixon's "Grand Design" for altering the international order. His oft-quoted remark in 1972 gives some indication: "I think it would be a safer world . . . if we can have a strong, healthy United States, Europe, Soviet Union, China, Japan, each balancing the other, not playing one against the other, an even balance."

Scholars are divided on what kind of new international order Nixon tried to construct. Did the president hope to institute a return to a balance of power or a revived concert system? A balance-of-power system is generally theorized as one composed of at least five actors. An astute analyst such as Nixon could discern the breakup of communism as a monolithic network of client states, much as he could see the rise of new powers in

Europe and the Pacific Rim. Balance of power also assumes an international arena relatively free of ideological and domestic constraints in
order for powers to adjust to challenges from hegemonic initiatives.
Nixon's anti-communist credentials were an ideal protection against
charges of appeasement. Such a system also required some recognition of
the parameters of international competition that Nixon attempted to
institute with his demands for "linkage" (such as a quid pro quo for
wheat sale) and the policy of détente with the Soviet Union. Skeptics of
Nixon's project have pointed out the incomplete character of each of
these features: the relative military and/or economic weakness of China,
Japan, and Germany as global powers; the still potent role of ideology
and the interpenetration of domestic and foreign policy in democracies;
the recalcitrance of the Soviets.

Still, the concert model gains some plausibility as a Nixon project
because of Henry Kissinger's aforementioned attraction to Metternich and
Nixon's reputation as a conservative. The Concert of Europe had been
very much a result of the great powers' effort to reconstitute stability in
the wake of the Napoleonic wars and to regularize colonialism. The Cold
War, too, had its own slow but calamitous effect on superpower budgets
and politics that became quite apparent in the 1980s and 1990s. Was Nixon
attempting to create some version of a concert through his policies of
détente and his overtures to China? Was the Nixon doctrine attempting to
regularize spheres of influence? Were the SALT agreements an effort to
lower costly defense budgets on both sides? Whatever were the outlines
of his Grand Design, even Nixon's most severe critics acknowledge his
success in foreign policy. According to Stephen Garrett, Nixon had set
America on a "wholly new course in its foreign relations. These policies,
irreversible in many areas, marked a most momentous shift in America's
posture toward allies and adversaries alike. Basic relationships were
realigned, and progressively, new truths were recognized."

Nixon's policies, both domestic and foreign, never proceeded
smoothly. His penchant for secrecy made Congress and the media suspicious, and what his aides call his "dark side" led him to lash out at critics
at every opportunity. Still, until the Watergate scandal, Nixon could point
to specific achievements. He could also initiate unanticipated new policy
turns to keep critics off guard and reassure his supporters. Seeking reelection in 1972, Nixon could report on his successes with détente and his
meetings with the Chinese, claim that "peace was at hand," and note his
bold efforts to contain inflation.

Nixon was aided by the Democratic Party as well. In an effort to
avoid the sort of disastrous situation that occurred in 1968 when protesters fought Chicago police outside the convention hall, the Democrats
established proportional quotas for delegates for racial minorities,
women, and youth (defined as those over 18 and under 30 years old). As
a result of these so-called "new politics," the convention was raucous and

undisciplined. On the night of George McGovern's nomination speech, his appearance was delayed until the early morning as delegates nominated Martha Mitchell and Mao Tse-Tung, made pleas for lowering the age of sexual consent, amnesty for war protesters, higher subsidies for Native American tribes, higher welfare payments, and rights for Mexican workers and illegal emigrants. Watching the speeches on television, Nixon happily concluded: "The scene had the air of a college skit that had gotten away with itself and didn't know how to stop." He ordered campaign officials to portray McGovern as a left-wing Goldwater. "This is the line," Nixon told John Ehrlichman: "McGovern . . . is a dedicated, radical, pacifist left winger." The strategy worked. The election results resembled those of 1964. Nixon won 60 percent of the vote and carried every state except Massachusetts.

The systematic cover-up of the attempted burglary at the Democratic Party Headquarters in 1972 posed special problems for the president. Although Nixon was quite used to facing adversaries, in this case he was confronted by four at once. The press, particularly the *Washington Post*, was determined to investigate the origins of the break-in as well as its ramifications. Reporters Carl Bernstein and Bob Woodward were the first to discover that those arrested had ties to the White House, the CIA, and the Committee to Reelect the President (CREEP), and hence the incident was not the "third-rate burglary" that the administration said it was.

The courts weighed in as well. Federal Judge John Sirica gave very long sentences for first-time offenders in order to force one or more of the defendants to talk about who ordered the break-in. The Supreme Court declared that tapes of conversations recorded by the president were not subject to executive privilege. A Democratically controlled Congress used its oversight powers to engage in televised investigations. Forced by intense political pressures, Nixon could no longer keep legal proceedings confined to his own Justice Department and was forced to appoint an independent Office of Special Prosecutor.

As the press, the courts, special prosecutors, and Congress investigated the break-in, other unsavory aspects of Nixon's presidency were exposed. In efforts to stop criticism and leaks of his policies, he authorized a "plumbers" unit. The most widely publicized activity of the plumbers was the break-in at Daniel Ellsberg's psychiatrist's office in an effort to copy his personal files. Nixon was angered by Ellsberg's release of a classified document known as the "Pentagon Papers" that scrutinized government policies in Vietnam. He hoped the medical files might damage the whistleblower's reputation. In addition, illegal activities by officials of the Committee to Reelect the President were exposed, including money laundering, fraud, forgery, and "dirty tricks" against opponents.

Nixon's classic response to these disclosures was, as usual, secrecy. He urged his aides to "stonewall" when faced with questions from Congress and prosecutors. He claimed that issues of national security required secrecy and that his conversations with aides were protected from scrutiny by executive privilege. All of these tactics actually fuelled the growing crisis, since secrecy itself was the political issue. Nixon's other common tactic was the bold, unexpected move. After a Senate investigating committee learned of the existence of tapes of White House conversations, Special Prosecutor Archibald Cox asked for a subpoena from Judge Sirica ordering Nixon to hand over the recordings. Nixon refused and again cited the practice of executive privilege. No president, Nixon argued, could receive candid counsel if advisors knew their conversations might later be scrutinized by Congress or the courts. Nixon did not mention that the tapes themselves eroded confidentiality, since a president could conceivably selectively release them.

The controversy would continue for a year. In a surprise move, the president ordered Attorney General Elliot Richardson to fire the special prosecutor. When Richardson refused and resigned, he ordered Deputy Attorney General William D. Ruckelshaus to follow his order. When Ruckelshaus also refused and resigned, he asked the third ranking official in the Justice Department, Robert Bork, to undertake the task. Bork complied, but these massive resignations were immediately called the "Saturday Night Massacre" by the press. This bold assertion of presidential power heightened the crisis rather than defusing it. Learning that this action severely eroded his support nationally and within his own party, Nixon agreed to release some tapes and was forced to agree to the appointment of a new special prosecutor. When experts discovered that one tape had an eighteen-minute erasure, Nixon claimed clerical error.

In the midst of impeachment hearings, the president tried one more surprise tactic. He appeared on television with a large number of volumes next to him and claimed that his release of this huge amount of transcripts would conclusively establish his innocence. Members of Congress, however, were suspicious of the edited transcripts, and their dissemination further embarrassed the president on several points, including his frequent use of strong language. Two months later, the House Judiciary Committee passed three articles of impeachment, citing obstruction of justice, violation of the constitutional rights of citizens, and contempt of Congress. Each article grounded the charges on the president's violation of his oath to "preserve, protect and defend the Constitution" and "to take care that the laws be faithfully executed." On the same day that the House Judiciary Committee began its debate on impeachment, the Supreme Court rejected the president's position on executive privilege in U.S. v. Nixon. The Court did acknowledge the right of executive privilege but denied Nixon's claim that unless such power was absolute, the constitutional principle of separation of powers would be violated. Faced with an order by the nation's highest court, Nixon released the tapes, which showed that he was aware of the break-in six days after it occurred and actively took steps to thwart an investigation by the FBI. On August 9,

1974, Nixon undertook one final bold action. He resigned. Later, out of office, Nixon himself speculated that had he destroyed the tapes after they were discovered (in what would have been yet another daring maneuver), perhaps his presidency would have survived.

Nixon is regarded by many as the epitome of the failures of the Cold War presidency. In this view, the president not only refused to sue for peace in 1968 but actually expanded the war in 1970, and he ultimately bore primary responsibility not only for America's only defeat in war but also for the terrible events that later befell Cambodia. He also exacerbated generational divisions at home, raised levels of distrust in government to levels that even today have yet to abate, and reduced respect for the office of president. Yet, even though he was the only president to be forced to resign from office, others contend that he was a visionary statesman who could both foresee and plan for American interests beyond Vietnam and even beyond the Cold War.

GERALD R. FORD (1974–1977)

Gerald Ford was certainly not the first president unelected in his own right. Presidents Tyler, Andrew Johnson, Theodore Roosevelt, and Lyndon Johnson assumed office as a result of the death of a president. Ford's position, however, was unique in another respect. He was not only the first to take office because a president had resigned, but he was also the first completely unelected president. During the Nixon administration in 1973, Vice President Spiro Agnew was forced to resign due to criminal charges of tax evasion. Under the provisions of the newly adopted Twenty-Fifth Amendment, the president was authorized to fill a vacancy in the office with the concurrence of a majority of the House and Senate. Nixon preferred to nominate John Connolly of Texas, a Democrat who had changed parties, but was concerned that he might not be able to win congressional approval. Instead he chose Gerald Ford, a congressman from Michigan and minority leader since 1965. Although Ford was a loyal supporter, Nixon had little respect for him, and some aides later reported that he also chose Ford as part of a poison-pill strategy: No Congress would impeach him and allow Jerry Ford to be president. When Nixon resigned and Ford too was required to appoint a vice president, he selected Nelson Rockefeller, who was serving his fifteenth year as governor of New York. Thus, both the president and vice president were officials unelected by the voters at large or by the constitutional provisions provided by the electoral college.

Ford struggled throughout his term to establish his legitimacy. When he had accepted the vice presidency under Nixon, he said that he was "a Ford, not a Lincoln." When he assumed the presidency on August 9, 1974, he insisted that his speech was not an inaugural address—"just a little straight talk." On this occasion, he announced that "our long national nightmare is over. Our constitution works. Our great republic is a government of laws and not men. Here, the people rule." He also carefully indicated his respect for the disgraced former president, saying that he hoped Richard Nixon, "who brought peace to millions, finds it for himself."

Ford's unique situation was not the only source of his difficulties. As a result of the Watergate scandal, Democrats enjoyed a 23-seat advantage in the Senate and 147 in the House. Many presidents have faced majorities of the opposite party, but the "Watergate Congress" represented the largest margin since 1936. In addition, the new administration included two powerful figures whose agendas were not necessarily the same as the president's. Henry Kissinger held two posts—national security advisor and secretary of state—and Vice President Rockefeller, who was a mentor to Kissinger earlier in his career, demanded and received overall authority to coordinate domestic policy. Rockefeller's plan was to make the Domestic Council the equivalent of the National Security Council in the Executive Office. Moreover, the Cold War was not over, the situation in Vietnam was rapidly deteriorating, the economic prosperity of the 1960s was faltering, and Watergate criminal charges and trials were ongoing.

Ford was thus faced with two difficult options. He could govern in a low-key and restricted manner, hoping to present a contrast to the Nixon administration. However, the danger in this strategy was that he could be seen as a president who was essentially a caretaker until the next election. Alternatively, he could be more assertive, developing and promoting his own policies. Either choice threatened to raise questions about his legitimacy as president: Did a president who was basically a clerk deserve reelection? What was the mandate for the first truly unelected president?

Ford wavered. Sometimes he seemed to take the first route. He retained the Nixon cabinet and the senior officials of his White House staff, including Al Haig, who had assumed the chief of staff position during Nixon's second term and was deeply involved in the events of the last days of the Nixon administration. Initially, Ford simply added his own appointments to this mix. The result was open warfare between the Ford team and what the new appointees called the "Praetorian guard of the deposed emperor." Cabinet members openly pursued their own agendas and sabotaged Ford's programs. William Simon, secretary of treasury, was opposed to Ford's WIN (Whip Inflation Now) program and ridiculed it before the press, and Haig ran the White House as if Nixon had never left.

Ford soon replaced Haig, and in November of 1975 he fired several cabinet members and replaced Kissinger with Brent Scowcroft as head of the National Security Council. Although he had reservations, Ford cooperated fully with a congressional investigation of the CIA and subsequently issued an executive order banning covert assassinations. He stopped Nixon's practice of impounding congressional appropriations. When North Vietnamese troops marched into Saigon in April of 1975 and

U.S. personnel and their South Vietnamese supporters struggled to leave on waiting planes, Ford minimized the event. He left for a vacation in Palm Springs and briefly noted, "The evacuation has been completed. . . . This action closes a chapter in the American experience." He ended by urging Americans to "avoid recriminations."

Many of Ford's actions were devoted to healing the political wounds inflicted by the Watergate scandal. He worked hard to convince the public he was ending the imperial presidency that critics associated with Nixon. While his predecessor had once attempted to outfit White House guards with special uniforms, Ford, in contrast, told the press he made his own breakfast each morning. On more substantive matters, Ford was willing to develop a policy of conditional clemency to draft resisters. About one percent of eligible men failed to register for service during the Vietnam war, and another one percent refused induction. Many fled to Canada. When Nixon received a staff memo reviewing the history of presidential policies toward draft resisters in 1972, he angrily rejected the precedents of Lincoln and Truman outlined in the report and scrawled, "Never, Never . . ." on the margin. Ford had supported Nixon's position when he was in Congress. In September of 1974, however, he announced the "Vietnam Era Reconciliation Program" and appointed Charles Goodell, a Republican congressman who had been blacklisted by Nixon for his criticism of the war, as head of the program. Although the program was controversial and difficult to administer, thousands of applicants were processed and most received either pardons or alternate service.

On September 8, 1974, Ford made a decision that rocked his presidency and was perhaps responsible for his failure to win reelection. He announced on television that he had pardoned Nixon for all crimes he "committed or may have committed or taken part in" while president. Ford's approval rating fell 21 points in a week. Ford's press secretary and longtime friend and supporter, J. H. terHorst, resigned. Many congressmen openly accused Ford of having made a deal while Nixon was still in the White House in order to assume the presidency. In order to quell these accusations, Ford appeared before the House Judiciary Committee on October 17. He was the first president since Lincoln to testify in person before a committee of Congress.

Questioning was detailed and acrimonious. The president angrily denied Representative Elizabeth Holtzman's characterization of the pardon as one that raised "very dark suspicions." He angrily interrupted her comments to say that "there was no deal, period, under no circumstances." In fact, the situation just before Nixon's resignation was very complex, and Alexander Haig did mention the issue of a pardon in his conversations with Ford. While there was no evidence of any collusion between Nixon and Ford, the pardon had few strong supporters. It is impossible to determine, however, what would have been the consequences for Ford had he not made this decision. The continued coverage of the former president as a witness in criminal trials of his aides (and perhaps his own) may have had a negative impact on the Republican ticket in the election as well.

Ford almost invariably found it difficult to initiate his own policies. In May of 1975, Cambodian forces captured an unarmed American merchant ship, the *Mayaguez*. Ford made a high-risk decision to send U.S. marines on a rescue mission and ordered the bombing of Cambodia. Fortunately, the crew were soon released, possibly as a result of the diplomatic efforts of China. Ford's poll ratings went up temporarily, and he attempted to portray the incident as evidence of America's continued power despite the outcome of the war in Vietnam. However, as John Robert Greene, one of Ford's biographers, has concluded, the *Mayaguez* was perhaps more important as a case of crisis management than of substantive policy implementation.

Ford was unable to reach an agreement with the Soviets on the SALT II negotiations, but he did sign the Helsinki Accords that resolved many outstanding issues with the Russians, including settlement of boundary disputes in Europe. In exchange for a recognition of the existing European borders, the United States received assurances that the Soviets would respect human rights in Eastern European nations under their control. Since this provision was unenforceable, many critics, especially the right wing of the Republican Party, complained that Ford participated in an agreement that met neither American interests nor moral duty. Ronald Reagan, in particular, suggested Ford made the same mistakes that FDR had made at Yalta. Ironically, the human rights provisions did rally dissidents in Eastern European countries (such as Vaclav Havel in Czechoslovakia) and may have contributed to the fall of Soviet-backed regimes in 1989. Ford also had little control over the congressional agenda and was reduced to exercising influence through his veto power, which he used 66 times in his term.

Eleven years after he left office Ford seemed to be content with a limited legacy, telling interviewers: "If I'm remembered, it will probably be for healing the land."

JIMMY CARTER (1977–1981)

Ford's problems continued throughout 1976. Although in his memoirs he denied that he forced Rockefeller to leave the ticket, most observers contend that he asked the vice president to retire in order to stave off a serious challenge from Ronald Reagan. Reagan damaged Ford's campaign in two ways. He reinforced the image of the president as both caretaker and insider in the primaries, and his dynamic personality clashed with Ford's quiet demeanor. Ford won about 60 percent of the contested primaries, but the vote total was close (53 percent to 46 percent), and he entered the convention twenty-seven votes short of the nomination. Sensing defeat, Reagan took the unprecedented step of announcing that if nominated he would recommend liberal Republican Richard Schweiker of Pennsylvania as vice president. The plan was ingenious, but it actually backfired since conservatives now found that Ford's first choice of the liberal Rockefeller was not so different from their hero, Reagan. Although Ford won the nomination, he was forced to accept what was fundamentally a Reagan platform that even included criticism of the Helsinki Accords that he himself had negotiated. Ford even considered asking Reagan to join the ticket. Without assurances that Reagan would accept, however, he chose another conservative, Robert Dole of Kansas.

Meanwhile Jimmy Carter, former governor of Georgia, became one of the surprise dark-horse phenomena of the century. Generally, dark horses (unexpected winning candidates) emerge from contested conventions, but the newly expanded primary system permitted a relative newcomer to gain momentum and arrive at the convention with a majority of the delegates.

Carter ran against two liberal candidates in the primaries, Frank Church and Morris Udall. He distinguished himself from both by suggesting a return to a pre-Watergate and to a certain extent even a pre-Sixties America. When Nixon came to the White House in 1968, according to Carter, the people lost hope. Carter's repeated promise "never to lie to the American people" was both an attack on the Nixon presidency and a suggestion of a return to a political atmosphere where reform as well as trust were possible. The Nixon presidency, according to Carter, proved that if a person "separates himself from you," his administration can do great harm. Carter promised to "restore to the country what has been lost." The "two basic questions" posed in his campaign tract, "Why Not the Best?" were: "Can our government be honest, decent, open, fair, and compassionate?" and "Can our government be competent?"

Carter proudly announced that he was a "born-again Christian" and emphasized his personal religious beliefs in a way that no other president had done. John F. Kennedy acknowledged but forthrightly pushed aside his own religious beliefs as an influence on public policy. Carter, on the other hand, was not only willing but anxious to discuss his beliefs including the moment of his being born again, describing his conversion in the fall of 1966 as the turning point in his life. Presumably like many Americans, Carter had been angry, confused, and troubled before his conversion. Now, he said, he was truly free—free of pride, free of despair—and although it was "a little bit embarrassing" to say so, free to express his feelings of love. Many Democrats found Carter's candor refreshing, even though he was less liberal than many party activists.

During the campaign, both candidates portrayed themselves as honest men who could restore American confidence. Ford charged that Carter was really under the control of liberals in his party, and Carter charged that under Ford "Mr. Kissinger has been the president of this country." The election result was nearly a draw. With very low voter turnout, Carter won with 49.9 percent of the vote and barely enough electoral votes (297) to avoid sending the decision to the House of Representatives. A change of 8,000 votes in Hawaii and Ohio would have reelected Ford.

Carter took office in January without any clear mandate. Moreover, although there were large Democratic majorities in Congress, the party was in the hands of liberals with whom Carter often disagreed. Americans were still suspicious of their government, and many presidential powers enjoyed by other Cold War presidents had been stripped away. Carter had no experience in national government. Moreover, the issues facing the president, such as energy policy, debt reduction, inflation and welfare reform, were difficult ones to solve, especially since they lacked a clear constituency.

Carter's approach to these challenges was to attempt to devise policies that were neither conventionally liberal nor conservative. He openly retreated from the symbolism of the imperial presidency. Recalling Jefferson, he chose to walk rather than ride in a limousine from the Capitol to the White House at his inaugural, and he temporarily banned "Hail to the Chief" as the introduction to his public appearances. On the other hand, unlike other presidents in a period of institutional eclipse, Carter was not particularly interested in following the lead of Congress. He was oblivious to congressional concerns about the impact on their constituencies of closing down military bases, weapons reduction, and a fifty-cent tax on gasoline. In fact, he flooded the congressional agenda with scores of complex, comprehensive proposals from executive reorganization to energy policy. While he vigorously appointed women and minorities to government positions, he also resisted liberal demands for comprehensive healthcare and job programs. Nevertheless, despite severe criticism on the part of congressional Democrats, Carter's early legislative achievements were respectable. There was civil service reform, airline deregulation, gas price legislation, and elimination of some pork-barrel projects.

In foreign policy, Carter actually followed in broad outline the policies initiated by Nixon. He continued efforts at détente with the Soviet Union and negotiated a new set of arms limitation agreements (SALT II). The Senate was reluctant to ratify the treaty, however, and when the Soviets invaded Afghanistan, Carter asked the Senate to delay action. Carter also established full diplomatic relations with China. The president did offer a major new revision to the Nixon-Kissinger balance-of-power approach. During the Cold War there had always been a tension in American policy between the critique of human rights violations in communist countries and a willingness to support authoritarian regimes that were anti-communist. At a speech before the United Nations General Assembly Carter announced that

> . . . all the signatories to the United Nations Charter have pledged
> themselves to observe and to respect basic human rights. Thus, no
> member of the United Nations can claim that mistreatment of its citi-
> zens is solely its own business. Equally, no member can avoid respon-
> sibilities to review and to speak when torture or unwarranted
> deprivation occurs in any part of the world.

In his presidential memoirs, Carter traced his interest in this question
to his own experiences growing up in Georgia during the period of racial
segregation, saying, "I know how easy it is to overlook the persecution of
others when your own rights are not in jeopardy."

Carter's human rights policy not only was controversial but also was
difficult to enforce. The Soviets naturally objected, contending that the
policy represented an effort to intensify the Cold War. But even some
allies raised doubts, including the chancellor of Germany, who accused
Carter of attempting to govern "from a pulpit." Others complained that
the policy was only symbolic and that the United States was not seriously
committed to alleviating the problem. Carter did, however, order the
State Department to issue reports on human rights violations worldwide
and restricted American aid to those countries that were the worst offenders. The most dramatic implementation was directed against South
Africa. With U.S. support, the U.N. issued an arms embargo against the
government, which was the first time such action was undertaken by the
U.N. against a member nation.

In addition to these initiatives, Carter decided that continued American ownership of the Panama Canal was both unnecessary and morally
inappropriate. Five previous presidents had promised major revisions in
the treaty, and Carter felt that it was necessary for him to "correct an
injustice." He concluded that the Panamanians were now so deeply
resentful of American ownership that acts of sabotage were likely and
even direct attacks were possible. Since America could always intervene
in the case of an international crisis, outright ownership was not required.
Unfortunately for Carter, few Americans agreed. Polls showed only 8
percent of the public favored his position. Nevertheless, Carter entered
negotiations with Panama, successfully managed to reject demands for
compensation, and reached agreement on a return of the canal by 1999.
He arranged an elaborate signing ceremony attended by representatives
of eighteen nations and invited General Torrijos, Panama's leader, to visit
with senators. These tactics did reduce public opposition to about 59 percent, and the Senate narrowly approved the treaty after extensive debate
in April of 1978. Although the treaty remained unpopular, especially
among conservatives, Carter's management of the negotiations and ratification impressed the public and the press.

The high watermark of the Carter presidency was the result of
another foreign policy initiative. The conflicts in the Middle East
remained a focus for all Cold War presidents. Not only was the region an

arena of competition for influence with the Soviets, but the oil reserves in the region were essential to the American economy. In addition, support for Israel's survival was always a basic feature of American policy. In 1973, for instance, a war resulted in an oil boycott of the United States by Arab nations. In 1977 Carter visited with President Anwar Sadat of Egypt and discovered that he might be receptive to a peace agreement. Encouraged by Carter, Sadat declared he would personally visit Israel for the cause of peace. Although other Arab nations refused to participate, formal negotiations began in Cairo in December of 1977. When the discussions faltered, Carter asked Sadat and Israeli Prime minister Manachem Begin to join him at the Camp David retreat. After thirteen days of secret negotiations, an agreement was reached. Before a television audience, Carter, Sadat, and Begin announced that Israel agreed to return land captured in the 1967 war, and Egypt would recognize Israel. The status of the Palestinians was left unresolved. When disagreements about portions of the treaty emerged later, Carter flew to the Middle East to personally resolve the disputed issues. The treaty was ratified by both nations in March, and a ceremonial signing was held at the White House.

Carter's success in brokering the first diplomatic recognition of Israel by an Arab state surprised the world. The Panama Canal Treaty and the Camp David Accords highlighted Carter's status as peacemaker and artful negotiator. In fact, regime changes in Nicaragua and Iran, in which long-standing dictators were removed, suggested the success of Carter's human rights policy. At this point, Carter was presented with some extraordinary and unanticipated challenges. The OPEC oil cartel announced major price increases, driving gasoline prices to record levels. In conjunction with the federal deficit, Japanese competition, and other factors, a new kind of economic crisis emerged. Generally, inflation emerged as a problem in a boom economy, but now it appeared in the context of slowed economic activity. The Consumer Price Index rose 13 percent in 1979, the largest increase since 1946. The press called the combination of high unemployment levels and inflation "stagflation." No president before Carter had been faced with the task of curing this particular economic problem.

In addition, the new regime in Iran was much more militant than expected. The Ayatollah Khomeini assumed control of the government and announced a program of fundamentalist Islam at home and anti-Americanism abroad. The new officials had particular grievances against the United States, since the CIA had helped restore the Shah to power in 1953. When the deposed Shah was permitted entry to the United States for medical treatment, the government demanded his return to Iran for trial. On November 4, 1979, at the instigation or acquiescence of the government, 500 militants seized the U.S. embassy and held 63 American officials hostage.

Six weeks later, Soviet troops entered Afghanistan, assassinated the prime minister, and installed a new government. The events that led to the invasion are complex and still not fully understood. A Marxist regime had been in power since April of 1978, and the new government's attempt to implement economic changes precipitated armed resistance that was supported by the CIA, China, and fundamentalist Muslims. Perhaps in an effort to forestall the loss of a client state, the Soviets decided direct military occupation was the only alternative. The action, however, could not have occurred at a worse time in Soviet–American relations, since the policy of détente was already under stress.

President Carter knew that the economic situation was unique. He had received poll data that showed a general deep estrangement from government on the part of Americans. He also knew that a failing economy was a disastrous backdrop for a reelection campaign. He cancelled a scheduled energy address and retreated to Camp David for time to read and reflect. A string of experts arrived to give advice. Carter left the retreat for quick visits to "average middle class" families in West Virginia and Pennsylvania. As a result of these efforts, Carter emerged from Camp David to deliver a speech that connected the energy crisis to much broader themes. Sixty-five million people tuned in to watch the address, twice the number of his previous telecasts.

Carter felt confident he had discovered the source of the current problem and he shared this newfound vision with the American people. There was a "fundamental threat to American democracy," though not from outside adversaries. The threat was "nearly invisible in ordinary ways." A "crisis of confidence" strikes "at the very heart and soul and spirit of our national will." The crisis had created doubt in people's personal lives and "the loss of unity of purpose for our nation." Carter acknowledged that before the last "extraordinary 10 days" he had not faced this crisis himself as a leader. His previous addresses had "become increasingly narrow, focused more and more on what the isolated world of Washington thinks is important." Now, however, he was prepared to lead the people out of this crisis, and "energy will be the immediate test of our ability" to recreate a national purpose.

One of the books that apparently influenced the president was Christopher Lasch's *The Culture of Narcissism*. Lasch argued that American individualism had metamorphosized into narcissism in the 1960s. Carter seemed to accept this assessment. Historically, America was a nation "proud of hard work, strong families, close-knit communities, and our faith in God." Now "too many of us . . . tend to worship self-indulgence and consumption." While Carter acknowledged there were events beyond the control of a national will, such as the assassinations of John and Robert Kennedy and Martin Luther King, Jr., there was still present the notion that the nation was bearing the fruit of past error. There was a "crisis of the spirit," of which "growing disrespect" for government, churches, and schools, along with declining productivity and personal savings, were signs. Carter warned that "down this road was a mistaken idea of freedom." Instead, Americans must move in a different direction at this "turning point in history" and take the path that leads to "common purpose and the restoration of American values."

But what was to be the nature of this path away from a mistaken idea of freedom? Carter announced that winning the energy war would restore confidence. In the days following the speech, he announced that he would "explore new ideas and new fronts," and he would "develop new points of attack." Carter used terms of martial rhetoric: "On this battlefield of energy, this democracy which we love is going to make its stand, and on that battlefield you and I, fighting side by side, will win the energy war."

Vice President Mondale's assessment just after the speech that "it went from sugar to shit" was eventually shared by the public and the press. In fact, the "Energy and Crisis of Confidence" speech quickly became a classic—perhaps *the* classic—case study of presidential rhetorical ineffectiveness. President Carter later blamed the failure of his address, despite the initial popular support, on the way he handled subsequent cabinet resignations. Others have placed emphasis on a skeptical media, Republican opposition, and factionalism within his own party. The derisive description of the address as the "malaise" speech reportedly came from Ted Kennedy and was quickly adopted by the press. Speakers at the Republican National Convention spoke repeatedly of the "malaise of the Carter years." Carter's effort to connect economic problems to a flaw in the American people themselves was a high-risk effort. Instead of galvanizing the public, Carter's own leadership became the focus of attention.

While still struggling with the economy and the aftermath of the energy address, Carter faced the intractable problem of recovering the hostages. Aiding American citizens in distress, of course, has always been a difficult task since the founding presidents faced the issues of impressment by the British navy and attacks by Indian tribes. In the Cold War, American citizens being charged with spying or caught in revolutionary turmoil was an ongoing problem. This crisis, however, was especially acute for several reasons. Since embassy officials were involved, the incident involved the government directly. The recent defeat in Vietnam was very much on the mind of politicians and policymakers, and this event seemed to underscore the limits of American power abroad. The election was less than a year away, Carter faced a primary challenge from his party's left wing by Ted Kennedy, and Governor Reagan announced his candidacy for the Republican nomination on November 13.

Carter moved cautiously to resolve the crisis. Although he refused to accede to the radicals' demands, he made arrangements for the Shah to leave the country, going first to Panama and then to Egypt. He banned the purchase of Iranian oil and froze Iranian assets in the United States. He did not, however, sever diplomatic relations with Iran and continued to negotiate through third parties. Although some hostages were released, no progress was made. The crisis filled the news in the following months and a new television show, "Nightline," was introduced to cover the crisis. Each evening the program began with the headline, "America Held Hostage" and contained the number of days Americans remained in captivity. In April, Carter made a high-risk decision to attempt a military rescue of the hostages, but the mission failed when three of the eight deployed helicopters crashed. When the Shah died the following July, there was still no movement to free the hostages. Throughout the 1980 campaign, the Republicans anxiously awaited some dramatic breakthrough that they called the "October Surprise," but no success ever occurred. Not until Reagan took his oath of office in January were the hostages released.

Carter reacted swiftly to the Soviet occupation of Afghanistan. He removed ratification of SALT II from the Senate's consideration, cancelled grain sales to the Soviet Union, forbade American athletes from attending the Olympics, cut back cultural exchanges, increased requests for military expenditures, and reinstituted registration for the draft. None of these measures had an immediate effect on the Soviet occupation and many were not popular with Americans. Farmers were concerned about the sudden loss of an important market. Young people were not pleased with the possible return of selective service. Segments of the public at large were frustrated that their finest Olympic athletes would not be able to compete.

In the last fifteen months of Carter's presidency these challenges decimated large parts of his agenda. His energy proposals failed to rally the public, and in an effort to defend himself against Ted Kennedy's challenge, he abandoned his attempt to form a new kind of liberalism and accepted traditional Democratic approaches to the economy. His human rights policy and focus on the developing world were overshadowed by the events in Iran and, in response to Soviet actions in Afghanistan, Carter returned to conventional Cold War policies.

RONALD REAGAN (1981–1989)

During the 1980 campaign, despite the severe economic problems facing the nation, President Carter attempted to portray Ronald Reagan as another Herbert Hoover. He suggested that if Reagan became president the nation would tumble into a severe depression. Reagan, however, artfully argued that it was Jimmy Carter who represented the persona of Hoover and that he himself was, in important ways, like FDR. This inversion seemed ludicrous to Democrats. As one union leader complained, "You know, this movie star's been making B movies all his life and he somehow convinced a lot of people who don't remember what the Depression was." But as Reagan presented his case, he suggested that

Carter was the defender of the past (in this case, the 1960s), as Hoover was of the 1920s. Like FDR, Reagan was the optimist and the innovator and Carter the cautious, timid figure who was immobilized by ideological blinders.

Carter vigorously denied Reagan's assertion that the country was suffering from a "severe depression," but the president's correction that the appropriate word was "recession" only seemed to reinforce the analogy to 1932. Moreover, Carter's economic orthodoxy seemed Hoover-like in its reiteration of the fundamental "great economic strength" of the American economy and his warnings against experimentation. We "must resist the temptation to overstimulate the economy," he warned as Reagan called for bold measures to reduce the "misery index." Reagan emphasized that the uniqueness of America's economic problems (inflation and high unemployment) required new thinking. He also assumed the role of humanitarian. "A recession is when your neighbor loses his job," Reagan repeated in his stump speech; "depression is when you lose yours." The definition always ended with a pause and the punch line, "Recovery is when Jimmy Carter loses his." Carter's defense also played into the Hoover analogy. Sometimes he attempted to portray Reagan as the "country squire" of the 1980s. Reagan was an "extremely engaging, charming man" who wanted to be president. Late in the campaign he presented Reagan as a dangerous man who was incompetent to manage the economy and whose ideas would bring the nation to war.

Reagan's supreme confidence and his unshakeable optimism, during the 1980 campaign and later, replicated FDR's style if not his substance. More than any post-Roosevelt president, Reagan successfully challenged the authority of FDR and initiated his own "revolution" in American politics. Yet the achievements of the "Reagan Revolution" were constructed from unusual elements. Reagan always referred to Roosevelt as his idol. His "Time for Choosing" speech in 1964, however, connected the New Deal to Karl Marx, and later he contended that New Dealers used fascism as their policy model. This paralleling of strident critiques of the New Deal and imitative gestures toward FDR characterized Reagan's entire presidency. Reagan repeatedly and readily admitted that he was a Roosevelt supporter *and* portrayed the New Deal in the Satanic mode of the new American Right, which puzzled even his supporters. Peggy Noonan, a Reagan speechwriter, insisted Reagan's Roosevelt was derived from a scene in the 1942 film *Yankee Doodle Dandy,* in which an actor playing FDR gives a presidential medal to George M. Cohan (played by Jimmy Cagney). Cohan/Cagney is rendered speechless by Roosevelt's comments about love of country as the president awards the medal for his authorship of "Over There" and "Grand Old Flag."

Reagan constantly acknowledged the influence of FDR in his own youth. He recalled Roosevelt's election victories, his father's jobs in New Deal relief programs, and FDR's speeches and personal appearances.

Reagan's remembrances of the Depression and FDR's heroic actions are quite vivid. The Great Depression hit his boyhood town of Dixon "like a cyclone" and "one of its first casualties was my father's dream." The Depression "had such an oppressive effect that it cast a dreary pall over everything." In these "cheerless, desperate days," Reagan remembered the "strong, gentle, confident voice" of FDR who "brought comfort and resilience to a nation caught up in a storm and reassured us that we could lick any problem. I shall never forget him for that."

This seemingly frank and fond oral history, however, also contained a critique. In his 1965 autobiography (*Where is the Rest of Me?*), Reagan tells the story of his father's job as New Deal relief administrator and then as local head of the WPA. Although he described the WPA as "one of the most productive elements of FDR's alphabet soup agencies," Reagan notes that his father had difficulty signing up participants. Jack Reagan later found that relief administrators discouraged able-bodied men from applying. Reagan the son concludes: "I wasn't sophisticated enough to realize what I learned later: The first rule of bureaucracy is to protect bureaucracy. If the people running the welfare program had let their clientele find other ways of making a living, that would have reduced their importance and their budget."

The young Reagan, however, was unaware of this danger. He confessed that he was a "very emotional New Dealer" and a "near-hopeless hemophiliac liberal" who was "blinded" by the brilliance of the president and "blindly" joined any organization that "would guarantee to save the world." These two narratives, one of affectionate youthful remembrance and one of youthful indiscretion and conversion, formed part of a general generational ambivalence that Reagan captured. Were FDR's reforms, although gratefully accepted at the time, still helpful to Americans? Even many union members who had become suspicious of the programs of the Great Society in the 1960s found Reagan's message appealing. The press named these voters "Reagan Democrats." Reagan justified cuts in domestic spending as necessary to free not only "professionals" and "industrialists" but also "shopkeepers, clerks, cabbies, and truck drivers" from an intrusive federal government.

No events in Reagan's youth were evoked more positively than the American experience in World War II. In a 1981 interview he reminisced about FDR's 1937 "quarantine" speech. "I remember when Hitler was arming and had built himself up—no one has created quite the military that the Soviet Union has, but comparatively he was in that way," he told Walter Cronkite. "Franklin Delano Roosevelt made a speech in Chicago at the dedication of a bridge over the Chicago River. In that speech, he called on the free world to quarantine Nazi Germany, to stop all communications, all trade, all relations with them," said Reagan, "until they gave up that militaristic course and agreed to join with the free nations of the world in a search for peace." Reagan continued to remember that "the funny thing was, he was attacked so here in our own country for having said such a thing. Can we honestly look back now and say World War II would have taken place if we had done what he wanted us to do back in 1938?"

Conventional Republican assessments of New Deal foreign policy centered upon the "treason" at Yalta, but Reagan generally interpreted the conference as evidence of Soviet betrayal. To him, FDR was "a great war leader." Under his leadership, "there were less of the tragic blunders that have characterized many wars in the past. . . ." Reagan was especially generous in his accounts of the efficiency of the American war effort. FDR took a nation completely unprepared for war and, forty-four months after Pearl Harbor, produced an awesome war machine. "We truly were an arsenal of democracy," he told one interviewer, as he noted that FDR was criticized for asking for 50,000 planes a year. The massive military budget increases in the 1980s were thus broadly justified by what Reagan regarded as FDR's own success in preparing to confront a hostile power despite the pessimism of his critics.

Reagan's memories of the war also focused on the battlefield valor and autobiographical remembrances of those who participated in the war effort. The centerpiece of his remarks at the Omaha Beach commemoration of D-Day in 1984 was the narrative of a daughter of one of the participants in the invasion. Reagan quoted Lisa Zanatta Henn, who wrote the president of the "bond she had with her father" and the tears she sheds even today when she thinks about him "as a twenty-year-old boy having to face that beach."

Reagan's memory of when he parted from the New Deal ideology varied. He did remain a Democrat until 1962, when he finally registered as a Republican. Reagan's electoral success then could be traced to his own status as a Democrat who left his party—or, as he preferred to say, the party left him. Unlike FDR, however, Reagan was a president who possessed a single vision. The remark in 1986 by François Mitterand, the socialist president of France, may be patronizing but does capture the combination of FDR's style with a Jacksonian resolve:

> [Reagan] is a man of common sense, gracious and pleasant. He communicates through jokes, by telling ultra-California stories, by speaking mainly about California and the Bible. He has two religions: free enterprise and God—the Christian God. . . . He is not a man who dwells on concepts, yet he has ideas and clings to them.

At a Conservative Political Action Conference in 1985, Reagan claimed that as FDR once had "ideas that were new" and "captured the imagination of the American people," now he led a movement that no longer was "diffuse and scattered" but had its own agenda. "We became the party of the most brilliant and dynamic of young minds; we are "not the defenders of the status quo but creators of the future." The "Reagan Revolution" was thus in major ways a reversal of FDR's, although the new president imitated aspects of FDR's style, especially his ability to speak effectively to popular sentiment. During his presidency, Reagan was named by the press as the "Great Communicator."

An excellent example of Reagan's rhetorical talent is his performance at the Liberty Weekend in 1986. The occasion for the celebration was Independence Day and the 100th anniversary of the Statue of Liberty. The event represented the culmination of a project begun in 1984 to restore the Statue as well as Ellis Island facilities. The weekend was planned by a Hollywood producer who designed what he described as a "50 goose-bump event." As David E. Proctor (*Enacting Political Culture*) has noted, the "celebration of a revered monument symbolizing Liberty on a national holiday traditionally representing Liberty provided a focal point resulting in a crush of Liberty rhetoric." The weekend included ceremonies of the relighting of the Statue, a swearing-in of new citizens by Chief Justice Berger, a naval review, a music concert and fireworks, a salute to sports and, of course, five speeches by the president.

Throughout these celebration addresses, Reagan said that he searched for the "common thread" in American history that united people. "What was it that tied these profoundly different people together?", he asked in his remarks at the relighting ceremony. His answer was that the bond is "an abiding love of liberty." The immigrant was the archetype of this desire for freedom, and Reagan highlighted the heroism of many of them in his address (including Justice Scalia who arrived in the United States at age 15, speaking "not a word of English"). But since all Americans were immigrants, recent arrivals were part of a long chain of men and women who had the "special courage that enabled them to leave their own land, leave their friends and countrymen, and come to this new and strange land to build a new world of peace and freedom and hope." The bond extended into the future in the "hope that our children will always find here the land of liberty in a land that is free."

Unlike FDR, however, Reagan did not win a landslide victory in 1980. He did win forty-four states in the electoral college, and Republicans gained control of the Senate. However, in a three-way race (Republican Representative John Anderson ran as an independent) he received only 51 percent of the popular vote, which was only three percentage points higher than Ford's in 1976. Reagan's challenge was to institute major changes in the federal government without an overwhelming mandate. The new president did have one advantage: He knew exactly, at least in general terms, what policies he wanted to implement.

In terms of the economy, Reagan believed the most effective way to reduce the budget deficit, inflation, and unemployment was to reduce taxes. Although his "supply-side" theory was controversial, it did have support among some economists, and the public in general was receptive to new economic initiatives. Certain of his direction, Reagan appointed David Stockman as his budget director. Stockman instituted a complete budget review and even reprogrammed the computers at the Office of Management and Budget. Neither Democrats, Republicans, nor even Reagan's cabinet members could keep up with Stockman's figures. He later admitted: "We were doing the whole budget-cutting exercise so frenetically. In other words, we were juggling details, pushing people, and going from one session to another, trying to cut housing programs here and rural electric there, and we were doing it so fast, we didn't know where we were going to end up." At the time, however, Stockman's reports so caught politicians of both parties off-guard that Congress only reluctantly worked from his figures.

Reagan himself proposed at a joint session of Congress an economic recovery plan that recommended reductions of over $40 billion in the budget, a 30 percent tax cut, plans to reduce bureaucratic waste, and reduction of the monetary supply. Reagan himself could institute many cost-saving measures in the executive branch, and the Federal Reserve independently continued anti-inflation policy, but Reagan needed congressional approval for budget and tax cuts. The Democratic House quickly rejected Reagan's proposals regarding cuts in Social Security benefits and derisively referred to the proposals as "Reaganomics." Reagan retrenched a bit. He gave in on Social Security reform but nevertheless insisted on tax cuts.

On March 30, the president was struck by an assassin's bullet. Reagan recovered, and the political atmosphere changed. The public rallied behind the president, and Reagan's bravery in the aftermath of the attack impressed citizens. In April, the president spoke in a televised national address complaining about the power of special interests and urging Americans to communicate with their representatives their support for his proposal. Speaker of the House Tip O'Neill described the effect of the address as "devastating" for Democrats, who were now willing to negotiate. The president signed the largest tax reduction legislation in American history on July 29. Reagan never enjoyed a year as successful as his first. Actually, Congress passed reductions in tax cuts in 1982 and 1984. Nevertheless, the spectacular achievement in 1981 provided a momentum that lasted until the Iran/Contra scandal in November of 1986.

The basic prediction of supply-side economics is that once people have more disposable income through tax cuts, they will spend more, the economy will grow, and tax revenues will rise despite lower tax rates. One complication in the experiment was Reagan's commitment to massive increases in military spending that totaled $2.4 trillion by the end of his administration. As a result, the national debt grew from $914 million in 1980 to $2.6 trillion in 1988. In Carter's last budget the deficit was $55 billion. Annual deficits averaged $180 million in the Reagan years. In the short term, the economy worsened as the unemployment rate rose to more than 10 percent in 1982, the highest since 1940. Despite the large deficits, however, the economy did recover. By 1984 inflation had been reduced to 4.4 percent and unemployment to 5.3 percent, and Reagan was able to claim that his policies worked.

Unlike recent Cold War presidents, Reagan was extremely suspicious of détente policy. In 1983 he reintroduced early Cold War rhetoric by calling the Soviet Union an "evil empire" and communism "the focus of evil in the world." Reagan's Cold War policies reflected these beliefs. In addition to large increases in military expenditures, he authorized construction of new intercontinental missiles at home and the installation of medium-range missiles in Europe, and he showed little interest in arms reduction or summits.

In March of 1983, Reagan advanced a foreign policy equivalent to his supply-side theory. As his economic policy was a high-risk experiment, so too was his new commitment to what he called the "Strategic Defense Initiative." Renamed by the press as the "Star Wars" plan, SDI was largely a theory, supported by some evidence, that a shield could be constructed to detect and destroy any incoming nuclear weapons. Reagan knew little about the technology required to make such a system operational, but he nevertheless was fascinated with the project. According to Lou Cannon, "missile defense was one of the few issues beyond his economic program that actively interested Reagan once he was in office." Critics, even in his own administration, raised questions about cost. But to Reagan, what was expense, compared to the creation of a future world without danger of mutual destruction? Others raised questions about feasibility, but Reagan thought there was no problem that American ingenuity could not solve. When others raised concerns that SDI would force the Soviets to greatly increase missile production and start a new arms race, Reagan offered to share the technology, once developed, with the Soviets.

Indeed, the Soviets were very concerned about SDI, but mostly because they could not afford to compete once more with the United States in an expensive project. After a major accident at the Chernobyl nuclear power plant in 1986, some members of the Soviet leadership lost confidence in their capacity to compete with the West. The new prime minister, Mikhail Gorbachev, was committing all his resources to reforming a sluggish economy. Thus, at Reykjavik, Iceland, in 1986, Gorbachev offered major concessions if Reagan would agree to postpone SDI. Reagan refused. What was so astounding in terms of Cold War practice, however, was that both leaders actually engaged in a rapid, competitive round of proposals to reduce weapons rather than threats to increase them. After Gorbachev offered a 50 percent cut in all nuclear weapons, Reagan responded with a plan to eliminate all ballistic missiles within a decade. Gorbachev countered with a proposal to eliminate all nuclear weapons and Reagan said: "All nuclear weapons! Well, Mikhail, that's exactly what I've been talking about all along. . . . That's been my goal." A year later, however, the Soviets agreed to an unprecedented reduction in nuclear weapons without a ban on SDI. The Intermediate Range Nuclear Force Treaty eliminated an entire class of missiles and provided for stringent on-site inspection. The latter was a requirement the Soviets had rejected since the Eisenhower administration.

Thus, by the end of the Reagan administration, Soviet–American relations were at a high point in the Cold War despite the president's open hostility to détente during the first term. Reagan had, in fact, been criticized by Democratic presidential nominee Walter Mondale for failing to meet with Soviet leaders as other Cold War presidents had done. Reagan replied that he would have sought discussions, but "they [the leaders] kept dying on me." Indeed, after Brezhnev's death, the Soviets selected in turn two aging leaders, Yuri Andrpov and Konstanin Chernenko, who both died in office. While many of Reagan's advisors were suspicious of Gorbachev and warned Reagan not to trust him, the president developed an instant liking to the general secretary. Donald Regan said the two leaders were "like a couple of fellows who had run into each other at a club and discovered they had a lot in common." When Reagan left office in 1989, as John Lewis Gaddis has remarked, "The point at issue no longer seemed to be 'how to fight the Cold War' but rather 'is the Cold War over?'."

Before the breakthrough in Soviet relations, Reagan foreign policy, while rhetorically militant, was generally cautious. The "Reagan Doctrine" provided American support, both covert and overt, to anti-communist resistance movements, and there were efforts to punish states that sponsored terrorist groups. The invasion of Grenada in 1983 to protect American medical students and prevent a government sympathetic to Cuba from assuming power involved only 1,700 soldiers who left in two months. The bombing of Libya in retaliation for terrorist acts was a single raid in which one airplane was lost. When 241 U.S. Marines stationed in Lebanon were killed by terrorists, the American garrison was later withdrawn. The CIA provided weapons to Afghanistan rebels, but no troops were involved.

In two areas, however, Reagan acted less cautiously. Concerned about the fate of American hostages held in Lebanon (and perhaps fearful of repeating Carter's fate), Reagan authorized the sale of weapons to Iran in return for their help in gaining the release of hostages. When the secret arms-for-hostages deals became public, Reagan initially insisted that the two actions were separate but later reluctantly admitted that the effect was the same. No sooner did the administration face charges of secretly negotiating with hostage-taking terrorists than another report became public. The Iranians were overcharged for the weapons and the "profits" were then diverted to an anti-communist insurgency movement in Nicaragua. This revelation was particularly damaging because Congress, fearing extensive U.S. military involvement, forbade the president from "expending any funds for the purpose of overthrowing the government of Nicaragua." Later, it was also learned that CIA Director William Casey was also soliciting secret "donations" from other states, including Saudi Arabia, to support the Contras.

The "Iran/Contra" affair, sometimes called "Irangate" by the press, nearly destroyed the Reagan presidency. Had Reagan admitted that he ordered the secret diversion of funds despite explicit congressional restriction, he would have faced a constitutional crisis and possible impeachment. If, on the other hand, he denied he was aware of these actions, he risked charges that he was an absentee president. Reagan took the second option, and no evidence was presented that the president knew about the actions of his advisors.

Reagan did feel very strongly about the justice of the Contra cause. Since the rebel force was fighting against a Marxist regime, Reagan compared them to the American revolutionaries. It is likely, therefore, that his subordinates followed the cues (if not the commands) of the president. National Security Advisor John Poindexter testified before Congress that he authorized the action and purposely did not inform the president to protect him from political criticism, although he was certain the president would have approved if presented with the plan. Poindexter's deputy, Oliver North, implicated William Casey, who died just as the congressional hearing began. Another investigation authorized by the president found Reagan innocent of knowledge of the affair. However, the report (chaired by former Republican Senator John Tower) offered a devastating image of Reagan as president. Tower wrote that the president was disinterested in most problems and rarely supervised subordinates. A special prosecutor was also appointed to investigate the affair. Poindexter and North, dismissed from their positions, were later indicted although the courts overturned their convictions, because evidence used in their trials was limited by the immunity granted by Congress for their testimony. With Reagan's term nearly over and because of his denials of knowledge about the affair, he avoided impeachment.

To some the Iran/Contra affair showed that the excesses of Cold War presidency were still evident even after Watergate, and that Reagan had indeed engaged in actions that were impeachable. To others, Reagan's actions were simply the result of a management style that gave too much authority to subordinates. Despite the seriousness of the scandal, Reagan retained his popularity with members of his own party and elements of the public at large. Commentators have questioned whether the changes Reagan instituted actually constituted a "revolution," since most federal entitlement and regulatory programs were left untouched. However, the decades of reluctant accommodation by Republicans with FDR and the New Deal were concluded as Reagan declared his own "rendezvous with destiny."

GEORGE H. W. BUSH (1989–1993)

When George Herbert Walker Bush took the oath of office in January of 1989, he faced some unique challenges as the last of the Cold War presidents. In many ways he was an ideal president for this moment, since he had already held a number of foreign policy positions as U.S. ambassador to the United Nations, chief liaison officer to China, and director of the CIA. Bush, of course, also served in a number of elected offices, including vice president in the Reagan administration and U.S. congressman. The new president knew that momentous changes in the international system were imminent although no one, including the CIA, knew how dramatic and sudden they would be. The major theme of his inaugural address was the prediction that a new era was emerging in which dictatorships were in decline and democracies were increasing. Bush remarked, "A new era is blowing, and a world refreshed by freedom seems reborn. The totalitarian era is passing, its old ideas blown away like leaves from an ancient, lifeless tree."

The relative rise and decline in democratic political versus dictatorial political systems worldwide seems to proceed in a broad historical fashion. The American and French revolutions initiated an increase in democracies until after World War I, when dictatorships emerged in Germany, Poland, Argentina, Spain, and other nations. Although fascist dictatorships were defeated in 1945, the number of communist regimes rose until a number of former European colonies won independence after World War II. Many of these new regimes reverted to authoritarian rule in the following years until what Samuel Huntington has called the "third wave" crested in 1989 and 1990.

Soon after Bush took office, communist and authoritarian governments began to collapse. A non-communist government, led by the trade union Solidarity movement, took power in Poland in August, followed in rapid succession by new democratic governments in East Germany, Czechoslovakia, Romania, and Hungary. Nelson Mandela was freed after 27 years in prison in South Africa in February of 1990, Sandinista rule ended in Nicaragua in the same month, and the Pinochet's Chilean dictatorship ended in March. Then the unthinkable happened. Boris Yelstin was elected president of the Russian Republic in July of 1991. A month later, Gorbachev survived an attempted coup by communist leaders just as he was ready to sign a treaty vastly increasing the power of the republics that comprised the Soviet Union. Upon his release, the parliament suspended all activities of the Communist Party. A short-lived commonwealth of former Soviet republics was formed, but nearly all of them soon declared their independence. The fall of the Berlin Wall in November of 1989 was a powerful symbol of the end of the Cold War. Also symbolic was the removal of the red flag from its place in the Kremlin on New Year's Eve, 1991. The one setback in this astonishing collapse of communism was the suppression of the student pro-democracy movement at Tiananmen Square by the Chinese Red Army in June of 1989.

How did President Bush react to these extraordinary developments? Despite his wide experience, Bush faced an extremely delicate situation. If he moved too quickly to support these new regimes in Eastern Europe and/or urged more changes within the Soviet Union, he risked a backlash that might include a Soviet invasion or a coup in the Soviet Union itself. Thus the president himself told his advisors:

> I don't want to do something that would inadvertently set back the progress that has been made in Eastern Europe. . . . And it is so delicate . . . I'm old enough to remember Hungary in 1956 where we exhorted people to go to the barricades, and a lot of people were left out there alone.

Moreover, many of Bush's advisors were suspicious of Gorbachev's intentions and thought President Reagan had created unjustified expectations about Soviet–American relations during his last year in office. James Baker, for example, recalled that "in 1989 [Gorbachev] was running around Europe trying to out-promise things in arms control and so forth. It looked like typical Soviet tactics [designed to] split the West." On the other hand, if the United States acted passively toward these developments and they were halted, critics could charge that the United States lost a unique opportunity to win the Cold War. Why not press the advantage when the Soviet Union was in a weakened state? Either Gorbachev's reforms would work and the Soviet Union would emerge as a stronger power, or they would fail and hardliners would take power. In either case, as Vice President Dan Quayle said, the Soviet Union "remains . . . our adversary."

For the most part, Bush elected to undertake the option of restraint. Even after the Berlin Wall fell, he remained silent—and there was no more potent symbol of the Cold War than the Berlin Wall. Not only was Berlin the strategic flashpoint during the entire Cold War, but it also stood for the brutality and bankruptcy of communism. Soldiers shot citizens who attempted to climb the wall, which had been built to stop emigration to the West. However, when Bush met with the press and was asked for comments, he said, "Don't think any single event is the end of what you might call the Iron Curtain. . . ." When a surprised reporter asked why he was not elated by the event, Bush replied, "I'm not an emotional kind of guy. . . ." Quickly, Democrats seized upon Bush's reticence. Richard Gephardt complained that "even as the walls of Jericho come tumbling down, we have a president who is inadequate to the occasion." Republicans openly stated that Reagan's response would have been quite different.

When Gorbachev was placed under house arrest by members of a coup, the president was also quite cautious. Only after there was evidence of resistance to the overthrow (CNN carried pictures of a defiant Boris Yelstin standing on a tank, announcing opposition to the coup) did he speak critically. Bush supported the election of a communist military leader in Poland, urged Hungarian anti-Communist Party leaders to be "prudent" and proceed slowly, and suggested that Ukraine not declare independence. (Critics referred to the latter as the "Chicken Kiev" address.) Shortly after the massacre in Tiananmen Square, Bush secretly sent advisors to China to discuss future relations, vetoed attempts by Congress to strengthen sanctions and extend the visas of Chinese students in the United States, and permitted sales of Boeing aircraft to China. Bush argued that only through the maintenance of continued relations could the United States hope to prevent further deterioration of human rights in China.

In some areas, however, Bush did react proactively. He arranged an early summit with Gorbachev at Malta to make the initial plans for a post–Cold War relationship with the Soviets. He also helped negotiate the peaceful withdrawal of the Baltic states from the Soviet Union. Perhaps the most difficult challenge in all these developments involved the reunification of Germany. He actively supported Chancellor Kohl's plan to reunify the country. Both the Soviets and many Western European nations regarded two Germanys as an important security measure after two wars. Bush urged Gorbachev to accept reunification on the grounds that a democratic, united Germany under American and NATO influence was less a security risk than a nonaligned Germany that might someday acquire nuclear weapons. Gorbachev had little power at this point to effectively resist reunification, but his acquiescence did speed up the process, which all parties initially estimated would take several years. Moreover, Bush's active support cut off the possibility that the Germans might negotiate a separate arrangement with Russia in which neutrality would be traded for unification.

Bush's general caution did succeed. Although the full impact is still not completely clear, the Soviet empire was dismantled quickly and almost without violence. During this same period, the president confronted the first crisis of a new post–Cold War period. While Bush was careful about employing American power as old Cold War patterns collapsed, he was more willing to do so in cases that seemed to him to presage features of the newly emerging international system. In each of the three instances in which Bush used force, the crisis can in part be traced to Cold War policies. In response to a series of aggressive acts in Panama, Bush sent 10,000 American troops to occupy the capital and capture General Manuel Norreiga. Noriega's troops had killed a U.S. military officer, declared the results of an election won by his opponents void, and engaged in drug trafficking. The Bush administration was particularly concerned about the fate of 35,000 Americans in the country and feared a hostage crisis similar to the one faced by President Carter. The surprise raid was successful, but the action did highlight Noreiga's long association with the CIA, including the period in which the president was director of the agency.

The single most important foreign policy action of the Bush administration was the decision to oppose Iraq's invasion of Kuwait. Saddam Hussein, like Noriega, was closely linked to American intelligence agencies during the Cold War. In the Iraq–Iran war (1980–1988), the Reagan administration supported Saddam with economic aid in an effort to limit the power of Iran. When Congress learned that Saddam had used chemical weapons against his own citizens, Senators Claiborne Pell, a liberal Democrat, and Jesse Helms, a conservative Republican, joined forces and offered legislation to impose sanctions. However, Bush not only resisted the effort but proposed an increase in economic credits. When Saddam discussed his grievances with Kuwait with the American ambassador a few months before the invasion, she offered an equivocal response.

What then accounts for the abrupt change in American foreign policy? Why was Saddam Hussein regarded as a valued de facto ally and then later as an enemy? One explanation is that the Bush administration was preoccupied with events in Europe and therefore missed signs that Saddam was moving toward a more aggressive position, not only in regard to Kuwait but toward Israel as well. More likely, the events in Europe had a different impact. If the Cold War was indeed in its last stages and the Soviet Union was likely to be a reduced world power, then American policy required a major global reevaluation. No longer would the United States be driven to engage in competition with the Soviets throughout the world. With a new international power vacuum, regional powers might feel free to prey on their neighbors. As the last superpower standing, the United States was now responsible for what President Bush began to call the "new world order." In his address before Congress on the crisis, Bush formally announced the first policy of the post–Cold War period:

> Out of troubled times, a new world order can emerge, a new era, freer from the threat of terror, stronger in the pursuit of justice, and more secure in the quest for peace. An era in which the nations of the world, east and west, north and south, can prosper and live in harmony.

It was possible, however, that this new order "struggling to be born" might instead be one in which the titanic struggle between superpowers would be replaced by a world in which many small wars were common. In order that the future not be one in which the "rule of the jungle" is dominant, aggression must be resisted. Bush was particularly influenced by the failure of the international community to check Hitler's aggression in the 1930s, and he saw the invasion of Kuwait as a similar destabilizing event.

Indeed, if Iraq had invaded Kuwait ten or twenty years earlier, the act would likely have received the approval of one of the superpowers and been subject to the exercise of the veto in the United Nations Security Council. The Russians were early supporters of Bush's coalition to challenge the occupation of Kuwait. But while the president quickly built a large coalition with U.N. authorization, he faced domestic opposition. Many in Congress were not anxious to approve a major use of force just when the possibility of a "peace dividend" was emerging with the end of the Cold War. Others feared another Vietnam. Bush contended that the current crisis was quite different and promised that victory would end the concerns about the effective use of force, which he called the "Vietnam syndrome." According to the administration, the goals of the operation were clear; the force requested would be overwhelming, not incremental; and a clear exit strategy was available. Initially, Bush had difficulty convincing the public as well. Giving birth to a "new world order" appeared to be a vague reason for using force, and Secretary of State James Baker's rationale that Iraq's occupation threatened the supply of oil seemed too cynical. Bush quickly focused on the status of hostages in Iraq, human rights violations in Kuwait, and the danger that Iraq might become a nuclear power.

The effort worked, although just barely. Some members of Bush's administration objected to a request for congressional authorization to use force. Richard Cheney publicly argued that Truman did not ask Congress to send troops to Korea and privately expressed concerns that Congress might reject Bush's request. Bush, however, felt that the risk was necessary. He had been reading Lyndon Johnson's memoirs and concluded that the absence of a clear congressional authorization had a significant impact on later criticism of the war in Vietnam. The vote mirrored public opinion itself, which was almost evenly divided. The House approved the authorization to use force 250–183 and the Senate 52–47. Not only was the request itself a novelty, since it was the first time Congress exercised its power to declare war throughout the long period of the Cold War, but so too was the spirited debate, much of which was broadcast on evening television. Most congressmen acknowledged the gravity of the occupation, but many urged the use of economic sanctions before force was used.

When Saddam Hussein refused to respond to Bush's demands for the unconditional evacuation of Kuwait, despite a last-minute effort to reach agreement by Secretary of State Baker, bombing began on January 16, 1991. Seven weeks later, coalition forces began land operations. This portion of the war lasted only 100 hours. Iraqi forces fled, setting fire to 600 Kuwaiti oil wells as they departed. There were several reasons for Bush's abrupt end to the conflict. General Colin Powell expressed concern that the decimation of the Iraqi army had the appearance of "slaughter for slaughter's sake." General Schwartzkopf raised doubts about the military wisdom of an occupation that would be like a "dinosaur in a tarpit." Bush himself was concerned that the international coalition might not bear the strain of a march on Baghdad. National Security Advisor Brent Scowcroft believed it was likely that Saddam would soon be overthrown. It is also likely the president calculated that a very weak and dismembered Iraq would not be desirable for the stability of the region, since it would leave Iran as the dominant power. Bush and his advisors, however, did not anticipate that Saddam would be able to use helicopters and elements of the Republican Guard reserved from the fighting to crush internal opposition and maintain power.

In 1991, however, few critics realized how momentous was the decision to end the war in 100 hours. Americans were enthralled by the success of the effort and Bush's approval poll ratings soared to over 90 percent, the highest ever recorded for a president. Buoyed by the triumph, Congress even supported U.N. military intervention in Somalia. The United States supported the repressive regime of Siad Barre during the Cold War, but by 1990 the air force base in the country was less important to American interests and Bush allowed the agreement, along with economic aid, to lapse. However, civil war and a drought led to a massive famine, and the president sent 500 marines to help distribute food in December of 1992. (The Somali mission was ended by Clinton after eighteen marines were killed by local military factions.)

In domestic policy, Bush never found a victory equivalent to the one that he enjoyed in the Persian Gulf, nor even the quiet successes he had in managing the end of the Cold War. During the 1988 campaign, in an effort to distinguish himself from President Reagan, Bush announced his support for a "kinder, gentler America" and proposed the revitalization of voluntary associations to help those in need. These groups would be "like a thousand points of light in a broad and peaceful sky." Although Bush made over 500 speeches for community services during his term of office and created an Office of National Service in the White House, he proposed no major legislation since he believed the effort was primarily inspirational.

Bush did attempt to revise some areas of Reagan domestic policy. The deregulation of savings-and-loan associations in the 1980s led to numerous scandals as officers made high-risk investments. When the real estate market sagged, over 350 institutions were bankrupt. Since the S&Ls were federally insured, the president and Congress were forced to find ways to pay for this failed experiment, which raised the budget deficit by $50 billion. Bush also supported major amendments to the Clean Air Act that had been opposed by Reagan and supported the Americans with Disabilities Act that forbade discrimination in employment. It was Bush's support of the Omnibus Budget and Reconciliation Act of 1990, however, that so angered Republican voters that it contributed to his reelection defeat in 1992. In 1988, Bush had pledged very forthrightly not to raise taxes. He said: "Congress will push me to raise taxes—and I'll say to them, read my lips, no new taxes." However, faced with the massive sums required to save the S&Ls and across-the-board cuts, Bush agreed to an increase in income taxes for the most wealthy Americans (28 percent to 31.5 percent).

In many ways, Bush, the last Cold War president, was similar to Truman, the first. Both men faced a new international system and attempted to devise policies, such as containment and the "new world order," to respond to the challenges they faced. Both too found it very difficult to govern domestically in the shadow of their predecessors, FDR and Ronald Reagan.

SUMMARY AND COMMENT

The Cold War greatly expanded the powers of the presidency. Prior to this period, the discretionary exercise of power and expanded bureaucratic structures to enforce and implement decisions had existed only for relatively brief moments. Lincoln's war powers were limited after his death in 1865, and the draft was discarded. The extraordinary powers bestowed upon Wilson in the Lever Act were soon withdrawn, and the Senate frustrated his attempt to create a new post-war international order. FDR enjoyed a vast increase in power primarily in the early stages of the Great Depression and during World War II. Even in the midst of the Depression crisis he faced opposition from the courts, and in 1938 the erosion of his electoral support. Cold War presidents, however, were presented with a steady accretion of personal and bureaucratic power for a period of over 50 years. Certainly, presidential power during the Cold War presidency rose and ebbed, particularly after the Watergate scandal. However, the demands of the Cold War—swift decision making, the need for global intelligence, and military preparedness—provided Cold War presidents with a great reservoir of authority.

There is a sense, however, in which Cold War presidents were also limited by the new authority they were granted. After 1948, presidents were highly constrained by the Cold War consensus on foreign policy. No president could abandon the policy of containment without severe electoral consequences. The charge that a president might be "soft on communism" was a deadly one, if it could be made with any plausibility. Kennedy struggled with the possibility that his response to the installation of missiles in Cuba might be considered "another Munich," and both presidents Johnson and Nixon worried that they would be charged with having "lost Vietnam." Innovative policies, from Eisenhower's "brinkmanship" to Nixon's "détente" to Carter's human rights initiative and the Reagan doctrine, were all closely scrutinized as measures that leaned either toward concession or toward war. Moreover, since the American political system became so executive-centered in foreign policy, presidents constantly faced the dilemma of failing to meet high expectations. By the 1950s the public did not expect dramatic Cold War victories, but they often were frustrated by the small movements that formed the pattern of bipolar international politics. The numerous summits with Soviet leaders invariably produced a temporary rise in presidential approval ratings but were not occasions for any major breakthroughs. International crises were a standard feature of the Cold War but none, despite the fears of the domino effect, significantly altered the balance of power between the two rivals.

In domestic politics, however, Cold War presidents confronted significant changes. The civil rights movement represented an ongoing challenge that required imagination and resolve in terms of both Congress and the public. As Russell Riley has demonstrated, the president's role as the prime "nation keeper" described by Alexander Hamilton in the *Federalist* as one responsible for the "preservation of peace and tranquility" conflicted with demands for social justice. Moreover, presidents were well aware that any action in this area might alter the political base of their parties. In addition, presidents in this period quickly discovered the election process itself was undergoing rapid transition. After 1968, no presidential candidate could afford to ignore the gauntlet of primaries. Nor could the impact of television on election outcomes and campaign funding be ignored. Despite the "Reagan Revolution," the economic policies created by modern presidents remained largely intact, but the economy itself was changing rapidly. Economic institutions were more global than national and more service-oriented than industrial.

Together, these demands required exceptional abilities. Cold War presidents were "imperial" in some spheres and custodial in others. They were required to carry the burden of what President Kennedy called a "long twilight struggle," but they also found that they must respond innovatively to change.

Bibliographic Essay

There are numerous narratives of the origin and progress of the Cold War. The following are especially helpful in their exploration of its theoretical aspects: Thomas G. Paterson, *On Every Front* (New York: W. W. Norton, 1979); John G. Stoessinger, *Crusaders and Pragmatics* (New York: W. W. Norton, 1979); John Lewis Gaddis, *Strategies of Containment* (New York: Oxford University Press, 1982); and Ralph B. Levering, *The Cold War, 1945–1987* (Arlington Heights, IL: Harlan Davidson, 1988). For two different accounts of impact of the Cold War on the American political system, see Aaron L. Friedberg, *In the Shadow of the Garrison State* (Princeton, NJ: Princeton University Press, 2000) and Stephen J. Whitfield, *The Culture of the Cold War* (Baltimore, MD: Johns Hopkins University Press, 1991). Friedberg emphasizes American anti-statism as a significant and salutary restraint on the growth of government, while Whitfield focuses on irrational aspects of the American response. While there is no general account of Cold War presidents, the works of two presidential advisors emphasize the changes in presidential authority as a result of the Cold War: Arthur Schlesinger, Jr., *The Imperial Presidency* (Boston: Houghton Mifflin, 1973) and George Reedy, *The Twilight of the Presidency* (New York: World, 1970).

Aaron Wildavsky advanced the "two presidency" thesis to attempt to account for the differences in presidential power domestically and internationally in "The Two Presidencies," Aaron Wildavsky, ed., *Perspectives on the Presidency* (Boston: Little, Brown, 1975). For the impact of the civil rights movement on the presidency, see Russell L. Riley, *The Presidency and the Politics of Racial Inequality* (New York: Columbia University Press, 1999), ch. 5–8; and Kenneth O'Reilly, *Nixon's Piano* (New York: Free Press, 1995), ch. 4–9. For accounts of the civil rights movement in general, see Aldon D. Morris, *The Origin of the Civil Rights* (New York: Free Press, 1984); Juan Williams, *Eyes on the Prize* (New York: Viking, 1987); and Taylor Branch, *Parting the Waters: America and the King Years, 1951–1963* (New

York: Simon & Schuster, 1988). On changes in political parties during this period, see Sidney M. Milkis, *The Presidency and Political Parties: The Transformation of the American Party System Since the New Deal* (New York: Oxford University Press, 1995) and Byron E. Schaeffer, *Bifurcated Politics: Evolution and Reform in the National Party Convention* (Cambridge: Harvard University Press, 1988).

There are many studies of Harry S. Truman and his presidency. Alonzo Hamby emphasizes domestic politics in the Truman administration, especially Truman's relationship with New Deal liberals, in *Beyond the New Deal: Harry S. Truman and American Liberalism* (New York: Columbia University Press, 1973). David McCulloch focuses upon the persona of Truman as a plain speaker in *Truman* (New York: Simon and Schuster, 1992). Donald R. McCoy concludes that Truman "made big government a permanent and major feature" of American life in *The Presidency of Harry S. Truman* (Lawrence: University Press of Kansas, 1984). William E. Leuchtenburg discusses Truman and FDR in *In the Shadow of FDR* (Ithaca, NY: Cornell University Press, 1983), ch. 1. Truman's Cold War decisions are evaluated in Gar Alperovitz, *Atomic Diplomacy: Hiroshima to Potsdam* (New York: Simon and Schuster, 1965) and Richard F. Haynes, *Awesome Power: Harry S. Truman as Commander in Chief* (Baton Rouge: Louisiana University Press, 1973). For analysis of the 1948 election, see Irwin Rose, *The Loneliest Campaign* (New York: New American Library, 1968) and Allen Yarnell, *Democrats and Progressives: The 1948 Campaign as a Test of Postwar Liberalism* (Berkeley: University of California Press, 1974).

The presidency of Dwight D. Eisenhower has been interpreted quite differently as scholars have reassessed the Cold War. Arthur Lawson, a member of Eisenhower's administration, provides an astute interpretation of the president's actions in *A Republican Looks at His Party* (New York: Harper, 1956). Marquis Child presented his influential portrait of the president as "captured hero" in *Eisenhower* (New York: Harcourt Brace, 1958). Both Fred Greenstein and Robert Griffith later offered reinterpretations: *The Hidden-Hand Presidency* (New York: Basic Books, 1982) and "Dwight D. Eisenhower and the Corporate Commonwealth," *American Historical Review* (1982), pp. 87–122. Martin Medhurst has collected recent interpretations that emphasize the success of Eisenhower's rhetorical strategies in Eisenhower's *War of Words* (East Lansing: Michigan State University Press, 1994). Robert F. Burk's biography traces Eisenhower's transition from war hero to "manager of the American national security state" in *Dwight D. Eisenhower: Hero and Politician* (Boston: Twayne, 1986). Michael S. Mayer discusses Eisenhower's civil rights positions in "'With Much Deliberation and Some Speed': Eisenhower and the *Brown* Decision," *Journal of Southern History* (1986), pp. 43–76.

Assessments of John F. Kennedy include William G. Carleton, "Kennedy in History: An Early Appraisal," *Antioch Review* XXIV (fall, 1964); Henry Pachter, "JFK as an Equestrian Statue: On Myth and Myth Makers," *Samagundi* I (1966); George Kateb, "Kennedy as Statesman," *Commentary* (June, 1966); Arthur Schlesinger, Jr., *A Thousand Days* (Boston: Houghton Mifflin, 1965); Theodore Sornson, *Kennedy* (New York: Bantam, 1966); Gary Wills, *The Kennedy Imprisonment* (Boston: Little, Brown, 1981); Henry Fairlie, *The Kennedy Promise* (Garden City, NY: Doubleday, 1973); Nancy Gager Clinch, *The Kennedy Neurosis* (New York: Grossett and Dunlap, 1973); Doris Kearns Goodwin, *The Fitzgeralds and the Kennedys* (New York: St. Martin's, 1987); Herbert S. Parmet, *The Struggles of John F. Kennedy* (New York: Dial, 1983) and *JFK* (New York: Dial, 1983); Harris Wofford,

Of Kennedys and Kings (New York: Farrar, Straus, Giroux, 1980); Thomas C. Reeves, *A Question of Character* (New York: Free Press, 1991); Irving Bernstein, *Promises Kept: John F. Kennedy's New Frontier* (New York: Oxford University Press,1991); and Nigel Hamilton, *JFK: Reckless Youth* (New York: Random House, 1992). The accounts of Wills, Clinch, Reeves, and Hamilton are quite negative; and those of Schlesinger, Sorensen, Wofford (members of the administration), and Bernstein are the most positive. See Thomas Brown, *JFK: History of an Image* (Bloomington: Indiana University Press, 1988) for a complete and insightful review of Kennedy scholarship. Richard Reeve's *President Kennedy: Profile of Power* (New York: Simon and Schuster, 1993) is the most balanced account of the administration.

The Cuban Missile Crisis has received extensive commentary. See Robert Thompson Smith, *The Missiles of October* (New York: Simon and Schuster, 1992) and Graham T. Allison, *The Essence of Decision* (Boston: Little, Brown, 1971) as well as Robert Kennedy's memoir, *Thirteen Days* (New York: Norton, 1969). For re-examination by some of the surviving participants, see James G. Blight and David A. Welch, eds., *On the Brink: Americans and Soviets Re-examine the Cuban Missile Crisis* (New York: Hill and Wang, 1989) and *Back to the Brink: Proceedings of the Moscow Conference on the Cuban Missile Crisis* (Lanham, MD: University Press of America, 1992).

Robert Caro offers different views of Johnson in his pre-presidential years in *Path to Power* (New York: Knopf, 1982); *Means of Ascent* (New York: Knopf, 1990); and *Master of the Senate* (New York: Knopf, 2002). Robert Dallek's biography is considerably more positive: *Lone Star Rising* (New York: Oxford University Press, 1991). Doris Kearns' *Lyndon Johnson and the American Dream* (New York: Signet, 1976) is a fascinating account based on extensive interviews with the president soon after he left office. *The Great Society: A Twenty Year Critique* (Austin, TX: LBJ Library, 1986) is a useful collection of assessments of Johnson's domestic initiatives that can be compared with analyses in the 1960s in *The Great Society Reader* (New York: Random House, 1968). Larry Berman reviews Johnson's decision making in Vietnam in *Planning a Tragedy* (New York: Norton, 1982) and *Lyndon Johnson's War* (New York: Norton, 1989).

Michael A. Genovese, *The Nixon Presidency* (Westport, CT: Greenwood Press, 1990) and Melvin Small, *The Presidency of Richard Nixon* (Lawrence: University Press of Kansas, 1998) are the most useful single-volume reviews of the Nixon administration. Stephen Ambrose's three-volume biography, *Education of a Politician* (New York, 1987), *Triumph of a Politician* (New York, 1989) and *Ruin and Recovery* (New York, 1991), emphasizes Nixon's grasp of politics. Joan Hoff Wilson presents an interesting re-evaluation in *Nixon Reconsidered* (New York: Basic Books, 1994), as does Dean T. Kotlowski in *Nixon's Civil Rights* (Cambridge: Harvard University Press, 2001). Gerald S. Strober and Deborah H. Strober, eds., *Nixon: An Oral History of His Presidency*, contains frank recollections of the president by members of his administration.

For attempts to discern and evaluate Nixon's foreign policy, see Stephen Garret, "Nixonian Foreign Policy: A New Balance of Power—or a Revived Concert?" *Polity* (spring, 1976), pp. 389–421; Stanley Hoffman, "Will the Balance Balance at Home?" *Foreign Affairs* (summer, 1972), pp. 60–86; James Chace, "The Concert of Europe," *Foreign Affairs* (October, 1973), pp. 96–108; and M. J. Brenner, "The Problem of Innovation and the Nixon-Kissinger Foreign Policy" *International Studies Quarterly* (September, 1973), pp. 255–94. William Shawcross's *Sideshow: Kissinger,*

Nixon and the Destruction of Cambodia (New York: Simon and Schuster, 1979) is an early and still influential moral critique.

There are many analyses of the Watergate scandal. See Stanley Kutler, *The Wars of Watergate: The Last Crisis of Richard Nixon* (New York: Knopf, 1990). Michael Schudson, *Watergate in American Memory* (New York: Basic Books, 1992) reviews various interpretations and attempts to assess its impact. Robert T. Hartman's *Palace Politics* (New York: McGraw Hill, 1980) describes the conflict in the Ford administration between Ford and Nixon appointees. Also see Richard Reeves' *A Ford, not a Lincoln* (New York: Harcourt, Brace, 1975) and John Robert Greene, *The Presidency of Gerald R. Ford* (Lawrence: University Press of Kansas, 1995). There are several reviews of the constitutional aspects of Ford's pardon of Nixon and the first application of the Twenty-fifth Amendment. See, for example, Patrick R. Cowlishaw, "The Conditional Presidential Pardon," *Stanford Law Review* (1975), pp. 149–77. For differing assessments of the *Mayaguez* incident, see Richard E. Neustadt and Ernest P. May, *Thinking in Time* (New York: Free Press, 1996) and Dan F. Hahn, "Corrupt Rhetoric: President Ford and the *Mayaguez* Incident" in *Essays in Presidential Rhetoric*, ed. Theodore Windt (Dubuque, IA: Kendall-Hunt, 1983).

Kenneth E. Morris, *Jimmy Carter: American Moralist* (Athens: University of Georgia Press, 1996) deftly examines Carter's ability to match his persona to the times in 1976 and his difficulties during his presidency. Betty Glad offers a psychological assessment in *Jimmy Carter* (New York: Norton, 1980). Carter's foreign-policy initiatives are reviewed in Gaddis Smith, *Reason and Power: American Diplomacy in the Carter Years* (New York: Hill and Wang, 1986). Carter himself offers a vigorous defense of his positions in regard to Panama and the Middle East in his memoir, *Keeping Faith* (New York: Bantam, 1982). For assessments of the "malaise" speech, see Dan F. Hahn, "Flailing the Profligate: Carter's Energy Speech of 1979," *Presidential Studies Quarterly* 10 (1980), pp. 583–87; and Robert A. Strong, "Recapturing Leadership: The Carter Administration and the Crisis of Confidence," *Presidential Studies Quarterly* 16 (1986), pp. 636–50. Gary Sick reviews the background to the hostage crisis in *America's Tragic Encounter with Iran* (New York: Random House, 1985).

The nature and extent of the "Reagan Revolution" is much debated. Martin Anderson's *Revolution* (New York: Harcourt, Brace Jovanovich, 1988) is an able account by a former advisor. Also see Charles O. Jones, ed., *The Reagan Legacy* (Chatham, NJ: Chatham House, 1988). For a more critical assessment that attempts to measure the Reagan rhetoric to reality, see Michael Schaller, *Reckoning with Reagan* (New York: Oxford University Press, 1992). Eric J. Schmertz, Natalie Datlof, and Alexej Ugrinsky present extensive evaluations by both academic and political actors based on the Hofstra University Conference on the Reagan Presidency: *Ronald Reagan's America*, 2 vols. (Westport, CT: Greenwood Press, 1997). Especially useful are works that attempt to examine Reagan's role as "Great Communicator." See Gary Wills, *Reagan's America* (Baltimore: Penguin, 1988); Paul D. Erickson, *Reagan Speaks* (New York: New York University Press, 1985); and David E. Proctor, *Enacting Political Culture* (Westport, CT: Praeger, 1986). Reagan's unique background has inspired many to base their analysis of the Reagan Revolution on the influence of Hollywood. Michael Paul Rogin, *Ronald Reagan, the Movie: And Other Episodes in Political Demonology* (Berkeley: University of California Press, 1987) considers the influence of the American cinema on Reagan's political outlook, and Alan Nadel, *Flatlining on the Field of Dreams: Cultural Narratives in the Films of President Reagan's America* (New Brunswick, NJ: Rutgers University Press, 1997), argues that Hollywood confirmed the Reagan outlook in films ranging from *Wall Street* to *The Little Mermaid.*

The dual memoir by President Bush and his national security advisor, Brent Scowcroft, is extremely valuable not only for its participant account of the final days of the Cold War but also as view of the relationship of a president and advisor: *A World Transformed* (New York: Knopf, 1998). For assessment of Bush's performance in the transition, see Steven Hurst, *The Foreign Policy of the Bush Administration* (New York: Cassel, 1999) and Ryan J. Barilleax and Mary E. Stuckey, eds., *Leadership and the Bush Presidency: Prudence or Drift in an Era of Change?* (Westport, CT: Praeger, 1992). General accounts include Herbert Parmet, *George Bush: The Life of a Lone Star Yankee* ((New York: Scribner's, 1997); John Robert Greene, *The Presidency of George Bush* (Lawrence: University Press of Kansas, 2000); and David Mervin, *George Bush and the Guardianship Presidency* (New York: St. Martins, 1996). Parmet focuses on the impact of Bush's hybrid cultural roots on his conception of politics. Greene generally defends Bush's policies of prudence, while Mervin is more critical. There are numerous and conflicting assessments of the Gulf War: Jean Edward Smith, *George Bush's War* (New York: Holt, 1992); Alex Hybel, *Power over Rationality: The Bush Administration and the Gulf Crisis* (Albany: State University of New York Press, 1993); and Marcia Lynn Whicker, James Pfiffner, and Raymond Moore, eds., *The Presidency and the Persian Gulf War* (Westport, CT: Praeger, 1993).

CHAPTER 7

THE POSTMODERN PRESIDENCY

Postmodern Presidents

President/ Political Party	Term of Office	Vice President	Percent Electoral Vote	Percent Popular Vote
Bill Clinton (D)	1993–1997	Albert Gore	69	43
Bill Clinton (D)	1997–2001	Albert Gore	66	49
George W. Bush (R)	2001–	Richard Cheney	52	48

In 1988 Richard Rose used the term "postmodern presidency" to describe a new form of governance. As he observed the last years of the Reagan administration, Rose not only anticipated the end of the Cold War but also the complex international system that would follow. He believed the outlines of the postmodern presidency could be seen as early as the Vietnam War. He suggested that Jimmy Carter might have been the first postmodern president but argued that the complete outlines of this new presidential system would be evident when a new president took office in 1989. In a subsequent edition of *The Post-Modern President*, Rose defined George H. W. Bush's presidency as postmodern and accurately predicted that, despite the success of the Persian Gulf War, Bush would be vulnerable since postmodern presidents face challenges that are very difficult to meet.

Two revisions are appropriate to Rose's prescient analysis. First, since President Bush was the last Cold War president, one can make the case that the features of a new presidential system were not yet fully in place.

Second, one can conclude that the definition of postmodern can be expanded. Rose defined the postmodern presidency as one in which "the resources of the White House are not sufficient to meet all of the President's international responsibilities." Hence, unlike modern presidents (which, for Rose, includes Cold War presidents), their successors no longer have the resources to effectively direct international change. "Postmodernism" as a philosophical and cultural concept includes elements that are helpful in delineating a possible new period in the development of the presidency.

Although postmodernists rarely agree on even major parts of their formulations, there are a number of themes relevant to the presidency. Most postmodernists agree that in the present era it is very difficult to make an effective case for large-scale political projects. François Lyotard (*The Postmodern Condition*) has called this phenomenon the "loss of the grand narrative." If one applies this observation to the American case, one might argue that the project that FDR outlined for America—an active government that promoted the economic welfare of its citizens through entitlement programs—no longer receives the unqualified support that it once did from large portions of the American electorate. Bill Clinton acknowledged the result of this erosion of confidence when he announced before Congress in 1996 that "the era of big government is over." Similarly, the confidence that America represented the forces of light and the Soviet Union the forces of darkness that Eisenhower and other Cold War presidents reiterated is now gone. Although the 9/11 terrorist attack may have changed public consciousness, the journalistic designations of "generation X" and "generation Y" are meant to convey an age cohort in which no transforming political event, such as the Civil War, the Great Depression, or the fight against fascism captures public consciousness.

Postmodernists also place great emphasis on the impact of modern technology on our thinking. The development of computer and information technology, including the Internet, have dramatically altered previous notions of time and space. Communication is now both quicker and more readily available. These changes create enormous opportunities for democratization. As President Clinton said in his second inaugural address, "Ten years ago, the Internet was the mystical province of physicists; today it is a commonplace encyclopedia for millions of schoolchildren." Consequently, dictators find it increasingly difficult to control the flow of information to their subjects. On the other hand, this new technology poses many dangers. The rights of privacy are threatened, and groups throughout the world that wish to maintain traditional cultures find themselves bombarded by cultural change. For postmodernists, the most significant aspect of these developments is how instant and constant electronic images alter our views about reality. For the French critic Jean Baudrillard (*Simulations*), the proliferation of signs threatens to create a media "hyper-reality" that is independent of the objects signified. The effects of this "virtual reality" were portrayed in the film *Wag the Dog*, in which a fictitious president created a phantom war based entirely on computer imagery.

The modern and Cold War presidents, of course, were well aware of the political impact of rhetoric and images, but some scholars now speculate that the ability to manipulate public opinion has reached a new level. The availability of mass communication has created great temptations to saturate the media with electronic images during primary and general elections. The media too has so significantly expanded that some critics contend events are covered beyond their newsworthiness and even manufactured to increase ratings. Bruce Miroff has suggested that presidents now use the new media to create "spectacles" for the public that often have little relation to actual events. The spectacle, he argues, is more like a wrestling than a boxing match, in which the gesture and the performance is the only point of the event. Miroff contends that President Clinton was the first president to employ the postmodern spectacle in which "fleeting images and fractured continuity, surfaces without depth, personae rather than personality" were the main features of his presidency.

If we have now entered the era of the postmodern presidency, we can expect presidents to confront a variety of new challenges. The nation-state itself is much more exposed, as Rose suggests, to largely uncontrollable forces. While the United States is at an unparalleled zenith in terms of military and economic power, it is also vulnerable to what defense analysts call "asymmetrical threats" by terrorists. Some nation-states have become "hollowed out" structures in which the government is unable or unwilling to control independent military forces, such as Afghanistan, the former Yugoslavia, Somalia, and Yemen. New economic structures have emerged, such as the European Union, that partially supersede individual states, and global corporations sometimes act independently. All the while, media-fueled presidential spectacles may encourage citizen passivity and undermine presidential accountability.

BILL CLINTON (1993–2001)

The presidency of William Jefferson Clinton exhibited all the contradictions described by postmodernists. The 1992 election was an unusual one. Most of the likely Democratic contenders, intimidated by President Bush's high approval ratings after the Gulf War, refused to run. Among the seven who entered the race was a young governor from Arkansas whose name recognition was quite low. Moreover, Clinton was plagued with accusations about his character that repeatedly threatened to remove him from consideration by primary voters. He was charged with adultery (which he denied). He was charged with draft evasion (which he denied). He was charged with marijuana use as a youth (which he denied). Many of these accusations were first made in tabloids and on Internet sites and later were carried by the conventional media. Clinton attempted to deal with what his opponents called the "character issue" by appearing through the media in intensely personal settings. For example, he pioneered the use of "electronic town meetings" in which ordinary citizens rather than professionals asked him questions.

The campaign was complicated by an independent candidate, Ross Perot, who entered the race, withdrew, and then reentered. Perot was able to mount an effective campaign largely focused on the budget deficit, in part because his vast personal wealth allowed him to avoid campaign finance restrictions. Meanwhile President Bush was damaged by persistent challenges from the right wing of his party. Former Nixon speechwriter Patrick Buchanan captured prime-time attention at the Republican Convention with a call for "culture war" in America. Elected with 43 percent of the vote, and with little support from liberal Congressional Democrats and determined opposition by Republicans, Clinton had little national experience to deal with a damaged economy and a fluid post–Cold War international system.

The Clinton administration was characterized by extraordinary roller-coaster-like periods of crisis, failure, and success. In the first two years of his presidency Clinton struggled to present an effective agenda. During the campaign, he successfully focused on the economy as the main issue facing the nation. He suggested that new ideas were necessary to deal with the problems of the American economy which, he argued, must find ways to compete globally. On the other hand, he spoke eloquently about his affection for John Kennedy and frequently showed empathy for the unemployed. His campaign policy pamphlet, entitled "Putting People First," pledged middle-class tax cuts, expansion of the income tax credit for the working poor, and job creation. Upon taking office, Clinton tried to follow both approaches. To the surprise of many of his campaign advisors, Clinton abandoned his promise of a tax cut and focused attention on deficit reduction. He initially proposed a tax on energy use, which was later discarded over the opposition of Democratic senators. The deficit reduction package passed by Congress included a tax increase on high-income families and on corporations as well as significant cuts in Medicare and defense. The legislation passed without a single Republican vote. Although the act called for a reduction in the deficit by $500 million over five years, the $241 million tax increase energized Republicans and disappointed Democrats, who saw no direct connection to unemployment relief.

Clinton, however, insisted that deficit reduction was an essential first step in reviving the economy. Shortly after assuming office, the president announced his general plan for national healthcare reform and appointed his wife, Hillary, to head a task force to make recommendations. Since healthcare costs had risen significantly and many Americans had no healthcare insurance, both the prospects and the expectations for legislation were high. The Democrats controlled both Houses and the press awaited a major piece of legislation equivalent to Lyndon Johnson's Medicare legislation in 1965. Instead, Clinton made a series of decisions that led to the defeat of healthcare reform. In fact, the legislation never reached the floor of the House or Senate for consideration.

Clinton's failure, which is now treated by presidential scholars as a classic case of a misused legislative opportunity, can be traced to a series of tactical errors. Liberal Democrats in the House favored a program of universal healthcare much like the Canadian system. Clinton employed the imagery of this plan in speaking before Congress by holding up a single card that would guarantee healthcare. He was convinced, however, that such a comprehensive plan would be too expensive, and he believed that he could not afford to raise taxes again. Another tactic might have been to promote a very modest plan. At this point, Republicans, particularly in the Senate, concerned that their opposition would be unpopular and obstructionist, were prepared to accept some reform. Clinton, however, rejected this alternative and eventually produced a complicated proposal of over 1,300 pages for "managed healthcare."

Hillary Clinton's task force, which submitted the plan to the president, was already a controversial group. Republicans complained about the secrecy with which the task force deliberated, and some Democrats complained that questions of important public policy should be addressed by elected officials. Interest groups opposed to the legislation used the eight-month period the task force took to produce results as testimony to their advantage. They spent $60 million on a media campaign that raised doubts about the plan. The most effective ad featured an average American couple, Harry and Louise, sitting at the their kitchen table puzzling over the plan. Opponents used Clinton's own populism to attack the legislation. By the time the president's plan came before Congress, public support had dropped to 50 percent. Republicans were emboldened and Democrats were unable to find a compromise.

There were administration victories during the 103rd Congress. The Family and Medical Leave Act guaranteed unpaid leave for employees. The legislation was passed earlier by Congress in 1990 but was vetoed by President Bush. The "Motor Voter" act permitted voter registration at state drivers license centers. One of Clinton's major legislative successes was won at considerable political cost. The president actively supported the North American Free Trade Agreement (NAFTA) despite the strong opposition of labor and environmental groups. Clinton argued that free trade would invigorate the American economy. Opponents argued that American jobs would be lost and pollution would increase, since Mexico had minimal environmental restrictions. The president went over the heads of the leaders of his own party. House Majority Whip David Bonior actually led the legislative opposition. Clinton held a free-trade bazaar on the White House lawn and spoke before a nationally televised town meeting sponsored by the U.S. Chamber of Commerce. With the help of Republicans who voted in favor in the House by 132–43, NAFTA was passed.

Clinton knew his early decisions were controversial since he had taken on, at various points, both the Congressional Republicans and Democrats. Although he expected to lose seats in the 1994 elections, he was completely unprepared for the result. Republicans took control of both the House and Senate for the first time in 40 years. Moreover, the House leadership, under the direction of Newt Gingrich, not only campaigned against Clinton policies but also campaigned for their own. Republicans signed a pledge, called the "Contract with America," to support their own reforms. Media attention shifted to the House, and Gingrich was given more media coverage than the president. The "eclipsed presidency" seemed to have made a surprising return. Privately, Clinton was devastated; publicly he announced, "I am still relevant."

Clinton's initial relations with the new Republican 104th Congress seem to represent the bottom of the roller-coaster ride, only to be followed by another steep ascent. Frustrated and hurt by the midterm elections, Clinton called an old advisor, Dick Morris, for help. Morris was so disliked by the White House staff that Clinton actually met regularly with him in secret. Morris presented to Clinton a recent historical analogy. When Jacques Chirac headed the National Assembly in 1985 on an antisocialist platform with the slogan "Under Socialism, I Have Nothing Left!", François Mitterrand, the president, did not directly challenge him. Rather, he "fast-forwarded" Chirac's agenda. According to Morris, Mitterand passed "enough of it to relieve the frustrations that led to Chirac's victory." Clinton noted that Mitterand lost in 1987, but Morris insisted that was not the point. Mitterand's strategy could work, since Gingrich was just like Chirac. He was "a born leader who loves nothing more" than to "march his followers into battle." Morris advised the president to permit Republicans to lower the deficit and reduce government spending while offering other agendas to achieve both, and to show leadership in areas where Congress cannot fully dominate, such as foreign policy.

Clinton followed Morris's advice. When Gingrich demanded severe budget cuts in Medicare and Social Security as well as a tax cut to reduce the deficit, Clinton offered to agree on a balanced budget in ten years but refused to accept cuts in entitlement programs, which he said were being used to give a tax break to the rich. Infuriated, Gingrich initiated a game of "chicken" in December of 1995. The government was shut down pending concessions by the president. Rather than exposing Clinton's incompetence, the government shutdown began to appear to the public as ideological rigidity on the part of Republicans. Sensing the change in public opinion, Republicans accepted an agreement on a balanced budget in seven years and smaller cuts. Republicans then proposed a welfare reform bill that eliminated federal aid to mothers with dependent children to be replaced by federal assistance for state "workfare" programs. Several of Clinton's cabinet members, as well as many Congressional Democrats, urged the president to veto the legislation. On Morris's advice, however, Clinton signed the legislation after demanding some revisions.

With both the balanced budget and welfare removed as issues in the upcoming election, Clinton pursued another strategy offered by Morris. Morris insisted that in addition to "fast-forwarding" the Republican agenda, the president should offer policy alternatives of his own that were neither imitations of the Republicans nor alternatives offered by liberal Democrats. He called the strategy "triangulation": ". . . create a third position, not just in between the old positions of the two parties but above them as well. Identify a new course that accommodates the needs Republicans address but does it in a way that is uniquely yours." In his 1996 State of the Union message Clinton announced that the "era of big government is over," a concession to the Republican agenda, but he also presented what came to be known as the "values agenda." Using Morris's strategy of triangulation, Clinton accepted Republican cultural issues but also presented his own policy solutions. He recommended, for example, the use of V-chips to help parents control what their children watched on television. In subsequent speeches over the next eight months, he offered proposals on handgun regulation, new regulations on tobacco, suggestions for local curfews for teens, and the use of cell phones by citizens to reduce crime. Liberal Democrats complained that Clinton was offering only "small-bore" micro-legislation to deal with large problems, but the president had effectively seized a major portion of the Republican agenda.

Clinton also knew that the end of the Cold War severely restricted the ability of a president in foreign policy. Shortly after assuming office, he paid the price for what military analysts call "mission creep" in Somalia. The Bush administration's humanitarian effort in 1992 slowly expanded to one of establishing peace between contending military factions. In an ambush by a local military leader, eighteen American soldiers were killed and one body was dragged through the streets of Mogadishu. Members of Congress and the public were outraged and demanded the withdrawal of American forces. Clinton complied. The lesson drawn from the experience was that the United States should not be involved with "regime-building" projects throughout the world. This admonition placed restrictions on Clinton's general post–Cold War foreign policy, which was described by his national security advisor, Anthony Lake, as "enlargement," designed to replace containment as a guiding principle for the new post–Cold War world. According to Lake, U.S. policy should be focused on ways in which the number of democracies can increase in the world. The policy was consistent with the advocacy of human rights but also had practical goals. According to the theory of "democratic peace" advanced by many scholars, democracies go to war with dictatorships but rarely fight one another. If the world could be transformed into a set of democracies, the problem of international violence could be reduced or even eliminated.

How could a president encourage democracies without becoming mired in attempts at regime building? Clinton faced this dilemma throughout his presidency as he surveyed events in the former Yugoslavia. When Yugoslavia disintegrated as a single state after communist rule ended, war broke out in the resulting new states of Serbia, Croatia, and Bosnia. Because the new states contained complex mixtures of ethnic minorities, there was fierce and brutal fighting intended to "ethnically cleanse" each region. During the 1992 campaign Clinton had criticized President Bush for his apparent indifference to the suffering. Once in office, however, Clinton was reluctant to commit American troops to the region. In 1995, he brokered a peace treaty among the warring states called the Dayton Accords. When these arrangements broke down, he initiated a series of air strikes in 1999 in order to force Serbian forces to withdraw from Kosovo. In 1994 Clinton took no action when an estimated one million people of the Tutsis tribe were killed by Hutu militias in a genocidal civil war in Rwanda. Just before the midterm elections, Clinton did insist that Haiti's military junta, which had invalidated a recent election, step down and threatened a U.S. invasion. Former President Carter negotiated a peaceful settlement, and a small contingent of military personnel supervised the transition.

Although Clinton helped produce a major breakthrough in the Middle East conflict in 1993 that promised Palestinian self-rule, he had few other opportunities to establish the kind of presidential leadership in foreign policy that was available to Cold War presidents. However, without the possibilities of a "rally effect" from international events, Clinton did enjoy significant assistance in his reelection campaign from domestic economic developments. Although most of his economic stimulus proposals were blocked by Republicans, in 1993 the American economy began its longest peacetime expansion in U.S. history. Clinton claimed his deficit reduction legislation was responsible for the boom, but there were other sources as well, including the impact of new developments in information technology. Unemployment declined rapidly (from seven percent in 1993 to four percent by 2000), the stock market soared, and associated domestic problems eased as well. Crime rates, welfare rolls, teenage birth rates, and infant mortality rates all declined. The economic boom, along with the impact of his "fast forward" and "triangulation" strategies, made Clinton's claim that he represented the bridge to the twenty-first century an appealing one. Clinton improved his popular vote total from 43 percent to 49 percent.

Clinton's moment of triumph, however, was very short-lived. Throughout his first term, he suffered from numerous allegations that he engaged in corrupt activities. In 1994, he was forced to request the appointment of a special prosecutor to investigate his investments in the

Whitewater Development Company while he was governor. Hillary Clinton was charged with illegal economic activities as well. Paula Jones filed a lawsuit in federal court accusing him of sexual harassment in the same year. The Clintons were charged with firing officials in the White House travel office in order to hire friends. There were also investigations of a White House cover-up of the suicide of White House advisor Vincent Forrester. In January of 1998 a new charge emerged that threatened to lead to the collapse of the Clinton presidency. Clinton was accused of having an affair with a twenty-one-year-old White House intern, Monica Lewinsky, and also of encouraging her to deny their relationship under oath.

Many presidents have had affairs in office, but these revelations assumed a new importance in this period of the postmodern presidency. Historically, the press has been reluctant to report these activities, but new Internet outlets showed no such restraint, and the conventional media picked up the allegations. Moreover, the scope of media coverage was greatly expanded. Print and electronic news was saturated with speculation over the following months. In addition, sexual activity in the workplace had been under close scrutiny in recent years. Also, partisan acrimony was at particularly high levels since 1994, and charges about the president's personal character were already widely reported.

Clinton survived the crisis. Although he was impeached by the House of Representatives on counts of perjury, obstruction of justice, and abuse of power, he was not convicted by the Senate. In fact, some of the unusual circumstances that created the crisis ultimately worked in the president's favor. The activities of the special prosecutor were regarded as time consuming and intrusive by the public. By the time Clinton admitted the affair in August, most Americans had accommodated themselves to the crisis and rejected impeachment as a remedy. Clinton's confident State of the Union address before a televised prime-time national audience in January reminded Americans of their extraordinary economic prosperity.

Despite avoiding resignation or impeachment, the Clinton presidency operated in a particularly defensive state for the remainder of the second term. The courts eroded Clinton's claims of executive privilege in ruling that a president could face civil trial while in office (*Clinton v. Jones*) and that the president's Secret Service and White House staff were not immune from testimony. In the last weeks of his presidency, the roller coaster dipped one final time. Clinton's pardons of campaign benefactors and his acceptance of a plea bargain that included temporary disbarment reduced his approval ratings once again. As perhaps the first of the postmodern presidents, Clinton offered the public a seemingly endless set of contradictions. He governed from both the left and the right. His presidency sometimes appeared weak and at other times strong; sometimes he seemed able to detect and direct forces of change, and at other times he seemed oblivious to them.

GEORGE W. BUSH (2001–)

It is, of course, much too early to evaluate the presidency of Clinton's successor, George Walker Bush. Bush's presidency, however, is thus far marked by three extraordinary events that may direct the course of his administration. First was the unusual outcome of the 2000 election itself; second was the 9/11 terrorist attack on the World Trade Center; and third was the resulting "war on terrorism" that encompassed both Afghanistan and Iraq.

Extremely close presidential elections are not uncommon, and several presidents who lost the popular vote have been elected (John Quincy Adams, Rutherford B. Hayes, and Benjamin Harrison). Moreover, controversies about voter fraud and accurate voter counts have occurred in the past (1876, 1916, and 1960). What was novel about the 2000 election was the fact that a close election, in which the winner of the popular vote failed to gain a majority of the electoral college under conditions of challenged ballots, occurred under the intense scrutiny of the news media.

The 2000 presidential campaign itself was a conventional one, although there were some noticeable postmodern elements. Governor Bush faced strong competition from Senator McCain, and Vice President Gore defeated a challenge from Senator Bill Bradley. Both challengers presented themselves as "outsiders" in terms of the party establishment. Both candidates participated in debates, and both candidates were faced with minor third-party candidates from their right and left, respectively. Pat Buchanan ran on a neo-isolationist and anti-immigration platform, and Ralph Nader on an anti-corporate and pro-environment one. Bush and Gore campaigned from their political bases but attempted to offer signs of independence as well. Thus Bush spoke of tax cuts and criticized the "Clinton–Gore" administration for its failed attempts at "regime building" internationally. He raised the "character" question without discussing the impeachment issue but also spoke of his commitment to "compassionate conservatism." Gore spoke of the strong economy and of his leadership experience and raised populist themes, but significantly he also refused to ask the president to campaign with him.

Novel factors included the first widespread use of the Internet as a source of both fundraising and candidate advertisement. John McCain surprised party leaders by raising $1 million on his Internet site in a single day after his win in the New Hampshire primary. Candidates experimented with interactive sites where leaders could respond to voters in chat rooms and "virtual town meetings." Links for voter registration and speeches were also provided. CNN actually covered these new Web sites as a news event. Marjorie Randon Hershey has discussed the predominance of "media frames" (story lines with a central visual and/or textual theme) in the 2000 campaign and has noted that presidential candidates are now evaluated on their "entertainment value":

> Coverage of a presidential election was more and more difficult to distinguish from the prime-time dramas and sports events on network television, except that the personality clashes and competitive action took place in a series of settings rather than in an emergency room or athletic stadium.

Indeed, both candidates appeared regularly as guests on late night entertainment shows, and one of the most common media frames centered on the personalities of both candidates. News stories focused on Bush's verbal nonchalance and on Gore's "stiffness."

As election day approached, the most prominent media frame was the closeness of the election itself. All the networks declared Bush the electoral winner shortly after 2 A.M., November 8. Gore made a personal call to Bush at 2: 30 A.M. Concession and victory speeches were scheduled to start in minutes; foreign governments sent initial congratulations. Gore's retraction thirty minutes later delayed the selection of a president for 36 days. In contested elections, some officials who engage in ceremonial or perfunctory legal functions in perfect elections become central actors. In 1876, as in 2000, certification by local boards of election and the electoral college became major obstacles instead of gates to pass through routinely. In 1800 and 1824, Congress assumed the central legitimizing role in what usually is a mere public count of electors' votes. In 2000, the courts and county canvassing boards were instrumental in this process. They were called on to decide what votes to recount, what votes to disqualify, when results were to be certified, whether deadlines could be altered, and whether new elections could be called.

Without a concession by one candidate, the campaign itself was extended. In contested elections, there is the possibility that the continued competition among leaders can lead to outbreaks of violence that can ultimately, as it did in 1860, lead to civil war and dual sovereigns. In 1800 Jefferson threatened to call a constitutional convention, which could have led to two competing constitutions and two presidents. General Sherman ordered four artillery divisions to Washington, DC on November 18, 1876. Although the November 22 "Brooks Brothers" protest in Miami-Dade County raised the issue of organized physical intimidation, violence in 2000 was minimal. Nevertheless, the two contesting princes eventually created two transition teams, and by December there was pressure in Congress to split the federal transition funds.

In 2000, neither party could effectively "open the gates." One candidate needed to receive Florida's twenty-five electoral votes in order to claim a majority of the electoral college. Since both parties also knew that media frames would be crucial in determining who would ultimately win, each developed competing narratives. Each campaign defined the post-election period in terms of retrieving the legitimacy of the election through its own interpretation of democratic theory. The position of the Bush campaign, particularly after the machine recount on November 10, was that he had won the election fairly. Certainly, argued Bush, the election was an extraordinarily close and exciting one but it was, after all, over. "Everyone in Florida has had his or her vote counted. Those votes were recounted. In some counties they have been counted a third and even a fourth time." Any further recounts threatened to "overturn" the results. The Gore campaign, on the other hand, insisted the election was not over until all disputed ballots had been reviewed. To declare a winner without counting everyone's vote would not be fair. Gore claimed, "I don't want to win the presidency by a few votes cast in error or misinterpreted or miscounted, and I don't think Governor Bush does either."

Both arguments then rested securely within the democratic standard of legitimacy. Once "the people have spoken" the successor's authority is established, and any further contest is illegitimate. But had the people spoken? The Bush campaign claimed that they had; the Gore campaign insisted they had not—yet.

The risk on both sides, of course, was that the winner could become so stigmatized that he would be unable to govern. In fact, the slogans that encapsulated each narrative potentially forced either side to ingest a poison pill of illegitimacy to gain formal victory. The Bush rallying cry, "Sore Loserman," portrayed the strategy of the Gore–Lieberman ticket as one that planned to win the election by stealth. On November 18, James Baker asserted, for example, that: "The Gore campaign strategy is crystal clear. Keep conducting selective recounts. Keep filing selective lawsuits, keep making false charges that divert attention, and keep refusing to accept any deadline until the results change." The Gore slogan of "Count Every Vote," which was carefully tested with focus groups, claimed the true winner had to be the one who "won the most votes." In a televised address on November 27, Gore justified continuing his challenge by contending that "ignoring votes means ignoring democracy itself." Gore's team portrayed the 2000 election as a systemic threat to democracy: "If we ignore the votes of thousands in Florida in this election, how can you or any American have confidence that your vote will not be ignored in a future election?"

An election in which votes were uncounted not only raised questions of fairness but also of overt discrimination. Jesse Jackson compared the election to tactics at Selma and drew analogies about the histories of oppressed peoples: "Once again, sons and daughters of slavery and Holocaust survivors are bound together. . . ." The issue of hand recounts only sharpened the credibility of each competing narrative. Were these recounts a reasonable method of determining the will of the people, or were they attempts to "harvest" and "invent" votes?

While these two narratives were intended to stigmatize each opponent, they also had other purposes. As basic theoretical devices with operational goals, each was designed to ultimately provide validation for legitimacy. Gore was constantly forced to justify any inconsistencies in his narrative that might expose the "Sore Loserman"/"Count Every Vote" narratives as simple opportunistic partisan interpretations. And as for Bush, if the election should not be "judicialized" and not rest within the domain of state authority, wasn't his recourse to the courts—especially the federal courts—hypocritical and opportunistic? If every vote should count, shouldn't the Gore campaign support the counting of overseas ballots and those in Seminole and Martin counties despite "technical" irregularities?

The selection of spokespersons for each candidate in the post-election phase was part of an effort to appear statesmanlike by relying on elder party statesmen, James Baker and Warren Christopher, rather than campaign apparats. As the dispute continued, prominent lawyers took over a large portion of this task. David Bois, Lawrence Tribe, Barry Richard, Ted Olson and others were characterized as learned constitutional counsels and their partisan ties deemphasized. In fact, an unusual aspect of the 2000 election is that both candidates were called upon to present themselves as president before the outcome was decided. The press constantly evaluated their ability to perform in a crisis. Was Bush too reclusive? Was Gore too desperate? In general, was each candidate exhibiting "grace under pressure"?

The competing narratives, carefully presented to the media for framing, were also designed to open the various gates that eventually would declare a winner. Each side had their own "friendly" gatekeepers who could conceivably open a gate that would decide the election and reinstall the transition ritual. For Bush, there was the secretary of state and the governor, the state legislature, and some of the election boards that accepted overseas ballots. For Gore, the Florida Supreme Court and the election boards in Broward, Palm Beach, and (initially) Miami-Dade counties stepped forward. The friendly status of other crucial gatekeepers was unknown (Judge Nikki Ann Clark, Judge Sanders Saul, the Supreme Court). Others, such as the press and the public in general, were divided.

Each side found it necessary to insure the continued public support of political elites who could conceivably close gates before them. For example, on November 14 and 15, Senators Bayh, Nelson, Hawkins, and Breaux supported hand recounts and Senators McCain, Lott, and Hatch questioned them. Senator Kerry, a Vietnam war veteran, arrived in Florida to support standards in counting ballots of military personnel; and Republican governors, including Raciot and Whitman, served as recount observers (and, of course, critics). The AFL-CIO and the Sierra Club publicly supported recounts. Nancy Coleman, a spokeswoman for People for the American Way, said: "Unless the public is satisfied that the election process has been done fairly and the winner has won fair and square, there's a real question about how the next president will govern, whoever he is." Tom Finton of the conservative advocacy group Judicial Watch announced, "We're going in to come up with numbers that are independent from the political partisans on the ground."

When the Supreme Court ended the 2000 election, its majority selected one of the competing narratives in its decision. In the *per curiam* portion of the decision, seven members supported the Bush narrative that hand recounts violated central precepts of democratic theory. The members reiterated that both parties acknowledged the principles of the vote as a fundamental right, including the principle that "equal weight" be "accorded to each vote and the equal dignity owed to each voter": "Respondents say that the very purpose of vindicating the right to vote justifies the recount procedures now at issue." The Court concluded, however, that "the recount mechanisms implemented in response to the decisions of the Florida Supreme Court do not satisfy the minimum requirement for non-arbitrary treatment of voters necessary to secure the fundamental right."

In effect, the majority of the Supreme Court endorsed those gatekeepers who were ready to declare Bush the winner after the machine recount (the secretary of state, the Florida legislature) and rejected those who were not (the Florida Supreme Court and some canvassing boards). The key operational decision of the bare majority of the Supreme Court—that no recount, however formulated, could be made before the deadline that provided immunity to the Florida electors from Congressional challenge—assured that this gateway remained open as well.

The post-election campaign resumed swiftly after its dramatic stall on November 8. Gore's concession speech mentioned the theme of unity ten times, the need to bury partisanship seven times, and the obligation to honor the rule of law four times. Both the concession and Bush's victory address compared the 2000 election to that of 1860. Gore placed himself in the role of Stephen Douglas as the defeated prince: "Almost a century and a half ago, Senator Stephen Douglas told Abraham Lincoln, who had just defeated him for the presidency, "Partisan feeling must yield to patriotism. I'm with you, Mr. President, and God bless you." Bush referred to a "nation divided."

However, like the imperfect elections of 1824 and 1876, the final resolution was highly contested. Charges of judicial partisanship were immediately made despite early indications of public support for the decision, first by candidate Bush against the Florida Supreme Court and subsequently (more persistently and intensely) by the Democrats against the U.S. Supreme Court.

A major challenge confronting George W. Bush when he took office was whether he should acknowledge or ignore the contested election in his inaugural address. The first option risked carrying the campaign directly into this important ritual, and the second risked vacating the ritual of its symbolic and emotive content. Of course, in selecting the first option he might hope to dilute its importance by issuing a statement *en passant*, but in the compressed poetic language of the inaugural and the scrutiny it receives by the media, this would be difficult. Jefferson's open admission of the severely contested campaign and post-election crisis in his conciliatory statement, "We are all Republicans, We are all Federal-ists," actually carried the nascent tradition of the inaugural to a new level because it acknowledged the legitimacy of a presidency decided by parti-san competition. Lincoln's first inaugural was an extended plea and brief against secession. The inaugural did not stop the movement to civil war, but it did establish this inaugural as one of the most profound. On the other hand, Hayes's acknowledgment ("Human judgment is unerring and is rarely regarded as otherwise than wrong by the unsuccessful party"), which was one of five subjects, did not lead to the reconciliation that was the general theme of the address.

The challenge of the Bush inaugural was to confront (by admission or omission) the 2000 election within this circumscribed context. There were some difficult particulars as well. He would be sworn in by Justice Reh-nquist, who was instrumental as friendly electoral gatekeeper and judged by some as a partisan. His campaign opponent would be on the podium. Bush certainly could have chosen someone else to administer the oath, but this would have broken a tradition of elected presidents initiated in Washington's second term. John Adams did not attend Jackson's inaugu-ral in 1828, but because all other defeated vice presidents did, he could anticipate Gore's presence. Bush kept to the script and honored Gore's presence at the ceremony in the address, noting especially the graceful-ness of his concession.

In addition to these concerns George W. Bush faced the prospect, common in many contested elections, of significant protests to the inau-gural itself. Hayes, for example, held no balls or parade on the grounds that the preparation time was too short, but concern about possible vio-lence was a factor in the decisions. During the recount, congressional leaders in both parties threatened to boycott the inaugural, but these threats were later retracted. Large numbers of protesters did arrive at the Capitol. Security arrangements were strengthened, and the parade route was shortened. Picket signs carried forward the themes of the imperfect election: "Thief," Fraud," "His Fraudulency," "Hail to the Thief," "Sto-len," "Silenced Majority," "Supreme Coup." The press noted that there were more protesters than at any inaugural since 1972, but overall the rit-ual closely approximated that following regular elections.

The inaugural address itself acknowledged the imperfect election by pairing the exceptional way Democratic regimes manage the succession problem with American exceptionalism in general: "The peaceful transfer of authority is rare in history, yet common in our country." Translated from the poetry of the occasion into the problem of establishing legiti-macy, this single statement could be read, "To challenge this presidency is equivalent to challenging democratic rules of succession and America's uniqueness among nations in history."

The remainder of the inaugural address noted basic American beliefs ("everyone belongs . . . everyone deserves a chance . . . no insignificant person was ever born") as well as notations concerning their incomplete fulfillment. Bush closed the address with a reaffirmation of America as a chosen nation by quoting Jefferson's observation that angels watch over the country. The president-elect restated his campaign pledges in general terms, claiming that reform is still required in moments of prosperity and that personal responsibility is the anchor of a free society.

After the inaugural, President Bush still faced significant obstacles to his legitimacy. A president's first major address before Congress provides a new president with an opportunity to display his leadership. In this case too, there were challenges. A very limited agenda would suggest to the opposition that a caretaker presidency was likely. An agenda that was too ambitious might revitalize claims of illegitimacy. Bush therefore offered a relatively limited number of proposals but did highlight a large tax cut as his agenda centerpiece. In March, Rep. John Doolittle (R-CA) claimed that Republicans on Capitol Hill were "exultant . . . that Bush is building the mandate that he didn't get at the polls. You don't hear any talk about a minority president now. He's functioning with the full power and imagery of the presidency. He has the bully pulpit and it's powerful." While this interpretation did resonate among Republican politicians, polls suggested that a broad public mandate still eluded the president at this point.

By the fall of 2001, President Bush had managed to establish the basic contours of a legitimate presidency despite the contested election in 2000. His tax cut was passed by Congress, and he resolved a potential international crisis over a spy plane that had crashed in China. Still, the press and party opposition continued to compare him to politically damaged one-term presidents such as John Quincy Adams and Rutherford B. Hayes. Then, on September 11, a momentous and horrible event occurred that suggests a major alteration of American politics for some time to come. The terrorist attack on the World Trade Center shocked, saddened, and angered all Americans. Tensions were heightened because no one knew if more attacks were imminent. Anthrax-laced letters were sent to congressional leaders. Airplanes were briefly grounded. Wall Street was closed.

Terrorists, acting either independently or with the support of some states, had engaged in numerous violent acts throughout the Cold War. Al Qaeda, the group responsible for the attacks of 9/11, had been in existence since the early 1990s and was responsible for several previous acts of terrorism against the United States, including the bombings of American embassies in 1998 and an attack on the *U.S.S. Cole* in 2000. While Al Qaeda is reported to have agents in 60 countries, its base of support in 2001 was in Afghanistan, where members were welcomed by the Taliban government. American policy in regard to terrorist attacks before 9/11 was focused on attempts to bring perpetrators to justice and punish states that sponsored terrorism. President Reagan had authorized the bombing of Libya in retaliation for the 1989 destruction of a Pan Am civilian aircraft, and President Clinton had authorized the bombing of Al Qaeda camps in Afghanistan in 1998 in response to their embassy attacks. While these efforts were controversial in their time, after 9/11 critics (including the *New York Times* editorialists) called them "fitful, short-lived and not terribly effective."

The president and Congress reacted swiftly to meet the threat of new attacks. Power to detain immigrants accused of terrorism was increased, aid was provided to New York City as well as loans to airlines, and the Office of Homeland Security was established. The centerpiece of the government's first responses was the Patriot Act signed by President Bush on October 26. The legislation included provisions for aid to the families of victims of the attacks, additional resources for intelligence agencies, and increased penalties for computer fraud. More dramatic changes included granting greater authority to law enforcement agencies for surveillance, including wire taps, tracking users of Internet sites if the information was deemed "relevant" to a crime by a judge, and partial repeal of barriers placed on the CIA regarding surveillance of U.S. citizens. New, broader definitions of terrorism and terrorist organizations were also added. In response to the concerns of some members of Congress, the portions of the legislation dealing with surveillance were scheduled to expire on December 31, 2005. On September 20, President Bush issued a series of demands to the Taliban, including deliverance of Al Qaeda leaders and dismantlement of all terrorist training camps in Afghanistan. When the Taliban leaders refused to comply, the United States undertook military action with international support called "Operation Enduring Freedom" on October 7. The war ended in December, and a new government was formed in Afghanistan. Although numerous Al Qaeda terrorists were killed or captured, their leader, Osama bin Laden, was not found.

In January, President Bush expanded the scope of the war on terrorism by announcing in his State of the Union address that three states—Iraq, North Korea, and Iran—constituted an "axis of evil" in the world. While he moved cautiously in the face of North Korea's subsequent decision to withdraw from the Nuclear Nonproliferation Treaty to begin reprocessing plutonium and Iran's continued purchase of nuclear material from Russia, the president spoke directly about the need for a "regime change" in Iraq. Unlike the action in Afghanistan, Bush's demand made before the United Nations in September 2002 that Iraq submit to renewed international inspection of weapons of mass destruction (WMD) or face military force was more controversial. The United Nations Security Council in a unanimous vote authorized the return of weapons inspectors in November, but this international consensus began to unravel.

As United Nations experts searched for WMD, the United States pressed for direct military action. In February of 2003, Secretary of State Colin Powell presented evidence of Iraq's weapons programs and support of terrorists derived from intelligence sources to the Security Council. Many Security Council members, however, preferred a policy of containment similar to the successful Cold War strategy used against the Soviet Union. Powell, however, disagreed: "The United States will not and cannot run the risk to the American people. Leaving Saddam Hussein in possession of weapons of mass destruction for a few more months or years is not an option, not in the post–September 11 world." France, Germany, Russia, and China opposed a U.N. military action. Unable to secure United Nations support, President Bush declared that since the Security Council "has not lived up to its responsibilities, so we will rise to ours." He pieced together his own "coalition of the willing," composed primarily of British troops and smaller commitments from other nations such as Spain, Poland, and the Czech Republic.

Meanwhile in the United States, Congress debated a resolution to authorize military force in Iraq. Some members expressed opposition to the breadth of the resolution. Representative Charles Rangel (D-New York) said that he made a vow to veterans of past conflicts that he would never delegate Congressional responsibility to declare war to the president. Senator Robert C. Byrd (D-West Virginia) said that the resolution unwisely placed the decision to declare war in one man rather than in "the people's branch":

> Are we going to present the face of America as the face of a bully that is ready to go out at high noon with both guns blazing, or are we going to maintain the face of America as a country which believes in justice, the rule of law and liberty and the rights of all people to work out their destiny?

Others expressed concern about the absence of U.N. authorization. Many, including Senator Bob Graham (D-Florida), questioned whether Iraq had WMD; some felt that another Iraqi war would divert resources and energy from the effort to destroy Al Qaeda. A large majority, however, supported the president. Democratic Minority Leader Representative Richard Gephardt concluded that "September 11 was the ultimate wake-up call. . . . In these new circumstances deterrence well may not work." Gephardt decided that "the 12-year history of the U.N. effort to disarm Iraq convinces me that Iraq is a problem that must be dealt with diplomatically if we can, militarily if we must." Senator John McCain (R-Arizona) argued that, given the failure of the United Nations to disarm Iraq and Saddam Hussein's own actions, the "burden of proof" rested on those who supported continued diplomacy. Only with "regime change" would the United States be safe. Congressional authorization to use force against Iraq passed the House by a vote of 296–133 and the Senate by 77–23.

The war against Iraq began on March 20, shortly after the president gave Saddam Hussein forty-eight hours to leave the country. A small but highly mobile and technologically advanced American and British troop force defeated Iraqi forces within three weeks, although no WMD were immediately discovered and Saddam Hussein was not captured. The war itself received extensive television coverage, both in the United Sates and abroad. The Defense Department decided to attach reporters to every major military unit. Unlike the coverage of the first Iraqi war, in which press access was limited to reporter pools, this conflict featured continuous broadcasts from "embedded" correspondents in the field. On April 9, U.S. troops helped Baghdad residents topple a giant statue of the Iraqi dictator. This symbol of regime change appeared in media around the world. After the hostilities, President Bush appeared in full flight uniform on an aircraft carrier to greet troops returning to California.

The controversy over the 2000 election and the events of 9/11 thus constitute two very different anchors for the presidency of George W. Bush. The first indicated that his presidency would be a very difficult one. His disapproval ratings by the public in the first fifteen weeks of his new administration averaged about 30 percent, which suggested that he would govern under the same difficult conditions as the first postmodern president, Bill Clinton, as well as those of other presidents who came to office after highly contested elections. On the other hand, the terrorist attacks placed Bush in the category of wartime presidents who enjoy wide public support and subdued partisan criticism. From 9/11 to the end of the Iraqi war his approval ratings ranged between 74 and 90 percent. Republican victories in the midterm elections, rather than the traditional loss of Congressional seats, showed that Bush could extend his personal support to his party. Indeed, the president's decision to campaign extensively for Republican candidates represented a willingness to undertake a high-risk decision that in this case brought significant results.

SUMMARY AND COMMENT

The events of 9/11 and the new war on terrorism produced several significant changes for President Bush and the presidency. In the wake of the attack, the focus of the public and the press shifted from how Bush became president to what he would do as president. The question of his legitimacy was thus erased or at least secluded.The power of the office itself, which was in decline from the last stages of the Cold War through the Clinton presidency, was revived. In periods of national emergency, increased executive authority is nearly unavoidable. Immediately after 9/11, Congress authorized the president to use all necessary measures to respond to the attack. In 2002, after more debate, Congress provided the president with even more authority to deal with Iraq than it did with North Vietnam in the 1964 Bay of Tonkin resolution. In addition, a major change in American political culture may have occurred. As Americans viewed the heroic acts of police and firefighters at the World Trade Center and the passengers of United Flight 93 who prevented an apparent attack on either the White House or the Capitol, they experienced a new sense of patriotism and political resolve that had been absent in American politics for a generation.

It is not clear whether all or any of these changes are permanent or temporary. If they represent long-term changes, it is possible that the features of the postmodern presidency will have been fleeting. John Lewis Gaddis, for example, concluded shortly after 9/11 that the period after the fall of the Berlin War and the events of 9/11 constituted a interregnum between the Cold War and a new era. Will a new kind of presidency emerge as well?

Several factors also indicate that future scenarios for George W. Bush and his successors may nevertheless be difficult ones that do not replicate the Cold War presidency. In the Cold War, while both adversaries regularly used spies and client states to advance their interests, each side knew that the source of any threat came from one another. In the war against terrorism, however, the adversary operates in secret and is mobile across states. As President Bush said in his September 20 speech before Congress:

> Americans should not expect one battle, but a lengthy campaign, unlike any other we have seen. It may include dramatic strikes, visible on TV, and covert operations. . . . We will starve terrorists of funding, turn one against another, drive them from place to place, until there is no refuge or no rest.

What will be the consequences for the presidency of a long-term war, fought partially in secret and on many different fronts throughout the world? Since no president is able to promise invulnerability against attack, it is possible that electoral politics may revolve around the question, "Are you safer today than you were four/eight years ago?" instead of the old question about economic progress ("Are you better off today than you were four/eight years ago?"). Certainly, after the Cuban Missile Crisis Americans became accustomed to a certain routinization of the Cold War. The danger of nuclear war was always a concern, as well as unexpected "hot wars," but Americans could expect to live their lives in relative calm. President Eisenhower laid out this more reassuring scenario in 1954 when he told Americans that worrying about the H-Bomb was really no different than worrying about how to meet the next mortgage payment. President Bush attempted to make a similar case after 9/11 when he urged Americans to be calm and continue about their daily lives. Is such tranquility possible in an era of constant or intermittent terrorist threat and/or actions? Will presidents be blamed for allegedly failing to prevent terrorist attacks? Or will presidents be blamed for pursuing policies that are too zealous or be accused of advancing their own partisan interests?

The Cold War was fought with the general policy of *containment*. President Bush has continued to support the post–Cold War strategy of *enlargement*. American military action in Afghanistan was justified partly on the grounds that a new democratic regime not only would better people's lives but would also help bring peace to the region. Bush has, however, questioned whether the policy of containment is applicable after the events of 9/11. On June 1, 2002, he noted that the Soviets as adversaries were generally "risk-adverse" but, "deterrence based upon the threat of retaliation is less likely to work against leaders of rogue states more willing to take risks, gambling with the lives of their people, and the wealth of their countries." He also observed that in the Cold War the use of weapons of mass destruction was reserved as an option of "last resort." "Today, our enemies see weapons of mass destruction as weapons of choice," to be used for blackmail or the "best means of overcoming the conventional superiority of the United States." Bush concluded that preemptive strikes will be necessary "in an age where the enemies of civilization openly and actively seek the world's most destructive technologies. . . ." Future presidents may face the challenge of defending the use of preemptive military actions to the American public and the world and also avoiding stretching resources beyond effectiveness. Moreover, presidents must weigh the costs of other preemptive actions such as detainment and surveillance in regard to American citizens and resident aliens who may pose security threats against civil liberties.

During the Cold War, alliances with the United States or the Soviet Union did occasionally shift. Castro soon joined the Soviet bloc after he took power. Indeed, Iraq moved from a pro-Soviet to a pro-American position during the Cold War. For the most part, however, allies of the two superpowers held firm—particularly in Europe, which was divided between NATO and Warsaw Pact signatories. There were, of course, periods of strained relations, but both sides could count on their own European allies. After the Cold War, the Warsaw Pact was disbanded but NATO continued to function as an active force. NATO actually invoked Article Five (the pledge to defend a member state under attack) in support of the American action in Afghanistan. As France and Germany grew more adamant about opposing military action in Iraq, however, Secretary of Defense Donald Rumsfeld made a distinction between the "old Europe" and the "new Europe." France and Germany represented the "old Europe," said Rumsfeld, "but if you look at other countries in Europe, they're not with France and Germany . . . they're with the U.S." He continued by claiming that the "center of gravity is shifting to the east." It is possible that the diplomatic coalitions over whether to use force in Iraq—France, Germany, Russia (a former Communist state), Communist China, the United States, Great Britain, Spain, and several former communist Warsaw Pact Eastern European nations—will be temporary ones. On other issues perhaps the old alliances will return.

On the other hand, as Rumsfeld indicated, perhaps new international coalitions are emerging in the aftermath of the Cold War. The Bush administration is clearly very willing to explore these new arrangements. When

National Security Advisor Condolezza Rice said that the period after September 11 is "analogous to 1945 to 1947," she emphasized the need to reevaluate international relationships and answer the question, "how do we capitalize on these opportunities?" President Bush and future presidents will therefore face an international order with less stable alliances. A basic prediction of international political theory is that whenever a single power emerges that is significantly more powerful than others, inevitably a counterbalancing coalition of weaker states emerges. Did this pattern actually form in the months before the war with Iraq? Will future presidents be able to successfully "contain" these efforts? Will efforts to shed old alliances and find new allies lead to a reliance on neither?

Finally, during the Cold War both superpowers accused the other of managing and extending their "empire." Even before the Vietnamese War, however, Americans were reluctant to conceive of themselves as an empire. In the context of an international order under terrorist threat and the rise of "hollowed out" states, will the United States occupy other nations for long periods, in addition to Afghanistan and Iraq? Even the most benevolent and shrewd imperialist administration faces resentment and resistance by the occupied. Will future presidents be able to convince Americans that this kind of service on the part of their sons and daughters is necessary and worthwhile?

Whether these factors constitute a dangerous and volatile version of the postmodern presidency or yet a new period is still unclear. We do know, however, that future presidents will continue to struggle to meet both old and new challenges.

Bibliographic Essay

Richard Rose presents the model for the postmodern presidency in *The Post-Modern President* (Chatham, NJ: Chatham House, 1988). Also see Steven E. Shier, ed., *The Post-Modern Presidency: Bill Clinton's Legacy in American Politics* (Pittsburgh: University of Pittsburgh Press, 2000). The classic statement of postmodernism in general as a new historical period is Jean François Lyotard, *The Post-Modern Condition* (Manchester: Manchester University Press, 1984). For reviews and assessments, see Stephen K. White, *Political Theory and Postmodernism* (Cambridge: Cambridge University Press, 1991) and David Harvey, *The Condition of Postmodernity* (Oxford: Blackwell, 1989). Michael Hardt and Antonio Negri present a controversial application of postmodernism to international politics in *Empire* (Cambridge: Harvard University Press, 2000). An accessible account of a postmodern American culture is Robert Kaplan, *Empire Wilderness: Travels to America's Future* (New York: Random House, 1999). Bruce Miroff applies some aspects of postmodernism to the presidency in "The Presidency and the Public: Leadership as Spectacle," in Michael Nelson, ed., *The Presidency and the Political System* (Washington, DC: CQ Press, 1998), pp. 299–322. Also see Marjorie Randon Hershey's analysis of the role of the media in the 2000 election: "The Campaign and the Media," in Gerald M. Pomper, ed., *The Election of 2000* (Chatham, NJ: Chatham House, 2001), pp. 46–72. George C. Edwards III and B. Dan Wood conclude in

their study of recent presidencies that "most of the time presidents react, respond-
ing to fluctuations in the media and, in the area of foreign policy, world events."
See their "Who Influences Whom? The President, Congress, and the Media,"
American Political Science Review (June, 1999), pp. 327–44.

An extremely influential prediction of the next possible international system
is Francis Fukuyama, "The End of History?" *National Interest* (summer, 1989):1–18.
Fukuyama expanded his views about the "democratic peace" in *The End of History
and the Last Man* (New York: Free Press, 1992). A contrasting prediction which
assumes severe national and ethnic conflicts is Samuel Huntington, *The Clash of
Civilizations and the Remaking of World Order* (New York: Simon and Schuster,
1996). Also see Robert D. Kaplan, *The Coming Anarchy: Shattering the Dreams of the
Post-Cold War* (New York: Random House, 2000). Philip Bobbitt's *The Shield of
Achilles: War, Peace, and the Course of History* (New York: Knopf, 2002) attempts to
place changes in international politics in historical perspective. A new approach
to decision making in international politics assumes that actors perceive the devastation of loss as greater than the benefit of gain. "Prospect theory" may be a productive model for analyzing presidential actions for the post–Cold War period.
See Barbara Farnham, ed., *Avoiding Losses/Taking Risks: Prospect Theory and International Politics* (Ann Arbor: University of Michigan Press, 1995) for theoretical and
empirical assessments. Raymond Tanter examines the impact of rogue states on
the international order in *Rogue States: Terrorism and Proliferation* (New York: St.
Martin's, 1999).

Colin Campbell and Bert A. Rockman present initial evaluations of the Clin-
ton presidency in *The Clinton Presidency: First Appraisals* (Chatham, NJ: Chatham
House, 1996) and later assessments in *The Clinton Legacy* (Chatham, NJ: Chatham
House, 2000). Also helpful is Paul C. Light's extension of his application of political capital to the Clinton administration: *The President's Agenda* (Baltimore, MD:
Johns Hopkins University Press, 1999), ch. 12. There are a number of studies that
attempt to apply postmodern concepts to the Clinton presidency. See especially
Shawn J. Parry-Giles and Trevor Parry-Giles, *Constructing Clinton* (New York:
Peter Lang, 2002). For an inside account of the deficit reduction proposals in 1993,
see Bob Woodward, *The Agenda: Inside the Clinton White House* (New York: Simon
and Schuster, 1994) and Elizabeth Drew, *On the Edge* (New York: Simon and
Schuster, 1994).

Biographies of Clinton have been quite critical. See Dick Maraniss, *First in His
Class* (New York: Simon and Schuster, 1995); Martin Walker, *The President We
Deserve* (New York: Crown Publishers, 1996); R. Emmett Tyrell, Jr., *Boy Clinton*
(Washington, DC: Regnery, 1996); Joe Klein, *The Natural* (New York: Doubleday,
2002). Klein's is the most positive but, like many observers, while he acknowl-
edges Clinton's accomplishments, he concludes that "his public service may be
defined by the smug, shallow serenity of his time." Four memoirs by members of
Clinton's administration are very insightful: George Stephanopolis, *All Too
Human: A Political Education* (Boston: Little, Brown, 1999); Robert B. Reich, *Locked
in the Cabinet* (New York: Knopf, 1997); Strobe Talbott, *The Russia Hand* (New York:
Random House, 2002); and Dick Morris, *Behind the Oval Office* (New York: Random House, 1997). Treatments of Clinton's impeachment are frequently very
shrill, but see Richard A. Posner, *An Affair of State* (Cambridge: Harvard University Press, 1999) and Mark Rozell and Clyde Wilcox, eds., *The Clinton Scandal and
the Future of American Government* (Washington, DC: Georgetown University

Press, 2000) for more balanced assessments. See also Dick Maraniss's dissection of Clinton's "apology address" in *The Clinton Enigma* (New York: Simon and Schuster, 1998) and analyses from the perspective of cultural studies in Lauren Berlant and Lisa Duggan, eds., *Our Monica Ourselves: The Clinton Affair and the National Interest* (New York: New York University Press, 2001).

Clinton's pre-presidential addresses are available in *Preface to the Presidency: Selected Speeches of Bill Clinton, 1974–1992* (Fayetteville: University of Arkansas Press, 1996). For an astute comparison of Perot's and Clinton's use of the "town meeting," see Janette Kenner Muir, "Clinton Goes to Town Hall," in Stephen A. Smith, ed., *Bill Clinton on Stump, State, and Stage* (Fayetteville: University of Arkansas Press, 1994), pp. 314–64.

On the contested election of 2000, see James W. Caesar and Andrew Busch, *The Perfect Tie* (Lanham, MD: Roman and Littlefield, 2001) and the *Washington Post* Political Staff, *Deadlock* (New York: Public Affairs Press, 2001). For relevant documents and commentary, see E. J. Dionne and William Kristol, eds., *Bush v. Gore* (Washington, DC: Brookings, 2001). Philip Abbott, Marjorie Sarbaugh Thompson, and Lyke Thompson attempt to place the 2000 election in the context of succession problems in democratic theory in "The Social Construction of a Legitimate Presidency," *Studies in American Political Development* (fall, 2002), pp. 208–30.

For early attempts to assess the impact of 9/11 on American policy, see the essays by John Lewis Gaddis and Paul Kennedy in Strobe Talbott and Nayan Chanda, eds., *The Age of Terror: America and the World after September 11* (New York: Basic Books, 2001). Frank Bruni's *Ambling into History* (Harper Collins, 2002) examines George W. Bush's agenda; and Bob Woodward presents an account of presidential decision making in the aftermath of 9/11 based on interviews with administration officials, including the president himself, in *Bush at War* (New York: Simon and Schuster, 2002). David Frum, the speechwriter who drafted the term "axis of evil," is the first member of the Bush administration to offer memoirs of his experience: *The Right Man: The Surprise Presidency of George W. Bush* (New York: Random House, 2003). Karl Rove is often considered the most influential and imaginative presidential advisor since Mark Hanna. James Moore and Wayne Slater examine his role in the Bush administration in *Bush's Brain: How Karl Rove Made George W. Bush* (Chicago: John Wiley, 2003).

The most comprehensive collection of material on the events leading to the Iraqi conflict is Micah L. Sifry and Christopher Cerf, eds., *The Iraq War Reader* (New York: Simon and Schuster, 2003). For two differing views on America as an empire, see Charles Krauthamer, "The Unipolar Moment Revisited: America, the Benevolent Empire" and Kevin Phillips, "Hegemony, Hubris and Overreach," both in this volume. An influential argument for American military intervention is Kenneth Pollack's *The Threatening Storm: The Case for Invading Iraq* (New York: Random House, 2002).

INDEX